Lecture Notes in Computer Science 5080

Commenced Publication in 1973
Founding and Former Series Editors:
Gerhard Goos, Juris Hartmanis, and Jan van Leeuwen

T0223238

Zhigeng Pan   Adrian David Cheok
Wolfgang Müller   Abdennour El Rhabili (Eds.)

Transactions on
Edutainment I

Editors-in-Chief

Zhigeng Pan
Zhejiang University, State Key Lab of CAD&CG
Hangzhou, China
E-mail: zgpan@cad.zju.edu.cn

Adrian David Cheok
National University of Singapore, IDM Institute
Singapore
E-mail: adriancheok@mixedrealitylab.org

Wolfgang Müller
University of Education, Media Education and Visualization Group
Weingarten, Germany
E-mail: mueller@md-phw.de

Volume Editor

Abdennour El Rhabili
Liverpool John Moores University
School of Computing
Liverpool, UK

Library of Congress Control Number: Applied for

CR Subject Classification (1998): K.3.1-2, I.2.1, H.5, H.3, I.3

LNCS Sublibrary: SL 3 – Information Systems and Application, incl. Internet/Web
and HCI

ISSN   0302-9743 (Lecture Notes in Computer Science)
ISBN-10   3-540-69737-3 Springer Berlin Heidelberg New York
ISBN-13   978-3-540-69737-4 Springer Berlin Heidelberg New York

Springer is a part of Springer Science+Business Media

springer.com

© Springer-Verlag Berlin Heidelberg 2008

Typesetting: Camera-ready by author, data conversion by Scientific Publishing Services, Chennai, India
Printed on acid-free paper   SPIN: 12282272   06/3180   5 4 3 2 1 0

Preface

With great pleasure we would like to present the first volume of a new journal, *Transactions on Edutainment*. This journal, part of the Springer series *Lecture Notes in Computer Science*, is devoted to research and development in the field of edutainment. Edutainment, also known as educational entertainment or entertainment-education, denotes all forms of entertainment designed to educate as well as to provide fun. This approach is motivated by the increasing demands on individuals for life-long learning and the need to integrate effective learning opportunities throughout life. As such, edutainment has attracted increasing interest in the last few years.

The first 12 articles of this first issue represent a selection of outstanding contributions from Edutainment 2008, the Third International Conference on E-Learning and Games held in Nanjing, China, in June 2008. These papers are complemented by individual contributions from international experts in this field.

The first six articles provide an introduction into the field of edutainment by presenting different application examples. In their article "Designing an Educational Game: Case Study of Euope 2045," Šisler and Brom discuss their experiences in the design of an on-line multi-player strategy game on political, economic, and social issues in contemporary Europe. The following examples point out the crucial role of interaction design and technolgies in the development of a successful edutainment application.

Jung et al. show the pontials in rehabilitation training when combining game-based approaches with motion capture devices in their article "Timed Automata-Based Rehabilitation Training Game Design for the Affected Lower Extremity of Hemiparetic Patients." Similarly, Sato et al. include haptic I/O into their educational VR application in "A Haptic Virtual Environment for Molecular Chemistry Education." Oh et al. utilize a method from augmented reality (AR) to simplify the interaction with the learning system and virtual tutor in their paper "AR Gardening: AR Edutainment System with an Augmented Learning Companion." Finally, Lo et al. describe their approach and experiences in the design of a learning game for elementary students in "Developing a Digital Game-Based Situated Learning System for Ocean Ecology." In their article "A Pen-Based 3D Role Modeling Tool for Children" Li et al. use pen-based I/O devices.

The following papers focus on different technological aspects. Hu presents a reusable eduventure framework in his paper, targeting to simplify the development of edutainment applications by extending a standard game platform by further core elements for eduventure game design. Shinozaki et al. focus on movement control of physical robots in their article "Construction and Evaluation of a Robot Dance System." Na et al. and Linaza et al. both address the field of interaction again, proposing the use of an interactive table-device and a specifically designed 3D visualization device, respectively.

The last two papers from Edutainment 2008 from Merabti et al. and Delgado-Mata et al. target the fields of interactive storytelling and believable agents. They also provide a perfect transition to contributions from Spierling and Paiva in the same fields. Merabti et al. give a general overview on approaches and techniques to achieve dynamic stories. Delgada-Mata et al. present a robotics-inspired behavioral AI technique to simulate characters' personalities. They also discuss the application of this model in a computer game and report from user studies. Spierling presents an application example with the "Killer Phrases" game and discusses design issues and first experiences. Paiva explores the role of tangibles as posible gateways for interactive storytelling systems, and adresses issues related to their design.

Martens et al. and Khine et al. widen the discussion in their papers "Game-Based Learning with Computers Learning, Simulations, and Games" and "Core Attributes of Interactive Computer Games and Adaptive Use for Edutainment." In these papers, general aspects of game-based learning applications are discussed. Goh et al. explain how interactive authoring and corresponding systems may be utilized in this context.

The following three papers focus on sophisticated approaches to human–computer interacton in the context of edutainment. Lee and Wong provide a detailed view on the state of the art of VR for learning. Peternier et al. present their concept for teaching, practicing, and researching with computer graphics and VR. Chang et al. transfer learning processes back into the real world, using techniques from the field of ubiquitous computing.

The final two papers present two application examples. Cai et al. explain how VR-based game technology may be applied for educational use, and they show two specific examples from the field of biology classes. Finally, Moreno-Ger et al. present a successful game-like interactive simulation for online learning of clinical procedures.

The papers in this first issue present a very good overview on the lively field of edutainment, and the large number of application examples already gives evidence on the high potential and impact of edutainment approaches. We are very confident that *Transactions on Edutainment* will provide a large number of very intersting contributions to the fields of education and training in the future.

April 2008   Wolfgang Müller
                                                                          Zhigeng Pan
                                                                Abdennour El Rhalibi

LNCS Transactions on Edutainment

This journal subline aims to provide a highly visible dissemination channel for remarkable work that in one way or another addresses research and development on issues related to this field. It targets to serve as a forum for stimulating and disseminating innovative research ideas, theories, emerging technologies, empirical investigations, state-of-the-art methods, and tools in all the different genres of Edutainment, such as game-based learning and serious games, interactive storytelling, virtual learning environments, VR-based education, and related fields. It will cover aspects of educational and game theories, human–computer interaction, computer graphics, artificial intelligence, and systems design.

Editorial Board

Ana Paiva (INESC-ID, Portugal)
Abdennour El Rhalibi (JMU, UK)
Daniel Thalmann (EPFL, Switzerland)
Kok-Wai Wong (Murdoch University, Australia)
Gangshan Wu (Nanjing University, China)
Hyun Seung Yang (KAIST, Korea)
Xiaopeng Zhang (IA-CAS, China)

Editorial Office

Edu-Game Research Center, School of Education Science
Nanjing Normal University, Ninghai Road 122, Nanjing 210097, China
E-mail: edutainment@njnu.edu.cn
Tel.: 86-25-83598655

Table of Contents

Papers from Edutainment 2008

Regular Papers

Designing an Educational Game:
Case Study of 'Europe 2045'

Vít Šisler[1,3] and Cyril Brom[2,3]

[1] Charles University, Faculty of Philosophy and Arts, Prague, Czech Republic
[2] Charles University, Faculty of Mathematics and Physics, Prague, Czech Republic
[3] Generation Europe, Prague, Czech Republic
vsisler@gmail.com, brom@ksvi.mff.cuni.cz

Abstract. This paper presents a theoretical framework, which has been adopted in designing an on-line multi-player strategy game *Europe 2045*. *Europe 2045* is an educational tool for high school social science courses, aimed at familiarizing students with political, economic, and social issues in contemporary Europe. Apart from learning facts, players develop a range of key skills: discussion ability, negotiation, teamwork, and group decision-making. The presented theoretical framework is based on a critical analysis of crucial issues, which seem to determine the success or failure of development and implementation of an educational game in the formal school environment. It demonstrates key approaches the authors of *Europe 2045* have adopted in order to overcome already known problems related to game-based learning. On a general level this paper discusses issues related to formal fact learning in educational systems and the possible role of educational games in enhancing these systems.

Keywords: Educational games, serious games, game design, immersive environments, game-based learning.

1 Introduction

The earliest-developed computer games have already been used to support training and learning objectives [4]. Since then, the concept of game-based learning has undergone substantial changes. The high expectations of early edutainment and e-learning have not actually been met by particularly successful outcomes. The reasons mentioned in this regard are that such tools were poorly designed, simplistic, and repetitive, and did not allow players any active exploration [16]. On the other hand, many commercial computer games often place the user in very complex environments and require them to complete highly demanding tasks with difficult objectives. Therefore some authors argue that at least some commercial games are actually based on well developed and sound theories of learning in order to engage the player and instruct him how to play and win the game [12]. In this respect several recent works have explored of the potential for commercial strategy games in formal education and their supposed advantages over classical e-learning and edutainment tools, e.g. [8, 23, 26]. The results from these case studies are promising but also ambiguous in some aspects, pointing out the difficulties in linking games' educational content with the context of formal education.

Z. Pan et al. (Eds.): Transactions on Edutainment I, LNCS 5080, pp. 1–16, 2008.
© Springer-Verlag Berlin Heidelberg 2008

Hence, so called *serious games* – full-fledged games in which education (in its various forms) is the primary goal, rather than entertainment [6] – are starting to gain an increasing amount of attention. The fact that these games are, contrary to commercial games, intentionally developed as educational tools arguably makes their integration into formal education easier. Several of these games have been already evaluated with generally positive outcomes [7, 11, 32].

With the rapid development of the Internet a new form of gaming has emerged. Drawing upon the concept laid down by multi-user dungeons (MUDs) in the 1980s, multi-player on-line games construct complex virtual worlds, allowing non-linear interactions and exploration, as well as various forms of collaboration/competition among groups of players. The distinctive features of multi-player, on-line games – team collaboration, problem solving, and group decision-making – have already attracted the interest of educators and instructors, including the U.S. Army [32].

Learning and training via computer games and simulations can be regarded as a part of a more general process in what de Freitas calls *learning in immersive worlds* [6]. Minsky and Papert define immersive worlds as given environments which may be explored in a non-linear way by learners. They include artifacts and objects and allow users to learn through exploring the environment and its objects in a relatively open-ended way [19; cited from 6]. The fundamental question of learning in immersive worlds is how to transfer the acquired experience into relevant knowledge and skills and similarly how to design an immersive learning environment in order to facilitate such transfers [8, 23].

The primary goal of this paper is to present the theoretical framework used in designing a complex learning environment, which combines the advantages of serious games (i.e. easier integration into formal education) with those of multi-player, on-line games (i.e. intrinsic facilitation of collaboration). Within this framework we have developed a multi-player, on-line strategy game *Europe 2045* aimed at educating high school students in economics, politics and other social sciences as well as training them in a range of key skills. The theoretical framework stems from research conducted prior to embarking on the game's development. It has been evolving during the development process, having been shaped by preliminary case studies carried out during the game's testing and implementation. Basically, it presents the desired learning objectives of *Europe 2045* and the strategies our team has adopted in order to ensure fulfilment of these objectives. It also reviews our approach in light of the results from pilot evaluations of the game. Evaluations were conducted on two groups of 34 high-school students.

As far as we know, *Europe 2045* is most likely the first multi-player strategy game worldwide that has been designed specifically for use in secondary schools. Therefore the secondary goal of our paper is to set theoretical and case-study-based background for researchers and designers involved in similar future projects. Thus, on a more general level, this paper analyzes the crucial issues that seem to determine the success or failure of developing an educational game and its insertion into formal secondary education programs. Finally, this paper argues that successful and effective implementation of an educational game requires reconsidering the very way in which one learns, the desired outcomes of formal education, and how the learning context should be enhanced in this respect.

Section 2 summarizes the key findings on game-based learning resulting from previous research and case studies. Essentially it is based on a study conducted in the initial phase of *Europe 2045*'s development. These findings were crucial for choosing the *Europe 2045* game platform and content, and for creating the methodology for its use in education. Section 3 describes the game *Europe 2045*, outlines in detail its fundamental learning features and theoretical approaches adopted in order to facilitate implementation. It also reflects upon which features and approaches proved to be/or not to be successful during the game's testing and pilot evaluation. Section 4 provides conclusions on the project assessment.

2 Key Findings on Game-Based Learning

As Piaget and Vygotsky have argued, play is a crucial method through which we test ideas, develop new skills, and participate in new social roles [20, 31]. In this respect early video games raised various expectations about their educational value. Given the fact that motivation is regarded to be a key aspect of effective learning, the popularity of games among younger generations inspired many educators. Indeed, early research on arcade-style games has demonstrated that games create intrinsic motivation through fantasy, control, challenge, curiosity, and competition [18, 5]. The high popularity and consumption of games even led some authors to suggest that children of the "videogame generation" do not respond to traditional instruction and developing educational games is thus a necessity [15, 21]. However, the facility with which one can transplant this intrinsic motivation from a leisure time activity into formal education structures is a different question that will be discussed in Section 3.

Commercial computer games construct oftentimes rich, complex environments that allow immersive exploration of numerous strategies for action and decision [10]. Many authors suggest that by situating players in immersive worlds, where they can freely move and act, these games can promote problem-solving, goal-related behavior, engagement and motivation, as well as social networking [13, 6, 28, 11, 23]. Other studies argue that games help develop strategic thinking, group decision-making, and higher cognitive skills [1, 6].

Several case studies have evaluated the implementation of commercial computer games in formal education – i.e. *The Sims 2*, *Civilization III*, and *Europe Universalis II* [23, 26, 8]. On a general level they have demonstrated that commercial games exhibit some of the positive learning effects mentioned above but have also revealed certain ambiguities and problems as discussed below. Egenfeldt-Nielsen conducted a case study on learning history with *Europe Universalis II* in Danish high schools and concluded that students using the game had, in the end, slightly worse factual knowledge than the control group (attending normal classes). But those test-group students exhibited better retention of the learned facts over the long-term and a greater willingness to search actively for additional information [8]. Similarly Gee and Steinkuehler argue that research is a core component of gameplay, and games stimulate an interest in topics related to a game's content, thus promoting various types of information literacy and developing information-seeking habits [29]. Another study has introduced *Civilization III* into secondary school history classes in the US. The study's author, Squire, argues that one group of students, in the end, exhibited a deeper understanding of the broader geographical, social, and economic conditions determining historical processes. At the same time, another group of students refused to continue in the course, opting for a normal history class instead [26].

Despite some positive outcomes, these studies point out a significant incompatibility of most commercial games with school environments [8]. Conclusions from the studies also suggest that a more theoretically grounded approach is needed for the development of educational games and their implementation in formal schooling. As has been already mentioned, such games are often being developed in the emerging field of so-called serious games, e.g. *Tactical Iraqi, Revolution,* or *Global Conflicts: Palestine* [17, 11, 7]. For example the latter is a 3-D role-playing game that deals with the Israeli-Palestinian conflict and is based on real personal stories. According to the evaluation study of the game prototype, players demonstrated significantly better comprehension of the complexity in the conflict, the ability to consider problems from a broad perspective, and higher personal involvement in learning via the game [7]. The majority of studies concerning serious games also demonstrate that the latter are useful for stimulating debates and discussions between peer learners concerning the taught topic [6, 7, 32, 10].

Generally speaking, it seems that games could be particularly useful for generating a deeper understanding of certain key principles of given topics, mainly when dealing with complicated and multifaceted issues, which are hard to comprehend through factual knowledge only. As Gee puts it, a large body of facts that resist out-of-context memorization becomes easier to assimilate if learners are immersed in activities and experiences that use these facts for plans, goals, and purposes within a coherent knowledge domain [12].

On the other hand, there exist some substantial problems in using (even serious) games in formal education. These known pitfalls will now be reviewed, and in Section 3 we will present how we have incorporated our solutions to these problems into our framework.

First and most notably, there has been a dominant perception, among the majority of teachers, of gaming as a leisure time activity with no pedagogic value – except for developing IT skills. Although recent surveys show that this perception is about to change, the deeply-rooted experience with videogames as entertainment may mitigate the educators' willingness to use games as educational tools [6, 24]. To some extent this applies also to students who, even when playing complex games in their leisure time, are skeptical of the learning effects of games in the school environment [8]. Such perceptions are also strengthened by the fact that learning in immersive environments generally does not promote awareness of – and more specifically how – we are developing our skills and knowledge. In the case of *Europe 2045* we have tried to overcome this problem by defining clear, desired learning outcomes in accordance with national curricula guidelines and by explaining these outcomes to teachers and students as we will discuss in Section 3.6.

Second, a substantial problem lies in transferring skills developed through game-based learning into a real environment. In educational research, this phenomenon is commonly referred to as the *transfer problem* [8, 23, 30]. It means that the players actually develop a number of skills and knowledge required to finish the game's objectives, but are not easily able to apply what they learned in different contexts and different social practices. The role of the teacher and his/her reflection upon and moderation of the learning process seem to be of critical importance in dealing with the transfer problem as we will discuss in Section 3.7.

Finally more practical barriers to using games in schools were cited by a majority of researchers. For example, they mention a lack of access to equipment and limited availability of up-to-date video cards [6], or barriers posed by fixed lesson times (mainly 45 or 50 minutes) which seem insufficient for game-based learning [23]. Also, in several cases, the commercial computer games chosen for educational purposes appeared to be overwhelmingly complicated both for teachers and some students to handle [8, 26]. These limitations have been central to the development of *Europe 2045* and its educational methodology.

3 Designing Europe 2045

3.1 Game Description

As a part of the European-funded project "Integration of IT Tools into Education of Humanities" we have developed a multi-player, on-line strategy game *Europe 2045*, designed to be supporting educational material for social science courses, attempting to familiarize players with political, economic and social issues in a united Europe and the present-day world. Apart from learning facts, the player should develop a range of key skills: the ability to discuss, to negotiate, to think critically, and to work in a team. In the course of the game's development, which finished at the end of 2007, seven preliminary studies were carried out, each involving about 10 high school students. A pilot evaluation has been conducted on two groups of 34 high school students (19 females, 15 males) in Prague, Czech Republic in January 2008. They include both qualitative and quantitative outcomes (here, for reasons of brevity, only some of the qualitative data are presented). The game is intended to be fully applied in the spring 2008.

Europe 2045 features three layers of game-play. In the game, each student (1) represents one EU member state and defines its domestic policy (beginning with tax levels and environmental protection and graduating on to issues such as legalization of same sex marriage and privacy protection policies). Also, the player offers subsidies designed to persuade domestic and foreign investors to invest in his/her country. On a diplomatic level (2), the player has an opportunity to present drafts for policy changes to the EU. At the beginning of the match, the situation closely copies the real state of affairs in Europe today. The players are free to cancel current policies or to introduce new ones. Additionally (3) players face various simulated scenarios and crises addressing contemporary key issues faced by the unified Europe, including migration, population aging, international relations, and energy independence. The players must react to all these events and, in co-operation with fellow players, seek out appropriate solutions. During the course of the game, they typically witness the short- and long-term effects of their decisions.

Moreover, each player (or team of players) has his or her own project to try to push through at the European level. A project is basically a vision of how the EU should look like in the future (e.g., the Green Europe project supports environmental protection and investment into alternative power resources, while the Conservative Europe project strives to preserve traditional values). The final appearance of Europe at the

end of each match is thus a result of discussions, voting, and intense diplomatic negotiations in a given player group. The discussions take place in the classroom, where
they are moderated by the teacher. Supplementary information, which is both relevant
for success in the game and which summarizes the real world information, is provided
by hints and the in-game encyclopedia (Fig. 4).

Technically, the game is a client-server application; the students play the game via
the Internet (Fig. 1). The server part comprises PHP scripts generating the game interface, the story manager is written in PHP as well, and the social-economical simulation is written in Java. Almost all parts of the interface are programmed in Flash
(Figs. 2, 3) in order to make the game suitable to technological equipment standards
in Czech secondary schools (e.g. slower Internet connections, etc.) and make it ready
to use without the need of special installations by end-users. These   seemed have
proven problematic in the past, according to many case studies [8, 26].

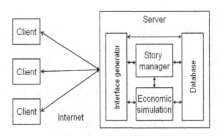

Fig. 1. Architecture of *Europe 2045*

Fig. 2. Flash interface; state management

Fig. 3. Flash interface; EU policies

Fig. 4. In-game encyclopedia

3.2   Development Framework

The following sections (3.3–3.7) describe fundamental features of *Europe 2045*. Emphasis is placed on the aspects of technological solution, gameplay and usage methodology, which are relevant to achieving learning objectives and integration of the
game into formal education structures. For better clarity we have summarized our
framework in a simplified graphical representation (Fig. 5). In the left column we
have listed key problems with and objectives for developing educational games,
which stem from Section 2 of this paper. The second column consists of our solutions

to these problems, while the last column reviews the solutions in relation to testing and pilot evaluations. Detailed descriptions, including working hypotheses and case studies, are provided below.

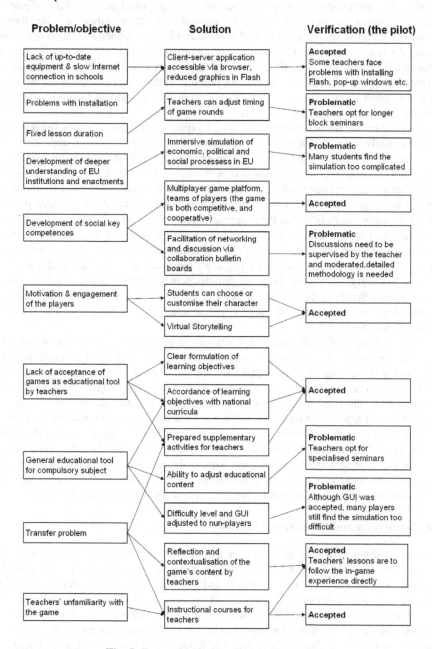

Fig. 5. *Europe 2045's* development framework

3.3 Collaboration and Multi-user Environment

As argued in [2, 27], multi-player, on-line games offer an ideal environment in which gamers can communicate with one another, accomplish shared goals, and participate in solving complex problems. In order to maintain the development of the above-mentioned social skills, the gameplay of *Europe 2045* was designed so that co-operation among the teammates (players sharing the same project) would be necessary in order to achieve the game's very objective, i.e. to put the project through at the European level. Changing particular EU policies is also not possible without careful diplomatic negotiations with other teams. Thus the learners are encouraged by gameplay to take an active part in the complex in-game diplomacy.

With regard to the development of social skills, several case studies suggest that cognitive tools, such as discussion forums and bulletin boards, play an important role in enhancing learning in multi-user environments through the mediation of social interaction and by encouraging discussion [6, 10]. *Europe 2045* is equipped with a multi-thread bulletin board, which enables communication on a variety of levels, from general message boards to peer-to-peer communication. Although it has been proven during the pilot evaluation that these supplementary tools actually play a vital role in enabling the players' collaboration, without proper teacher moderation discussions soon digressed into utter chaos. After several rounds the dominant players took over the discussion and the arguments started to be personal and irrelevant to the game's content. Similarly, the voting about EU policies was heavily influenced by the persuasive power of these dominant players. As a result we have developed a more detailed methodology for managing the players' discussions and voting processes. We will present this in Section 3.7.

Previous case studies also argue that students in multi-player environments need to have the opportunity to choose their roles or at least to customize their characters [6, 22]. During the testing of *Europe 2045* we applied various approaches, ranging from random distribution of the players' roles (i.e. the state and the project) to students' free selection from the roles available. It becomes evident that the identification with the player's virtual representation is crucial. When students had the opportunity to deliberately choose their roles and their motivation, then their level of engagement in the game and in the subsequent negotiations was significantly higher. On the other hand, when they have to represent states and projects without the possibility of choosing them, discussions soon became short, lacking in content and rather formal (i.e. most of the students were simply trading support for various laws or regulatory measures).

3.4 Simulation and Educational Content

From the findings demonstrated in Section 2 it seems that simulation is an essential feature of game-based learning [8, 12, 23, 26]. As argued in [10], simulation can respond to students' actions, provide rapid feedback, and gradually increase the degree to which they are challenged. *Europe 2045* puts students into an immersive simulation of the European Union, its economic and political dynamic, etc., where they can experience its processes in a complex way. Our hope was that this can assist students in better understanding the underlying logic for key issues addressed by the European Union. These are issues that are otherwise overwhelmingly complex and unfamiliar to most of them.

Conceptually, our model is a multi-agent simulation, where each agent is either a country, or an abstract representation of an EU industry. In a simplified fashion, at the end of each round, an agent-country computes the next state of the country, while an agent-industry carries out decisions which lead the country to build new factories, mines etc. based on particular variables related to the countries. Similarly, our model simulates a vast number of other variables, e.g. comfort, unemployment, crime levels, immigration, etc.

Essentially, the pilot evaluation has proved that students definitely appreciate a simulation based on real data and benefit from exploring its logic (see also [25]). At the same time some of the features of simulation-based learning turned out to be problematic.

First, although we intended for the model to be designed in a relatively simple way, and we have tried to explain it to students via introductory lectures, hints, and an in-game encyclopedia, a substantial number of students have found the simulation too complicated and have failed to successfully manage their states. This applies particularly to non-players, i.e. students who do not play computer games regularly in their leisure time (see also [8, 26]). As a result, it seems that educational games intended to be used in general education need to lower substantially the difficulty level set as a standard by the gaming culture for various game genres. In this respect it has to be noted that most commercial computer games are designed for relatively longer periods of use (e.g. weeks or months), which gives the player more time to explore, challenge and master the game's rule system.

Second, given that the simulation inherently provides a schematized picture of the world, some teachers have expressed concerns that by merely exploring the relationships between various phenomena in the game, students might develop naïve concepts of how the economies of the European Union work. Other researchers formulated a similar concern as well [25]. During the pilot evaluation it appeared that the role of reflection of the game's content through additional educational materials, active interpretation, classroom discussions, and teachers' explanations is of paramount importance. The methodology designed for this reflection will be detailed in Section 3.7.

3.5 Virtual Storytelling

Storytelling has played an important role in humanities education since the advent of formal schooling [6]. Our working hypothesis was that stories help to build a learning context. Through stories students can better understand certain issues. Stories increase their involvement and, consequently, their motivation.

The narrative structure of *Europe 2045* serves three purposes. First, it introduces new topics and agendas for students' discussions. Second, by tying new events to players' previous decisions, it serves as a global feedback mechanism for students and as a method for sharpening discussions. The third class of events provides individual players with feedback on the results of their previous actions concerning their own states.

The game proceeds in rounds, one round is one game year. An atomic "beat" of a scenario is called an *affair*. It is an event that takes place in one round and can be triggered by players' actions or results from the economic and social model or events from previous rounds. An event is communicated to the player via a textual description in the game newspaper (Fig. 7) or via a short animated clip on TV (Fig. 6). In some cases, an event also has an impact on the economic and social model, i.e. it influences state of one country or that of the whole EU.

Fig. 6. The TV News; Darfur conflict

Fig. 7. The Newsletter

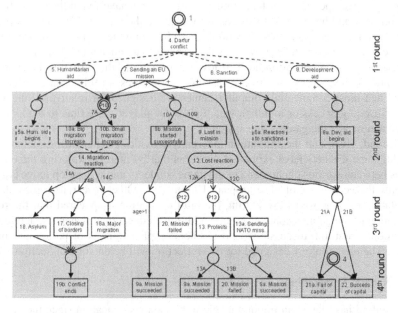

Fig. 8. Darfur scenario. The elements of the plot are organised in rounds for clarity's sake.

Some events introduce issues that require decisions to be taken by the players (e.g. accepting another state's proposal, sending a humanitarian mission to a conflict area, etc.). These decisions are intended to be taken during a discussion, typically in the class under the teacher's supervision (see Sec. 3.7), and voted on via ballot. One event often triggers more ballots, each containing a precisely-formulated question ("Do you support sending a European humanitarian mission to the Darfur Region?") with three possible answers (yes/no/abstain). The ballots chosen by the game designers aim to cover all the main possible solutions usually proposed by real policy-makers in similar cases. When the answers cannot be schematized to fit a yes or no option, the ballot contains a number (3-4) of more detailed solutions. The decision chosen by the players again influences the economic and social model and the events to be triggered in the next round.

We have adopted a modified version of Petri Nets for *Europe 2045's* plot specification [3]. Fig. 8 provides an example of specifications for the Darfur scenario: one of the largest, and perhaps most informative, scenarios in the game. This scenario starts in the first round with an event communicating via TV that the crisis in Darfur has escalated and requiring four ballot proposals. Based on the results of the ballots (i.e. the actions of the students), the crises evolves further. The important point is that it can develop in several aspects at the same time. For example, if students agree both on a form of development aid (Ballot 8) and of humanitarian aid (Ballot 5), both the events "Development aid begins" (8a) as well as "Humanitarian aid begins" (5a) follow through to (or lead to a) the second round. Additionally, either Affair 10a "Big migration increase", or Affair 10b "Small migration increase" ensues. Which affair is started depends on conditions 7A and 7B. In a similar manner, the scenario then evolves further and provides the students with direct feedback on their actions. In the basic campaign of *Europe 2045*, there are two additional scenarios of similar size to the "Darfur" one and several dozens of small scenarios consisting of one to three actions.

During the pilot evaluation it became evident that well-designed virtual storytelling is a key element in *Europe 2045*. The students appreciated scenarios which provided them with more alternative solutions and evolved according to their own actions. At the same time, they were more skeptical about smaller and simpler scenarios, which they perceived as schematizing. Nevertheless, the narrative structure appeared to be an important factor for students' motivation. During various phases of testing *Europe 2045*, the game was played on several occasions without any events at all. In most of these cases the students' engagement in the game was significantly lower after several rounds.

3.6 Educational Framing: Learning Context

From the findings demonstrated in Section 2 [1, 25, 28] and our pilot evaluations outlined in Section 3.1 it essentially seems that when a game is supposed to be used in a formal school environment, the context of game-based learning is probably more important than the specific features and/or content of the game itself. By context here we mean both the contemporary educational practice, i.e. the national curricula, and the learning activities and discourse surrounding the particular educational game (e.g. supportive educational materials, students' presentations, teachers' lectures following the in-game experience, etc.). These last two sections of our paper (3.6 and 3.7) discuss the necessity of articulating clear learning outcomes, the role of the teacher in explaining the game's content, and our methodology for using *Europe 2045* in formal classes.

In the Czech Republic, the Education Ministry recently adopted a the new *General Educational Program*, which is a fundamental framework for secondary school education. It is aimed at enhancing the traditional form of face-to-face education by promoting development of key skills and a broader and multidisciplinary approach towards traditional subjects [14]. At the beginning of *Europe 2045*'s development, we defined its learning objectives as described in Section 3.1 in accordance with this new *General Education Program*. During our evaluations, it appeared that this step simplified our collaboration with Czech secondary school teachers. Ultimately, teachers demonstrated greater interest in the game and were more likely to integrate it into learning plans, when it was presented within the framework of the new national curricula.

However, we do not suggest that educational game designers should try to incorporate into a game the same scope of factual information prescribed by the national curriculum for particular subjects. More precisely they should construct the game's environment such that it can draw upon students' already existing knowledge and understanding [9]. What we have found essential is that specific knowledge and skills developed through a game need to be clearly explained to teachers and students and integrated into accepted teaching formats in order to ensure effective learning (see also [6]).

3.7 Role of the Teacher

As Facer et al. state the role of the teacher in the game-based learning process should be one of translation – between immersion and reflection, between implicit and explicit knowledge, between the game world and the world of formal, summative assessment [10]. This role is by no means a simple task; yet it fundamentally determines the learning outcomes. From the testing of *Europe 2045* it is clear that the teacher has to be very familiar with the learning environment and has to experience the whole game-based learning process related to a particular game. In some cases during the pilot evaluation the teacher's lack of familiarity and preparation substantially corrupted the results of the implementation (see also [6]).

During the development of the *Europe 2045* game, we designed a teachers' preparation program that included seminars on how to use the game in various settings, model lectures, handouts, and suggested additional activities for students. After the first pilot evaluation, it became clear that a more detailed methodology document for helping to facilitate student discussions would be needed (see Section 3.3). Basically, it was obvious that discussions and subsequent negotiations are more productive when managed within a specified timeframe (i.e. between managing players' own states and voting about EU policies during each round), space (e.g. normal classroom instead of computer room), and moderated by the teacher. Fig. 9 outlines the model structure of a lesson based on this methodology.

The teacher's reflection on the development of the simulation and his or her lecture introduction to the corresponding real-world issues proved to be critical in reaching the desired learning outcomes of *Europe 2045*. The results of the pilot evaluation also suggest that this lecture has to follow directly the students' in-game experience and has to be clearly linked to the actual game's content. See also [7].

In order to use *Europe 2045* in of the general teaching of compulsory subjects we have designed the instructor's interface in a way that allows him or her to change the in-game scenario of events and thus adjust it to a particular curriculum (e.g. stressing environmental issues, economics, international relations, internal affairs of the European Union, or specific regional issues). Although teachers generally appreciated this feature, in most cases they opted for using *Europe 2045* in specialized, elective seminars. When they expressed willingness to use the game for compulsory subjects, it was mostly motivated by the above-mentioned need for compliance of learning objectives in *Europe 2045* with the new national curricula (especially development of key competencies and European Union issues). During the instructional seminars it also became clear that computer games, as an educational tool, do not appeal to every teacher. As such it seems such games will remain a supplementary – rather than mainstream – educational tool in the near future: at least in Czech Republic.

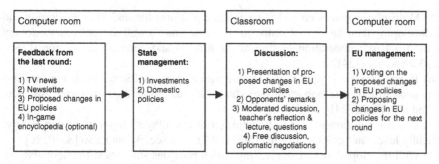

Fig. 9. Methodology for using *Europe 2045* in classes; model lecture

4 Conclusions

In this paper we have discussed key findings on game-based learning with emphasis placed on already known problems related to using computer games in formal education processes. Drawing upon these previous findings and case studies we have put together a theoretical framework, which has been adopted in designing the multi-player educational game, *Europe 2045*. The main purpose of this framework was to ease the development of *Europe 2045* and facilitate its implementation in Czech secondary formal education structures. On a general level this framework is intended to provide theoretical and case-study-based background information for similar projects.

The case studies conducted during testing *Europe 2045* underscored findings already come across in several earlier studies [1, 6, 28] that the context of game-based learning (i.e. national curricula and educational practices surrounding the game) is more important then the actual content of the game. Finally, we had started to formulate the theoretical framework for designing an educational game combining the features of serious games and multi-player on-line games prior to the development of *Europe 2045*. This framework has been further refined in the course of the game's development and has grown to include the following items:

1) Learning objectives must be clearly formulated and set out in accordance with accepted educational practice (e.g. national curricula) before development starts (i.e. accepted at least by teachers that are willing to use the product). See Sec. 3.6 and also [6, 7, 25, 27].

2) Supplementary collaborative activities, educational materials, and teaching methodologies need to be prepared in advance, but in co-operation with end-users. Further improvements in the course of development by means of evaluative studies is vital. See Sec. 3.7 and also [1, 6, 28].

3) The teacher has to be able to provide the students with reflection and contextualization of the learned skills and knowledge into meaningful real-world scenarios. We also suggest that teachers' lectures directly follow the in-game experience and are clearly linked to the game's content. See Sec. 3.7 and also [7].

4) It follows from (2) and (3) that the instructional courses for teachers are essential. The teachers have to be very familiar with both the game's interface and the whole game-based learning process (concept). See Sec. 3.7 and also [6, 25].

5) Multi-player games proved to be an ideal platform for student collaboration and for developing their key social skills. At the same time, a well-designed methodology for the teachers' moderation of student discussions and negotiations is crucial. See Sec. 3.3 and also [24].

6) If role-playing is part of the learning process in multi-user environments students need to have the opportunity to choose or customize their character. See Sec. 3.3 and also [6, 22, 24].

7) Educational games need to be adjusted to non-players in terms of complexity, difficulty level, and graphic user interface (GUI). See Sec. 3.4 and also [8, 10, 26].

8) Well-developed virtual storytelling which provides students with alternative solutions and evolves according to their actions has proven to be an important factor affecting their motivation and engagement. See Sec. 3.5.

9) Educational games need to be designed in accordance with the technological and personal limitations of individual educational institutions. Client-server applications that remove the need for end-user installations proved successful.

10) Fixed lesson times (i.e. 45 minutes) need to be adjusted for the implementation of game-based learning programmes. Most teachers opted for longer block seminars.

This list is, by no means, intended to provide a full and comprehensive or fixed framework for game-learning; rather, we recommend that it be taken as a set of working hypotheses. And of course, there are open questions. First, given the fact that games are often aimed at the development of key skills and broader and cross-disciplinary learning objectives, new ways for assessment of students' progress must be developed. This requires substantial re-thinking on how and what we learn, which is a long-term process that will require rather broad changes in formal educational systems.

Second, from the instructional seminars, that we have already conducted, it also seems that computer games as a learning tool do not appeal to every teacher. Similarly, several authors have suggested that some learners do not like using simulations or games for learning [6]. If an educational game is intended to be used as a general tool for compulsory subjects, educators should definitely have additional choices for presentation of learning materials and more differentiated activities planned [6].

Last but not least, as the field of game-based learning matures, it is probably time to start calculating the per student cost of development for educational games: in terms of money and time spent on development and instructing teachers how to use these specific tools.

Acknowledgments. *Europe 2045* was developed as part of the project "The Integration of IT Tools into Education of Humanities", financed by the European Social Fund, the budget of the Czech Republic, and the City of Prague (CZ.04.3.07/3.1.01.3/ 3213). The simulation was developed by a non-profit organization, Generation Europe, in cooperation with Charles University in Prague, the Association for International Affairs, The International Center for Art and New Technologies in Prague, and the Sázavská secondary school in Prague. The technical research related to the game was partially supported by the Czech Ministry of Education (Res. Project MSM0021620838), and the project "Information Society" under project 1ET100300517. The authors would like to thank the development team: namely Tomáš Holan, Martin Klíma, Petr Jakubíček, Edita Krausová, Veronika Hrozinková, Klára Pešková and Radek Slavík.

References

1. Arnseth, H.C.: Learning to Play or Playing to Learn - A Critical Account of the Models of Communication Informing Educational Research on Computer Gameplay. Gamestudies 6 (2006)
2. Barab, S., Thomas, M., Dodge, T., Carteaux, R., Tuzun, H.: Making learning fun: Quest Atlantis, a game without guns. Educational Technology Research & Development 53(1), 86–107 (2005)
3. Brom, C., Sisler, V., Holan, T.: Story Manager in 'Europe 2045' Uses Petri Nets. In: Cavazza, M., Donikian, S. (eds.) ICVS-VirtStory 2007. LNCS, vol. 4871, pp. 38–50. Springer, Heidelberg (2007)
4. Coleman, J.: Learning through games. In: Avedon, E., Sutton-Smith, B. (eds.) The study of games, pp. 322–329. John Wiley, New York and London (1971)
5. Cordova, D.I., Lepper, M.R.: Intrinsic motivation and the process of learning: Beneficial effects of contextualization, personalization, and choice. Journal of Educational Psychology 88, 715–730 (1996)
6. de Freitas, S.: Learning in Immersive worlds: A review of game-based learning. JISC (Joint informational Systems Committee) report (2006) [6.6.2007], http://www.jisc.ac.uk/eli_outcomes.html
7. Egenfeldt-Nielsen, S., Buch, T.: The learning effect of Global Conflicts: Middle East. In: Santorineos, M., Dimitriadi, N. (eds.) Gaming Realities: A Challenge for Digital Culture, Fournos, Athens, pp. 93–97 (2006)
8. Egenfeldt-Nielsen, S.: Beyond Edutainment: Exploring the Educational Potential of Computer Games. PhD Thesis. University of Copenhagen (2005)
9. Facer, K.: Computer Games and Learning: Why do we think it's worth talking about games and learning in the same breath. Nesta Futurelab discussion paper [6.6.2007], http://www.nestafuturelab.org/research/discuss/02discuss01.htm
10. Facer, K., Ulicsak, M., Sandford, R.: Can Computer Games Go to School? In: Becta. Emerging Technologies for Learning. British Educational Communications and Technology Agency, Coventry (2007) [6.6.2007], http://partners.becta.org.uk/index.php?section=rh&catcode=_re_rp_ap_03&rid=11380
11. Francis, R.: Revolution: Student's experiences of virtual role play within a virtual reconstruction of 18th century colonial Williamsburg (An unpublished manuscript)
12. Gee, J.P.: What would a state of the art instructional video game look like? Innovate 1(6) (2005) [6.6.2007], http://www.innovateonline.info/index.php?view=article&id=80
13. Gee, J.P.: What video games have to teach us about learning and literacy. Palgrave/St. Martin's, New York (2003)
14. General Educational Program in the Czech Republic [7.1.2007], http://www.rvp.cz/
15. Katz, J.: Up, up, down, down. Slashdot.org (2000) [7.1.2007], http://slashdot.org/features/00/11/27/1648231.shtml
16. Kirriemuir, J., McFarlane, A.: Literature Review in Games and Learning, Nesta Futurelab series, Report 8, Bristol (2004)
17. Losh, E.: In Country with Tactical Iraqi: Trust, Identity, and Language Learning in a Military Video Game. In: Digital Experience: Design, Aesthetics, Practice, pp. 69–78. University of Copenhagen, Copenhagen (2005)
18. Malone, T.W.: Toward a theory of intrinsically motivating instruction. Cognitive Science 4, 333–369 (1981)
19. Minsky, M., Papert, S.: Progress report on Artificial Intelligence (1971)
20. Piaget, J.: Play, dreams and imitation in childhood. Norton, New York (1962)
21. Prensky, M.: Digital Game-Based Learning. McGraw Hill, New York (2000)

22. Royle, K.: Games-based Learning: A Different Perspective. Innovative: Journal of Online Education 6 (2007) [7.10.2007], http://innovateonline.info/index.php?view=article&id=433
23. Sandford, R., Ulicsak, M., Facer, K., Rudd, T.: Teaching with Games. Using commercial off-the-shelf computer games in formal education. Futurelab, Bristol (2007) [6.6.2007], http://www.futurelab.org.uk/download/pdfs/research/TWG_report.pdf
24. Schrader, P., Zheng, D., Young, M.: Teachers' perceptions of video games: MMOGs and the future of preservice teacher education. Innovate 2 (3) (2006) [6.6.2007], http://www.innovateonline.info/index.php?view=article&id=125
25. Squire, K.: Cultural Framing of Computer/Video Games. Gamestudies 2 (2002)
26. Squire, K.: Replaying history: Learning World History through playing Civilization III. PhD thesis. Indiana University (2004)
27. Squire, K.D.: From content to context: Games as ideological spaces. In: the International Conference on Education and Information Systems Technologies and Applications (EISTA), Orlando (2004)
28. Squire, K.: Game-based Learning: Present and Future State of the Field. An x-Learn Perspective Paper. MASIE Center (2005) [6.6.2007], http://elearning.fe.up.pt/documentos/e-learning-geral/Game-Based_Learning.pdf
29. Squire, K., Steinkuehler, C.: Meet the Gamers. Library Journal (2005)[6.6.2007], http://www.libraryjournal.com/article/CA516033.html
30. Thorndike, E.L., Woodworth, R.S.: The influence of improvement in one mental function upon the efficacy of other functions. Psychological Review 8, 247–261 (1901)
31. Vygotsky, L.: Mind in society: The development of higher psychological processes. Harvard University Press, Massachusetts, Cambridge (1978)
32. Li, Z.: The Potential of America's Army - the Video Game as Civilian-Military Public Sphere, Master Thesis in Comparative Media Studies, MIT (2004)

Timed Automata-Based Rehabilitation Training Game Design for the Affected Lower Extremity of Hemiparetic Patient

Gi Sook Jung[1], Sang Yun Kim[1], Soon Ki Jung[1],
Seung Deuk Byun[2], and Yang Soo Lee[3]

[1] VR Lab., Department of Computer Engineering,
Kyungpook National University, Korea
[2] Department of Rehabilitation Medicine,
Daegu Fatima Hospital, Korea
[3] Department of Rehabilitation Medicine,
Kyungpook National University College of Medicine, Korea
{gsjung,yun}@vr.knu.ac.kr, skjung@knu.ac.kr,
sato1009@hanmail.net, leeyangsoo@knu.ac.kr

Abstract. This paper presents a timed automata based rehabilitation training game design to effectively strengthen the affected leg of the hemiparetic patient. The proposed system is implemented by applying a simple motion capture technique to a rhythm game. Especially, for the rapid prototyping of the game and a patient-customized game storyline reflecting isometric training as well as dynamic training, the timed automata concept and tool are adopted. The system, which consists of a training generator, rehabilitation training game, and sensor, shows the close correlation with existing physical training.

Keywords: timed automata, motion capture, rehabilitation training game, isometric training, hemiparetic patient.

1 Introduction

In the medical field, there have been various rehabilitation training methods to improve the affected lower extremity of hemiparetic patient, who have incomplete paralysis affecting one side of the body. However, existing rehabilitation training systems, in general, have some disadvantages in that the training methods are boring and stressful. Additionally, depending on the involved muscle and its strength, the patient's ability to train is so various that the training methods cannot be easily customized at a low cost. Hence, it is necessary to present a new rehabilitation training system that lets the patient concentrate on the process at a low stress level and can be somewhat customized for each patient at a low cost. Therefore, this paper presents a training system for a hemiparetic patient implemented by applying a simple motion capture technique to a rhythm game. To allow the rapid prototyping of the game and patient-customized game scenarios reflecting isometric training as well as dynamic training, a timed automata concept and tool were adopted.

Z. Pan et al. (Eds.): Transactions on Edutainment I, LNCS 5080, pp. 17–27, 2008.

2 Related Work

Related works can be described as either rehabilitation training systems [6, 7, 8, 12], dynamic and isometric training [4, 14], or real-time software modeling tools [11, 13].

2.1 Rehabilitation Training System

In the case of the rehabilitation training systems, there are several ones available such as CAREN [12], TheraGames [8], and Kim's walking training game [6, 7].

CAREN [12] is a full body-motion capture system that consists of a moving platform, an optical and magnetic system registering human movements in real-time, and a 3D projector for the projection of the virtual surroundings. The CAREN platform can be applied in areas of physiotherapy, orthopedics, neurology and the early diagnostics of a wide range of balance or coordination disorders. However, even though giving a meaningful methodology to analyze and train human balance, posture and locomotion behavior, the system cannot be directly adopted for hemiparetic patients in paralysis, since their numb muscles are too incomplete to sustain the body on the moving platform.

TheraGames[8] is a home-based rehabilitation game operated on a standard PC with a simple webcam, which requires combinations of motor and cognitive abilities such as memory, planning, and visual scanning. Since the inputs in the TheraGame are left and right arrows, or one or both arms' motion, this system cannot be applied for the hemiparetic patient.

Kim [6, 7] proposed a motion capture-based rehabilitation game for hemiparetic patient's balanced walking training including weight shifting and knee flexion. To sense patient's position information, the degree of horizontal weight shifting and vertical knee flexion angle, the sensor module is composed of two digital indicators and IR filtered camera. However, since it considers only dynamic training, it is necessary to add other training elements such as isometric training in order to increase the training effects.

2.2 Dynamic and Isometric Training

Isometric training is a type of strength training in which the joint angle and muscle length do not change during contraction. Isometric exercise is done in static positions, rather than being dynamic through a range of motion. The joint and muscle are either worked against an immovable force or are held in a static position while opposed by resistance [14].

Isometric exercises have some differences in training effect as compared to dynamic exercises. While isometric training increases strength at the specific joint angles of the exercises performed, dynamic exercises increase strength throughout the full range of motion. A study has shown that while dynamic exercises are 5% better at enhancing the twitch force of a muscle than isometric exercises, isometrics are 32% better than dynamic exercises at increasing maximal muscle power [14, 4].

2.3 Real Time Software Modeling Tool

From the result of the study conducted by J. Duchateau and K. Hainaut [4], it is assumed that maintaining a specific posture for some time is a key factor to increase muscle strength when a hemiparetic patient trains the affected muscles. Hence, when designing a rehabilitation training game, it is important to effectively express the duration time of the specific pose. For real time software modeling tools including that kind of timing features, UML state chart and Uppaal has been proposed [11, 13].

Uppaal is an integrated tool environment for modeling, validation and verification of real-time systems modeled as networks of timed automata, extended with data types. While the UML state charts are weak in their support for absolute time and do not formally support verification methods, timed automata models are rich in support of real time modeling and support formal verification solutions. Additionally, while the UML state chart appropriate for medium complexity systems that do not require exhaustive timing representation and verification, Uppal is suitable for relatively small systems with a stringent timing requirement [11].

Therefore, it is concluded that Uppaal based on timed automata theory is more appropriate for designing a rehabilitation game including isometric training as well as dynamic training. By using Uppaal, the system can be easily modeled, and simulated and verified before the development.

The proposed system in this paper upgrades Kim [6, 7]'s game by way of adding isometric exercise, defining the game with timed automata theory, and modeling the system by using Uppaal. Beside that, the output data of Uppaal can be used as an input to generate the game story. Through the above methods, the system can be a patient-customized rehabilitation game having a close correlation with traditional physical evaluations.

3 System Configuration

The system consists of a training generator, rehabilitation training game, and sensor as shown in Fig. 1.

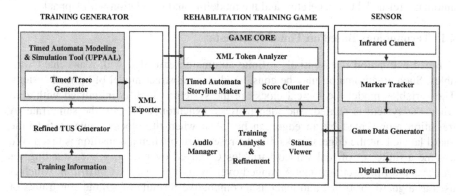

Fig. 1. System diagram

The training generator makes a *timed trace*, which is a sequence of training units, after refining *training unit set* from the basic training information determined by doctor or expert. The generated *timed trace* can be modeled and simulated by using Uppaal and exported to the rehabilitation training game in the form of XML file.

The rehabilitation training game module implements a music action game, since the rhythm game has the features that timing is an important game factor and player's posture can be used as a game input. While a patient plays the game, the game storyline is made from the tokenized *timed trace*, the audio manager deals with the game music, and the status viewer displays the patient's posture in a graph. After playing the game, the patient or expert can check the training results and modify the *training unit set* through training analysis and refinement module.

Since the proposed system basically adopts the previous sensor module [6, 7, 9, 10], the posture information, which is captured from two digital weight indicators and IR filtered camera, is the degree of weight shifting and knee flexion angle like previous system (Fig. 2). The details of sensor module including marker tracker and the game data generation are omitted in this paper.

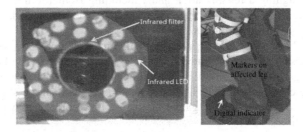

Fig. 2. IR filtered camera and digital indicators [7]

4 Training Generator

The training generator can be described in terms of terminology based on timed automata, refined TUS generator, and the modeling and simulation with Uppaal.

4.1 Terminology Based on Timed Automata

A timed automaton is essentially a finite automaton extended with real-valued variables. Such an automaton may be considered as an abstract model of a timed system. The variables model the logical clocks in the system, which is initialized with zero when the system is started, and then increase synchronously with the same rate. A transition represented by an edge can be taken when the clocks values satisfy the guard labeled on the edge. Clocks may be reset to zero when a transition is taken. We assume a finite set of real-valued variables C ranged over by x, y, etc. standing for *clocks* and a finite set alphabet $\sum$ ranged over by a, b etc. *Clock Constraint*, which is used as a guard for timed automata, is a conjunctive formula of atomic constraints of the form $x \sim n$ or x-$y \sim n$ for $x, y \in C$, $\sim \in \{\leq, <, =, >, \geq\}$ and $n \in N$. $B(C)$ is a set of clock constraints, ranged over by g [1, 2, 3].

Definition: *Timed Automata A* is a tuple $<\sum, S, S_0, C, E>$ such that

1. $\sum$ is a finite set of alphabets called *actions*.
2. S is a finite set of states.
3. $S_0 \subseteq S$ is a set of initial states.
4. C is a finite set of clocks.
5. $E \subseteq S \times B(C) \times \sum \times 2^C \times S'$ is a set of edge. If $(s, g, a, r, s') \in E$, where $r \subseteq C$,
we also write $S \xrightarrow{g,a,r} S'$.

From the basic concepts including *timed automata* and *clock constraint* [1, 2, 3], the terminology such as *action, timed action, pose maintenance time, training unit, training unit set*, and *concurrency* can be newly derived or redefined as follows.

Action, a is a tuple (TT, UT, LT) in which TT, UT, and LT stand for Training Type, Upper Threshold, and Lower Threshold respectively. When the hemiparetic patient does walking training, the more the position is closed to the thresholds, the more patient feels pain.

Timed Action, a pair (t, a), where $a \in \sum$ is an action taken by an automaton A at $t \in R^+$ time after A started. An absolute time t is called a time-stamp of an action a.

Pose Maintenance Time (PMT) is a time for which the patient should maintain specific training posture, where $(x \leq \text{PMT}) \in B(C)$ for $x \in C$ and $\text{PMT} \in R^+$.

Training Unit (TU) is a tuple (TT, UT, LT, PMT, *rate, level*). The TTs are Weight Right Balance (WRB) and Weight Left Balance (WLB) for horizontal weight shifting and Knee Bending (KB) for vertical knee flexion, in which WRB and WLB are the weight difference between the two digital indicators. The UT tells the patient's maximum knee bending angle or weight difference and the LT means the patient's minimum knee bending angle or weight difference. The *rate* stands for a frequency in a sequence of TUs with time-stamps called *Timed Trace*, and the *level* is a value chosen from the difficulty continuum for training.

Training Unit Set (TUS) is a set of TUs that can be described as $\{TU_1, TU_2,..., TU_i\}$, in which i is determined by training planer. *Timed Trace* is $\delta = (t_1, TU_1)(t_2, TU_2)...(t_j, TU_j)$ such that $t_j \leq$ playing time of music for all $j \geq 1$.

Concurrency means that timed automata can be extended with a parallel composition. In the proposed system, easy training having low *level* can be composite with other easy training units.

4.2 Refined TUS Generator

From the training information composed of initial TUS, *range*, and *easy training rate*, this module makes a refined TUS, in which the initial TUS is described as $\{TU_{WRB}, TU_{WLB}, TU_{KB}\}$ shown in Table 1 and the refined TUS is a new set of refined TUs, $\{TU_{WRB1}, ..., TU_{WRBi}, TU_{WLB1}, ..., TU_{WLBj}, TU_{KB1}, ..., TU_{KBk}\}$.

When determining the training information, it is necessary to analyze a patient's physical state to be reflected in the training units for patient-customized training. As the patient's training information, doctor or expert inputs the initial TUS, the *range* which determines how many refined TUs can be generated from |refined UT – refined

Table 1. Initial TUS

	TT	UT	LT	PMT	rate	level
TU_{WRB}	WRB	Max. Weight Diff.	Min. Weight Diff.	time	0	0
TU_{WLB}	WLB	Max. Weight Diff.	Min. Weight Diff.	time	0	0
TU_{KB}	KB	Max. Knee Angle	Min. Knee Angle	time	0	0

LT|, and an *easy training rate* which is the rate of TUs having the level of easy train-
ing in the *Timed Trace*.

The refined TUS, RTUS consists of the refined TUs, in which each TU is a tuple
(TT, RUT, RLT, RPMT, Rrate, Rlevel) such that RUT, RLT, RPMT, Rrate, and
Rlevel stand for refined UT, refined LT, refined PMT, refined *rate*, and refined *level*
respectively. The *easy training rate* in the *Timed Trace*, which is an area between LT
and UT, is newly determined as an area between the RLT and RUT by manipulating
the sigma of the Gaussian distribution function as shown in Fig. 3. Naturally, the *hard
training rate* can be achieved from the rest of the whole area.

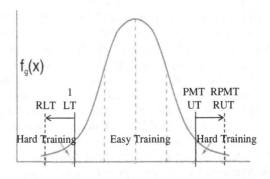

Fig. 3. Easy training rate in the Timed Trace

The concept of making the *easy training rate* or the *hard training rate* in the *Timed
Trace* is also applied to the PMT. From the *easy training rate* and the *range*, the
whole normalized section with the Gaussian distribution can be split into the various
easy and hard refined TUs, in which the split position for easy training units is determined by the following equation (1).

$$split\ position = (RLT + range \times i), where\ 0 \leq i \leq \frac{|RLT - RUT|}{range}\ and\ i \in N \qquad (1)$$

The refined *rate* of the split section can be found by following equation (2) as shown
in Fig.4.

$$rate = range \times f_g(X),\ where\ X = RLT + range \times (i - 1/2) \qquad (2)$$

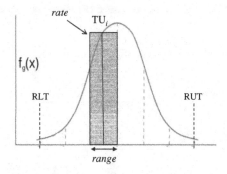

Fig. 4. The rate of TU_i in the Timed Trace

After the splitting process using equation (1) and (2) is repeated for each TU of the initial TUS, the RTUS is made in the form of a set $\{TU_1, TU_2, \ldots, TU_i\}$, that is, $\{(TT_1, RUT_1, RLT_1, RPMT_1, Rrate_1, Rlevel_1), \ldots, (TT_i, RUT_i, RLT_i, RPMT_i, Rrate_i, Rlevel_i)\}$.

When an element of RTUS is included in the easy training section, it can be composed with another easy element of RTUS. Since the system has to consider the limitations of human physical action, the composition of easy trainings has to be processed between the KB and the WRB or between the KB and the WLB. The composition equation is as follow.

$$(TU_{l,rate} + TU_{m,rate}) / easy\ training\ rate \cong ((TU_{k,rate} + TU_{0,rate}) / easy\ training\ rate,$$

$$(3)$$

$$where\ k = \frac{|LT - UT|}{2 \times range}\ and\ 0 \le l, m \le \frac{|LT - UT|}{range}$$

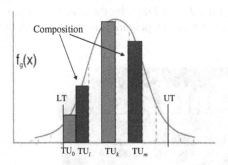

Fig. 5. Composition of two easy trainings

4.3 Modeling and Simulation with UPPAAL

The *Timed Trace* is generated from the RTUS and can be modeled, verified, and simulated by using the Uppaal [13]. The expert can simulate and modify the *Timed Trace*, because artificially generated *Timed Trace* is not always customized for the specific patient even though the expert inputs the patient's information. The screen shot of the Uppaal used in the proposed system is shown in Fig. 6.

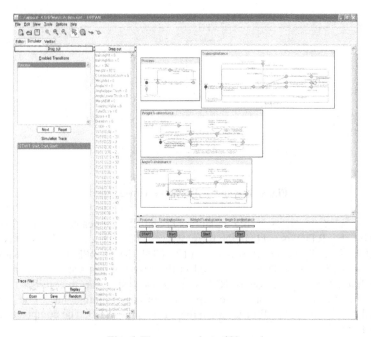

Fig. 6. The screen shot of Uppaal

5   Rehabilitation Training Game

The implemented rhythm game is "Music Action", in which the XML token analyzer splits the Uppaal file into the TUS and the *Timed Trace*. The game story is made from the tokenized TUS and the *Timed Trace* by the timed automata storyline maker. The Status Viewer receives the patient's posture information from the Sensor Module and

Fig. 7. The screen shot of the Music Action

visualizes it. The score counter compares patient's posture with the TU of the *Timed Trace* to mark the game score. After the game ends, the player or expert can analyze and refine the training results.

Fig. 7 shows the screen shot of the Music Action game, in which the length of the bar tells the PMT and the patient trains the postures directed by training instructions. When the patient maintains the right pose in the hitting state, a back-light turns on and percussion is added to the original music.

6 Experimental Results

The two experiments were conducted in terms of the correlation with previous physical trainings and the number of the training methods.

6.1 Correlation with Previous Physical Trainings

The related experiment was conducted at the Department of Rehabilitation Medicine in Daegu Fatima Hospital and the Department of Rehabilitation Medicine in Kyungpook National University College of Medicine. The experiments show how much the proposed system is correlated with existing physical training.

The following items are the evaluation tools in a clinical demonstration for patient with hemiplegia [10].

1. Functional Ambulation Category (FAC)
2. Berg Balance Scale (BBS)
3. 10 meter Walking Time (10mWT)
4. Timed Up & Go test (TUG)
5. Modified Barthel Index (MBI)
6. Maunal Muscle Test (MMT)

Table 2 shows the experimental results for Music Action, in which the figures represent the correlation coefficients between the existing evaluation methods and the game's training elements and score. When the coefficient is higher than 0.4, the parameters are correlated. For the coefficient above 0.6, the two parameters are closely correlated.

Table 2. Correlation with the Music Action and the existing evaluation tools

	FAC	BBS	10mWT	TUG	KMBI	MMT
weight shift to affected leg	0.398	0.516	-0.206	-0.379	0.331	0.220
knee flexion angle	0.629	0.740	-0.620	-0.770	0.460	0.530
game score	0.647	0.699	-0.326	-0.448	0.604	0.526

From the Table 2, it can be concluded that the proposed Music Action has closer correlations than the previous game contents implementing only dynamic training [7]. Therefore, it can be considered that reflecting the isometric trainings as well as the dynamic trainings to the rehabilitation game is more effective for the hemiparetic patients.

6.2 The Number of Training Methods

This paper compares the Music Action with a previous rehabilitation game [7] in terms of the number of training methods. While all the previous games have the training methods under six, the Music Action makes a lot of training methods for each TU of the initial TUS as in the equation below (4). In this equation, the first term means the number of easy and hard trainings, and the second tells the combinations of easy trainings.

$$\frac{|RLT-RUT|}{range}+\frac{|LT-UT|}{2\times range} \tag{4}$$

The previous games such as juggling running, avoiding a fire bomb, virtual walk, and erase board have the isometric training methods under four. As for the Music Action, it satisfies the equation below (5).

$$time\times\frac{|RLT-RUT|}{range}+time\times\frac{|LT-UT|}{2\times range}, where\ time \geq Isometric\ Time \tag{5}$$

Because the presented system designs the training by using timed automata, the training methods can be increased as shown in Fig. 8.

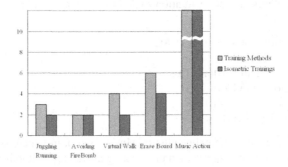

Fig. 8. The number of training methods

7 Conclusion and Future Work

In this paper, the patient-customized training system by using timed automata has been presented. The proposed system has three good points in the rehabilitation training area. First, it presents the elaborate training generator for the patient-customized training, which makes the *Training Unit* and *Timed Trace* based on the patient's information. Second, it adopts the isometric training as well as dynamic training, which results in the close correlation with existing physical training standards. Third, it increases the number of training methods by applying a time parameter and the combination of easy trainings.

The future work is as follows. Because the system provides only semi-automatic tools, it needs to upgrade the manual tools in the Uppaal. Additionally, since it does not have the special tool to generate an optimized *Timed Trace*, the optimization technique for more effective rehabilitation is required. Actually, there was not enough time to conduct various experiments because the experiment takes at least 6 months. Hence, the system needs to be improved for enough time to conduct various experiments, and with a lot of patients suffering from different symptoms.

References

1. Alur, R., Dill, D.L.: A Theory of Timed Automata. In: Proceedings of the 17th International Collquium on Automata, Language, and Programming, vol. 126(2), pp. 183–236 (1994)
2. Bengtsson, J., Yi, W.: Timed Automata: Semantics, Algorithms and Tools, UNU-IIST Report No.316 (2004)
3. Bouyer, P., Fleury, E., Larsen, K.G.: Optimal Strategies in Priced Timed Game Automata, BRICS, Department of Computer Science, University of Aarhus (2004)
4. Duchateau, J., Hainaut, K.: Isometric or dynamic training: differential effects on mechanical properties of a human muscle. Journal of applied physiology: respiratory, environmental and exercise physiology 56(2), 296–301 (1984)
5. Jonathan, P., Folland, A., Hawker, K., Leach, B., Little, T., Jones, D.A.: Strength Training: Isometric Training at a Range of Joint Angles versus Dynamic Training. Journal of Sports Sciences, 817–824 (2005)
6. Kim, S.Y., Jung, S.D., Kim, S.H., Jung, S.K., Lee, Y.S., Kim, C.H.: Rehabilitation Training System for Leg Rehabilitation Based on Motion Capture. In: Proceedings of HCI, South Korea, vol. 1, pp. 109–114 (2007)
7. Kim, S.Y., Jung, G.S., Oh, S.H., Lee, Y.S., Jung, S.K.: A Motion Capture Based Rehabilitation Training System for the Affected Lower Extremity of Hemiparetic Patient. In: Proceedings of the 7th International Conference on Applications and Principles of Information Science, Auckland, New Zealand, pp. 583–587 (2008)
8. Kizony, R., Weiss, P.L., Shahar, M., Rand, D.: TheraGame–a Home Based Virtual Reality Rehabilitation System. In: Proc. of 6th Intl Conf. Disability, pp. 265–269. Virtual Reality & Assoc. Tech, Esbjerg, Denmark (2006)
9. Lee, Y.S.: Appraratus for Rehabilitation Training and Method of the Rehabilitation Training Using the Weight Load and the Angel of Articulation For Variable, Korea Patent: 10-2005-0024333 (2005)
10. Lee, Y.S., Kim, C.H., Byun, S.D.: Correlation between Maximal Inclination of Sliding Rehabilitation Machine and Gait Parameters. Journal of Korean Academy of Rehabilitation Medicine 31(2), 196–201 (2007)
11. Naughton, M., McGrath, J., Heffernan, D.: Real-time Software Modeling Using Statecharts and Timed Automata Approaches. In: IEE Irish Signals and Systems Conference, Dublin, June 28-30 (2006)
12. CAREN (Computer Assisted Rehabilitation Environment),
    http://www.motekmedical.com
13. Uppaal, http://www.Uppaal.com
14. Wikipedia, http://www.wikipedia.org

A Haptic Virtual Environment for Molecular Chemistry Education

Makoto Sato, Xiangning Liu, Jun Murayama,
Katsuhito Akahane, and Masaharu Isshiki

Precision and Intelligence Laboratory - Tokyo Institute of Technology
msato@pi.titech.ac.jp,
{liu,jmy,kakahane,m_isshiki}@hi.pi.titech.ac.jp

Abstract. We attempted to produce an environment for education.
Subjects such as mathematics or sciences are usually studied on a desk
in a classroom. Our research goal is to allow students to study scientific
contents more viscerally than existing studying methods by haptic interaction. To construct the environment, we have to make a user-friendly
haptic interface. The study is described in two parts. The first part is
defining what a useful haptic interface is. In this part, we focused on the
grip of a haptic interface. SPIDAR-G is a haptic interface, which is ma-
nipulated by a grip with 8 strings.. Grip size is an important parameter
for usability. We have found an optimal sphere size through SPIDAR-G
usability testing. The other part is defining how teachers can use the
interactive system with haptic interaction as a teaching aid. In this part
, we focused on the interaction between two water molecules. First, we
constructed an environment to feel Van der Waals force as well as electrostatic force with haptic interaction. Then, we observe the effectiveness
of the environment when used by a class of students.

1 Introduction

Education is defined asthe field of study related to the pedagogy of teaching and
learning. The approach for carrying the teaching-learning cycle has been changing along with the evolvement of technology. In recent years, the wide availability of technological tools, such as, computers, networks, Virtual environments,
among others has allowed the development of a new educational method known
as e-learning (electronic learning).

The development of educational tools must aim to the overall improvement of
the learning cycle, for that, we must combine and use technology in a way that
does not interfere or distract user s attention from learning.

To enhance students' scientific learning, interactive technologies such as haptic
virtual environments have been increasingly used on the basis that students understand scientific ideas best when they are allowed to take a hands-on approach,
particularly when receiving haptic sensory feedback [5][7][22][24]. It is now well
known that virtual environments combined with haptic feedback can provide
students with very unique learning opportunities. Being allowed to investigate

Z. Pan et al. (Eds.): Transactions on Edutainment I, LNCS 5080, pp. 28–39, 2008.
© Springer-Verlag Berlin Heidelberg 2008

and experiment with abstract concepts that are not easy to be controlled in the real world (e.g., gravity), can help students think critically and gain confidence in their problem-solving abilities [22], evoke the tacit, embodied knowledge which has proved useful for formal science learning [20], and have a positive effect on reasoning about scientific ideas [21].

This exploratory study attempted to address these overarching issues by designing, developing, and evaluating interactive, haptic virtual learning environments that can support scientific learning. In addition, the overall quality of a string-based haptic device, SPIDAR [18], used to interact with the haptic virtual learning environments, was evaluated to obtain usability data. First, we review the potentials of sensory experience through haptic feedback in science education. In addition, previous interactive learning systems developed to support molecular learning will be reviewed. Second, an empirical experiment conducted to evaluate performance of the SPIDAR haptic device will be described, with an emphasis on the operability of SPIDAR-G's spherical grip [6]. We will also report the results of our experiment conducted to assess the educational effectiveness of a haptic virtual learning system we developed to support understanding of intermolecular forces. Finally, we will discuss the practical implications of haptic virtual learning systems and introduce a new haptic device.

2 Background

Throughout the years instructors have followed different approaches when teaching chemistry. Laboratory practices are a "must" when conducting lessons on molecular concepts. If we take a look back into our high school years we may remember learning about molecular geometry using balloons, constructing molecules using plastic models, learning by experimenting with substances and many other activities that helped us understand certain concepts when theory alone was not enough.

The reason laboratory practices or hands-on activities reinforce learning has been widely subjected to research and different studies have concluded and agreed on the positive effect of stimulating and combining various senses for knowledge acquisition. How we acquire knowledge? What conditions are needed for faster learning? Why does a group of students have different level of understanding of a lesson taught using equal resources? These are just some of the questions asked when trying to understand human's learning process (branch of cognitive science), and some of the answers found, help us create better methods, tools and resources o be used when teaching.

Some concepts and theories considered in this research, which served to justify the importance of developing alternative tools, were based on studies concerning learning and will be briefly introduced.

Each individual has his/her own channel preference when learning. We may stimulate one or various senses to fasten the acquisition of knowledge. Traditional lectures are usually classified as passive learning and are often limited to the stimulation of visual and auditory channels. The development of e-learning tools generates new resources capable of stimulating various learning channels; it is a tool that transforms passive learning into active learning, allowing students to learn at their own pace.

3   Overview of Haptic Virtual Learning Systems

3.1   SPIDAR-G Haptic Device and Usability Evaluation

A ground-based haptic device, called PHANToM, has been largely used to interact with most of the previous haptic learning systems [17]. PHANToM's pen-shaped grip may interfere with user's natural manipulation (i.e. when moving objects at certain postures). Sato et al. developed a 3D interface called SPIDAR-G, consisting of a grip attached to 8 strings connected to motors and encoders inside a cubical frame. Users manipulate virtual objects by rotating and translating the grip, which is initially located on the center of SPIDAR-G's frames. An experiment was conducted to assess the effect of the size of SPIDAR-G's grip on the manipulation of objects in 3D virtual spaces.

1) Method

Subject: Eight male subjects participated in the experiment: six in the age range of 20-29, one in the range of 30-39, and one in the range of 50-59. None of the subjects had any hand-related handicaps. The average hand length is 19.7cm according to the AIST Anthropometrics Database [16] in Japan. All subjects were within 5% range of the standard hand length.

The Shape: SPIDAR-G is a 6DOF haptic interface that is operated using a spherical grip as shown in Figure 1. SPIDAR-G's grip is attached to 8 strings that are connected to 8 motors and encoders.

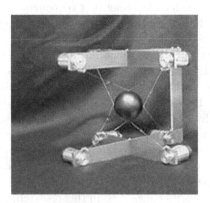

Fig. 1. SPIDAR-G

The basic structure of SPIDAR-G is shown in Figure 2. As the grip is being operated, SPIDAR-G obtains data regarding the string's lengths from the encoders every $t + \Delta t$.

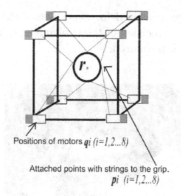

Positions of motors q_i $(i=1,2...8)$

Attached points with strings to the grip.
p_i $(i=1,2...8)$

Fig. 2. Structure of the SPIDAR-G

Experimental Task: Docking tasks were implemented in a 3D virtual space, in which participants moved a 3D cursor from a starting position into a target position as Fig.3. The cursor and target were created as 3-simplex (tetrahedron) where the edges of the tetrahedron were displayed as white with colored spheres attached on each of its vertices. The spheres were drawn using different colors to provide subjects with a sense of direction and orientation when matching cursor and target. In addition, to differentiate between cursor and target, brightness levels were used in different proportion for each object. A visual stimulus was displayed to subjects when docking was achieved (cursor and target matched their postures). The visual stimulus consisted on changing the tetrahedron's edges from white to red.

Target

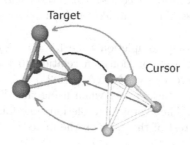

Cursor

Fig. 3. The task for the experiment

Measurements: Rotation, translation, and mixed (both rotation and translation) movements had to be executed by a subject in order to dock a cursor into its target. The translational task measured cursor movement while the rotational task measured cursor rotation. 12 targets were given for each movement (rotation, translation, mixed). Each subject needed to execute a set of tasks (12 targets for each movement rotation, translation, mixed) twice to complete a set.

Completion times were measured for every set of the experiment for use in evaluation. To confirm the precision of the movements in the task, the trajectory in the mixed task was also measured.

Fig. 4. Environment for the experiment

Procedure: Subject operates SPIDAR-G's grip to adjust and move the 3D cursor and match the target as Fig.4. When cursor and target match in regards of their vertices positions, the edges of the tetrahedron change colors from white to red representing a matching state. The matching state must be maintained for 0.7 seconds for the docking to occur. A cycle of steps 1-5 is repeated 2 times to complete a set. 7. 3 completed sets constitute one session. For each of the four different grips (30mm, 48mm, 60mm, and 77mm) one session is executed.

2) Results

As shown in both Fig. 5 and Fig. 6, the average completion time for each of the tasks (translation and rotation executed separately) had little variation when using different grips. However, we noticed a slight increase in task times when using larger grips.

Fig. 7 shows the average completion time for all subjects when executing mixed tasks (translation and rotation). In relation to the combined task, we can observe a slight difference by ANOVA ($F(3;21) = 2:46;P > 0:1$) that subjects completed the mixed tasks faster when using the 48mm diameter-grip as compared to other grips. The average completion time for all subjects tends to increase when using the rest of the grips on the mixed tasks.

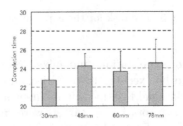

Fig. 5. Completion time – Translation task

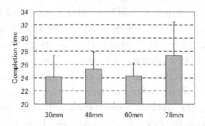

Fig. 6. Completion time – Rotation task

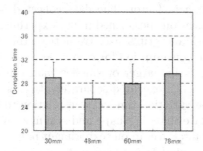

Fig. 7. Completion time – Mixed task

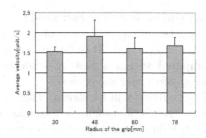

Fig. 8. Average velocities – Mixed task

Translation task results show slight variation in all subject task times when operating different grips. On the other hand, rotation task results show significant variations in subject task times. To confirm the handling quantity effect, Fig 8 shows the average trajectories, obtained by the four apexes on the cursor, from the task execution of the mixed tasks.

As shown in Fig. 8, ANOVA results showed a significant difference in the velocity of the cursor's apex ($F(3;21) = 6.67; P > 0:05$).

As a whole, the results displayed show that the 48mm diameter grip results in faster user task completion.

3) Discussion

The general assumption - if we take into account the concept of human coordinate movements - is that the use of larger grips would result in better task times. When designing a grip for a 3D interface, we need to consider the coordinate movements that occur between arm, wrist and fingers. For example, if we decide to use a large diameter spherical grip, users would need to open and separate fingers to hold and operate the grip. Thus, the user's arm and wrist movements will affect the range and speed of the grip's manipulation. Adversely, if we settle on using a small diameter spherical grip, users will use mostly fingers to operate the grip and the overall movements will tend to be more subtle, and therefore faster and more precise. As we can see, human arm and hand movement plays an important role when designing an optimal grip for 3D interfaces. In our research, by testing grips of different diameter, we were considering the human coordinate movement factor. The data collected from the mixed tasks (both rotation and translation) performed in our experiments showed a concave relationship between task and grip's size. We noticed that the 48 mm diameter grip had the lowest time consumption for combined tasks. Correspondingly, the task times increased for grips larger or smaller than the 48mm grip. We also observed that the tasks when executed separately, that is, either translation or rotation tasks, had little variation time-wise in relation to the grip's size. From the results we can validate that the shape and size must be evaluated when developing an optimal 3D interface. In our experiment based on SPIDAR-G's grip, a sphere shaped grip of around 48mm of diameter is considered the optimal grip.

3.2 Haptic Virtual Learning System for Intermolecular

This section shows the comparison between traditional teaching methods, which utilize visual and auditory interaction, and our proposed system, which utilizes haptic, visual, and auditory interaction. Traditional teaching methods and our proposed system are compared within a class of students by considering the interactional forces between two water molecules.

First, the contents of our system will be shown. Then, to measure the effectiveness of our system, two groups of students are compared. One group learns the content from a teacher, followed by a question/answer session. The second group learns through our haptic environment, followed by a question/answer session. The results will show the effectiveness of haptic interaction in the aforementioned scientific learning environment.

1) Method

Subject: 19 subjects participated in the experiment. Subjects were in the age range of 17–18 years old. All subjects are students of Electronics at Salesian Polytechnics.

Intermolecular Learning System: The system consists of a computer generated virtual environment and one SPIDAR-G device, as in Fig 9. The virtual environment was developed using OpenGL [10]. SPRINGHEAD [12] was used to calculate the coordination system.

The structures of molecules were taken from PDB files. [8][9] The algorithm used to calculate the force vector and generate the force feedback is outlined as follow:

Fig. 9. Intermolecular learning system

1. Obtain distance between atoms of molecules.
2. Calculate Energy Potential Functions, Van der Waals energy as (1) and electrostatic energy as (2) based on CHARMM. [7]

$$\mathbf{E}_{e_{ij}} = \frac{1}{2\pi\varepsilon_0 r} q_1 q_2 \tag{1}$$

$$\mathbf{E}_{v_{ij}} = \frac{A_i}{r_{ij}^{12}} - \frac{A_i}{r_{ij}^{6}} \tag{2}$$

Aij and Cij denote constant dependent upon atoms, and rij denotes distance between two atoms, and q1 and q2 denote carriers.
3. Differentiate the Potential energy
   (a) Calculate Energy between atoms as (3)

$$\mathbf{E}_{ij} = \mathbf{E}_{v_{ij}} + \mathbf{E}_{e_{ij}} \tag{3}$$

   (b) Calculate Energy based on an estimated distance (d+Δ d) as (4).

$$\Delta\mathbf{E}_{ij} = \mathbf{E}_{v_{ij}}(\mathbf{d}) + \mathbf{E}_{e_{ij}}(\mathbf{d} + \mathbf{\Delta d}) \tag{4}$$

4. Calculate Force for each atom as (5).

$$\mathbf{f}_{ij} = \frac{d}{d_d}\mathbf{E}_{ij} = \frac{\Delta\mathbf{E}_{ij}}{\Delta\mathbf{d}} \tag{5}$$

5. Add Force Values as (6)

$$\mathbf{f} = \sum_i \sum_j \mathbf{f}_{ij} \tag{6}$$

6. Present force feedback to SPIDAR-G with fixed number as (7). In the case, we set k as $k = 1 \times 10^{13}$.

$$\mathbf{f}_p = k\mathbf{f} \tag{7}$$

Experimental Task: For the experiment we set the system and task as following: Two water molecules were displayed on screen. One molecule had a fixed position but could be rotated using the keyboard. A second molecule was moved using one SPIDAR-G device, which also provided the force feedback.

Before the experiment, a specialist conducted a lecture on the topics of In-termolecular Forces Concepts and equations were provided to students by tra-ditional teaching methods.

Measurements: To measure the system's functionality, we conducted a test that consisted of six questions that inquired students' understanding of Inter-molecular Concepts. A sample of the questions asked are shown below:

1. What kind of force exists between hydrogen and oxygen?
2. What kind of force exists between oxygen and oxygen?
   (a) What kind of force exists between hydrogen and hydrogen?

We also evaluated usability and learner's engagement through a ranked questionnaire.

Procedure: After the lecture was conducted, the class was randomly divided into two groups randomly. Groups that will be referred to as Group A and Group B. Group A consisted of 10 students and Group B consisted of 9 students. Both groups interacted with the system as Fig.10 and took a short test that inquired student's understanding on the lesson. Timing for taking the test varied for each group.

Students from Group A were asked to use the system after the lecture was conducted. After each student from Group A had interacted with the system, they were allowed some extra time to try the system again either by themselves or in small groups. Once they had used the system they were given the test.

Group B, on the other hand, was tested following the lecture. Students from this group were able to use the system only after completing the test. Follow-ing the test, every student from Group B tried the system and gave feedback regarding their experience.

2) Results

Effective to the score: The results of Group A and Group B are shown in Fig.11. From the results we can imply that using the system after the lesson contributed to the students' understanding of concepts. Students were able to reinforce the theory learned by using the system. Having both a lesson on Inter-molecular concepts and a hands-on experience contributed to the good results obtained by Group A - whose participants scored a higher number of correct answers. Results obtained from Group B shows a large number of incorrect an-swers. Group B's test performance was low when compared to results obtained from Group A. We can imply that merely listening to explanations may not be sufficient for understanding Intermolecular Forces Concepts.

Effective to the motivation of students: From the results we notice how using an alternative learning tool capable of stimulating the haptic channel as well as recreating forces contributes to students' understanding on the subject of Intermolecular Forces.

In concern to the users' impressions on the system, Fig. 12 shows that most students felt the system was easy to use, ranking the system's usage from a range of four to five being the highest possible rank. Regarding user engagement, most

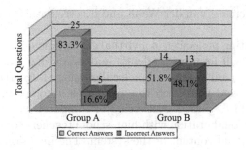

Fig. 10. The result of the test

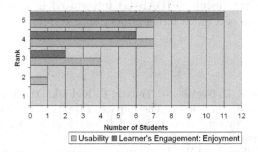

Fig. 11. Result of the questionnaire

students gave rankings from 4 to 5, showing that students enjoyed using the system.

3) Discussion

Overall, positive comments were received from students. Some students expressed how they found the activity to be fun and interesting. Others commented on how by using the system concepts became clearer and easier to understand. Positive feedback was also received from the professor who conducted the lesson. The professor pointed out a noticeable increase in students' interest on the concepts taught, expressing that throughout the lesson student's seemed more motivated and excited than usual.

Overall, the evaluation of the system showed positive response from both students and teachers towards the use of alternative learning tools to help reinforce the understanding of concepts. Based on the results obtained we recommend the incorporation of these type of learning tools in regular classroom, when learning molecular concepts such as the one targeted with our system (Intermolecular Forces).

4 Discussion and Conclusions

The system was presented as an alternative tool for the study of Intermolecular Force. To enhance the system manipulation, we tested and found a suitable grip.

We were able to recreate Van der Waals and Electrostatic forces using SPIDAR-G devices

Easily manipulating molecules in a virtual environment is an important aspect for students, as it will improve student's understanding. Analysis of the users' responses supports manipulation of molecules using the SPIDAR-G.

In order to test and transform the system as a complete educational tool, new modules should be added. Authoring of computer based training software could be planned. Collaboration with high school teachers could be conducted to define the instructional content of the system. The inclusion of media (graphs, videos, sounds, interactive evaluations, hyperlinks) and system navigation needs to be designed so that users can learn and navigate content at their own pace. The developed system (using SPIDAR-G) introduced in this paper, could be included as a module of a much larger educational system.

References

1. Jones, M.G., Andre, T., Negishi, A., Tretter, T., Kubasko, D., Bokinsky, A., Taylor, R.: Superfine, Hands-On Science: The Impact of Haptic Experiences on Attitudes and Concepts.In: National Association of Research in Science Teaching Annual Meeting, Philadelphia, PA (2003)
2. James, W.B., Galbraith, M.W.: Perceptual learning styles: Implications and techniques for the practitioner. Lifelong Learning 3, 20–23 (1985)
3. Wu, H.-K., Krajcik, J.S., Soloway, E.: Promoting conceptual understanding of chemical representations: students' use of a visualization tool in the classroom. Journal of Research in Science Teaching 38, 821–842 (2001)
4. Sankaranarayanan, G., Weghorst, S., Sanner, M., Gillet, A., Olson, A.: Role of Haptics in Teaching Structural Molecular Biology. In: Proceedings of the 11th Symposium of Haptic Interfaces for Virtual Environments and Teleoperator Systems (HAPTICS 2003), p. 363-366 (2003)
5. Sauer, C.M., Hastings, W.A., Okamura, A.M.: Virtual Environment for Exploring Atomic Bonding. In: Proceedings of EuroHaptics 2004, p. 232-239 (2004)
6. Kim, S., Ishii, M., Koike, Y., Sato, M.: Design a Tension Based Haptic Interface: SPIDAR-G. In: World Multiconference on Systemics, Cybernetics and Informatics (SCI 2000), pp. 422–427 (2000)
7. Brooks, B.R., Broccoleri, R.E., Olafson, B.D., Stales, D.J., Swaminathan, S., Karplus, M.: CHARMM: A program for macromolecular energy, minimization, and dynamics calculations. J. Comp. Chem. 4, 187–217 (1983)
8. http://www.pdb.org
9. Berman, H.M., Westbrook, J., Feng, Z., Gilliland, G., Bhat, T.N., Weissig, H., Shindyalov, I.N., Bourne, P.E.: The Protein Data Bank. Nucleic Acids Research 28, 235–242 (2000)
10. The OpenGL Utility Toolkit, http://www.opengl.org/resources/libraries/
11. Yanlin, L., Murayama, J., Akahane, K., Hasegawa, S., Sato, M.: Development of new force feedback interface for two- handed 6DOF manipulation SPIDARG-G system. In: ICAT 2003, pp. 166–172 (2003)
12. Hasegawa, S., Okada, N., Baba, J., Tazaki, Y., Ichikawa, H., Shirai, A., Koike, Y., Sato, M.: Springhead: Open source haptic software for virtual worlds with dynamics simulations. In: EuroHaptics 2004 (2004)

13. Ardito, C., De Marisco, M., Lanzilotti, R., Levialdi, S., Roselli, T., Rossano, V., Tersigni, M.: Usability of E-Learning Tools. In: Proceedings of the working conference on Advanced visual interfaces, pp. 80–84 (2004)
14. Fill, K.: Student-focused evaluation of elearning activities. In: European Conference on Educational Research (2005)
15. Chua, B.B., Dyson, L.E.: Applying the ISO9126 model to the evaluation of an e-learning system. In: Atkinson, R., McBeath, C., Jonas-Dwyer, D., Phillips, R. (eds.) Beyond the comfort zone: Proceedings of the 21st ASCILITE Conference, pp. 184–190 (2004)
16. Kouchi, M., Mochimaru, M.: AISTAnthropometric Database, National Institute of Advanced Industrial Science and Technology, H16PRO 287 (2005)
17. Massie, T.H., Salisbury, J.K.: The PHANTOMHaptic Interface: A Device for Probing Virtual Objects. In: Proc. ASME Winter Annual Meeting, Symposium on HapticInterfaces for Virtual Environmentand Teleoperator Systems (1994)
18. Ishii, M., Sato, M.: 3D Spatial Interface DeviceUsing Tensed Strings. PRESENCE-Teleoperatorsand Virtual Environments, vol. 3(1), pp. 81–86. MIT Press, Cambridge (1994)
19. Nam, C.S., Shafieloo, I.: Haptic Virtual Environments as a Science Learning Supporting Tool: A Preliminary Study. In: Proceedings of the IASTED International Conference on Educational Technology, Calgary, Alberta, Canada, pp. 40–44 (2006)
20. Reiner, M.: Conceptual construction of fields through tactile interface. Interactive Learning Environments 7, 31–55 (1999)
21. Bussell, L.: Haptic interfaces: Getting in touch with web-based learning. Educational Technology 41, 27–32 (2001)
22. Paulu, N., Martin, M.: Helping your child learn science. U.S. Department of Education Office of Educational Research and Improvement (1991)
23. Brooks, F.P., Ouh-Young, M., Batter, J.J., Kilpatrick, P.J.: Project GROPE—Haptic displays for scientific visualization. ACM Computer Graphics 24, 177–185 (1990)
24. Kilpatrick, P.J.: The use of kinesthetic supplement in an interactive system. Ph.D dissertation, ComputerScience Department, University of North Carolina at Chapel Hill (1976)

ARGarden: Augmented Edutainment System with a Learning Companion*

Sejin Oh and Woontack Woo

GIST U-VR Lab.
Gwangju, 500-712, S.Korea
{sejinoh,wwoo}@gist.ac.kr

Abstract. Recently, many researchers have studied on agent-based edutainment systems to improve students' learning experiences. In this paper, we present ARGarden which makes users experience an interactive flower gardening with a learning companion squatting on an augmented picture. The companion perceives users' actions as well as situations in the learning environment and appraises the perceived information autonomously. Then, it presents peer support to help participants' problem-solving through anthropomorphic expressions. We developed our system on a mobile device and visualized a learning companion as an animated bluebird. We also demonstrated the implemented system at an exhibition and evaluated the effectiveness of our system through the observation of participants' responses to the demonstration. In this evaluation, we found that the bluebird as a learning companion helped users to experience how to properly grow the flower in our edutainment setting. Finally, we expect possibilities that an augmented learning companion is one of the key factors for developing effective edutainment applications.

1 Introduction

In enhancing the effectiveness of educational applications, researchers have studied how they could increase students' engagements in learning experiences. Since the pedagogical agents can provide students with advice in response to their problem-solving activities, many researchers have applied the pedagogical agents to their educational systems for improving students' abilities [1], [2], [3], [4]. Moreover, the animated pedagogical agents have persona effect which makes their presences increase students' motivation on their learning experiences [5]. Although the research on animated pedagogical agents has been progressed, they rarely presented a connection to the real environment where the users actually exist. The spatial gap between users and pedagogical agents can be one of reasons why the users lose their interests in current educational systems.

To reduce the discontinuity between users and learning environments, there have been studies on augmented reality (AR) technology based educational systems [6], [7],

---

* This research was supported by the Foundation of UCN Projects, the MKE, and the 21C Frontier R&D Program in Korea as a result of subproject UCN 08B3-O1-20S.

Z. Pan et al. (Eds.): Transactions on Edutainment I, LNCS 5080, pp. 40–50, 2008.

[8], [9]. Furthermore, many researchers have developed augmented pedagogical agents in their educational settings [10], [11], [12]. Since AR technology allows users to experience computer generated contents embedded into the real world [6], it can make pedagogical agents coexisted with users in the same real space. Moreover, it enables the users to interact with the agents over a physical environment. Finally, it reduces the spatial seam between the users and the agents.

The pedagogical agents in AR setting express the guidance suitable for problem-solving situations in the real space. In the *Welbo* system, an animated agent guided users who wear HMD to simulate virtual furniture in an MR space [10]. The *AR Lego* exploited the augmented agent to educate an untrained user for assembling LEGO Mindstorms robot [11]. Wagner et al. introduced *Mr. Virtuoso* as an augmented expert which taught users about art history in an educational game [12]. In these systems, it lets users perceive the reduced spatial gap to agents and receive more benefits on their learning abilities from educational systems. However, since the augmented agents only have focused on guiding users explicitly as instructors, it sometimes disturbs the users and reduces their motivation on the educational settings. To offer more effective ways to improve users' learning experiences, edutainment systems need to give them less intrusive guidance for motivating them to engage in the systems.

In this paper, we present ARGarden which provides users with flower gardening experiences with a learning companion in real space. This system supports users to explore environmental considerations that affect gardening. Thus, the users can simulate specific factors, e.g., water, fertilizer, and light, to an animated flower in the augmented scene. In addition, we visualize an interactive learning companion as an animated bluebird. The bluebird presents pedagogical strategies with peer support through anthropomorphic expressions. Furthermore, users can collaborate on a work with the bluebird in our edutainment settings. We have implemented the proposed system on a mobile device attached with a camera. Then, we demonstrated our system at an exhibition and evaluated the effectiveness of the installed system. In the demonstration, participants presented better engagement in their learning experiences by interacting with a bluebird as a learning companion. Therefore, we can see indications that the augmented learning companion in edutainment system can be one of factors for improving students' engagement in their learning experiences.

The presented ARGarden has following characteristics. It presents a learning companion that responds to the users' interaction and shows peer support for helping the users to solve the problem situation. It offers a believable situated environment in which human learners can experience environmental consideration for the flowering in the real space where the learners actually exist. Moreover, it motivates users to engage in our learning environment by making them cooperate with the learning companion. Ultimately, we expect possibilities that a learning companion can increase users' engagement in learning experiences and improve the users' learning abilities in edutainment systems.

This paper is organized as follows. Section 2 introduces our augmented edutainment system. Section 3 describes detailed explanation of components in the implemented results. Then, section 4 shows the observation of users' responses to demonstration at an exhibition. Section 5 presents some general observations and remarks in our system and directions for future research.

2 ARGarden: Augmented Edutainment System

We have developed ARGarden that allows users to experience the flower gardening with a learning companion. In our system, users can see an augmented scene, which is consisted of simulated factors, a virtual flower and an animated learning companion, through their mobile devices. In addition, it enables users to explore environmental considerations that govern gardening and to interact with an augmented learning companion in the learning environment. The companion perceives users' interaction and changes of the augmented gardening environment, and then assists the users to solve the problem-solving situation. Fig.1 shows the overview of ARGarden.

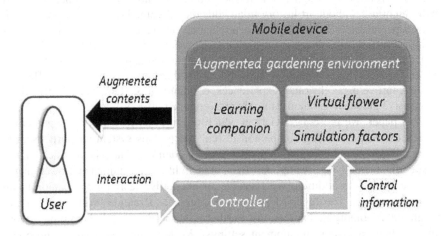

Fig. 1. The proposed ARGarden

2.1 Interactive Gardening Environment

We design an interactive learning environment which allows users to experience the gardening in real space. To support users to simulate environmental considerations on gardening, we offer a user interface for enabling the users to choose a specific factor, e.g., water, light, and fertilizer, which they can apply to a virtual flower in an augmented environment. We also provide users with the interaction metaphor for applying the selected factor to the virtual flower. According to users' simulation, the status of an augmented flower is changed. Therefore, participants can not only experience the gardening, but also learn influences of a specific environmental factor on the flower gardening.

We let users collaborate with an augmented learning companion by assigning collaborative working problems on the flower gardening to the users. In achieving the assigned work, users try to select a simulation factor and apply it to an augmented flower. In addition, the learning companion expresses peer support to the users' interaction by offering pedagogical comments to assist the users to solve the problem. Therefore, users can learn how to cooperate with their companions to achieve the desirable results.

2.2 A Learning Companion

Our learning companion generates autonomous behaviors to provide learners with problem-solving advice with peer support. The companion has the capability to perceive learners' action and changes generated from the augmented learning environment. In addition, it appraises the perceived information according to its own internal state, e.g., belief, desire, and intention [13]. Then, it generates responses suitable for problem-solving contexts [14]. Fig. 2 describes the response generation process of the learning companion.

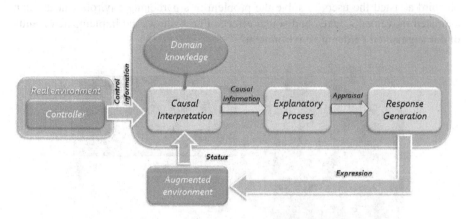

Fig. 2. The response generation process of the learning companion

A learning companion appraises the problem circumstance through the causal interpretation based on its domain knowledge. The knowledge contains the companion's mental state concerning actions and states [15]. Each state can be assigned a numerical value in the interval [-100, 100] denoting the companion's utility, which implies how much the state contributes to achieve the goal. Thus, a state associated with a positive value of utility is desirable for helping the companion to accomplish its intended goal. In addition, the relationship between actions and states is represented by causal establishment or threat relation, i.e. the effect of action can establish or threaten the goals. A plan to achieve the intended goal is composed of a set of actions, states and their relationships. Moreover, each state is appraised in accordance with computational appraisal theory, in terms of appraisal variables: relevance, likelihood, controllability, changeability, and can result in an emotional response [16].

To increase users' engagement with the learning companion, we allow the companion to show less intrusive responses than an instructor. Thus, the companion appraises the users' selection based on the status of the simulated environment. Then, it generates its own emotional state about the situation and presents the state for motivating the users to achieve desirable results. Therefore, the companion sympathizes with the users' actions in edutainment settings instead of explicit advice for problem-solving contexts. Ultimately, we expect that this kind of the learning companion can contribute to participants' better leaning experiences in edutainment systems.

3 Implementation

We have developed the proposed ARGarden on an ultra mobile personal computer (UMPC) attached with a camera. In Fig. 3, we made users experience the implemented system over a physical book which describes contents related to gardening. To overlay the interactive gardening environment on the book, we attached fiducial markers, which are exploited to ARToolkit [17], to pages of the book. Then, we augmented an animated flower and simulated factors, such as water, light, and fertilizer. Users could also interact with an animated bluebird as a learning companion. The bluebird assisted the users to solve the problem in a gardening environment through animated movements, texts, and sound effects. Fig. 4 shows the implemented results of our augmented gardening environment.

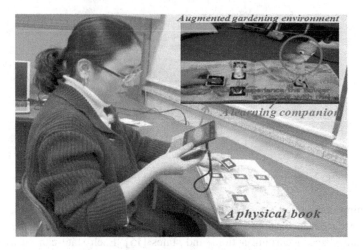

Fig. 3. The implemented ARGarden

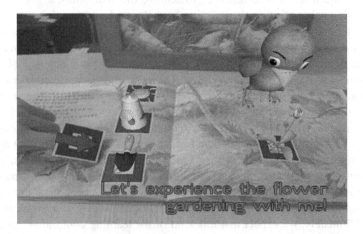

Fig. 4. Interactive gardening environment augmented over a physical book

In our system, we attached several fiducial makers to pages of the book. As shown in Fig. 5 (a) each marker indicates its function through an understandable picture. For example, if an object is the controller for adjusting the amount of water, a marker contains a sprinkler. Moreover, as shown in Fig. 5 (b), users can see augmented 3D CG models indicating specified simulated factors, such as water, light, and fertilizer, through their devices.

(a)   (b)

Fig. 5. (a) Fiducial markers over pages of a book (b) Augmented models over the markers

3.1 Interaction Metaphor

We offered a simple interaction metaphor which enables users to experience our AR-Garden in a natural manner. To allow users to select a specific factor which users want to simulate to the flowering, we designed a ring-type controller attached with a fiducial marker. Thus, the users could choose and apply the factor to the augmented flower with the controller. When they approached the controller to a marker attached to pages of a book, the 3D model overlaid on the fiducial marker was transmitted and augmented over the controller. Fig. 6 shows the interaction metaphor for the selection. In addition, we allowed users to apply the selected factor to the augmented flower through simple actions. Fig. 7 describes examples of the interaction metaphor. According to an applied factor, the augmented flower showed several changes represented by animation sequences of 3D models, such as growing up, withering, and waving. Therefore, participants could experience the gardening and learn the effects of the factors on the flower gardening.

(a)   (b)

Fig. 6. The interaction for selection (a) Initial state (b) Selecting a watering factor

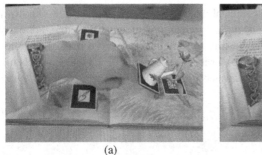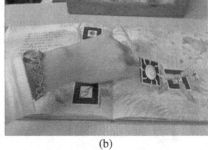

(a)	(b)

Fig. 7. The interaction for applying the selected factor (a) Sprinkling water (b) Shining the light

3.2 A Learning Companion's Expression

In the implemented ARGarden, we visualized a learning companion as an animated bluebird. Then, we made the bluebird present anthropomorphic visual and verbal responses autonomously. It showed visual expressions by changing animation sequences. Especially, the bluebird had capabilities to express the internal state, e.g., emotion, desire, through animated movements. Fig. 8 shows examples of the visual expressions reflecting the bluebird's states. In addition, to engage users' interests in the interaction with our bluebird, we displayed texts as bluebird's verbal actions. We also generated sound effect suitable for the verbal responses to the users' interaction.

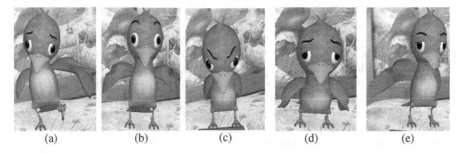

(a)	(b)	(c)	(d)	(e)

Fig. 8. Visual expressions (a) Fear (b) Joy (c) Anger (d) Tiredness (e) Encouragement

We customized the implemented bluebird's dynamic gestures and verbal responses suitable for a user's problem-solving situations as a learning companion. The implemented bluebird appraised the user's selection for assisting the user to solve the situation. Then, it presented its own comments or advice on the situation. For example, when a user selected an improper factor for the flowering, the bluebird recommended the user to select other factors. However, if the user ignored the bluebird's comment and applied the incorrect factor to the flower, the bluebird became fearful because they could not achieve the goal of flower gardening. Then, the bluebird showed corresponding visual expression and displayed texts indicating "fear" state, instead of explicit guidance like an instructor. Fig. 9 describes examples of the bluebird's expressions in a positive/negative circumstance.

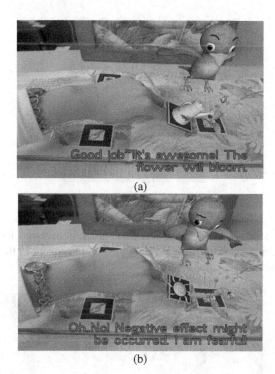

(a)

(b)

Fig. 9. The bluebird's expressions (a) A positive response (b) A negative response

4 Evaluation

To review users' response to the implemented ARGarden, we demonstrated our system at iDAT (Interactive Digital Art and Technology) 2007 [18]. In this demonstration, participants experienced the interactive gardening environment. Then, we observed participants' responses to the installed system. We could know that a learning companion made better participants' engagements in the installed learning environments. Finally, we found possibilities that an interactive learning companion in augmented educational setting could improve students' learning experiences in educational system.

4.1 Demonstration

In this exhibition, we allowed participants to experience ARGarden through a mobile device and to interact with other participants. Thus, a user could see the virtual gardening environment over the book and experience the flower gardening with his or her hands. Other participants could see the interactive gardening environment through large LCD monitor at the same time. Fig. 10 shows the setup of our system at the exhibition.

Since major participants of the exhibition were children, aged 8 to 13, we could collect and evaluate children's responses about our system. In this demonstration, we assigned a simple task, *help-to-blooming*, to them and offered collaboration condition by making the implemented bluebird present its movements and sound effects like a

Fig. 10. The setup of our system at iDAT

companion. While using our system, we noted their impression for indicating how they felt our bluebird's responses, and how engaged they were in the interaction with the bluebird as a learning companion.

Fig. 11. Participants to ARGarden at the exhibition

4.2 Observation

In these considerations, we observed children's impression of learning experiences in our system. At first, they actually liked to use ring-type controller and to see changes of 3D models over the controller by approaching it to markers on the book. Since they tried to change a 3D model on the controller repeatedly, we found that they had interests in the offered interaction metaphor. However, we also found inconveniences of current metaphor. Some children could not perceive the depth information when they saw the augmented scene with a mobile device. Since it was difficult for some of them to select a factor and to apply it to the augmented flower, we need to add more cues, such as the shadow of 3D model, for offering depth information.

Especially, we found how participants felt about our bluebird in our installation. Most children presented positive responses to the bluebird's expression according to their interaction. They tried to talk with the bluebird and to touch the animated bluebird with their own hands directly. In addition, we found their interesting responses to the bluebird. That is, they really liked the bluebird's positive responses, such as expression of joy and encouragement. Contrarily, they hated the bluebird's negative responses, e.g. anger and sad. When they experienced the negative responses, they tried to find the solution for changing the bluebird's response toward positive expressions. However, some children complained that why the bluebird did not make an eye contact with them like their friends. In addition, some of them could not understand the bluebird's response to their interaction. Thus, we need the bluebird to provide more customized peer support and more companion-like responses with participants about problem-solving situation. Even if current bluebird responses are limited to offer fully friend-like impression to participants, we could see that most children showed curiosity to an augmented bluebird, and expressed joyful engagement to experiences, especially the interaction with the bluebird, in our edutainment setting.

5 Conclusion and Future Work

In this paper, we described ARGarden which allowed users to experience an interactive flower gardening with a bluebird, a learning companion. The proposed system augmented a picture with the animated bluebird to provide interactive edutainment experiences with users. The bluebird could perceive the users' actions as well as the status of the learning environment. It also could appraise the information to provide participants with problem-solving advice. Moreover, the bluebird presented less intrusive responses than an instructor through anthropomorphic expressions. Furthermore, we exhibited the implemented system and evaluated its effectiveness through observation of participants' responses to our system at the exhibition. Furthermore, we found indications that the augmented learning companion in augmented edutainment system has possibilities to motivate participants' engagement in their learning experiences.

Current implemented system has limitations as revealed from comments of participants' responses to our exhibition. At first, it was insufficient to allow participants to understand a bluebird's explanations about social events. Therefore, we plan to specify and design the bluebird's more detailed guidance for improving the participants' understanding of the bluebird's explanation in edutainment setting. We also need to improve the bluebird's expressiveness to offer peer support as a companion than an instructor. Moreover, we plan to evaluate the effectiveness of a learning companion through usability tests on our edutainment system.

Acknowledgement

We give thanks to Sangchol Seo and Jaeseok Kim for their support in designing and modeling CG contents of the implemented ARGarden.

References

1. Lester, J., Stone, B., Stelling, G.D.: Lifelike pedagogical agents for mixed-initiative problem solving in constructivist learning environments. User modeling and user adapted interaction 9(1), 1–44 (1999)

2. Johnson, W., Rickel, J., Lester, J.: Animated pedagogical agents: face-to-face interaction in interactive learning environments. International Journal of Artificial Intelligence in Education 11, 47–78 (2000)

3. Gulz, A., Haake, M.: Design of animated pedagogical agents—A look at their look. International Journal of Human-Computer Studies 64(4), 322–339 (2006)

4. Sklar, E., Richards, D.: The Use of Agents in Human Learning Systems. In: International Joint Conference on Autonomous Agents and Multiagent Systems, pp. 767–774 (2006)

5. Lester, J., Converse, S., Kahler, S., Barlow, T., Stone, B., Bhoga, R.: The Persona Effect: Affective Impact of Animated Pedagogical Agents. In: Conference on human factors in computing systems, pp. 359–366 (1997)

6. Azuma, R., Baillot, Y., Behringer, R., Feiner, S., Julier, S., MacIntyre, B.: Recent Advances in Augmented Reality. IEEE Computer Graphics and Applications 21(6), 34–47 (2001)

7. Billinghurst, M., Kato, H., Poupyrev, I.: The MagicBook: a transitional AR interface. Computers and Graphics 25(5), 745–753 (2001)

8. MacIntyre, B., Bolter, J.D., Moreno, E., Hannigan, B.: Augmented Reality as a New Media Experience. In: International Symposium on Augmented Reality (ISAR), pp. 197–206 (2001)

9. Andreas, D., Eva, H.: An observational study of children interacting with an augmented story book. In: Hui, K.-c., Pan, Z., Chung, R.C.-k., Wang, C.C.L., Jin, X., Göbel, S., Li, E.C.-L. (eds.) EDUTAINMENT 2007. LNCS, vol. 4469, pp. 305–315. Springer, Heidelberg (2007)

10. Anabuki, M., Kakuta, H., Yamamoto, H., Tamura, H.: Welbo: an embodied conversational agent living in mixed reality space. In: Conference on human factors in computing systems, pp. 10–11 (2000)

11. Barakonyi, I., Psik, T., Schmalstieg, D.: Agents That Talk And Hit Back: Animated Agents in Augmented Reality. In: IEEE and ACM International Symposium on Mixed and Augmented Reality, pp. 141–150 (2004)

12. Wagner, D., Billinghurst, M., Schmalstieg, D.: How Real Should Virtual Characters Be? In: International Conference on Advances in Computer Entertainment Technology (2006)

13. Bratman, M.E.: Intentions, Plans, and Practical Reason. Harvard University Press, Cambridge (1987)

14. Oh, S., Gratch, J., Woo, W.: Explanatory Style for Socially Interactive Agents. In: Paiva, A., Prada, R., Picard, R.W. (eds.) ACII 2007. LNCS, vol. 4738, pp. 534–545. Springer, Heidelberg (2007)

15. Gratch, J., Marsella, S.: Technical details of a domain independent framework for modeling emotion from, http://www.ict.usc.edu/~gratch/EMA_Details.pdf

16. Gratch, J., Marsella, S.: A Domain-independent framework for modeling emotion. Journal of Cognitive Systems Research 5(4), 269–306 (2004)

17. http://www.hitl.washington.edu/artoolkit/

18. http://idat.wikidot.com/

Developing a Digital Game-Based Situated Learning System for Ocean Ecology

Jia-Jiunn Lo, Nai-Wei Ji, Ya-Huei Syu, Wan-Jyun You, and Yi-Ting Chen

Department of Information Management,
Chung-Hua University Taiwan, Republic of China
{jlo, b9210086, b9210116, b9210078, b9210004}@chu.edu.tw

Abstract. Digital game-based learning integrates computer games and learning content so that makes learning processes more engaging and attractive to learners. It embodies well-established principles and models of constructive view of learning. It has a number of advantages for learning environments, primarily, the ability that effectively motivate learners. Situated learning is an approach that puts learners into an environment that is similar to where the educational content will be applied in the future. Digital game-based situated learning integrates concepts of situated learning into digital game-based learning so that the learning process can take place unintentionally. This study developed a digital game-based situated learning system with nonlinear scenario paths aiming at 4-6 grades elementary students for ocean ecology learning. The main scenario of the game is centered on the life of a sea turtle heading for growing up. Paths with different ending alternatives of this turtle, formed by different combination of events, are designed to increase the motivation of users to play the game many times. Each event presents a situation and presents information of one ocean ecology concept. Non-player characters (NPCs) designed for each ocean ecology situation. The main knowledge resource is delivered through interactions between the sea turtle and NPCs. In addition to the scenario presented in an event, an observation screen is used to introduce more information about this event. Types of "small games" are designed to fit characteristics of every event. The branch to be followed along the path depends on the result of playing a "small game". In this study, the ocean ecology situations are presented in a vivid animated cartoon to attract children to learn in an interactive manner. Through experiencing different situated learning environments regarding ocean ecology situations, the user can have a better understanding of sea ecology, making their experience in the adventure more engaging and meaningful.

Keywords: game-based learning, situated learning, nonlinear path, animation.

1 Introduction

Online learning has been a fast growing field in education worldwide. Currently, there are abundant of online learning materials designed for children. However, not all of these learning materials that are available online have high attractiveness to children in that they seldom consider the psychological characteristics of children. As Liu (2006)

Z. Pan et al. (Eds.): Transactions on Edutainment I, LNCS 5080, pp. 51–61, 2008.
© Springer-Verlag Berlin Heidelberg 2008

mentioned, children like visual and interesting things and their knowledge roots in cognitive construction for objective world. Therefore, construction of learning environment is critical to raise children's learning interests and learning effects. Digital games have a number of advantages for construction of leaning environments for children. Primarily, they can effectively motivate learners. Digital games are believed to enhance intrinsic rather than extrinsic motivation of learners. In addition to "motivation", certain types of digital games can offer more advantages in learning. For example, adventure games can facilitate the integration of knowledge and skills across a number of content areas (Alessi and Trollip, 2001).

This study developed a digital game-based e-learning system aiming at 4-6 grades elementary students for ocean ecology learning. The main scenario of the game is centered on the life of a sea turtle. It is somewhat like an "adventure game" with implicit goals, in which the user becomes a sea turtle heading for growing up. Through experiencing different situated learning environments regarding ocean ecology situations, the user can make their experiences in the adventure more engaging and meaningful and have a better understanding of sea ecology. In this study, the ocean ecology situations are presented in a vivid animated cartoon to attract children to learn in an interactive manner.

2 Literature Review

2.1 Digital Game-Based Learning

According to the constructive view of learning, knowledge is not received from the outside or from someone else; rather, it is the individual learner's interpretation and processing of what is received through the senses that creates knowledge. Learners construct personal knowledge from the active learning experience rather than passive transmission (Ally, 2004; Zualkernan, 2006). Games embody well-established principles and models of constructive view of learning. They are effective because the learning takes place within a meaningful context. The learning is not only relevant but also applied and practiced within that context. Learning that occurs in meaningful and relevant contexts is more effective than learning that occurs outside of those contexts. Researchers refer to this principle as situated cognition. Researchers have also pointed out that play is a primary socialization and learning mechanism common to all human cultures. Games, clearly, make use of the principle of play as a constructive learning strategy (Eck, 2006).

Games are powerful educational tools if used appropriately. According to Crawford (1982), there are five major regions of games: board games, card games, athletic games, children's games, and computer games, which have common fundamental concepts such as representation, interaction, conflict, and safety. Crawford further divides computer games into two broad categories: skill-and-action (S&A) games and strategy games. The major factor that distinguishes between S&A games and strategy games is the emphasis on motor skills. All S&A games require some perceptual and motor skills. They are characterized by real-time play, heavy emphasis on graphics and sound, and use of joysticks or paddles. On the other hand, strategy games emphasize cogitation rather than manipulation and do not emphasize motor skills. They typically require more time to play than S&A games.

From a learning perspective, Charsky (2004) organize computer games into three categories: content driven didactic, business/training simulation, and recreational. *Content driven didactic games*, the type concerned in this study, embed the content or instruction in the game and can be referred to as edutainment. The game and content is well organized and sequenced. The game characteristics are used to make learning fun. This game type is consistent with a learning philosophy that centered on the transmission of information. The content is the information and the applied game strategy is merely a vehicle to deliver that information. In content driven didactic games, valuable learning is very explicit. *Business/training simulation games* teach learners basic skills through the simulation activities and teach higher order complex thinking skills through replicating the context and aspects of the real world. They require the learner to assume a role and give the learner a virtual feel for the role the learner is playing. Valuable learning is explicit in the sense that it transfer to a similar job/role. *Recreational games* typically have more fantasy elements. Usually, they are designed to make money. Therefore the gaming experience takes precedence over any learning goals. Valuable learning is not planned or facilitated.

Digital game-based learning integrates computer games and learning content so that makes learning processes more engaging and attractive to learners. It has a number of advantages for learning environments. Primarily, it can effectively motivate learners. Digital game-based learning works for the following reasons: (1) the added engagement that comes from putting the learning into a game context; (2) the interactive learning process employed; and (3) the way the two are integrated (Alessi and Trollip, 2001; Prensky, 2001). As cited in Prensky (2001), Kernan argued the following logic to make children learning at home: (1) since there is no time to use it in schools, the best way to make a difference for technology in schools is not in schools, but at home; (2) these programs have to be able to beat the other things that interest children; (3) to get the learning at home, it has to be fun. In this context, digital game-based learning encourages learners to study material they might not otherwise choose to study at all and learners will spend more time and invest more effort with the program than they would if other methodologies were used (Alessy and Trollip, 2001).

Brown et al. (1989) suggested that knowledge is influenced by, and cannot be separated from the situations within which knowledge is exerted, i.e., it is situation-based. Situated learning is an approach that puts learners into an environment that is similar to where the educational content will be applied in the future. When students learn in such environment, they benefit not only from the educational content but also from the culture that is in the environment. Digital game-based learning does particular well in creating highly realistic and immersed environment (Jong et al., 2006; Prensky, 2001).

Computer technology nowadays makes digital game-based learning possibly created into near real-life virtual worlds, which give players the feeling of living in a real situation and assuming a role in there (Shang et al., 2006). Thus, situated learning and computer technology work well together. Digital game-based situated e-learning integrates concepts of situated learning into digital game-based learning so that the learning process can take place unintentionally rather than deliberately. It is favored, interesting, explanatory, stimulating, challenging and capable to empower students to learn with confidence and retain the learnt knowledge (Jong et al., 2006).

2.2 Designing of Digital Game-Based Learning

According to Alessi and Trollip (2001), creating successful educational games must satisfy three basic requirements: the game must have worthwhile learning objectives; the game must be fun; and the game's goal must reinforce the learning goals. Prensky (2001) suggested that a good digital game-based learning comes only when engagement and learning are at a high level. Both dimensions have to be considered all the time. Therefore, a game style that engages and teaches what is required is needed.

Prensky (2001) summarized elements for designing enjoyable educational experiences such as challenges, fantasy, curiosity, imaginary situation, progressive difficulty, outcome uncertainty, etc. Alessi and Trollip (2001) also proposed seven general factors in designing of digital game-based learning: goals, rules, competition, challenge, fantasy, safety, and entertainment. In addition to the above general factors, they also suggested many important unique factors that impact learning and motivation as the game begins: scenario, level of reality, cast, role of the players, presence of uncertainty, presence of curiosity, nature of competition, relationship of learning to the educational objectives, skill versus chance, wins and losses, choices, information flow, turns, types of actions, and modes of interaction. Prensky (2001) further established a set of principles to create effective digital game-based learning by answering the following questions: Is this game fun enough that someone who is not in its target audience would want to play it (and would learn from it)? Do people using it think of themselves as "players" rather than "students"? Do users want to play again and again? Are the players' skills in the subject matter and learning content of the game? Does the game encourage reflection about what has been learned?

Construction of learning environment is critical to raise children's learning interests and learning effects. As multimedia technology has become widely available, learners are exposed to material in verbal and pictorial forms. One of the most exciting forms of pictorial presentation is animation. As cited in Charsky (2004), Keller proposed the ARCS model of motivation. The ARCS model suggests that student motivation includes four aspects: Attention, Relevance, Confidence, and Satisfaction. Animation can effectively receive users' attention on the learning content. Recently, animations have been increasingly incorporated into learning materials and it is believed that animation would be helpful for learning. Animated characters and graphics allow designers a great deal of freedom. They can be made to look and sound any way the designer want. Their actions can be preprogrammed and reprogrammed as necessary (Presnsky, 2001). One of the main reasons for the growing popularity of animation is the belief that animation is more interesting, aesthetically appealing, and therefore more motivating. Researchers have shown that animations are much preferred for their perceptual attractiveness. If learners find animations interesting, they will spend more time and resources attending to them (Mayer and Moreno, 2002; Kim et al., 2007). For children, an animated cartoon game can play an important role in education and effectively attract them to learn in an interactive manner. Learning by animated cartoon game has the advantage that traditional education methods cannot compare with, especially for children (Liu, 2006).

Keeping users motivated is the most important key element for digital game-based learning. In addition to animation, curiosity can effectively motivate users to learn beyond what they currently know or to explore further than they have come. It compels users to seek new knowledge. Player curiosity is usually used as a motivator. Enjoyable games will both evoke players' curiosity and provide a means for satisfying it through learning the knowledge embedded in the game (Alessi and Trollip, 2001). Moreover, uncertainty can increase users' motivation to learn, too. As cited by Alessi and Trollip (2001), Malone believes that a game needs to be uncertain to be challenging the attainment of its goal.

Games with nonlinear scenarios allow the player to experience different stories by being guided or making choices at each branching point. Alternative scenarios are designed to be explored and direct the player to different results. Such nonlinear scenario structure can arouse users' curiosity and offer uncertainty for challenging the attainment of its goal, hence motivates users to learn The player expects to play the game many times, trying different strategies each time. A game's representational value increases with each playing until the player has explored a representative subset of the branches in the game net (Alessi and Trollip, 2001; Charsky, 2004; Crawford, 1982).

Based on the above discussions, using the life of a sea turtle, this study developed a digital game-based situated e-learning system in animation with nonlinear scenario paths aiming at 4-6 grades elementary students for ocean ecology learning.

3   The Digital Game-Based Situated E-Learning System

3.1   Overview

The main scenario of the game developed in this study is centered on the life of a sea turtle to introduce ocean ecology to 4-6 grades elementary students. This game weaves facts and faces of ocean ecology into the journey of the sea turtle since it was hatched. It is somewhat like an "adventure game" with implicit goals, in which the user becomes a character (the sea turtle) heading for growing up. The journey is highlighted by different adventure scenes. This story about the sea turtle gives users a better understanding of sea ecology, making their experience in the adventure more engaging and meaningful. While traveling in the ocean, users will see animated scenes of the sea turtle and things around it. After the animated scenes, users can access more information by clicking objects, such as knowledge chunks and overview map, in the corresponding observation screens. Then the user is required to play a game or answer questions related to this scene to determine the following adventure scene.

Almost every game contains fantasy elements in an attempt to motivate and excite users. Many games use graphics, audios, videos, and animations to enhance game play (Charsky, 2004). An animated cartoon has the force of exaggerative expression and can effectively attract children to learn in an interactive manner (Liu, 2006). Therefore, in this study, the ocean ecology situations are presented in a vivid animated cartoon.

3.2 Game Structure

The scenario of a game is the "world" of in which the action takes place. This game is constructed with an intrinsic scenario, in which the nature of what is being learned is practically identical to the scenario and the learner activities within the scenario. In an

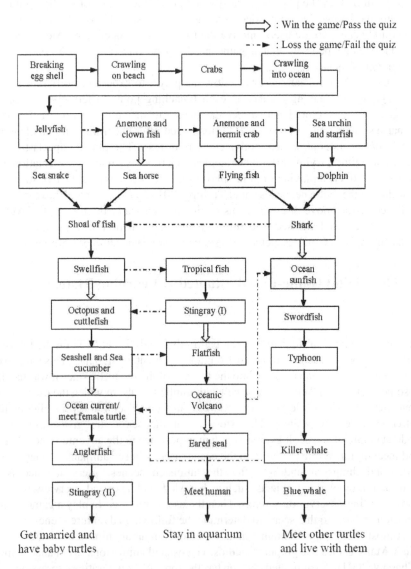

Fig. 1. The nonlinear scenarios of ocean ecology learning system

intrinsic game, the content is an integral part of the game structure (Alessi and Trollip, 2001; Prensky, 2001). In this study, gaming space is built to make ongoing scenarios with nonlinear paths formed by different combination of events. Paths with different ending alternatives of a sea turtle are designed to increase the motivation of users to play the game many times (see Fig. 1). A path is a series of connected events in context. Each event presents a situation of one ocean ecology concept with animations. These ocean ecology concepts can be oceanic creatures, such as shark and dolphin, or natural phenomenon, such as typhoon and ocean current. Such event-driven nonlinear structure allows users to play the game many times and each time the gaming experience will be different. The game space evokes users' curiosity because they are encouraged to explore and discover. Furthermore, the nonlinear scenario structure of this game can offer uncertainty for challenging the attainment of its goal and arouse users' cognitive curiosity (curiosity about information), hence motivates users to learn (Alessi and Trollip, 2001; Charsky, 2004).

A digital game can define or constrain the roles of participants more than a traditional game (Alessi and Trollip, 2001). Especially, in a digital game, it is possible to define non player characters (NPCs) to increase its attractiveness. In this game, NPCs are designed for ocean ecology situations. The main resource for knowledge about sea ecology situations is delivered through interactions between the sea turtle and NPCs. Such knowledge includes not only biological features and behaviors of oceanic creatures but also other natural phenomenon such as typhoon and ocean current. For example, in the "Anemone and clown fish" event (see Fig. 2), knowledge about the commensal relationships between anemone and the clown fish is presented by interactions and dialogues among the sea turtle and NPCs (anemone and the clown fish).

After the user experiencing a situation, an observation screen, embedded with every event, will be presented (see Fig. 3). The user may interact with observation screens by clicking objects, such as knowledge chunks, overview map, and animated objects, to obtain more supplementary information about this event. The knowledge chunk gives basic information about this event, e.g., the number of species of clown fishes. This basic information may or may not be directly related to the scenario of this situation. The overview map is designed to allow the user to see the current location of this event, such as beach, coral reef, oceanic volcano, etc., for better understanding of ocean ecology (see Fig. 4). In addition to knowledge chunks and overview map, the user can click animated objects in an observation screen. As an animated object is selected, a corresponding animation will be shown. Some animated objects are designed to present more information about this event whereas some are just designed to stimulate users' curiosity to retain their interests for continuous learning by showing "surprised" animated cartoon.

The structure of the game developed in this study is a combination of many "small games". After the observation screen, the user is required to play a "small game" or answer questions accompanied with this event. Types of games are designed to fit characteristics of every event. For example, for the "Anemone and clown fish" event, a jigsaw puzzle of anemone and clown fish is designed (see Fig. 5) and for the "Shark" event, a splatman-like game using the sea turtle and shark is used (see Fig. 6). This

Fig. 2. Situation screen of "the "Anemone and clown fish" event"

Fig. 3. Observation screen of the "Anemone and clown fish" event

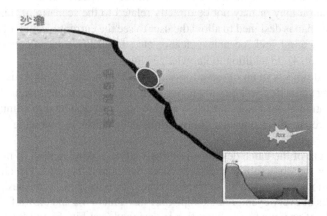

Fig. 4. Overview Map of the "Anemone and clown fish" event

program is designed with a branching structure to motivate the user to play the game many times. Some events are designed as branch points. As the user played the game in one event, he/she moves on to another event. The next event to be followed along the path depends on the result of playing the small game or answering the questions (see Fig. 1). For example, if the user passes the jigsaw puzzle of the "Anemone and clown fish" event, the next event will be the "Sea horse" event. Otherwise, the next event will be the "Anemone and hermit crab" event.

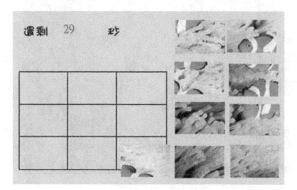

Fig. 5. The game (jigsaw puzzle) of the "Anemone and clown fish" event

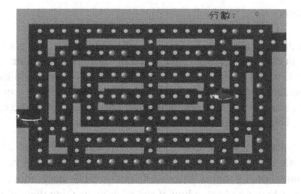

Fig. 6. The splatman-like game of the "Shark" event

As suggested by Alessi and Trollip (2001), competition has both positive and negative characteristics. It can be motivating for those students who win the game and demotivating for other students who lose the game. Though "wins and losses" are the results of playing a game in general, playing the game developed in this study does not have "real" winner or loser to avoid the negative effects of losing a game, especially for children. No matter a user wins or loses the small game accompanied with an event, he or she can always continue the learning process till the end. The only difference is the following event to experience. The motivation of learning roots in the uncertainty and curiosity resulted from the nonlinear structure of paths and different ending alternatives.

As the user completes a path to reach one of the three ending alternatives, he/she will be given a password. With this password, the user will be able to access all the "small games" and questions accompanied with events as well as knowledge chunks included in observation screens through the main menu (see Fig. 7).

Fig. 7. Main menu

4 Conclusions

The design of a digital game-based e-learning system aiming at 4-6 grades elementary students for ocean ecology learning is presented in this paper. The main scenario of the game is centered on the life of a sea turtle. Through experiencing different situated learning environments regarding ocean ecology situations, the user can have a better understanding of sea ecology, making their experience in the adventure more engaging and meaningful. This game includes the following characteristics:

(a) Situated learning environment: This study integrates concepts of situated learning into digital game-based learning so that the learning process can take place unintentionally rather than deliberately. This story about the sea turtle gives users a better understanding of sea ecology, making their experience in the adventure more engaging and meaningful.

(b) Nonlinear scenario structure: Paths with different ending alternatives of a sea turtle are designed to increase the motivation of users to play the game many times. Such nonlinear scenario structure of this game can offer uncertainty for challenging the attainment of its goal and arouse users' cognitive curiosity, hence motivates users to learn. In addition, to avoid the negative effects of losing a game, especially for children, the user can always continue the learning process till the end no matter he/she wins or loses the small game accompanied with an event.

(c) Interactive learning environment: In this game, NPCs are designed for ocean ecology situations. The main resource for knowledge about sea ecology situations is delivered through interactions between the sea turtle and NPCs. In addition, an observation screen, which the user may interact with to obtain more supplementary information, is designed to be embedded with every event.

The game developed in this study can be accesses through the following URL: http://www.chu.edu.tw/~jlo/CAI/Ocean/Main.swf

References

1. Alessi, S.M., Trollip, S.R.: Multimedia for Learning: Methods and Development. 3rd edn. Allyn & Bacon, Needham Heights Massachusetts, USA (2001)
2. Ally, M.: Foundations of Educational Theory for Online Learning. In: Anderson, T., Elloumi, F. (eds.) Theory and Practice for Online Learning, ch. 2, pp. 3–32 (2004), http://cde.athabascau.ca/online_book/pdf/TPOL_book.pdf
3. Brown, J.S., Collins, A., Duguid, P.: Situated cognition and the culture of learning. Educational Researcher 18(1), 32–42 (1989)
4. Charsky, D.G.: Evaluation of the Effectiveness of Integrating Concept Maps and Computer Games to Teach Historical Understanding. Ph.D. Dissertation, U. of Northern Colorado, USA (2004)
5. Crawford, C.: The Art of Computer Game Design (1982), http://www.vancouver.wsu.edu/fac/peabody/game-book/ACGD.pdf
6. Eck, R.V.: Digital Game-Based Learning: It's Not Just the Digital Natives Who Are Restless. EDUCAUSE Review 41(2), 16–30 (2006)
7. Jong, M.S.Y., Shang, J.J., Lee, F.L., Lee, J.H.M., Law, H.Y.: Learning Online: A Comparative Study of a Situated Game-Based Approach and a Traditional Web-Based Approach. In: Pan, Z., Aylett, R.S., Diener, H., Jin, X., Göbel, S., Li, L. (eds.) Edutainment 2006. LNCS, vol. 3942, pp. 541–551. Springer, Heidelberg (2006)
8. Kim, S., Yoon, M., Whang, S.-M., Tversky, B., Morrison, J.B.: The Effect of Animation on Comprehension and Interest. Journal of Computer Assisted Learning 23(3), 260–270 (2007)
9. Liu, Z.: Design of a Cartoon Game for Traffic Safety Education of Children in China. In: Pan, Z., Aylett, R.S., Diener, H., Jin, X., Göbel, S., Li, L. (eds.) Edutainment 2006. LNCS, vol. 3942, pp. 589–592. Springer, Heidelberg (2006)
10. Mayer, R.E., Moreno, R.: Animation as an Aid to Multimedia Learning. Educational Psychology Review 14(1), 87–99 (2002)
11. Prensky, M.: Digital Game-Based Learning. McGraw-Hill, USA (2001)
12. Shang, J., Jong, M.S.Y., Lee, F.L., Lee, J.H.M.: VISOLE: A New Game-based Situated Learning Paradigm. In: Proceedings of the Sixth International Conference on Advanced Learning Technologies (ICALT 2006) (2006)
13. Zualkernan, I.A.: A framework and a methodology for developing authentic constructivist e-Learning environments. Educational Technology & Society 9(2), 198–212 (2006)

A Pen-Based 3D Role Modeling Tool for Children

Jie Li, Danli Wang, and Guozhong Dai

Institute of Software,
The Chinese Academy of Sciences,
Beijing 100190, China
mumu1109@gmail.com, danli@ios.cn,
guozhong@admin.iscas.ac.cn

Abstract. Storytelling for children has received more and more attention. With the development of computer technology, many researchers put forward their novel storytelling systems to change the traditional way of storytelling. However, most of these systems have limited roles. Current modeling tools are mainly for professional users, so it's hard for children to add roles or props into the storytelling systems. In order to provide a larger space for children's creation, we present a pen-based 3D role modeling tool. The tool uses a pen-based interface, gesture recognition technology and role templates. With this tool, children can create various roles for their stories easily and enjoy the storytelling experience more.

Keywords: storytelling, pen-based interface, sketch, gesture recognition, 3D role modeling.

1 Introduction

Storytelling has been a multi-disciplinary research subject, which involves pedagogy, anthropology, sociology, psychology, linguistics and so on. Storytelling plays an important part in the growth of children. It can effectively improve children's language expression, logic thinking, imagination and creativity [1]. On the one hand, parents can teach their children basic moral rules and communication skills with the help of stories. On the other hand, children are all fond of listening to and telling stories. It brings them a lot of joy that they can play different roles in different stories. In the process of storytelling, Children can improve their language and expression ability happily. Researches show that storytelling is a powerful medium for education [2]. It can cultivate children's creativity and artistic expression and help them know more about themselves.

The traditional mediums of storytelling, such as books and games, are always have the fixed contents. They can only give children finite space of creation. If we make good use of computer, the freedom and creativity of the children can be increased. With the rapid development of the technology, many researchers have studied how to use computers to provide better environments and tools for children's storytelling.

Z. Pan et al. (Eds.): Transactions on Edutainment I, LNCS 5080, pp. 62–73, 2008.

There have been a lot of wonderful software products and research results. Among them are SAGE [3], KidPad [4], StoryRoom [5], Dolltalk [6] and so on. Our lab also developed a multimodal 3D storytelling system based on the specific needs of the Chinese children. Some children participated in the evaluation and all of them thought the system was good [7]. However, they hoped that there could be more roles in the system. All the above systems have limitations in common. That is children can hardly create their own roles. Moreover, children like new things and every child has his own imagination. The limited roles and props are not enough to make children enjoy storytelling longer and create their stories more freely.

To enlarge the imagination space and creativity space for children, and to attract their long-term interests in storytelling, we developed a pen-based 3D role modeling tool for children. In order to make the role creation process free and not too difficult for children, we use role templates in the tool. Children can use simple sketch gestures to create various roles based on the templates. And pen-based operations make roles adjustment easy and natural.

The organization for the remainder of this paper is as following: Section two discusses the related works. Section three presents the design of the 3D modeling tool for children. Section four describes this 3D modeling tool. Section five gives the informal evaluation of the tool. Finally the conclusion and future work are provided in Section six.

2 Related Work

Large commercial modeling software, such as 3Dmax and AutoCAD, are very powerful. They can assist users in building models accurately. However, the powerful functions of the software have two sides. On the bad side, it needs to be operated accurately, which makes the software too complex to use. Many researchers have presented different modeling method and tools to reduce the complexity of the traditional modeling. Quick-Sketch [8] and GIDeS [9] can be used to create ideal solid models, but not suitable for free-form modeling. Some modeling systems use 3D information input to make the modeling operation more intuitionistic and more efficient for the users. Nishino used data gloves and gesture recognition to achieve the 3D input, which made the modeling just like a procedure using plasticine [10]. Matsumiya used electronics glove, mediamask and other devices to provide the users with an immersed environment to modeling [11]. ArtNova [12] used force-feedback device to seamlessly integrate the haptic and visual presentation, and this 3D-touch technology can help the users create models naturally. They are all wonderful technologies. However, they are not easy to get popular in ordinary families, considering the cost of the interactive devices.

In 1996, Zeleznik et al. [13] developed SKETCH system which firstly used gesture to create 3D scenes and use Constructive Solid Geometry to describe the 3D models. Based on the Zeleznik's work, Igarashi firstly advanced the sketch-based method to construct 3D shapes from 2D freeform strokes and implemented Teddy system [14].

The sketch-based method brought a breakthrough to the 3D modeling. Sketch systems reduce the complexity of modeling effectively. Instead of requiring the users to work with traditional buttons, menus, and dragging operations, sketch systems allow them to directly express their thoughts in the form of freehand sketching. It can make 3D graphics authoring accessible to users with no special skills and knowledge. From then on, many researches have been studied on sketch system. Alexe [15] provided a sketch-based system using spherical implicit functions, in which users could adjust the model easily. Cherlin et al provided a method, with which users can construct 3D geometry entity with few strokes [16]. SmoothSketch [17] can greatly infer the hidden contours and create a corresponding 3D shape, which can be viewed from any direction. Moreover, some commercial software also uses sketch-based method for modeling. SketchUp help the architects to draw plane sketches to create 3D models. VRMesh can make the curved surfaces be easily changed. Curvy 3D use 2D sketch to author models with complex surface. These above system greatly improve the convenience of modeling for the non-expert users. However, they can not raise the children's interests largely. Because some of them require abstract ability of users, some of them don't provide intuitionistic operations and some of them need a lot of study and training.

At present, there are few tools for children's modeling. GollyGee Blocks [18], [19] is one of the modeling software for children. Children can use it to create their scenes happily and easily. But it is not suitable for the role modeling.

In order to allow children to model their roles for the storytelling easily, our role modeling tool adopts the design rules as follows:

1) Firstly, it uses pen-based interface to enhance the natural interaction.

2) Secondly, it takes advantage of the sketch-based idea which helps children create and adjust their models with simple gestures.

3) Thirdly, it provides several templates for the children. Because earlier tests result shows that children always don't know how to begin the creating of their roles, but as soon as they see the existed roles, they can give a lot of opinions about the color or shape of the roles.

3   Design of 3D Role Modeling Tool for Children

3.1 Pen-Based Interface

Pen-based Human-Computer Interaction Techniques is a very important research direction in the Human-Computer field. Pen-based interface is one of the hot spots of the next generation interface [20]. Natural and humanized interface is the development trend of Human-Computer Interaction [21]. Compared to the traditional interactive mode such as mouse and keyboard, pen-based interface is more natural and harmonious. It is also in accordance with users' interaction habit and convenient to capture users' intention. For children users, pen-based interface reduces the cognitive load of operations and plays advantage of harmoniousness and nature [22]. From the former work, we found children like pen-based interface. So we adopt pen-based interface in our role modeling tool.

3.2 Sketch-Based Modeling

As children are inclined to use natural and simple expression mode, there should not be too many gestures for them to remember. We use sketch gestures whose strokes are similar to the shapes that children want to create. In this way, we can reduce children's memory burden and make the sketch-based modeling more easily. Considering that children can't understand the 3D space concept, they are not very clear about the difference between 3D figures and plane figures. It would be very difficult when asking children to use gesture to create a cube just like figure 1 shows. On the contrary, we can simply let them draw a 2D figure to create a corresponding 3D figure. Just like figure 2 shows, when a child draws a rectangle stroke, a cube is created

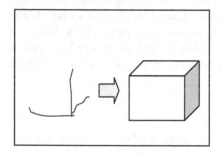
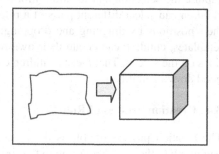

Fig. 1. 3D information gesture for modeling   **Fig. 2.** 2D information gesture for modeling

Furthermore, considering it will be more reliable and easier to modeling roles with single stroke, we use the single stroke gestures to create basic shapes as figure 3 shows.

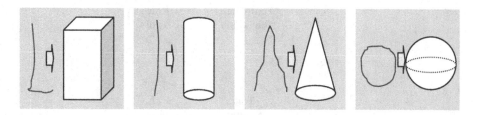

Fig. 3. Gestures for basic shapes

3.3 Role Template

During the former evaluation of the storytelling system [7], children all wanted more roles. In order to collect children's idea, we gave each of them a paint tool and asked them to draw roles they wanted. However, we found that most of them didn't know what they exactly wanted and how to draw them. Some children did draw some figures, but they thought those figures were not exactly the roles in their mind. It's very important for the children to create freely. But if they are given too much freedom, they will also get into trouble and meet difficulty in creation. We find it not easy to let children create their roles freely and to guard them against creation difficulty. In order to balance this dilemma, we use role templates in the tool. With these templates, children can still create their roles freely. Moreover, with the help of templates, they won't feel at a loss when beginning their creation. Considering roles which are often used when children tell their stories have limited types as following: two-leg animals, four-leg animals, none-leg animals and winged animals, we provide these types templates for children to create and adjust their own roles in our tool.

In a system with space information, pen is a very effective locating and pointing tool. Therefore, besides the sketch strokes information mentioned above, we mainly capture the selection and location information of pen. According to this information, children can select different parts of a role; adjust their color, size and shape; change their positions by dragging and dropping; even change their perspectives. Based on templates, children can create their own role models through some very basic operations on the screen. That means children can intuitively create roles they want without good drawing ability.

3.4   Creation Process of Role

The creation process of role is the process of creating a whole role from the very beginning to the end. According to the former design, the creation process is as shown

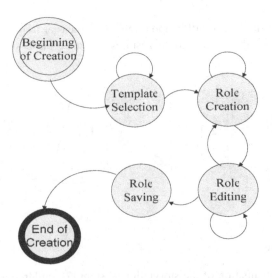

Fig. 4. The creation process

in figure 4. First, children should decide which kind of role they want and select the corresponding template (e.g. the two-leg template or the four-leg template); Then, based on the selected template, they can create the role's profile by inputting some creation gestures; if they are not satisfied with the initial role, they can adjust its shape, size, position and color by inputting some editing gestures; What's more, they can also change the perspective; At last, children can save their 3D role models for the use in future.

4   Implementation of the Role Modeling Tool

According to the above design, we implemented the pen-based story role modeling tool for children

4.1   Framework of the Tool

Figure 5 shows the tool's overall framework. The upper layer is the pen-based inter-face; the middle layer within the dotted-line shows the system process flow; while the bottom layer contains the template library, the gesture library and the rule library.

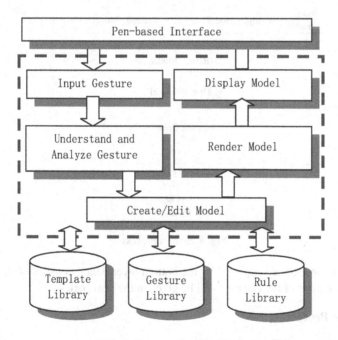

Fig. 5. Framework of the Tool

Users interact with the system through the pen-based interface. They input some gestures to the system. When the system gets these gestures, it will analyze and un-derstand these gestures to get the operating object and operational semantics. Then the system will create or modify the model according to the results of analysis and understanding. As long as the model is changed, it will be rendered. At last, the system will display the render result on the pen-based interface.

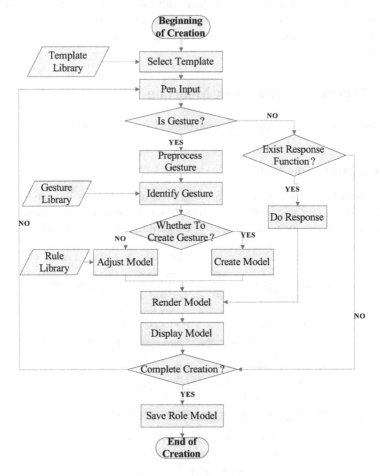

Fig. 6. System Process

The whole process is supported by the bottom layer which consists of three libraries. And the details of the libraries will be given in the next part.

4.2 System Process

The system process is just as figure 6 shows.

1) After users select their templates, they will input some pen-based information.

2) The system will capture this information and check whether it is a gesture or not. If it is not a gesture and it triggers a response function, the corresponding function will be executed. If it is a gesture, the system will preprocess it and generate the ultimate gesture.

3) After that, based on the gesture library, the system can identify the gestures. If the gesture is a creating gesture, the system will do the corresponding creating operation. Otherwise, it will be an editing gesture, and the system will do the corresponding editing operation.

4) When adjusting models, the system will analyze the editing gestures within the 3D model context and adjust the model under the restriction of rules in the rule library.

5) Every change will result in a new rendering. And the system will display the new model on the screen.

6) At last, when users finish their role creation, they can save them and use them in the storytelling system in the future.

We will briefly introduce the three libraries mentioned above. Their main functions for the system are as following:

Template Library. It provides templates for several kinds of roles.
On the one hand, the template library facilitates the creation process of roles. On the other hand, it assures that roles created by the system can be correctly used in the storytelling system.

Gesture Library. It provides some rules which restrict the model adjusting operation.
The gesture library is adequately exercised before applied in the system. After adding the

Fig. 7. Two-leg template

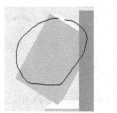

Fig. 8. Create body part using the creation gesture

characteristic information generated by the exercise, the gesture library is more effective to distinguish between the valid gestures and the invalid ones.

Rule Library. It provides templates for several kinds of roles.
Under the restriction of rules in the rule library, related information will change together when adjusting a certain part of the model. This will make the adjusting operations more simple and natural. For example, every part of the body is related with others, and a certain rule assures that these parts won't break away from each other after adjusting the size or position of some part.

These three above libraries help children create their own roles with pen more conveniently in the role modeling system.

4.3 An Example

Now, let's create a bear role using the role modeling tool.

1) Select the two-leg role template, which is shown by figure 7.
2) Create each part of the bear using the creation gestures. As Figure 8.
3) Select a certain part and adjust its color, size, position, etc. See Figure 9.
4) Repeat step 3 until completing the whole bear. Figure 10 shows the final bear.

(a) Select the head and move the pen up to zoom in the head

(b) Drag one ear to a new position, then both of the ears will change symmetrically

Fig. 9. Various operations of adjusting model

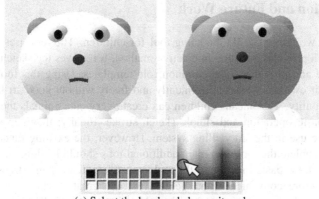

(c) Select the head and change its color

Fig. 9. (*continued*)

Fig. 10. The final bear

5   Informal Evaluation

We have invited six users to use and evaluate our 3D role modeling tool. Responses from the users were quite positive. They all thought that it was very easy for them to learn how to use the tool and the using process was very natural, efficient, and reliable. When they used the tool to create their roles, all of them felt it interesting and satisfactory. Most of them would like to use it in the future. Besides, they gave us some valuable suggestions for improvements. We made a summarization as follows:

(1) Using the templates can create roles easily and efficiently. However, if we can add a free-form template, it will be better;

(2) If they can draw some texture and import personalize accessories for their roles, it will make the modeling process more amazing;

(3) If they can customize the animation for the certain roles, it will cheer them up.

6 Conclusion and Future Work

In this paper, we present a 3D modeling tool for children. The tool uses pen-based interface which provides a natural interactive method. It reserves the sketch modeling creation mode and provides some common role templates. Using this tool, children can create their own story roles conveniently and freely without good art knowledge and drawing ability. That means children can create very cute animals they want by doing some basic operation and simple sketch stroke. Finally, they can save these roles for future use in the storytelling system. However, the existing function is not enough. To complete the tool, two main additional jobs should be done in the future: on the one hand, the basic function of the tool should be extended and strengthened to give children more convenience and flexibility when creation roles; On the other hand, animation design function should be added into the tool. With this function, children could not only create their story roles, but also customize certain personalized animation for their roles.

Acknowledgments. The research is supported by National Grand Fundamental Research 973 Program (Grant No. 2002CB312103), the National Natural Science Foundation of China (Grant No. 60373056), National Facilities and Information Infrastructure Foundation for Science and Technology (Grant No. 2005DKA46300-05-32) and the CAS Pilot Project of the National Knowledge Innovation Program (KIP) (Grant No. KGCX2—YW—606).

References

1. Wright, A.: Creating stories with children. Oxford University Press, England (1995)
2. Ruth, A.: And They Both Lived Happily Ever After?——Digital stories and learning. Sense Publishers (2005)
3. Bers, M., Cassell, J.: Interactive Storytelling Systems for Children: Using Technology to Explore Language and Identity. Journal of Interactive Learning Research, AACE 9(2), 603–609 (1999)
4. Hourcade, J.P., Bederson, B.B., Druin, A., Taxen, G.: KidPad: Collaborative Storytelling for Children. In: Extended Abstracts of Human Factors in Computing Systems (2002)
5. Alborzi, H., Druin, A., Montemayor, J., Sherman, L., Taxen, G., Best, J., Hammer, J., Kruskal, A., Lal, A., Plaisant Schwenn, T., Sumida, L., Wagner, R., Hendler, J.: Designing StoryRooms: Interactive Storytelling Spaces for Children. In: Proc. Desiging Interactive Systems, pp. 95–100. ACM Press, New York (2000)
6. Vaucelle, C., Jehan, T.: Dolltalk: a computational toy to enhance children's creativity. In: Proc. CHI 2002, pp. 776–777. ACM Press, New York (2002)
7. Danli, W., Jie, Z., Jie, L., Guozhong, D., Qiang, L.: A Multimodal 3D Storytelling System for Chinese Children. In: Hui, K.-c., Pan, Z., Chung, R.C.-k., Wang, C.C.L., Jin, X., Göbel, S., Li, E.C.-L. (eds.) EDUTAINMENT 2007. LNCS, vol. 4469, pp. 511–526. Springer, Heidelberg (2007)
8. Eggli, L., Hsu, C., Bruderlin, B., Elber, G.: Inferring 3D models from freehand sketches and constraints. Computer-Aided Design 29(2), 101–112 (1997)

9. Pereira, J.P., Branco, V.A., Jorge, J.A., Silva, N.F., Cardoso, T.D., Ferreira, F.N.: Cascading recognizers for ambiguous calligraphic interaction. In: Proc. of the Eurographics Workshop on Sketch-Based Modeling (2004)

10. Nishino, H., Utsumiya, K., Korida, K.: 3D object modeling using spatial and pictographic gestures. In: Proc. of the ACM symposium on virtual reality software and technology, pp. 51–58. ACM Press, New York (1998)

11. Matsumiya, M., Takemura, H., Yokoya, N.: An immersive modeling system for 3d free-form design using implicit surfaces. In: Proceedings of the ACM symposium on virtual reality software and technology, pp. 67–74. ACM Press, New York (2000)

12. Mark, F., Miguel, A.O., Ming, C.L.: ArtNova: Touch-Enabled 3D Model Design. In: Proceedings of the IEEE (2002)

13. Zeleznik, R.C., Herndon, K.P., Hughes, J.: SKETCH: An Interface for Sketching 3D Scenes. In: Proceedings of SIGGRAPH 1996. ACM Press, New York (1996)

14. Igarashi, T., Matsuoka, S., Tanaka, H.: Teddy: A sketching interface for 3d freeform design. In: Proc. of SIGGRAPH 1999, pp. 409–416 (1999)

15. Alexe, A., Gaildrat, V., Barthe, L.: Interactive Modelling from Sketches using Spherical Implicit Functions. In: Proceedings of the 3rd international conference on Computer graphics, virtual reality, visualisation and interaction in Africa (2004)

16. Cherlin, J.J., Samavati, F., Sousa, M.C., Jorge, J.A.: Sketch-based modeling with few strokes. In: Proc. of the 21st spring conference on Computer Graphics (2005)

17. Olga, A.K., John, F.H.: SmoothSketch: 3D free-form shapes from complex sketches. In: Proceedings of ACM SIGGRAPH (2006)

18. Jonathan, T.B.: GollyGee BlocksTM: A 3D Modeler for Children. In: ACM SIGGRAPH conference (2002)

19. Website for GollyGee, http://www.gollygee.com

20. Jurgen, Z.: Interactive Techniques. ACM Computer Survey 28(1), 185–187 (1996)

21. Jianming, D., Liming, F., Salvendy, G.: Human-Computer Interaction: User Centered Design and Evaluation. Tsinghua Press (2002)

22. Jie, Z.: A Speech- and Pen-based Multimodal Storytelling System for Children, M.D. Thesis. Chinese Academy of Sciences, Beijing (2007)

A Reusable Eduventure Game Framework

Wenfeng Hu

Institute of Computer Science,
Communication University of China,
China No.1 Dingfuzhuang East Street, Chaoyang District,
Beijing, 100024, P.R. China
Tel.: 0086-010-65783396
huwf@cuc.edu.cn

Abstract. Adventure games for educational purpose, which is termed of eduventure, show many advantages. In this paper, a group of core concepts which is essential to eduventure game design is found. In order to prevent eduventure game designer from continually rediscovering of these core elements, we clarify the functionalities of these core concepts and form them into a collaborated conceptual framework. We also show how the Conceptual Eduventure Framework can be reused in eduventure game design and how it can serve as a tool which can adjust the balance between instruction and entertainment. Furthermore, we implement the Conceptual Eduventure Framework in TorqueScript so that it becomes a library of building blocks which can be reused in eduventure game development based on Torque Game Engine. As evaluation and application, an eduventure game project is built based on the Torque-Script Eduventure Framework which can be applied in freshman training.

Keywords: adventure game, educational game, eduventure, reuse, Torque game engine.

1   Introduction

Computer games used for educational purposes offer great advantages over conventional instructional ways [1]. Among all genres of computer games, adventure game has many unique characteristics helpful for educational use. One of the characteristics is the strong sense of place or context in these games. The fantasy world of a typical adventure game consists of a network of distinct physical contexts such as the rooms or caves. Associated with each such context is a set of tasks or puzzles that must be completed if the player is to advance in the game or even change context. Another characteristic of adventure game for instruction is that challenges of this kind of game mainly stem from puzzles to be solved. Reaction time and coordination are rarely factors.

In scientific or technical education, many subjects can be characterized by a network of concepts which is structured by prerequisite relation between concepts in that some concepts cannot be mastered before others. Obviously, adventure game offers a natural way of mapping the structure of the instructional subject

Z. Pan et al. (Eds.): Transactions on Edutainment I, LNCS 5080, pp. 74–85, 2008.
© Springer-Verlag Berlin Heidelberg 2008

to the topology of an adventure game. Every physical place in adventure game can be associated to an instructional sub-objective. Constrains encountered by the player walking through the set of contexts represent the prerequisite relation between instructional sub-objectives. Having determined what basic knowledge or skills the learner should have acquired by this context, a series of puzzles can be designed to check on their proficiency at these knowledge or skills. These tests are then woven into the network of the plot to form a consistent whole educational objective.

Many research works [2] [3] have found the characteristic of the network structure in adventure games and realized that adventure game is very suitable for conveying systematized or hierarchical knowledge to player. Then a new term of eduventure is introduced [4].

Besides the network structure of eduventure game, furthermore, we find that a group of core concepts appears again and again which is believed to be essential to eduventure game design. Clarifying these core concepts and their correlation can prevent eduventure designer from continually rediscovering and reinventing of these concepts and give great help in obtaining high productivity and quality of eduventure game.

In the reminder of this paper, we will discuss the functionalities of each key concept of eduventure and illustrate how they collaborate into a coupled framework-Conceptual Eduventure Framework (CEF) in section 2. The emphasis of section 2 is to show how this CEF can be used in eduventure game design time and how it can serve as a tool which can adjust the game balance between instruction and entertainment. In section 3, we instantiate CEF based on Torque Game Engine so that it become a library of reusable building blocks which can be reused in eduventure game development time. In section 4, we will introduce an eduventure game project named "Adventure Journey of Computer" whose foundation is the TorqueScript Eduventure Framework. We conclude with some possible future works in section 5.

2   Conceptual Eduventure Framework – A Tool for Eduventure Game Design

In section 1, it is mentioned that there is a set of concepts essential to eduventure game design. In this section, we will clarify functionalities of these concepts and illustrate how they collaborate with each other and form into a coupled framework-Conceptual Eduventure Framework (CEF). Then we verify the cross-platform reusability of CEF and show how CEF can be used in eduventure game design.

2.1   The Conceptual Eduventure Framework

There are eleven elements in the CEF, that is: *Curriculum, Achievement, Course, Classroom, Puzzle, Examination, Textbook, Teacher, Obstacle* and *Reward*. First we discuss the functionality of each concept.

Curriculum: The concept of *Curriculum* is a metaphor representing the whole educational objective of an eduventure game. One of the main functionalities of *Curriculum* is holding references to all *Courses* which is a metaphor for educational sub-objective discussed below. We consider it reasonable that *Curriculum* take the responsibility to hold the prerequisite-relationship among *Courses*. Then *Curriculum* provides an important service which can list all prerequisite *Courses* of a given *Course*.

Achievement: When a player walking through an eduventure game, exploring each region associated with a *Course*, learning knowledge, solving puzzles, etc, his performance should be recorded and attached to him. The concept of *Achievement* takes the responsibility to record performance of player and offers an interface for querying them.

Course: Course is the most important concept which embodies the educational sub-objective associated to a single physical region in eduventure games. This concept contains so much content and functionalities that it is too coarse-grained to be used or reused. Therefore we extract four separate conceptual components from *Course*: *Classroom* where a *Course* is taught, *Teacher* who teaches a *Course*, *Textbook* what is taught in a *Course*, and *Puzzle* by which a *Course* tests player. Each of these four components holds a reference to its corresponding Course object. A *Course* object only provides some basic information, e.g. Course's ID, Course's name.

Classroom: Classroom is a physical region where a *Course* is taught. *Classroom* should reflect the prerequisite constraint which means that a player cannot enter a *Classroom* except he has accomplished some prerequisite *Courses*, and a player cannot leave a *Classroom* except he has demonstrated his proficiency or mastering of the subject associated to this *Classroom*. To accomplish above functions, *Classroom* must has three capabilities: (1) being aware of when a player enters or leaves; (2) knowing which prerequisite *Courses* should be accomplished by a player; (3) knowing the player's performance in those prerequisite *Courses*.

Puzzle and *Examination:* Having entered a *Classroom*, a player must explore the space and try to find his way escaping from the *Classroom*. But there are a lot of *Puzzles* blocking his way. A *Puzzle* object comprise of two parts: a question and a standard answer. *Puzzle* can evaluate whether player's input is consistent with its standard answer. *Puzzle* also takes the responsibility to update the *Achievement* attached to the player according to his performance. Only having resolved a series of *Puzzles* in a *Classroom*, a player can escape from its confinement. The set of *Puzzles* of a *Course* is called *Examination*, or Task.

Textbook: In order to pass an *Examination*, the player has strong motivation to acquire related knowledge. *Textbook* is what a *Course* teaches where the answers to *Puzzles* can be found. *Textbook*'s responsibility is relatively simple, that is, holding and showing knowledge associated to a *Course*. But the content of a *Textbook* may take various forms, e.g. plain text, hyper text, FAQs, picture, video, speech, etc.

Teacher: In order to obtain high flexibility and diversity of gameplay, *Teacher* is not a specific NPC but a role or an interface in term of software. Any game objects can play the role of *Teacher* as long as they are attached a *Textbook* object.

Obstacle: In order to increase challenge, it is attractive to place some *Obstacles* in player's way. In fact, the nature of *Obstacle* is some physical restraint to a player in the virtual game world. A blocking door, a too steep cliff, a deep river, etc, are some examples of *Obstacle*. Overcoming an *Obstacle* needs some conditions which a player must try to satisfy. A player with some particular game object can overcome a corresponding *Obstacle*.

Reward: If a player does a good work in his journey, some prize awarding him is fair and encouraging. *Rewards* are game objects with some particular properties which can help player to overcome *Obstacles*. Key is an example of *Reward* which can unlock a Door-a kind of *Obstacle*. The opportunities to obtain *Rewards* are varied, such as, solving a *Puzzle*, getting a high grade in a *Course*, killing a guard, or finding a box of treasure, etc.

Prompter: In all probability, a new player maybe gets lost in his first journey without any guide. It is necessary to assign a role of *Prompter* in eduventure games whose main responsibility is to show player his location in the network of tasks and indicate player what to do next.

These eduventure core concepts are not isolated. They collaborate with each other and form into a coupled framework. In figure 1, we use Unified Modeling Language (UML) to illustrate the Object-Model of CEF.

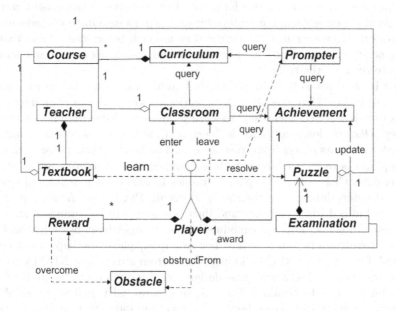

Fig. 1. Object-Model of Conceptual Eduventure Framework

2.2   Cross-Platform Reusability

It's easy to see that elements in our conceptual eduventure framework are specified in terms of interfaces rather than implementation details. That means that CEF is independent of game development platform (game engine). Moreover, the functionalities of CEF can be supported by any modern game engine. So CEF can be reused by game designer who can concentrate on their design work without worrying about any implementation technique.

2.3   A Tool for Eduventure Game Design

The CEF can be reused in game design time and provides eduventure game designer with a design blueprint. With the aid of CEF, an eduventure game designer can do the following works: (1) Decomposing the whole educational objective into many sub-objectives; (2) Designing game plot according to the prerequisite relationship network; (3) Assigning specific roles of CEF to various game elements. For example, an eduventure game designer can consider the following questions: who hold a *Textbook* or a *Puzzle* instance? What *Reward* an *Examination* should spawn? What kind of *Obstacle* should be placed and where to place? And so on.

2.4   A Tool for Regulating the Balance between Instruction and Entertainment

It's well known that the balance between instruction and entertainment is of key importance to the success of an eduventure project. An eduventure with excessive preaching doesn't have attraction for player. But excessive entertainment may let an eduventure game deviate from its educational purpose. Obviously, addressing the problem of balance in early design time is much better than doing that in last game testing time. The CEF provides eduventure game designer an operable means to regulate the balance.

That is, *Textbook* is the educational content and exploring the fantastic game world, on the other hand, is player's recreational motive. *Puzzle* is an important means to induce, or compel player to learn serious knowledge from his immersive journey. *Obstacle* leads to more challenge and entertainment, on the contrary, *Prompter* prevents player from frustration and make the journey easier. *Reward* brings player both sense of accomplishment and equipment to overcome *Obstacle*.

Therefore, CEF contains explicit variables to affect the two sides of education and entertainment. Furthermore, *Textbook*, *Puzzle* and *Reward*, etc, are abstracted into distinct concepts and their instances can be composed into any other game objects. This high modularization brings about flexibility and diversity in eduventure game design. For examples, player perhaps must get a *Textbook* from a guard NPC by killing him or from a merchant NPC by paying money, etc. So an eduventure game designer can easily adjust the grade of difficulty for a player to obtain a *Textbook*. In general, CEF makes it possible to do fine adjustment of balance between instruction and entertainment in game design time.

3   The TorqueScript Eduventure Framework

In section 2, we show the CEF is a game design tool independent of any game engine. In this section, we instantiate the CEF into a library of software building blocks which can be reused in game development time based on Torque Game Engine.

3.1   Torque Game Engine

In order to obtain high production standards (good artwork, animation, and sound) and diversity of gameplay experience, commercial non-educational game engines are introduced to build educational games [5]. Torque Game Engine (TGE) provided by GarageGames [6] is our choice to use to build our eduventure project. TGE is a fully featured AAA game engine with award winning multi-player network code, seamless indoor/outdoor rendering engines, state of the art skeletal animation, drag and drop GUI creation, a built in world editor, and a C-like scripting language (TorqueScript). Unlike most commercial game engines, low cost license ($100) is very suitable for indie game development, especially for educational game. Moreover, because of the availability of C++ source code, any additions to the engine can be easily made.

3.2   Modification and Extension in TGE

Ordinary commercial game engines often lack of elements or components designed deliberately for educational purpose but hold excessive entertainment elements, so adapting, extending, and even changing to TGE are necessary [7].

The Torque Game Engine was designed to use scripting (TorqueScript) to implement specific game objects and elements. One can build his games by making modification (MOD) from existing torque game.

In TorqueScript, Namespace is a powerful tool to define general behavior for game objects and then more and more specific behavior as needed. In order to get needed behavior not from default, one can add a new Namespace and define specific functions under this Namespace. Then any game object created under the new namespace can inherit its all behaviors. The general syntax of namespace mechanism is as follows.

```
//Define functions under a new namespace
function aNewNameSpace::fooFunction(){
    . . . . . .
}
//one way to create an object under a namespace
%handle = new SomeGameObject(){
    className = aNewNameSpace;
    . . . . . .
};
//another way to create an object under a namespace
```

```
%handle = new SomeGameObject(aNewNameSpace){
    ......
};
//%handle can be called under aNewNameSpace.
%handle. fooFunction();
```

By the mechanism of Namespace, existing game object's behavior can not only be inherited but also be extended as needed.

3.3   A Reusable TorqueScript Eduventure Framework

TorqueScript Implementation of CEF. In order to instantiate CEF in TorqueScript, we should select suitable building blocks provided by Torque platform to extend.

In TGE, there is a class named "ScriptObject" provided to the creation of TorqueScript-only classes. This class provides the ability to group data fields and associate the class with one or more namespace. ScriptObject is our choice to be extended to instantiate these concepts: *Curriculum, Achievement, Course, Textbook, Puzzle,* and *Prompter,* all of which are new namespaces associated to ScriptObject class. Figure 2 illustrates the instantiation of *Puzzle* which currently has one form of multi-choice.

"Trigger" is an API class provided by TGE which is a cubic region in a 3D game world. When player enters or leave the region of a Trigger instance, two

Fig. 2. A multi-choice Puzzle

callback functions, that is, onEnterTrigger() and onleaveTrigger(), are called automatically by the engine. So Trigger can perfectly fulfill *Classroom*'s first capability: being aware of when a player enters or leaves. We create a new TriggerData whose "className" of field is set to *"Classroom"*. Under the new namespace of *"Classroom"*, onEnterTrigger() and onleaveTrigger() are overridden as follows.

```
function Classroom::onEnterTrigger(%datablock,%classroom,%player)
{
  %prerequisiteCourses
    = Curriculum::getPrerequisiteCourses(%classroom.getCourse());
  %achievement = %player.getAchievement();
  if(Curriculum::accessable(%prerequisiteCourses,%achievement)){
    Classroom::doSomePreparatoryWorks(%player);
  }else{
    Classroom::pushPlayerOutAndShowSomeRefusageInfo(%player);
  }
}

function Classroom::onLeaveTrigger(%datablock,%classroom,%player)
{
  %achievement = %player.getAchievement();
  %scroe=%achievement.getScore(%classroom.getCourse());
  if(isPassed(%scroe)){
    letPlayerOut(%player);
  }else{
    pushPlayerBackAndShowSomeRefusageInfo(%player);
  }
}
```

Figure 3 and figure 4 illustrate what happens when a player tries to leave or enter a classroom but he hasn't the qualification.

Since TGE comprises of a powerful physical engine, the concept of *Obstacle* can be implemented in plenty varieties. All *Obstacles* can be classified into two categories: physical restraint and physical damage. Physical restraints come from collision and gravity provided by TGE physical engine. For example, ordinary player cannot pass through a stone door, cannot get over too steep cliff, cannot fly in air, etc. Physical damages come from some nature force or hostile creature, e.g. a lava river, a mass of poison gas, a fire wall, a wolf, or an enemy NPC. With the aid of Torque physical engine, we construct many kinds of *Obstacle* which can easily be placed in eduventure game to add challenge and enjoyment.

All sort of *Reward* are extended from "Item" which is another Torque API class. Item object can be picked up and used by a player. For example, we create a new sort of Item with namespace of FlyingGem. Under the namespace of FlyingGem, a callback function named onUsed() is overridden in which we alter the some property of player. So an ordinary player can break the restriction of gravity to fly in the air if he uses a FlyingGem object.

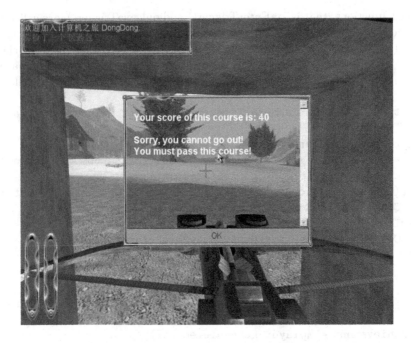

Fig. 3. Cannot escape from a classroom

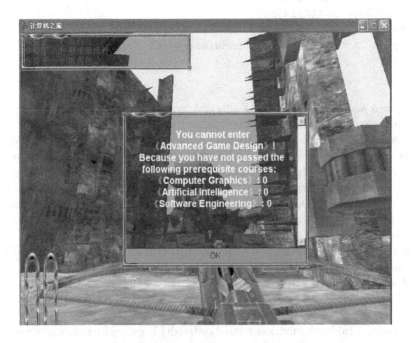

Fig. 4. Cannot enter a classroom

High Modularity of TEF. Each element of TorqueScript Eduventure Framework (TEF) is a namespace with the same name as the corresponding concept in CEF. All TorqueScript source codes related to a element of TEF is well encapsulated and packaged into two files: one is a server-side file containing all server-side logic discussed above; another is a client-side file containing the specification and behaviors of corresponding GUI. Now TEF is available as a library of reusable building blocks which can be used in eduventure game development time based on TGE.

4 A Case Study: "Adventure Journey of Computer"

4.1 Background of Our Eduventure Project

At beginning of September of each year, freshmen of Computer College, Communication University of China, routinely receive introduction of computer science curriculum. Each freshman is offered a booklet which lists brief introduction of all courses students will learn. The objective is to convey an overview of undergraduate curriculum to freshmen and hope to inspire them with some passion for computer science. But results often are unsatisfactory. Few freshmen have enough ability and patience to read through the booklet which is full of abstruse jargons. In order to let curriculum introduction more attractive to freshmen, we decided to make an educational game for them, which is named "Adventure Journey of Computer".

Obviously, the undergraduate curriculum is a good example to illustrate the network structure of eduventure game. Our educational objective can be decomposed into Courses naturally and embedded into an eduventure game perfectly. In our project, currently only those courses which are helpful for game development are involved, including, for example, "C++ Programming Language", "Data Structure", "Operation System", "The Principle of the Computer Graphics", "Artificial Intelligence", "Primary Game Programming", "Software Engineering", "Advanced Game Design", etc.

4.2 Development of Our Eduventure Project

Torque includes a basic game shell to get one started called "starter.fps" with all source code written in TorqueScript. We build our eduventure project by making modification (MOD) from "starter.fps" which provides some basic support for building games of genre of "First Person Shooter": weapon system, inventory system, etc. In order to fulfill our project, some other features were added to "starter.fps", e.g. conversation system and AI system.

Of course, TorqueScript Eduventure Framework is another foundation of our project. Reusing TEF is very simple: copying all files of TEF into project, loading them into memory with exec() statement and creating objects of TEF by setting corresponding namespace.

In our fantastic 3D game world, *Classroom* of involved *Courses* are scattered in varied regions such as island, cave, ruins, building, castle, etc. A great many of NPCs undertake various responsibilities such as teacher, examiner, merchant, guard, patrol, etc. Furthermore, players may pick up various game objects which act as roles of *Textbook*, *Examination*, and *Reward* etc above-mentioned. Freshmen must overcome many *Obstacles* and explore through all the *Classroom* following the prerequisite relation between them within given time limit. Figure 5 gives an airscape of our eduventure game world.

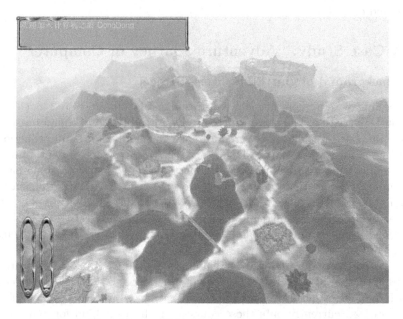

Fig. 5. The airscape of "Adventure Journey of Computer"

5   Future Works

The game of "Adventure Journey of Computer" attracted almost all of freshmen to play it. Most of the players won the game finally and acquired some overview of undergraduate curriculum as we hoped. But some defects in our game design have emerged:

(1) Game scene is too broad and average distance between *Classrooms* is too long which result in that players have more interest in rambling about for fun but addressing them to game tasks. In the future eduventure development, we will make game scene more compact and closed so that players can achieve tasks without disturbance.

(2) In the TorqueScript Eduventure Framework, currently there are only one type of *Puzzle* and two types of *Textbook* which is very monotonous. So designing various types of *Puzzle* and *Textbook* used in eduventure is our future works.

In addition, instantiating CEF into other game engine is our future work too.

6   Conclusions

In this paper, our work can be divided into three layers from bottom to top: CEF, TEF and an eduventure application. The CEF is the bottom layer because it is independent of game engine and can be used in game design time. The TEF is an instantiation of CEF in a specific game engine of TGE. Also, the TEF is a library of reusable TorqueScript building blocks which can be reused in any eduventure game development based on TGE. Finally, "Adventure Journey of Computer" is an application which is built upon TEF.

References

1. Mitchell, A., Savill-Smith, C.: The use of computer and video games for learning. Learning and Skills Development Agency, London (2004)
2. Parkkinen, P., Sutinen, E.: A fantasy adventure game as a learning environment: why learning to program is so difficult and what can be done about it. Bridging Ancient and Modern Cultures: Folklore in Multimedia British Journal of Educational Technology 30(3), 277–279 (1999) doi:10.1111/1467-8535.00116
3. Halff, H.M.: Adventure games for science education: Generative methods in exploratory environments. In: the Workshop on Educational Games as Intelligent Learning Environments, 12th International Conference on Artificial Intelligence in Education, AI ED 2005, Amsterdam, The Netherlands (August 2005)
4. Ferdinand, P., Mller, S., Ritschel, T., Wechselberger, U.: The Eduventure - A New Approach of Digital Game Based Learning Combining Virtual and Mobile Augmented Reality Games Episodes. In: Pre-Conference Workshop Game based Learning of DeLFI 2005 and GMW 2005 Conference, Rostock, Germany, September 13, 2005 (2005)
5. Noh, S.S., Hong, S.D., Park, J.W.: Using a Game Engine Technique to Produce 3D Entertainment Contents. In: Pan, Z., Cheok, A.D., Haller, M., Lau, R.W.H., Saito, H., Liang, R. (eds.) ICAT 2006. LNCS, vol. 4282, pp. 246–251. Springer, Heidelberg (2006)
6. GarageGames Inc. (2007), http://www.garagegames.com/
7. Carbonaro, M., Cutumisu, M., Duff, H., Gillis, S., Onuczko, C., Schaeffer, J., Schumacher, A., Siegel, J., Szafron, D., Waugh, K.: Adapting a Commercial Role-Playing Game for Educational Computer Game Production. GameOn North America, 54–61 (September 2006)
8. Nieborg, D.B.: Am I Mod or Not? - an Analysis of First Person Shooter Modification Culture. In: Creative Gamers Seminar - Exploring Participatory Culture in Gaming, Hypermedia Laboratory (University of Tampere) (2005), GameSpace.nl/research.htm

Construction and Evaluation of a Robot Dance System

Kuniya Shinozaki[1], Akitsugu Iwatani[2], and Ryohei Nakatsu[1,3]

[1] Kwansei Gakuin University, School of Science and Technology
2-1 Gakuen, Sanda Japan, 669-1337
{scbc0052,nakatsu}@kwansei.ac.jp
[2] Universal Studios Japan, Osaka, Japan
[3] National University of Singapore, Interactive & Digital Media Institute
Blk E3A #02-04, 7 Engineering Drive 1, Singapore 117574
idmdir@nus.edu.sg

Abstract. Dance is one form of entertainment where physical movement is the key factor. The main reason why robots are experiencing a kind of "boom" is that they have a physical body. We propose a robot dance system that combines these two elements. First, various factors concerning entertainment and dance are studied. Then we propose the dance system by robot using motion unit and the synthetic rule referring the speech synthesis. Also we describe the details of the system by focusing on its software functions. Finally we show the evaluation results of robot dance performances.

Keywords: Humanoid robot, dance, dance generation, text-to-speech.

1 Introduction

The research and development of various kinds of robots is actively being carried out, especially in Japan [1][2][3][4][5]. Several reasons explain the current robot boom. One main reason is that robots have physical bodies, and so human-robot interaction extends beyond human-computer interaction.

Although in the future these robots are expected to support various aspects of our daily life, so far their capabilities are very limited. At present, installing such a task in robots remains very difficult. To break through such a situation, entertainment might be a good application area for robots.

Developing a dancing robot would be remarkable from various points of view. First, it might become a new form of entertainment, activates both the body and brain. Watching humans dance is already one established type of entertainment. Second, we might develop a new type of communication with computers, because dance can be considered one of the most sophisticated nonverbal communication methods.

Based on the above considerations we started to research dancing robots. In this paper we clarify the relationship among entertainment, humans, and robots and propose a robot dance system by robot using motion unit and the synthetic rule referring the speech synthesis. Also we will describe an evaluation experiment carried out to test this basic concept's feasibility.

Z. Pan et al. (Eds.): Transactions on Edutainment I, LNCS 5080, pp. 86–95, 2008.

2 Dance Entertainment and Robots

2.1 Entertainment

The role of entertainment in our daily life is very important. It offers relaxation and thus contributes to our mental health. Many aspects concerning entertainment must be considered and discussed [6]. One of the most important may be the existence of two sides: entertainer and audience. Although these two sides change positions depending on the case, the existence of performers and spectators is an absolute prerequisite for entertainment. Many entertainments have both entertainer and spectator characteristics. In the case of dance, people sometimes go to theaters to watch good dance performances, and they sometimes go to dance clubs or discos to dance themselves.

Furthermore, when viewed from a different aspect entertainment can be classified into two types. One is a real-time type that includes performers or entertainers performing live in front of an audience. Good examples include plays and/or concerts. Another is the non-real-time type; reading books and watching movies are good examples.

Following this classification, dance basically belongs to the real-time type of entertainment. For robot dancing, however, as described later, its position is somewhat special.

2.2 Dance Robot

One main reason why we choose dance as an entertainment for robots is that dance is quite sophisticated [7]. Based on the considerations described above, what is the role of robots in dance entertainment? Dance robots allow us to become both entertainers and spectators. When watching a robot dance, we are spectators. On the other side, many people will probably want to install dance motions on their robots and show these actions to others. In this case they are entertainers. For the classification between real-time and non-real-time entertainment, dance robots also have significant characteristics. If we want to show people the robot dance, we have to install the dance actions beforehand, meaning that the robot dance is non-real-time entertainment. At the same time, by developing interactive capabilities, the robot would show impromptu dancing behaviors. For example, it could change the dance depending on audience requests. Or it could sense the audience mood and could adopt its dancing behaviors to reflect the sensor results. A dance robot could provide flexible entertainment that ranges between real-time and non-real-time entertainment.

3 Dance Robot System

3.1 Basic Concept

Based on the above considerations we want to develop a system that can generate various dance motions. Since different dance genres exist, it is necessary to restrict dance genres to a specific one. Then the system would generate various dance motions by selecting several basic dance motions and by concatenating them. This basic idea resembles text-to-speech synthesis (TTS) [8], where by restricting the language to be synthesized and by selecting a basic speech unit, any kind of text described by the language can be generated. The following is the basic concept adopted in TTS:

(1) Speech consists of a concatenation of basic speech units.
(2) Selection of the speech unit is crucial.
(3) Connection of speech units is also crucial.

As basic speech units, various basic units such as phonemes, phoneme pairs, CV (consonant-vowel concatenation), CVC, VCV and so on have been studied [8]. Based on research of the last several decades, phonemes including variations that depend on previous and following phonemes are widely used as speech units. Taking these situations into consideration, the basic concept of dance generation is as follows:

(1) We restrict the generated dance to a specific genre.
(2) All dance motions consist of a concatenation of several basic dance motions.
(3) Deciding what to select dance units as basic dance motions is very important.
(4) Connecting dance units is crucial.
(5) Also it is crucial how to express a dance unit as robot motion.

In the following sections, we answer the above questions.

3.2 Dance Genre

For basic dance motions, there are several researches on classic ballet [9]. The classification of ballet motions is based on several leg positions and movements called steps. Although each leg position and step has its own name, basically no rules describe the details of whole body motions. We chose hip-hop as the dance genre because all of its dance steps and motions are classified into several categories, so it is easier to handle the whole body motions of hip-hop than ballet.

3.3 Dance Unit

Next we must decide the basic unit for dance motions. As described above, since each hip-hop step/body motion has its own name, it can be selected as a dance unit. However, it is difficult for an amateur to extract them from continuous dance motions. Therefore we collaborated with a professional dancer to simplify the extraction of basic motions from continuous dance motions. In addition, when constructing robot motions based on human motions, we must deform complicated human motions into rather simple robot motions. In this deformation process, a professional dancer's advice is also of great help.

3.4 Concatenation of Dance Units

The next question is how to connect each motion unit. One method interpolates the last posture of the previous motion and the first posture of the next motion. The difficulty in the case of a dancing robot is how to connect these two motions and prevent the robot from falling down. We introduced a method in which a neutral posture represented by a standing still pose is used as a transition posture between two dance units. In this case developing an algorithm is unnecessary to generate a transitional motion that connects two different motions.

3.5 Realization of Robot Dance Motion

The next issue is transforming human dance motions into the motions of robots. One common method adopts a motion capture system that is used to generate the motion of CG characters. For a robot, however, due to the limitations of the degree of freedom at each joint, directly transforming the motion captured by the system into robot motion does not work well. Research that transforms captured motions into robot motions is described in [10] that treats a Japanese traditional dance whose motions include legs moving slowly and smoothly front/back and left/right instead of dynamically. In this case it is relatively easy to maintain balance. However, hip-hop motions include dynamic body motions, and therefore it is difficult to maintain balance. Taking these situations into considerations, we chose a method where each motion unit extracted from continuous motion is transformed manually.

3.6 System Architecture

Based on the above considerations, we constructed the first prototype of a robot dance system, as shown in Fig. 1, that consists of dance unit sequence generation, a dance unit database, and dance unit concatenation.

(1) Dance unit database
A large amount of dance units are stored here; each one corresponds to a basic short dance motion and is expressed as robot motion data.

(2) Dance unit sequence generation
An input data that expresses a dance motion is analyzed and converted into a sequence of dance units by this part. At the present stage a sequence of dance units is directly used as input data and fed into the system.

(3) Dance unit concatenation
As is described in 3.4, a neutral posture is introduced as an intermediate posture between two dance units, and therefore, they can be easily connected.

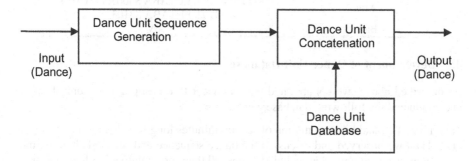

Fig. 1. Structure of dance robot system

4 System Development and Evaluation

4.1 Humanoid Robot

From the several humanoid robots already available on the market, we selected a humanoid robot developed by Nirvana Technology [11] and installed dance motions on it. Figure 2 shows its appearance, and Table 1 shows its basic specifications. Various robot motions can be designed and produced on PC using a "motion editor" realized by motion making and editing software.

Fig. 2. Humanoid robot

Table 1. Specifications of humanoid robot

Size/Weight	34 cm / 1.7 kg
Degree of flexibility	22 (12 legs, 8 arms, 1 waist, 1 head)
CPU	SH2/7047F
Motor	KO PDS-2144, FUTABA S3003, FUTABA S3102, FUTABA S3103
Battery	DC6V

4.2 Development of Dance Unit Database

As described above, we collaborated with a dancer to develop a dance unit database and conducted the following database generation:

(1) First, a typical hip-hop motion of several minutes long was recorded.
(2) Then we observed and discussed the dance sequence and selected about 60 motions as dance units that included almost all the representative hip-hop motions.
(3) We asked the dancer to separately perform each motion corresponding to each dance unit and recorded it. At the same time we asked him to start each dance motion from a "natural standing posture" and to finish in the same posture.

(4) By watching each dance motion being performed, we tried to create a robot dance motion that corresponds to human dance motion using motion editor.

4.3 Evaluation of Robot Dancing

Using the system described above we carried out simple evaluation experiments.

4.3.1 Comparison of the Two Types of Robot Dance Units

We evaluated the two types of dance units; one was generated by the professional dancer (type 1) and the other by non-experts (type 2). First we classified all the dance motions into three categories according to the complications of the motions; primary, intermediate, and advanced. And we selected one representative motion for each category. These dance motions are "Lock"(primary), "Rolling Arm" (intermediate), and "Club"(advanced). Then we generated two types of robot dance motions for each of these motions.

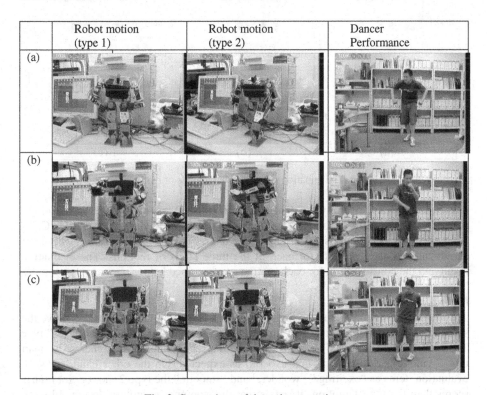

Fig. 3. Comparison of three dance motions

Ten subjects were asked to compare these two types of robot dance motions by giving a score ranging from 1 to 5 to each dance motion (1 is the worst and 5 is the best). Figure 3 shows the comparison between the two types of dance motions; robot

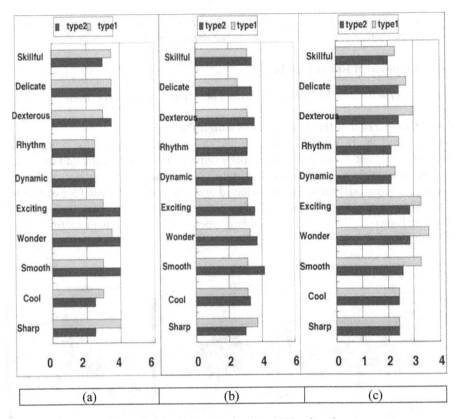

Fig. 4. Evaluation results for three kinds of motions

dance motions developed by the dancer himself (type 1) and those developed by non-experts (type 2) for three kinds of motions; (a) Lock, (b) Rolling arm, and (c) Crab. Also the live dance motions performed by the dancer is shown as references. Figure 4 shows the evaluation results for each of the three kinds of motions. The evaluation result and the consideration for each motion are described below.

(1)Lock
This is a repeating motion of moving and stopping like being locked. In this move the sharpness of stopping motion is an important factor as a dance. For "sharpness," type 1 motion (motion designed by a professional dancer) obtained the higher score than type 2 (motions designed by non-experts) as expected. On the other hand, for such evaluation items as "exciting," "wonder," and "smooth," the type 2 motion got higher scores than the type 1 motion. It seems that the stop-and-go motion designed by the dancer was judged awkward by the subjects.

(2)Rolling arm
This is a motion of moving body while turning arms smoothly. For the sharpness, the type 1 motion obtained higher score than the type 2. But for other evaluation items, the type 2 motions generally got slightly higher scores. Especially for "smooth" type 2

received much higher scores against type 1. Originally this motion contains a step raising legs, and the type 1 motion precisely simulates this process and in the case of sharpness it worked well and obtained the high score. On the other hand, the type 2 motion achieves this move by sliding legs without raising legs. As a result, it was judged that the type 2 motion looked smoother than the type 1, and this gave a influence to the result of smoothness evaluation and others.

(3)Crab

This motion is a move peculiar to the Hip-hop dance. It includes a move of sliding legs sideways without raising them and fixing their backside on floor and thus moving the body sideways. The motion designed by the professional dancer (type 1) receives higher scores than the motion designed by non-expert (type 2) for almost all evaluation items. Especially, important evaluation items for this move such as "exciting," "wonder," and "smooth," the type 1 obtains fairly higher evaluation scores than the type 2.

These result shows that as the robot dance motions become more complex, they can get higher scores. The reason for this would be that the professional dancer understands so well the characteristics of each dance motion and his knowledge and now-how is reflected on the robot dance motion. Even though it does not appear so well in the case of simple motions, this characteristic reveals itself in the case of complicated motions. On the other hand, the motion designed by non-expert (type 2) obtained higher evaluation scores than the type 1 for simple motions. The explanation for this would be that the subjects got good impressions for the over-actions and the unstableness that the type 2 motions generally contain and express themselves. Contrarily, the type 1 motions designed by a professional dancer are sophisticated without containing such over-action nor unstableness. This characteristic sometimes leads to rather low evaluation scores as the subjects are non-expert of dances and thus could not understand the details of the dance motions where the knowledge and now-how of the professional are stored.

4.3.2 Evaluation of the Continuous Dance Motion

Then we carried out the experiment to evaluate the feasibility of the dance generation system. We compared two types of continuous dance motions. One is a continuous dance motion which is automatically generated by this system and has the length of about one minute (type 3). Another is the same dance motion where instead of automatic generation the professional dancer designed the whole continuous dance motion from scratch (type 4).

For evaluation twelve items generally used for the sensibility evaluation such as "stable," "soft", "smooth," and so on were selected. Each evaluation item has a seven level score ranging from -3 to 3. For example, for the evaluation item "stable" the 0 means neutral, 3 means very stable, and -3 is very unstable. Figure 5 shows the evaluation result. The type 4 obtained fairly good results for most of the evaluation items. This means that the evaluation items were fairly well selected. Generally the dance motion generated by this dance generation system (type 3) obtained lower evaluation scores than the type 4 motion. Especially, for such evaluation items as "harmony," "lightness," and "tempo, " the type 3 motion obtained minus evaluation

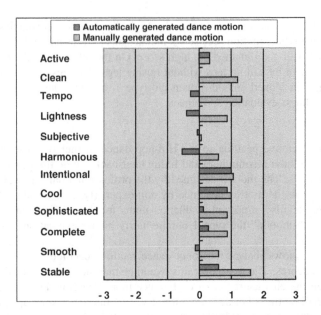

Fig. 5. Comparison between automatically generated motions and manually generated motions

scores. This is because the subject felt unnaturalness due to the neutral posture effect used to connect the two dance units. This means that the system still needs further improvement to generate continuous dance motion, especially for the connection of two dance units. At the same time, however, the type 3 motion got plus scores for "stability", "cool", and "intentional." Especially for "cool" and "intentional" the evaluation results are almost as high as the results of the type 4 motion. This shows that the continuous dance motion generated by this system would be effective as far as it is used as a performance even at the present stage.

The difference between type 3 and type 4 motions are that in the case of type 3 motion it goes back to a neutral position at the point of the dance unit connection. It is necessary to improve this point by introducing better neutral posture or introducing multiple neutral postures.

5 Conclusion

In this paper we proposed a dance robot system as a new application area for humanoid robots. We clarified several distinctive entertainment characteristics and investigated the role of robots in entertainment.

Based on these basic considerations we proposed a dance robot system in which a humanoid robot performs various dance motions. We hypothesized that any dance motion consists of a concatenation of short dance motions called dance units. This basic idea was imported from TTS, where any text can be converted into speech by concatenating short basic speech called speech units. Based on this basic idea, we collaborated with a professional dancer. After recording and analyzing his hip-hop dancing, we extracted about sixty dance units and converted them into the motions of a humanoid robot. By concatenating these dance units we found that a huge amount of dance variations for the hip-hop genre could be achieved.

Then we carried out two types of evaluation experiments. First we compared dance motions designed by the professional dancer and the ones by non-experts of dancing. We found that as the dance motions become more complicated and sophisticated, the dance motions by the dancer got higher evaluation results. Then we compared a continuous dance motion automatically generated by this system and one fully manually designed. Although the automatically generated dance got lower evaluation results, for some evaluation items it got almost the same scores. This means that this system is promising from a point of automatic dance generation. Further studies must address the following issues. First we have to investigate how many dance units are enough to generate any type of hip-hop dance. Also we have to investigate the feasibility of a neutral posture that connects two dance units. As only one type of neutral posture was used so far, still there is some unnaturalness for the automatically generated continuous dance motion. We expect that by introducing several other neutral postures, continuous dance motions achieved by the robot would become more natural.

References

1. Golubovic, D., Li, B., Hu, H.: A Hybrid Software Platform for Sony AIBO Robots. In: Polani, D., Browning, B., Bonarini, A., Yoshida, K. (eds.) RoboCup 2003. LNCS (LNAI), vol. 3020, pp. 478–486. Springer, Heidelberg (2004)
2. Ishimura, T., Kato, T., Oda, T., Ohashi, T.: An Open Robot Simulator Environment. In: Polani, D., Browning, B., Bonarini, A., Yoshida, K. (eds.) RoboCup 2003. LNCS (LNAI), vol. 3020, pp. 621–627. Springer, Heidelberg (2004)
3. Kerepesi, A., Kubinyi, E., Jonsson, G.K., Magnusson, M.S., Kiklosi, A.: Behavioural Comparison of Human-Animal (Dog) and Human-Robot (AIBO) Interactions. Behavioural Processes 73(1), 92–99 (2006)
4. Wama, T., Higuchi, M., Sakamoto, H., Nakatsu, R.: Realization of Tai-chi Motion Using a Humanoid Robot. In: Loeckx, J. (ed.) ICALP 1974. LNCS, pp. 14–19. Springer, Heidelberg (1974)
5. http://www.expo2005.or.jp/en/index.html
6. Callois, R.: Les Jeux et les Hommes. Callimard, Paris (1958)
7. Laban, R.: The Mastery of Movement. Macdonald and Evans. 4th edn (1980) (revised and enlarged edition)
8. Kleijn, W.B., Paliwal, K.K. (eds.): Speech Coding and Synthesis. Elsevier, Amsterdam (1995)
9. Lee, C.: Ballet in Western Culture: A History of Its Origins and Evolution, Routledge, London (2002)
10. Nakaoka, S., Nakazawa, A., Yokoi, K., Hirukawa, H., Ikeuchi, K.: Generating Whole Body Motions for a Biped Humanoid Robot from Captured Human Dances. In: IEEE 2003 International Conference on Robotics and Automation (2003)
11. http://www.nirvana.ne.jp/

TMAR: Extension of a Tabletop Interface Using Mobile Augmented Reality

Sewon Na[1], Mark Billinghurst[2], and Woontack Woo[1]

[1] GIST U-VR Lab., Gwangju, 500-712, South Korea
{sna,wwoo}@gist.ac.kr
[2] The HITLabNZ, University of Canterbury, New Zealand
mark.billinghurst@hitlabnz.org

Abstract. Recently, many researchers have worked on tabletop systems. One issue with tabletop interfaces is how to control the table without using conventional desktop input devices such as a keyboard or mouse. A second issue is allowing multiple users to simultaneously share the tabletop system. In this paper we explore how Augmented/mixed reality (AR/MR) technology can be used to explore these issues. One advantage of AR technology is being able to bring 3D virtual objects into the real world without needing to use a desktop monitor and allows users to intuitively interact with the objects. In this paper we describe a Tabletop Mobile AR system that combines a tabletop and a mobile interface. The Tabletop system can recognize user gestures and objects and intuitively manipulate and control them. In addition, multiple users have equal access for information on the table enabling them to easily share digital content. This makes possible unique entertainment and education applications. In this paper we describe the technology, sample entertainment interfaces and initial user feedback.

Keywords: Tabletop user interface, Mobile augmented reality, Tabletop mobile augmented reality, 3D interaction, Tangible user interface, Mobile interaction.

1 Introduction

In everyday life, tables provide space for entertainment, education and supporting meetings between multiple persons. For example, we sometimes play games around the table or talk with friends while having drinks on the table. In this case it forces people to concentrate on one point and it allows everyone equal access to the table.

Recently, many researchers have worked on electronic tabletop systems. One important issue of with tabletop systems is how to control the table without using conventional desktop input devices such as a keyboard or mouse. Some researchers have proposed input methods using graspable or tangible objects [1][13] while others have developed multi-touch technology.[2] For example, Microsoft's Surface computing project allows users to intuitively interact tabletop system by using multi-touch technology. However, touch screen manufacturing is difficult and the bigger the screen is, the more expensive it is.

Z. Pan et al. (Eds.): Transactions on Edutainment I, LNCS 5080, pp. 96–106, 2008.

In addition, other research has been conducted on how to enable multiple users to share tabletop interfaces simultaneously. Information on the screen is usually shown for only one user from one direction which limits concurrent accessibility from a variety of direction. The ability to sharing the table with multiple users allows users to access data significantly different way from desktop environments. [14] Some ways of doing this including splitting the table screen according to user number or using a spherical screen which can rotate left or right. [3][4] However, the former is insufficient for accessibility in sharing and collaboration manner because each split screen view is still shown for one person. A spherical screen is also difficult because the users often continuously compete to get the authority of control. Thus it is difficult to ensure simultaneous control opportunity of the table.

Augmented/mixed reality (AR/MR) technology has also been studied by many researchers in mobile and wearable computing field. [15][16] The main advantage of AR technology is to ability to bring virtual 3D objects into real space without having any vertical monitor. In addition, AR interaction technology allows users to intuitively interact with the 3D virtual objects. Since AR technology does not reply on a physical screen in the real world, it may be used to overcome the problems of view sharing and intuitive object manipulation.

In the research described in this paper, we present a tabletop mobile AR system which combines a tabletop interface with a mobile interface using AR. It extend tabletop interface and get out of limitation of scope of tabletop screen. It provides intuitively augmented 3D information by using a mobile device with attached camera as well as convenient 2D interaction through recognizing objects put on the table and touch input. The use of personal mobile device ensures that anyone can easily accessibility the tabletop interface and unlike previous tabletop systems. Users can easily manipulate 3D virtual objects.

This paper is organized as six sections. Section 2 explains an initial prototype system called ARTable [13] which identified several problems with tabletop systems. While section 3 explains a novel system we developed to overcome these problems. Section 4 explains how to implement the system. Finally we present conclusions in Section 5.

2 ARTable [13]

We briefly explain an earlier tabletop system we developed called ARTable which identified several problems common to desktop interfaces. Our current research is based on this earlier work and overcomes these problems. The ARTable is consists of a tabletop display with a projector and camera underneath it connected to a computer (see Fig. 1a). The top of the table is a semi transparent material so it can be projected onto and objects placed on it can be seen by the camera underneath. Using computer vision software [9] can recognize and track objects placed on the table.

Objects placed on the table have a square fidducial marker on their base which can be detected by the camera under the table and so the object position is known in table coordinates. For each object the 2D position and rotation relative to the table is found and so objects can be used to trigger events on the table. However, with rear-projector, rear-camera systems, there can be difficulty with marker detection due to projected imagery shown on the marker (see Fig. 1b). This makes it difficult for the marker tracking software to find the fidducial marker. One solution (shown in Fig. 2b) is to project a white circle around the object, enabling the tracking marker to be easily seen. However in order for this to work and initial object position must be known.

Fig. 1. ARTable (a) upper surface of the table (b) back surface of the table through underneath camera

There are two ways to find the initial object position and so change the projected imagery so that the object can be tracked. First, the system can make the entire screen white and waits until the first object is detected before projecting the application image. If the entire screen color is white, the objects placed on the table are not obscured by any projected images. Once the object is detected, the screen is restored to the desired image, and when the user gets rid of the object from table, the white screen again shown awaiting object detection. Although this is a very simple method, it has a critical problem in that there can be only one tracked object. After one object is detected, the table image is no longer white and further objects are obscured by the projected imagery.

A second method is to use additional device for finding the position of objects on the table. In our prototype we used the cost effective NextWindow touch frame [12] placed over the table. This uses cameras in the frame to touch enable any surface and so provides an initial position of any object placed on the table. We can use the coordinates given from the touch frame to provide the object position and enables us to project a white circle around the object. The camera under the table can then be used to find the object orientation. The advantage of this approach is that many objects can be tracked at once.

Our initial ARTable was used in a number of applications. For example, Dream of Mee-luck was interactive storytelling system on a Korean traditional tale, and ARTable was used as interaction tool for its virtual world navigation. [6]

However there were a number of limitations with this system. First users around the table did not have a view of the application aligned to their position, so the ARTable did not solve the view problem mentioned in section 1. Second, users could not see 3D virtual content and there was no intuitive support for 3D interaction. In the next section we describe our current tabletop mobile AR system which overcomes both of these problems.

3 Tabletop Mobile AR SYSTEM

3.1 System Overview

Our tabletop mobile augmented reality (AR) system consists of two types of interfaces: a table interface (the previous ARTable) and a mobile interface (see Fig. 2). The table interface consists of the modules for input and output, and networking. The mobile interface also consists of the modules for input and output, and networking but it also adds a tracking module which use a camera attached to back of the mobile device.

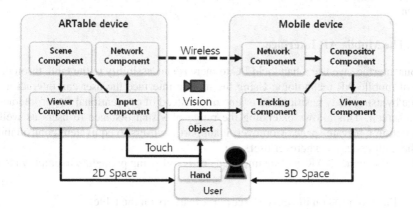

Fig. 2. The system diagram of the tabletop mobile AR system

The tabletop interface is a version of the ARTable previously describe. So the user can interact with projected images on the tabletop by using hand gestures or tangible objects in various ways. However, the mobile device allows the user to see 3D virtual images overlaid on live video from its camera through mobile device's screen. The user can also manipulate these 3D virtual images on the handheld device.

3.2 Table Interface

The tabletop interface can recognize and track the user's hands or other objects using a camera under the table and NextWindow touch frame as described in section 2 (see Fig. 3). The physical objects used are cardboard squares representing materials, selection tools or other control widgets (see Fig. 3d). In the future, these could be substituted by real symbolic objects such as a souvenir taken from travels. The NextWindow touch-frame technology can only detect one object position at a time and so will not report the correct position of a second object once the first is placed on the table. We overcome this by raising the touch frame a centimeter off the table surface (see Fig. 3b). In this way when an object marker is placed on the table its position is detected when it is being placed or removed, but whiles on the table it sits below the touch frame and so does not interfere with the detection of other object positions. Of course, once the object is on the table it can be tracked by the camera under the table.

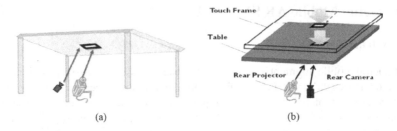

Fig. 3. Table system (a) concept of tabletop interface (b) the gap between touch-frame and the screen

3.3 The Mobile AR Interface

In our interface we use a handheld PC to increase accessibility to the table through the use of mobile AR technology. Using the mobile interface the user can interact in 3D space by using body position and orientation instead of conventional finger interaction on a screen. This allows extending the range of visual distance to users as well as supporting a private space. Moreover, it support for users to equivalent controllability in the mobile device wherever users are.

Likewise general AR, mobile interface needs following procedure to employ mobile AR.

 - Place objects on the table (User place markers on the table)
 - Object recognition and tracking (by camera attached in mobile device)
 - Augment 3D contents (User see 3D Contents registered on the video image)
 - Interact with 3D contents (It is similar with interaction on the table, so user will not be confused the interaction methods and there are no seam between table interaction and mobile interaction)

Object Tracking & Augmentation. In order to track and recognize the objects placed on the table, objects on the table have tracking markers on their top and bottom. The handheld PC tracks the markers on the top using the ARToolkitPlus tracking library. [9] This identifies the specific object being tracked and determines the pose of the handheld PC relative to the tracked objects. In this way 3D virtual imagery can be overlaid on the real objects and viewed through the handheld PC in real time. In the Mobile AR interface we use a Tangible AR user interface metaphor [20] to interact between the table and the mobile device. By using one tangible object as an input object, the users can see 3D virtual objects superimposed over live video on the screen of the mobile display device.

Interaction. In the mobile AR, the user will interact with 3D Contents. So, we basically can think selecting and manipulating 3D contents. User can explicitly select 3D objects through touch panel on the mobile interface as well as on the table. Because touch panel is 2D surface, we use ray tracing methodology to select 3D contents. Ray-tracing algorithm is usually used in the computer graphics area. In addition, user can select implicitly objects placed at the center of mobile devices without any selection because

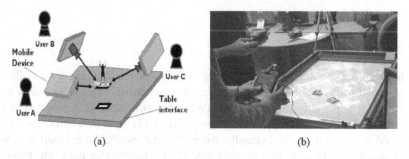

Fig. 4. Mobile Interface (a) sharing table using mobile device around the table (b) users with the handheld device around the tabletop interface

it is trivial that object seen through mobile device is user's interest object. Practically, user carry mobile device on one hand, the hand is not free. So we use button interaction method to manipulate the objects. If the object is selected, mobile device shows buttons about actions with respect to the object.

3.4 Common Space

One of our goals is to ensure that the users feel as through the two interfaces (tabletop, mobile AR) support seamless interaction in one common space on and above the table. In order to achieve this goal, we have to correctly align the two spatial coordinates systems, and provide temporal synchronization and unified data sharing. Aligning the spatial coordinates can be done through the placing reference objects on the table. As shown in Fig 5a, we can obtain absolute 3D coordinates by the combination of relative 3D coordinates of the object in the mobile AR devices frame of reference and 2D Absolute coordinates of objects put on the table. 'w' in the figure represents a obtained absolute coordinate result. 'u' represents a 2D Absolute coordinate of table. 'v' is a 3D coordinate in the mobile AR devices. When two devices transfer the coordinate data through networking, we conduct temporal synchronization to prevent data overflow or congestion by latency. Thus, we make pipe for data serialization as first-in first-out (FIFO) and control data (see Fig. 5b). This structure waste out-of-time data and reduce unnecessary data.

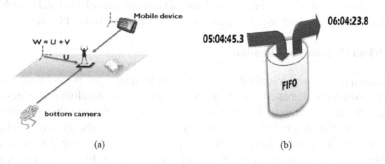

Fig. 5. Constructing common space (a) spatial coordinates correction (b) temporal synchronization

4   Implementation

4.1   System Setup

We have implemented a prototype tabletop mobile AR interface using the following hardware and software. First of all, the table interface consists of glass with semi transparent tracing paper attached and the NextWindow touch frame [12] mounted on top. Under the table, there is a NEC short throw projector [21] and Dragonfly camera [10] connected to workstation PC. Secondly, the mobile AR interface was based on a Sony VAIO ultra mobile PC [21] with an embedded USB camera on the back. The two computers are connected with wireless Ethernet networking. The software running on the tabletop interface was based on the OpenSceneGraph [7] library, while on the handheld PC we used osgART Library. [8] The projected table view was based on the osgViewer module of OSG and all virtual objects are represented as Scene-Graph objects. On the handheld device through the use of osgART library, we can easily represent augment reality areas combined with virtual world and computer vision. In addition, we used Point Grey Library to capture images. [10] To communicate between two interfaces, we employed TAO library which follows the CORBA specifications based on ACE. [11]

4.2   TMAR System

The TMAR system mainly consists of two interfaces: the tabletop interface and the mobile AR interface. The tabletop interface uses two types of input devices from the user. First one is tracking hands by using touch frame as we explained above. The user can intuitively select 3D contents or buttons (see Fig. 6a). The second one is recognizing and tracking physical objects on the table by underneath camera. The user usually put the physical objects on the 3D contents of the table screen (see Fig. 6b). It plays a role of carriers allowing coupling of both interfaces (mobile/toabletop) seamlessly.

While the mobile interface uses touch panel input device. Thus, the user can touch the panel on the handheld device and select 3D contents. 3D contents are displayed on the physical objects as one by one with it. The user can see registered image with video image (see Fig. 7a). After that, Fig. 7b shows that the user selects 3D content (a scribed building represent selected one) and then buttons which are applicable become displayed below it. As push the button, the user can rotate buildings (see Fig. 7c) or raise it (see Fig. 7d). Especially, in the case of Fig. 7d, multiple 3D contents are selected and then they are modified at once. Also the user can create or delete the contents (see Fig. 7e).

4.3   Urban Planning Application

The prototype interface described above could be used in many possible applications. We are particularly interested in how this could facilitate the development of new types of edutainment applications. Our first test application was for an urban planning task (see Fig. 8). Urban planning is to plan the city's structure or landscapes by architects. It has been utilized by researchers of AR area. [18][19] We made simple map consist of 3x2 roads and 9 sites (shown in Fig. 8a). Users can create buildings on it or manipulate

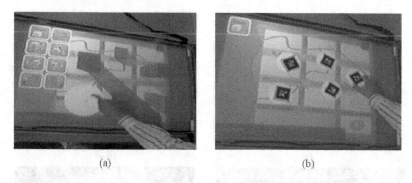

(a)   (b)

Fig. 6. The tabletop interface (a) tabletop interface recognizing hand gesture (the white circle is a clicked position) (b) physical objects on the table

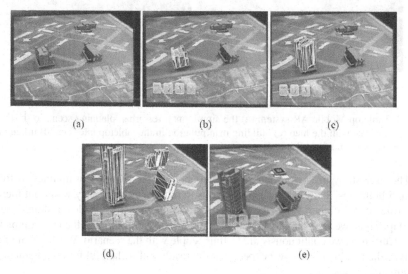

(a)   (b)   (c)

(d)   (e)

Fig. 7. Mobile AR interface views and Interactions (a) Augmented buildings on the markers (b) Selection and showing button (c) rotating a building (d) raising buildings (e) deleting a building

through tabletop interface (shown in Fig. 8b, 8c). Also it is possible to see and interact through mobile AR interface (shown in Fig. 8d).

4.4 User Study

To asset usability of the proposed system, we have conducted a simple user study with the prototype application. The experiment goal is to conduct an urban planning project. Each person is tested 3 kinds of system with that goal. First, they use fingers to touch the screen instead of mouse or keyboard. Second, they use some markers and a mobile device to achieve the same goal. Lastly, they will combine the first and second methods.

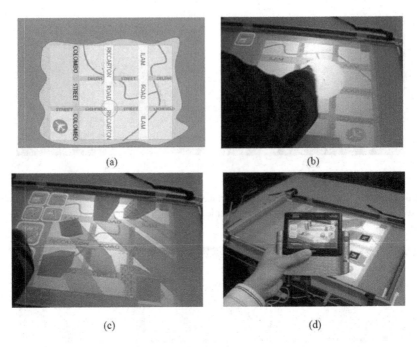

(a)   (b)

(c)   (d)

Fig. 8. Tabletop Mobile AR system (a) the simple map for urban planning scenario (b) the tabletop interface with the map (c) building manipulation in the tabletop interface (d) urban planning through the mobile AR interface

The user study procedure is like followings. We give them few minutes to freely place 5 buildings. They may use any buttons to make a city that they want, but there is one rule to remember when they are constructing the city: shadows should never overlap. Thus, we are going to be able to compare 3 systems through the task completion time. Currently, we continuously are testing people with the scenario. We are planning to analyze the results. Finally, we expect that the result will be helpful for complement our system and enhancing it.

5   Conclusion and Future Work

In this paper we have presented a prototype tabletop mobile AR interface which supports AR Interaction between virtual and physical objects. The Tabletop interface can recognize user's hand and objects and intuitively manipulate and control them. The advantage and novelty of our research is that multiple users had equal access for information on the table enabling them to easily share digital content. This made possible unique entertainment and education applications. In the future, each module is integrated and executed on one mobile device. We are going to study more about mobile collaboration in complex situation. The users may want to reflect a result of their manipulation to only the selected user. According to authority or position, the user's manipulation ability can be differentiated among users. For example, engineers of urban planning system have more power than consumers. Moreover, even if users see same buildings, they may want to see different building or landscapes according to their preference. Therefore, it is necessary to personalize the mobile AR interface. We believe that the proposed system is applicable for both education and entertainment.

Acknowledgements

This research is supported by the UCN Project, the MIC 21C Frontier R&D Program in South Korea.

References

1. Ullmer, B., Ishii, H.: The metaDESK: models and prototypes for tangible user interfaces. In: Proceedings of the 10th annual ACM symposium on User interface software and technology, pp. 223–232 (1997)
2. Han, J.Y.: Low-Cost Multi-Touch Sensing through Frustrated Total Internal Reflection. In: Proceedings of the 18th Annual ACM Symposium on User Interface Software and Technology, pp. 115–118 (2005)
3. Shen, C., Vernier, F.D., Forlines, C., Ringel, M.: DiamondSpin: An Extensible Toolkit for Around-the-Table Interaction. In: ACM Conference on Human Factors in Computing Systems (CHI), pp. 167–174 (2004)
4. Scott, S.D., Carpendale, M.S.T., Inkpen, K.: Territoriality in Collaborative Tabletop Workspaces. In: Proceedings of CSCW, pp. 294–303 (2004)
5. http://www.microsoft.com/surface/
6. Lee, Y., Kim, D., Lim, Y., Kim, K., Kim, H., Woo, W.: Dream of Mee-luck: Aspiration for a New Dawn. In: Subsol, G. (ed.) ICVS-VirtStory 2005. LNCS, vol. 3805, pp. 280–283. Springer, Heidelberg (2005)
7. http://www.openscenegraph.org/projects/osg
8. http://www.artoolworks.com/community/osgart/
9. http://studierstube.icg.tu-graz.ac.at/handheld_ar/artoolkitplus.php
10. http://www.ptgrey.com/
11. http://www.cs.wustl.edu/~schmidt/ACE.html
12. http://www.nextwindow.com/
13. Park, Y., Woo, W.: The ARTable: An AR-based Tangible User Interface System. In: Pan, Z., Aylett, R.S., Diener, H., Jin, X., Göbel, S., Li, L. (eds.) Edutainment 2006. LNCS, vol. 3942, pp. 1198–1207. Springer, Heidelberg (2006)
14. Carsten, M., Timo, E., Daniel, H.G.: A component based architecture for distributed, pervasive gaming applications. Advances in Computer Entertainment Technology (2006)
15. Güven, S., Feiner, S.: Authoring 3D Hypermedia for Wearable Augmented and Virtual Reality. In: Proc. ISWC 2003 (Seventh International Symposium on Wearable Computers), White Plains, NY, pp. 118-226 (2003)
16. Azuma, R.T.: A Survey of Augmented Reality. Presence: Teleoperators and Virtual Environments 6(4), 355–385 (1997)

17. Scott, S., Sheelagh, M., Carpendale, T., Inkpen, K.: Tabletop design: Territoriality in collaborative tabletop workspaces. In: Proceedings of the 2004 ACM conference on Computer supported cooperative work. ACM Press, New York (2004)
18. Buchmann, V., Violich, S., Billigust, M., Cockburn, A.: FingARtips: gesture based direct manipulation in Augmented Reality. In: Proceedings of the 2nd international conference on Computer graphics and interactive techniques in Australasia and South East Asia, pp. 212–221 (2004)
19. Broll, W., Stoerring, M., Mottram, C.: The Augmented Round Table – a new Interface to Urban Planning and Architectural Design. In: Ninth IFIP TC13 International Conference on Human-Computer Interaction, pp. 1103–1104 (2003)
20. Ishii, H., Ullmer, B.: Tangible bits: towards seamless interfaces between people, bits and atoms. In: Proceedings of the SIGCHI conference on Human factors in computing systems, pp. 234–241 (1997)
21. http://www.nec.co.jp/techrep/en/journal/g06/n03/060319.html

Interacting with Augmented Assets in Cultural Tourism

Maria Teresa Linaza[1], Ander García[1], Isabel Torre[1], and Jose Ignacio Torres[2]

[1] Department of Tourism, Heritage and Creativity, VICOMTech, Paseo Mikeletegi 57
20009 Donostia-San Sebastian, Spain
{mtlinaza,agarcia,itorre}@vicomtech.org
[2] The Movie Virtual, Paseo de los Olmos
2000 Donostia-San Sebastian, Spain
jitorres@themovie.org

Abstract. This paper presents the results of the PRISMA project, where a proposal to include a zoom-lens camera into an outdoor marker-less AR system for the cultural tourism sector has been developed and assessed. The key issue of PRISMA is the combination of the commonly known concept of tourist binoculars and AR technologies. PRISMA presents tourist information from a new point of view, allowing the user to interact with multimedia information. An panoramic view from one of the hills of Donostia-San Sebastian city in the North of Spain has been chosen as the real validation environment.

Keywords: Augmented Reality, multimedia management, cultural storytelling.

1 Introduction

Augmented Reality (AR) is not that much of innovation any more. Several number of projects and applications concerning AR using different types of registration techniques or recording cameras have been published. Regarding registration techniques, the use of marker-based tracking is widely extended due to its robustness. The position and rotation of the markers is extracted from the image recorded by a camera using image processing algorithms. Nevertheless, these techniques can not always provide the best solution, mainly in wide areas where the addition of markers is not always possible or can be cumbersome. Therefore, other technologies are used to track rotation and position of the user during the registration process. A variety of motion trackers can be found on the market, based on infrared, magnetic fields, inertial forces or other technologies.

However, the adquisiton of position and rotation data alone still is not enough to get an acceptable registration of an augmented scene. Further inaccuracies in the registration process can appear due to the specific parameters of the tracking cameras, like focus, opening-angle and distortions. To adjust these parameters, AR systems must include methods to calibrate the system according to the specifications of the selected camera. Thus, registration is still an up-to-date research topic with a wide potential for improvement, as synchronizing the virtual and the real worlds, and rendering the graphical interface from the point of view of the users is a crucial factor.

Z. Pan et al. (Eds.): Transactions on Edutainment I, LNCS 5080, pp. 107–117, 2008.

Up to now, few AR applications with zoom-lens cameras have been developed. Zoom-lens require an interactive adjustment of not just the position and orientation of the system, but also of the internal parameters of the camera like opening angle, distortions and focus. Marker-based tracking systems can overtake the difficulties associated to the usage of zoom-lens cameras implementing complex image processing algorithms for tracking. However, marker-less approaches including outdoor applications require additional developments to achieve proper registration.

This paper presents the results of the PRISMA project, where a proposal to include a zoom-lens camera into an outdoor marker-less AR system for the cultural tourism sector has been developed and assessed. The concept of binoculars on hills expecting tourists to put a coin in to see the surrounding area for a couple of minutes is widely known. They offer an overview over the buildings and streets of a city, nature and cultural sites as well as the chance to zoom tourist assets closer to the user. The view can increase the interest of tourists in visiting places and help them in choosing further targets to visit later on. However, it may often be hard to find anything except the nearby woods or the sky in the field of view of the binoculars. Even when a nice looking attraction is found, it turns out to be sparsely interesting because of the lack of sight and information about the resource.

Moreover, existing multimedia content presentations are distant from the real environment which means that users have to leave the tourist site to obtain additional information. If tourist organizations wished to reach wider audiences, they would have to build attractive multimedia content available on site. Therefore, new systems that support these innovative applications and provide added-value content are required.

The paper is organized as follows. Section 2 presents a brief state of the art of AR technologies and their application to cultural tourism applications. The following section includes a brief description of the PRISMA project and the validation scenario. Section 4 gives a technical overview of the prototype, including its components and performance. The assessment of the prototype in a real scenario is presented in Section 5. Finally, Section 6 presents some conclusions and further work.

2   State of the Art

Augmented Reality (AR) is a technique in which the view of the user is enhanced or augmented with additional information generated from a computer model [1]. In contrast to Virtual Reality, where the user is immersed in a completely computer-generated world, AR allows the user to interact with the real world in a natural way. In order to make AR systems effective, the computer-generated objects and the real scene must be combined seamlessly so that virtual objects align well with the real ones. It is therefore essential to determine accurately the location and the optical properties of the registration cameras. The registration task must be achieved with special care because the human visual system is very sensible to even small misregistrations.

Many researchers believe that AR is an excellent user interface for cultural tourism applications, because it allows intuitive browsing of location-based information. Using AR, the perception of the user of the real world is enhanced by computer-generated entities such as 3D objects and spatialized audio. The interaction with these entities takes place in real time to provide convincing feedback to the user, giving the impression of natural interaction.

It can not be denied that the standard equipment used in the traditional tourism activity has remained unaffected by the common attitude to embrace the latest and greatest technological solutions. When visiting a tourist asset, the traditional visitor's guide and a trusty map remain as the standard equipment. Although everybody is familiar to such scenario, it shall shortly undergo a rapid metamorphosis. The standard equipment will change into Personal Digital Assistants (PDA); instead of a map, an electronic map enhanced with a reliable position sensing mechanism is envisaged; guides will change into online access to a data repository endowed with rich multimedia content, spatial data and other relevant up-to-date content.

As a key element in the standard equipment, maps are abstractions of the real world and are well suited to give an overview of an area. However, some cognitive effort is needed to determine the orientation of the user from looking at maps. On the other hand, AR allows matching the scene with reality immediately, although it could be difficult to provide location-based information without positioning and orientation errors.

Questions like "What can I see and do in he city?" or "What is important to know about it?" will be answered by future tourist guides or the so called Pedestrian Navigation Systems (PNS). When reviewing literature on PNS, it can be observed that most of current concepts have been developed in one of two following research approaches: location-based services and outdoor AR systems.

Some well-known systems that have been developed within the location-based services approach are Cyberguide [2], GUIDE [3], Deep Map [4], and Lol@ [5]. The presentation of the location of the tourist is mainly based on maps, which are displayed on mobile devices connected to wireless networks. Further multimedia information such as photos, videos and audio about landmarks and points of interest are linked to the map.

Concerning outdoor AR systems, different projects can be mentioned, such as the Touring Machine, ARREAL [6] and Studierstube Mobile AR [7]. In the Touring Machine project [8], users stand in the middle of the campus, wearing a prototype which includes a Head Mounted Display (HMD). The system overlays textual labels over campus buildings. However, the relative inaccuracy of the trackers is not a significant problem for the success and acceptance of the final application by the user. Although the approaches for PNS differ substantially, both of them mix reality and virtuality to support orientation and wayfinding; location-based services adding real information to virtual maps and Augmented Reality systems adding virtual objects to real scene views.

From the state of the art, it can be concluded that there is a shift towards more active, cultural and urban destinations. The attractiveness of urban culture and other aspects of the tourist resources of the city receive growing attention from tourists. How to deal with these opportunities is a challenge for the tourist industry as well as for local and regional governments. In order to manage quality tourism in tourist destinations, it is necessary to create new possibilities for services and dynamic ways of experiencing the destination.

3 The PRISMA Project

The aim of the PRISMA project is the design, development and implementation of a new 3D visualization device based on AR technologies and storytelling techniques for cultural tourism applications (Fig. 1). The emphasis within the project has been focused on developing experimental user interface software, not on designing hardware [9][10]. Therefore, commercially available hardware has been integrated in order to build the prototype.

Fig. 1. PRISMA prototype in the real environment

The key issue of PRISMA is the combination of the commonly known concept of tourist binoculars and AR technologies. PRISMA presents tourist information from a new point of view, allowing the spectator to interact with multimedia information. By means of these technologies, the real scene can be enhanced by virtual information to increase the experience of the user and provide added value interactive personalized multimedia content about the current view. The proposed techniques are highly visual and interactive in order to access and understand tourism information.

A panoramic view from one of the hills of Donostia-San Sebastian city in the North of Spain has been chosen as the real validation environment. For the assessment of the prototype, the binoculars have been placed at the middle height of the hill to allow tourists and also local citizens to "visit" some of the interesting cultural and tourist attractions of the city, such as the Cathedral and Santa Clara Island in the middle of the bay, as shown in Fig. 2. PRISMA overlays graphical labels over cultural tourist attractions. The relative accuracy of the labels is crucial so that the spectator chooses the correct cultural asset and not another one in the nearby.

When the user discovers a tourist asset about which he/she is interested in getting additional information, it is enough to click on the graphical representation of the object and a menu with the available choices for the content (cultural and tourist information, historical data, interactive models) is displayed. PRISMA allows tourists to

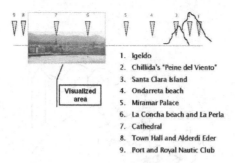

1. Igeldo
2. Chillida's "Peine del Viento"
3. Santa Clara Island
4. Ondarreta beach
5. Miramar Palace
6. La Concha beach and La Perla
7. Cathedral
8. Town Hall and Alderdi Eder
9. Port and Royal Nautic Club

Fig. 2. Selected tourist attractions for the augmentation

obtain multimedia personalized information about these cultural tourist assets, including textual information (timetables, directions, telephone numbers), 2D photographs and maps, or even videos and 3D reconstructions. The user interface is based on simple buttons placed on the system.

4   Technical Description of the Prototype

4.1   Components of the Prototype

As shown in Fig. 3, the prototype basically comprises a camera that records a real time image from the point of view of the user, and sends the image to a processing unit. The camera used in the prototype is the Sony SNC-Z20N, which incorporates a highly sensitive 1/4 type CCD. Equipped with auto-focus 18x optical zoom lens, this camera can zoom in on small or distant objects with exceptional resolution. Moreover, the camera can be controlled from an external control device, allowing local control of zoom parameteres of the camera over a serial RS-232C connection.

The prototype further includes a visualization device through which the user can view the augmented scene. Our current setup uses a 5DT HMD 800-40 Head Mounted Display fixed to the structure as an output device. It is basically a metaphor of conventional binoculars, including a video non see-through visualization system.

As an essential device involved in the registration process, the tracking of the system is achieved by an Intersense Inertiacube2 orientation sensor for inertial tracking as the prototype is mainly supposed to be moved in two dimensions (left/right, up/down). As seen in Fig. 3, the visualization device and the camera are mounted on the same mechanical axis so that they move in a synchronous way. Therefore, the tracking system calculates the position of the visualization device and thus, the position of the camera.

The prototype also includes seven buttons distributed among the left and right sides of the prototype for simple and ergonomic interaction. On the one hand, the two buttons on the left side allow the user zooming in or out over the augmented scene. On the other hand, there are five buttons on the right side: one button in the middle which can be used to click on the augmented graphical objects and also to choose among the menus of the additional multimedia content; and four buttons distributed around the middle button, allow browsing through the menus for selecting the additional multimedia content.

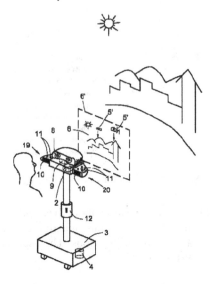

Fig. 3. Technical components of the PRISMA system

Additionally, some sound speakers are included so that the user can listen to presentations or other audio information included in the additional multimedia content.

Content is stored in two different databases in the processing unit: an augmentation database and an auto-administrable content database. The augmentation database stores the 3D graphical objects, including the name of the main tourist attractions and other graphical objects that are superimposed to the points of interest for the spectator through applicable AR methods. These methods convert 3D graphical objects into 2D graphical representations, which are superimposed to the real scene, resulting in an augmented scene. The auto-administrable content database stores the additional multimedia content, including videos, movie clips, interactive 3D panoramas or even 3D models of existing and reconstructed cultural tourist attractions.

We have used ARToolKit as the software platform for developing the applications. ARToolkit is a software library for building AR applications, which offers the possibility of augmenting a video stream with graphical objects. The graphics supported are principally OpenGL, but also a VRML import PlugIn exists which allows importing 2D as well as 3D objects and animations. The ARToolkit is based on marker-based tracking that detects special markers in the video stream by means of computer vision algorithms and calculates the real camera position and orientation relative to the physical markers in real time. As the tracking approach used in PRISMA depends on inertial sensors fixed to the binoculars, the ARToolKit has been modified.

Finally, an Authoring Tool has been implemented in order to simplify the manipulation of the 3D graphical objects, their placement in the augmented scene and the associated additional multimedia content they are supposed to show. The programme can load XML files to change them or to create new ones in the proper style for the main programme. The prototype includes up to ten points of interest with up to five subobjects to choose within the menu. 3D graphical objects include tourist points of interest and their corresponding markers in the augmented scene, while subobjects stand for different types of additional multimedia content shown when choosing 2D graphical representations.

4.2 Performance of the Prototype

Fig. 4 shows the functional schema of the PRISMA prototype. As explained previously, the real camera captures the Field of View (FoV) of the user. The tracking system calculates and sends certain positioning information to the processing unit, informing about the current location and orientation of the visualization device. The processing unit then runs a graphics adaptation process which converts 3D graphical objects into 2D graphical representations depending on an orientation vector obtained from the positioning information. In other words, the processing unit adapts a shot of the 3D graphical objects to obtain a virtual scene, controlling a "virtual camera" using the orientation vector of the real camera. Therefore, the real scene and the 2D graphical representations are synchronized according to the position of the camera. This synchronization allows composing the real and the virtual scenes of the augmented scene.

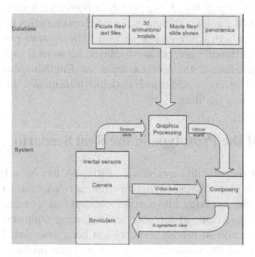

Fig. 4. Functional scheme of the PRISMA system

If the user moves the prototype to the left or to the right, the tracking system informs the processing unit about this change. The graphics adaptation process then updates the 2D graphical representations of the 3D graphical objects so that they match the new real scene. As a result, when the user changes the position of the prototype, the augmented view changes as a whole.

In order to clarify the above mentioned concepts, Fig. 5 depicts an example of the performance of the PRISMA prototype. In the real validation scenario, the augmented scene viewed by the user is formed by the real view of the Bay of San Sebastian and some hills, some of the buildings and one of the hills being pointed out by corresponding 2D graphical representations.

As the user sees an interesting object about which he/she would like to get more information - for example, the high building in the middle of the screen pointed out by the text "obj1"-, he/she presses on the buttons on the right side of the prototype until selecting the 2D graphical representation of that interesting object. Then, the prototype displays the additional multimedia content regarding the selected 2D graphical representation.

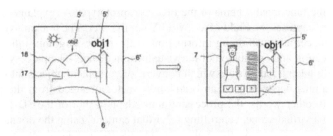

Fig. 5. Example of the performance of the PRISMA system

For example, as shown in Fig. 5, the prototype pops up a screen showing some text and playing a video of a guide explaining certain characteristics of the selected tourist asset, and/or offering extra navigation options. The system provides personalized information, where different contents are displayed for several user profiles, including aspects such as multilingualism. For example, an English-speaking tourist with a cultural background receives additional in-depth information in English about the history of the interesting building.

5   Assesment of the Prototype in the Real Scenario

The overall aim of the usability analysis of PRISMA has been the development of typologies of users and standards, so that new interactive tourist experiences could be personalized in the future taking into account concepts such as usefulness and ease of use. Therefore, the behaviour of the user when dealing with new technologies as a means of communication of tourist contents has been assessed. In order to achieve this aim, the quality of the communication between the prototype and the user has also been measured. Therefore, it is crucial to assess the impact of PRISMA within the added-value experience with the innovative 3D visualization prototype.

Concerning the sample, about 100 people took part in the usability study, from which 47 answered in-depth questionnaires, at the real scenario at the Monte Urgull in San Sebastian (Spain) in March 2006. The average profile of the participant is a man between 20 and 35 years old (61% of the sample) and quite familiar with the use of new technologies (mobile devices, laptops, digital cameras, Internet). Most of the participants worked in the tourism sector, including destination managers and content providers.

In order to measure the scope of the results and conclusions, it must be mentioned that the profile of the sample has been biased, as most of the selected participants worked in the tourism sector. They had a double role within the usability study: a common tourist role for the quantitative analysis and a professional of the tourist sector role for the qualitative one. The participants provided a critical vision taking into account not only their personal point of view, but also an extended discussion about further developments of the prototype. The conclusions have been grouped on the basis of the issues that have been highlighted within the evaluation process.

Most of the participants agreed that the approach of using advanced visualization technologies such as Augmented Reality enhances the interactive experience with tourist content. The interviews concluded that the device provides added-value multimedia contents in an interactive way. This way, information is more accessible with new visualization means and innovative interaction metaphors. Moreover, more than 80% of the participants were willing to pay up to three euros for the experience. As a conclusion, the participants have positively assessed the usefulness of the prototype as a tourist information point for urban environments due to its capability of providing Location-Based contents to allow better route planning.

Concerning the ease of use, the results of the quantitative analysis were mostly positive, although issues related to interaction, comfort and simplicity in the access to contents have to be improved. Many limitations or usability problems were related to the fixed height and the restricted physical adaptability of the prototype to the physical conditions of the user. Position of legs, arms and hands of the user was influenced by the binoculars, the interaction devices, the mechanical rotation of the visualization device and the design of the device as a whole. Further improvements in the physical design of the device will have a great impact not only on a more comfortable experience for the user, but also on a smaller damage when using the device. A final recommendation was the need of the contextualization of the prototype in order to facilitate its usage.

Regarding the contents, more than half of the sample found them usable, interesting and innovative. Moreover, two thirds of the users were impressed by the historical images that were displayed. Interactive contents based on QuickTime panoramas had the greatest impact, specially the navigation and zooming inside the Cathedral of the city. However, the potential of the prototype could be extended by panoramic approaches, holograms or non-linear story-telling techniques. As a final conclusion, it can be said that PRISMA can be considered as a prototype with a great potential impact over the tourist sector. Further application scenarios such as environmental impact of architecture planning projects have been suggested.

6 Conclusions

This paper presents the results of the PRISMA project, where a proposal to include a zoom-lens camera into an outdoor marker-less AR system for the cultural tourism sector has been developed and assessed. The main objective of the project was the implementation of user interfaces and personalized contents, and not the hardware development. Therefore, commercially state-of-the-art equipment has been integrated to build the prototype.

Regarding the hardware, the inertial tracker works quite accurately although the answer is quite slow in some cases. Therefore, when the system was moved too fast left to right, the delay of the tracking system got very obvious, limiting the immersion effect of the 3D graphical objects. Further refinements of the prototype should include complementary hybrid tracking systems depending on further outdoor tracking possibilities.

The main technical challenge in the programming of the prototype has been the implementation of the augmented zoom. Although many different alternatives were tested to achieve appropriate results, it can be concluded that there are two possible ways of programming the zoom algorithms: implementing the linear interpolation of the changes in the FoV with slow change rates, or using absolute zoom positions with the most correct overlay but minor delays of the real behind the change of the virtual position. As a general statement, it can be affirmed that a higher precision of the information about the position of the zoom provided by the real camera as well as a higher communication speed could be a possible solution.

As the merging of the 3D graphical objects with the real data is crucial in AR, the overlay of the graphics on the video-stream in PRISMA is also a key issue. Due to several reasons, the graphics merged with the real environment suffer from some slight inaccuracies. Main shortcomings are the synchronisation of the zoom between the real and virtual cameras, the change of the rotation centre as the camera lens move from the centre while zooming and the delay of the inertial sensor on fast movements. These problems may be solved using another type of camera or some kind of mechanical mechanism to move the camera, as the lens must be kept in the centre of the rotation.

Other optional features for further refinements of the prototype are the option to see the surrounding area during different seasons of the year, i.e. with snow, or in summer, or without clouds, or the possibility to combine the AR aspecta with a virtual immersive enhancement. By selecting an object of interest such as a cultural building in the area, a virtual walkthrough is started. This application "moves" the user from the real position into the building, letting him/her move around and discover the virtual interior of the building.

This paper can be considered as an example of how an AR system can annotate the environment of a user to visualize related information. Unlike desktop visualization environments in which the system can control what the user sees, in tourism applications, the tourist determines the viewing specification and the physical environment determines which tourist assets are visible.

As cultural tourism is dominated by visual experiences to a large extent, it can be regarded as a rich site for both the 'creation' and analysis of visual evidence, by both researchers and practitioners. Despite the importance of the visual sight in tourism, image-based research methods are simply not on the agenda for many tourism researchers. When visual images are used, it is often only to support the use of written text. PRISMA aims at developing specialised language or standardized methodologies and modes of using and analysing image-based sites.

As concurrence gets harder, it will become increasingly important that tourist destinations develop products tailored to their main consumer groups. Thus, it becomes ever more important to understand visitors' perceptions of destinations. Urban environments serve multiple functions and often become ideal destinations for both business and pleasure travellers as they increase in size and importance.

Acknowledgements

This paper is part of the project "PRISMA- Augmented vision for Cultural Tourism Applications", financed by The Movie Virtual and Ereiten Kultur Zerbitzuak within the INTEK program of the Department of Industry of the Basque Government.

References

1. Azuma, R.: A Survey of Augmented Reality. Presence: Teleoperators and Virtual Environment 6(4), 355–385 (1997)
2. Abowd, G.D., Atkeson, C.G., Hong, J., Long, S., Kooper, R., Pinkerton, M.: CYBER-GUIDE: A Mobile Context-Aware Tour Guide. ACM Wireless Networks 3, 421–433 (1997)
3. Cheverst, K., Davies, N., Mitchell, K., Friday, A., Efstratiou, C.: Developing a Context-aware Electronic Tourist Guide: Some issues and experiences. In: 2000 Conference on Human Factors in Computing System, pp. 17–24 (2000)
4. Malaka, R., Zinf, A.: DEEP-MAP- Challenging IT Research in the Framework of a Tourist Information System. In: Information and Communication Technologies in Tourism ENTER 2000 (2000)
5. Gartner, G., Uhrlitz, S.: Cartographic Concepts for Realizing a Location-based UMTS Service: Vienna City Guide LOL@. In: 20th Int. Cartographic Conference ICC (2001)
6. Baus, J., Krüger, A., Wahlster, W.: A Resource-Adaptive Mobile Navigation System. In: Int. Conference on Intelligent User Interfaces IUI, San Francisco (2002)
7. Reitmayer, G., Schmalstieg, D.: Location-based Applications for Mobile Augmented Reality. In: 4th Australasian User Interface Conference AUIC 2003 (2003)
8. Feiner, S., MacIntyre, B., Höllerer, T., Webster, A.: A Touring Machine: Prototype 3D Mobile Augmented Reality Systems for Exploring the Urban Environment. In: Int. Symp. On Wearable Computing ISWC. IEEE Press, Los Alamitos (1997)
9. Alzua-Sorzabal, A., Linaza, M.T., Susperregui, A.: Providing On-Site Augmented Information to Tourists. In: Hitz, M., Sigala, M., Murphy, J. (eds.) Information and Communication Technologies in Tourism 2006. SpringlerWien, New-York (2006)
10. Fritz, F., Susperregui, A., Linaza, M.T.: Enhancing Cultural Tourism Experiences with Augmented Reality Technologies. In: Proc. of the 6th International Symposium on Virtual Reality, Archaeology and Intelligent Cultural Heritage VAST 2006(2006)

Interactive Storytelling: Approaches and Techniques to Achieve Dynamic Stories

Madjid Merabti[1], Abdennour El Rhalibi[1], Yuanyuan Shen[1],
Jorge Daniel[1], Alcantara Melendez[1], and Marc Price[2]

[1] School of Computing and Mathematical Sciences.
Liverpool John Moores University,
Byrom Street, L3 3AF, UK
{M.Merabti,A.Elrhalibi,Y.Shen}@ljmu.ac.uk
[2] BBC Research, Kingswood Warren, Tadworth
Surrey, KT20 6NP, UK
Marc.Price@bbc.co.uk

Abstract. In this paper we review different techniques which can be used to achieve interactive storytelling in games, most notably the employment of planning algorithms to decide which and how events should be presented to the player at a given time, and the definition of non playing characters actions and behaviours as a response to the player's actions. Furthermore we will consider game world with more interesting characters that react to other characters actions and behaviour, while forming bonds and relationships with them and the player. We will consider the use of emotional characters to this effect. The incorporation of narrative techniques into the storytelling used in games can help not only to increment the level of interaction between the player and the world and characters, but also to keep the story fluent, thus achieving more realistic narrative. We will examine and discuss some of them, along with some existing approaches and possible applications for interactive storyline generation. We will also review and discuss some areas in which emotional characters have been used to support the player, and in the development of interactive storytelling.

Keywords: Interactive Storytelling, Planning, Emotional Model.

1 Introduction

Similar to other entertainment media, stories in games play a big role in increasing immersion, building tension and adding interest to the player [1]. However, one main difference from the games to those other media is that games are interactive; they expect participation from the player and in turn, players expect to participate and get involved in the events the game is presenting and the outcomes of those events [2, 3].

Stories can be presented in different ways: they can be linear, branching, parallel or threaded [14]. Games typically follow a linear storyline, where the events of the story are presented in a defined sequence. Nevertheless, it can be argued that making a player follow a defined story can diminish the interactivity level of a game; the player is, after all, following a preset path laid for him [1]. So in order to benefit the most of the story

Z. Pan et al. (Eds.): Transactions on Edutainment I, LNCS 5080, pp. 118–134, 2008.

and still allow the player to feel a high degree of interactivity, the concept of interactive or non linear storytelling has to be introduced. Simply put, interactive storytelling presents the opportunity for players to create their story, to have an input on what is happening in the game world they are placed in, to be the ones who dictate how certain events may come to pass [1, 2, 3, 6]. This in turn will help players to be more immersed in the game and enjoy them in a greater degree, since as stated by Laurel in [4], "story making is a pleasurable activity", as seen by recent studies[4, 5].

Furthermore, when the player is playing a game, he is presented with a fictional environment which he can explore and interact with; but this world is not desolate, as it is populated by several other characters that can interact with the player. Whether a simple digital opponent as in Pong, a complete town full of villagers as in most Multiplayer Massive Online Games, or the diverse NPCs controlled by a game master in the traditional pen and paper role playing games, those characters are placed in the game world in order to help or challenge the players while they try to achieve a specific goal, or simply to make the game world feel more believable and realistic. Additionally, creating NPCs that can react and adapt their behaviours in response to external factors such as the player's actions or changes in the game world, will increase the player's level of immersion with the game itself, as they are more likely to feel identified with the characters' motivations and troubles [2], thus desiring to continue playing the game and getting more involved with those characters.

Based on this premise, we can appreciate the importance of employing more deep and interesting characters to populate a game world, characters that the player will feel motivated to talk to, rather than simple and apparently void characters with only one line of dialogue and which react only when directly addressed by the player [20]; characters that will demonstrate a 'genuine' interest in the events occurring in the game world as they will affect them directly, thus giving a more realistic feeling to the player [22]. As mentioned in [21], "expression of emotion is crucial for increasing believability" and, these interactions may also provide players with a sense of belonging to the game world, as they will be affecting it directly with their own actions and decisions, thus becoming actors in the game world rather than just spectators.

The question now is how to provide the player with an interactive storytelling experience. The most common techniques used, and as noted in [3], are branching storylines which enable the player to select the order of the missions available. However, to achieve this goal, we can employ other techniques, such as parallel paths, threaded stories or dynamic object oriented narrative [14]. On this paper, we will examine and discuss some of them, along with some existing approaches and possible applications for interactive storyline generation. On this paper we will also examine and discuss some current techniques being employed to create emotional NPCs, that is, characters that can simulate emotions and behave according to their current state; we will also mention and review some areas where they can be used and how they can affect the game experience for the player.

The structure of the paper is as follows: in section 2, we propose an overview or planning based interactive storytelling approaches; in section 3, we will introduce emotions controlled interactive storytelling based techniques; in section 4 we will discuss the issues of implementation and future possible direction; before summarising the main points of the paper in the section 5 as conclusions.

2 Planning Based Interactive Storytelling

As noted in [3], one example of interactive story telling can be found in a game of Dungeons and Dragons where the person in charge of the narrative, the Dungeon Master (DM), can adapt the way the story unfolds in accordance to the way the players behave and interact with their environment; so in a normal D&D game, whenever the players do something completely unexpected by the DM, he can adapt the story to take into account those events. Of course, the DM may want to stick to the original storyline and he can use several resources, such as NPC's to keep the players in track, but it is the players who ultimately decide how they want to behave and act, and the story moves according to these variations.

What we can see from this example is that we can create interactive storytelling by having a larger entity controlling and adapting the story in accordance to the players' actions. Champagnat et al [6] suggest a narrative framework to simulate this activity. In this framework, they suggest having a set of agents in charge of evaluating the current state of the game, and one director agent, who "chooses a set of relevant actions to be executed" [6].

Another approach to generate interactive storytelling is described by Cai et al [7]; in this approach, a tool based on Goal Net is used to plan the story and Fuzzy Cognitive Maps are employed to analyze the user inputs and decide which path should be followed; they were selected due the fact that they act as "collection of the rules such that it not only concerns the relationships between the causes and effects, but also considers their relationships among the causes". Similar to the work described in Champagnat et al [6], this approach implements an agent, modelled using the Goal Net tool, which will be in charge of presenting the story in accordance to the user actions. In order to accomplish this, a controlling agent keeps information related to the states required to achieve a goal, and the relationships or transitions that connect those states [7].

What makes the Goal Net tool a good fit for creating interactive storytelling is that it can divide goals into simpler states; that way, each scene in the story can be divided into simpler scenes, thus creating several paths that can lead to the conclusion of the defined story; having four different ways of connecting the states (sequence, concurrency, choice and synchronization) allows for flexible and more interesting transitions between the different sates, which leads to the creation of more complex stories. Important to note is that using Goal Net as planning tool instead of Hierarchical Task Networks yields better results in terms of interactive storytelling, since it provides the ability to select scenes on real-time, according to the current context and user input [7].

The engine created by Cai et al consists of a knowledge database, where the scenes and their relations are stored, the fuzzy cognitive goal net engine, a container for the agents to be used, known as the Drama Manager, and a Multi Agent Development Environment (MADE) [8] platform to implement the agents' system; using fuzzy cognitive maps, the engine will decide, at runtime, which scenes from the knowledge database should be loaded into the agents in order to better suit the path selected by the user [7].

Three main advantages can be distinguished from employing this method to create interactive storytelling [7]:

- All events are simplified into less complex scenes
- The engine can react not only to the user inputs but also to the actual state of the game, and look for the best path.
- Since all the events are loaded into the engine on real time, its performance is increased.

While the approach presented by Cai et al addresses the issues of letting players interact with their environments and creates its own story, it only uses defined actions to determine how the story will be told. Ciarlini et al [9] suggest an approach in which player's actions affect not only the scenes of the story, but also the behaviour of non playing characters directly related to those actions. What they propose is to use a "formal logic model" for defining "events and characters' behaviour" [9].

Ciarlini et al state that the user should be able to "intervene in the story" but their actions should not "violate the rules of the intended genre" [9]. The architecture used in order to achieve this is comprised of a plot manager, which will serve as the interaction point for the user and will manage the story as it is being created; an Interactive Plot Generator which will take the input from the user and generate and order possible sequences, which in turn will be passed onto the plot manager; finally, a drama manager will control the characters in the game world in order to add appropriate drama to the story; it will also be in contact with the interactive plot generator to maintain the "coherence between logical and graphical representations" [9].

The Interactive Plot Generator (IPG) uses Prolog files that contain the logic to be used for creating stories; in order to generate the storyline, the IPG requires 3 main items:

- An initial state for all the characters and scenarios. These states are described using Prolog and they are contained in a database. An example, as presented in [9], would be: character (villain, dragon) which will represent that the dragon is a villain.
- The logic rules, which will be used to infer the goals for each character as the plot is generated.
- The list of operations available for the characters. Each operation should indicate which events should happen before it (preconditions), which events will come to pass after the operation (post-conditions), the representation of the operation, that is, the smaller actions involved in the performance of the operation (getting close to the victim, etc.) and the actors involved in the event, whether characters or other features.

When plots are generated, partial ordering is used to arrange the events comprising the story; this will allow the creation of more dynamic and diverse stories, as the outcome of each event will be affected by the order in which they are defined to occur. So in some stories, the hero may be stronger before he faces the enemy, and in some other, it will be the other way around.

For every character in the story, a set of goals will be defined following the inference rules created; these rules employ "meta-predicates to speak about the occurrence of an event or the truth value of a literal at certain time" [9]. For example, to represent the motivation of a hero to rescue a victim that has been kidnapped, the predicate rule will be something like 'whenever there is a villain and a victim, if at time1 it is established that the villain kidnapped the victim, therefore it exists a time2 on which the victim should not be kidnapped by the villain and time1 should be lesser than time2'. We can observe here that there's no actual mention of the hero rescuing the victim, but what it is modelled is the motivation; there should be a later time on which the victim is freed. Using this approach, the goal of freeing the victim may be assigned to any suitable character, and not just a specific one.

At the initial state, goals will be defined for each character and a planner will decide which events will allow the characters to achieve their goals. When all goals have been either met or abandoned, a new set of goals will be inferred for the characters, and this process will be affected by the past outcome of past events [9]. What one can appreciate from this approach is that it takes into account all previous events, whether they were successful or not, thus affecting the development of the storyline, a feature that is not supported by conventional plan generators [9].

The approach used by Ciarlini et al shows that mixing player's participation, the generation of plans and the inference of goals can yield positive results. The use of predicate logic to construct the scenes and behaviour of characters in the story increases the level of interaction and the degree of interactivity perceived by the player. It is also implied that this model to construct interactive stories can be used in other entertainment media, such as TV or cinema, as a tool for authors to create adaptive stories, and it may even be applied to other non-gaming related applications, like information systems [9].

As it has been suggested, one can employ non playing characters' actions and be-haviours to generate interactive storytelling since it will be them with whom the player will be interacting the most while playing the game. In our personal experience while playing D&D and generating dynamic storylines on the fly, we believe that NPCs are a very useful resources for helping the players shape the story to their own liking while maintaining a sense of coherence on it: they might encourage them to keep going in a certain path, point them into the right direction or simply be used to maintain the story interesting.

Barros and Musse [10] suggest an approach that employs this mechanism and two other narrative practices into a storytelling generator based on the usage of planning algorithms and STRIPS domains. The architecture they propose is divided into 3 modules

- A module who will be dedicated to defining the actions that can be performed by the NPCs.
- A module in charge of executing the available actions for the NPCs and keep the state of the world
- A module responsible of resolving conflicts that may appear whenever a new plan of actions is generated.

In order to progress the story, a plan of actions should be created for the characters to follow; each action is described in a language similar to STRIP and it is composed of a prerequisite, used to decide if the action is coherent given the current state of the world, and an effect, which indicates the repercussions of performing the action. For example, the action of giving a present to someone may have as prerequisites having the present and being at the same place as the receiver, while the effects would be to be more liked by the receiver. The implementation made by Barros and Musse "treats the planning problem as a state space search problem, and uses the A* algorithm to solve it"[10].

What Barros and Musse incorporate into their model for creating interactive story-lines is three narrative principles:

- View story as a whole: By considering the overall storyline as a set of sequential plans, which in turn are sets of sequential actions, one can make sure that each plan will try to include the best actions to take in order to continue with the main plot; this kind of control will yield more coherent and believable stories.
- Three act storylines: Being the most common format for stories, it presents the opportunity to group together events that help develop the story: the first act introduces the overall problem, the second one helps increase tension and develop solutions and the third one presents the resolution of the story [2, 10]
- Avoid narrative stalls: Being the focal point of the story, the player may sometimes decide to not follow the plan set in order to continue the story. To avoid this, the actions of the NPCs can be prioritized, so that they can act and accomplish goals before the player. This will allow the story to be fluent even when the player gets stuck.

By combining the narrative techniques and the described architecture, Barros and Musse [10] were able to create interactive storylines that would adapt to the player's actions, even if those actions were not doing well in keeping the story fluent. One possible drawback might be the use of "predicate logic to represent the world state" [10] due the fact that it does not helps us to deal with the most complex aspects of narrating stories [10, 11]; however, as stated by Barros and Musse, it can help us understand the problems and their solutions in an easier manner.

What can be definitely useful for future work is the employment of the narrative principles to create more interactive stories; by defining both the actions and behaviour for the NPCs as a results of the player's actions, will help increase the interactivity of the story: the state of the world and their inhabitants will change to adapt to whatever path the player decided to follow. Allowing the story to keep going whenever he gets stuck can be viewed as both beneficial and detrimental for the player: on one side, the story is still flowing, even when the player cannot find a solution to achieve a certain goal; on the other hand, events performed by the NPCs in order to advance into he story may not be noticed by the player, which in turn can later lead to confusion [10].

Similar to the approach used in [10], the Storytron engine [15] employs a set of verbs to define all the possible actions and it also describes the conditions and consequences for that action. However, and differently from the approaches mentioned early, the creation of plans to be executed by the characters is not handled by a single planning manager, but instead by the characters themselves; that way, each character will decide how to react to a given event.

Plans are created in a 'Reaction Cycle', which allows the characters to examine the event that is occurring and then evaluate the better course of action for them in order to respond to that even; and then executed in an 'Action Cycle' in which the characters will evaluate if all the requirements are met for the execution of their plan and if possible, execute the planned actions. For example, if a character punches another, all witnesses of that event will analyze their possible options (i.e. run away, hide) and will select the one to which they feel most inclined and immediately create a plan to perform that action whenever all the conditions are met.

By employing verbs to define actions, the Storytron engine provides an approach to generate interactive storytelling that implements the strong points of branching narratives, but without the complex managing of the nodes created in that kind of technique[15, 14]. The very interesting feature is the implementation of the Response Cycle, as the idea to allow each character to generate its own plan in response to the events happening in the world allows for more freedom and dynamic interaction of the players, thus providing the sense of interactive storytelling as the events presented will be as responses to the actions of not only the payer, but the whole lot of characters.

3   Emotions Controlled Interactive Storytelling

On this section we will examine and discuss some current techniques being employed to create emotional NPCs. We will also mention and review some areas where they can be used and how they can affect the game experience for the player.

3.1   Modelling Emotions

As the player explores and travels the world he is placed in, he will eventually have to interact with the different NPCs that populate the world; furthermore his actions and behaviours will also affect the world he lives in and indirectly, the lives of the other characters in the game. Placing the player in a situation where their actions and behaviours have a lasting effect on the characters he interacts with can be a very rewarding experience [12]; so the main issue is how to model the non-playing characters behaviours in a way that they react accordingly to their emotions, the environment and their changes.

One approach described in [23] is to use a simple flag system to define the current affective states of a given character in response to actions by the player; this approach however results are very simplistic and not very realistic: after all, human behaviours and feelings are related to a more wide range of variables. However, trying to represent all emotions present in humans within one game character might be a nearly impossible task, especially since, as mentioned by [24, p 377], the term might sometimes be used to refer not only to feelings but also to biological needs such as thirst, hunger or sleepiness.

To deal with this issue, Sheldon [20] presents an approach on which each character has a personality chart containing individual scores for six different areas: Love, Admiration, Trust, Loyalty, Respect, Like. Each score can take a predefined value ranging from negative to positive six; the addition of those values will determine the overall character's personality towards the rest of the world inhabitants. In order to determine the relation between the player and a given character, we need to calculate a relationship modifier value, which ranges from negative to positive six and might increment or decrement as a result of the actions of the player, for example, completing specific quests. The relation score between a player and a certain character is then calculated as the addition of both the player's modifiers and the character's personality scores; this score will be compared with a behaviour table to define the attitude for the character towards the player [20].

Another approach is the one presented in [23], which consists of an affinity system that indicates how comfortable a certain character feels towards another character or object. The different situations being presented over the course of the game will increase or reduce the affinity score by a defined amount; a set of rules should be established to define, based on this affinity score, which behaviour should a certain character present when interacting with the player.

3.2 Motivations and Social Relationships

While these approaches address the relationships between players and NPCs and help construct more realistic interactions between them, they do not consider other factors that might affect the relationships between characters, such as personal motivations or social networks; these factors are something that should also be considered when designing reacting and emotional characters, as the actions that those characters might be able to do or the behaviour they could exhibit and the consequences of the player's actions might be completely different depending on the social network that a character belongs to [20].

Bailie-De Byl, in [24], presents and reviews some existing architectures oriented towards the creation of emotional NPCs while taking into consideration their inner motivations and desires:

- Blumberg's Silas T Dog: On this architecture, an artificial agent is composed of three main layers: Geometry system, Motor Controller and Behaviour System. The firs two are in charge of the movement of the agent in a 3D environment, while the latter is the one that handles the responses the agent exhibits to external stimuli; it consists of a hierarchical network of modules, each representing a defined goal which can be either general or specific. When a stimulus is received by the agent, the Behaviour System analyzes that stimuli and employs the motivation and goal variables from the agent in order to determine which behaviour module should be activated. If the selected behaviour has any child behaviours in the hierarchy, all those children modules begin competing between themselves to define the one that should take control of the agent at a given moment; this competition is made by analyzing the internal goals, motivation and the behaviour's importance. Once selected, the behaviour module will inform the Motor Controller and Geometry system of the actions that the agent should perform in order to reflect the change in attitude.

PETEEI (A PET with Evolving Emotional Intelligence): Composed of three main process models (emotional, cognitive and learning), this architecture waits for an event to occur and then processes this stimuli to define its desirability. The agent then takes into account its own motivations and processes both internal and external stimulus to define the emotion that should surface. Once the emotion has been defined, the agent evaluates, by employing a set of defined rules, the behaviour that should be exhibited. One interesting aspect that the architecture employs is the fact that the emotions decay over time and the internal variables are evaluated and updated after a fixed time, in order to define if a change on the agent's current behaviour should be made.

Emotion-Based Control (EBC) Framework for Autonomous Agent: Whenever the agent receives an external stimulus, a Perception System is activated to determine its emotional significance, which will affect the resulting behaviour used by the agent; this data is then sent to the Emotion System and the Behaviour System, which also receive internal information from a Drive System in charge of storing all information regarding the agent's motivations and desires. After analyzing the provided information, the Behaviour System, using affect programs (internal pre-defined systems that describe and represent primary emotions), decides which behaviour the agent should present and instructs the Motor System to act accordingly. Something of note is that each affect program has a decay value that represents the time that the actual emotion will be activated; another interesting feature is the possibility to actually combine the basic emotions in order to simulate more complex behaviours, i.e. combine fear and joy to create guilt.

Emotionally Motivated Artificial Intelligence: Whenever an agent receives an external stimulus, a first mechanism activates the drivers controlling the motivations for the agent; these drivers describe the source and current strength of all the agent's motivations and will serve as indicators of the behaviour the agent should take. The drivers will remain active until a certain threshold is reached, meaning that a necessity has been covered. Higher emotions are represented in this architecture as coordinate points in a six-dimensional space, known as the affective space; based on this coordinate system, the agent can asses their importance and impact to decide which behaviour should be shown. One aspect of this architecture is that all external stimuli is positioned in the affective space and then processed, along with the motivations of the agent; this means that the resulting behaviour will not only be dependant on the external factors and motivations, but also in the current affective state of the agent.

As we have discussed, these architectures try to create deeper characters in terms of the emotions and behaviours they display by taking into account not only the external factors but the agent's motivations as well, but we still have to take into account the effect that social networks existing between the NPCs and the character itself might render into their interactions.

Lankoski and Björk [13] mention that humans, being social by nature, feel more compelled to get involved with games when social relationships exist between the characters populating the world [13]. Social relationships are an important aspect to be considered when trying to create realistic worlds and societies within it. Even the most emotional accurate characters will feel somewhat unreal if they do not seem to have an interest on the world they are living on or if they do not interact directly with other characters living in the same place [22]. As [25, pp 1] explains it, "to create believable agents we must not only have some internal model of emotion, but also a way to communicate with the user based on these models".

As with human societies, the proximity of NPCs between one another and to the player, their frequent interaction and their personal goals and motivations will result in the creation of relationships between those characters and the formation of groups or factions that share interests or goals [20, 24]. Depending on the existing relations that a player has with different NPCs and the diverse factions that exist in the world, he might gain more or less information, obtain a varying degree of rewards or be faced with different challenges; we have seen this in games such as The Elder Scrolls: Morrowind or Fable, were the player's actions and allegiance directly affect the behavior and responses he gets from NPCs and the events that are presented to him. However, the modification of those relationships are normally done as scripted events presented in the form of cut-scenes, or by providing the player with a limited set of choices to select from, thus reducing the input of the player and limiting the number of possible reactions and consequences to just a handful of pre-defined results [13].

So what we now must address is how we can generate and maintain those relationships, both between the NPCs and the player and between the NPCs themselves. Lankoski and Björk present two methods to analyze social networks between characters and to apply them into the game:

- Social Network Analysis: This approach represents people as the nodes of a graph and their relationships are represented as nodes; since this approach is based on graph models, we can employ mathematical measures to represent diverse characteristics of the relationships. Some examples of the subgroups that we might find within networks are N-cliques (everyone in a group is connected to the rest of the nodes by at most N relationships), K-plexes (members are related to each other node with the exception of K nodes), isolated communities (star shaped groups where each member is related to each other through one central member) and singletons (members with no relationships to the groups) [13, 26]. This kind of analysis can help us to describe how a character fits within one group and how they perceive and are perceived by other members of that group, thus helping us understand why they exhibit certain behavior [26].

- Actor Network Theory: This theory states that nodes or members in social relationships should not only be defined as humans or characters, but rather as "collections of heterogeneous entities consisting of humans, human-tool combinations and non humans (e.g. technologies, machines or materials)" [13, pp. 2]. Basically, actor network theory suggests that relationships and behaviours of human actors in a network are defined by other external factors such as experience, existing regulations or a given tool's capacity and characteristics [27]. One approach that Actor Network Theory employs is the consideration that social groups are not static entities and they are changing constantly, meaning that goals and motivations for the group and its internal actors might be changing constantly; therefore, NPCs and players themselves will have to adapt their actions and behaviours constantly in order to satisfy their new needs and achieve new goals, thus creating more realistic and interesting social groups [13].

3.3 Cooperation between Characters

Aside from interaction between characters, social networks are defined by each individual's goals and motivations [25], which in turn can lead to either cooperation or conflict between NPCs and the players [13]. This presents a more realistic approach to the representation of social groups and character behaviours, as relations between NPCs seem more real when each of them follow their own motivations and the cooperation and social relationships appear as a result of this fact[28]. After all, each character is a single entity looking to satisfy its own goals and necessities; working together with other characters might help them to faster satisfy their needs.

Studies have been made applying the Iterated Prisoner's Dilemma to model cooperation between agents and satisfaction of each agent's own needs [12, 29]. Cohen et al point out that the IPD can be used to represent a real social life problem: "how to sustain over time a pattern of cooperation between agents that may be quite beneficial to both" [29]; in their study, they point out that a number of playing agents using the IPD behave and present characteristics similar to human social networks: groups are formed and cooperation within them exists to varying degrees, always changing according to each agent's own motivations and the current member of that group.

One interesting aspect of the study by Cohen et al [29] is that they allowed agents to change strategies over time as a result of their interaction with other agents; that way each agent would try to adapt himself to the strategy that better allowed him to satisfy his own needs while still cooperating with the rest of the group. To represent this change in strategies, Cohen et al make use of probability values for the initial movement of the agent when no history is present, the probability to cooperate after other has cooperated and the probability of cooperation after other has defected; they also included a noisy environment in which sometimes the messages between agents were not perceived correctly, which helped create more realistic interactions between agents as "real interactions may always involve failures to execute what was intended, misperceptions of the actions of others, misjudgements of the experience of others and errors in understanding and emulating the strategies of others"[29, pp. 6].

The obtained results showed that agents tend to be more cooperative when they were able to adapt and change their strategy after some interactions with other agents; they also showed that populations and groups managed to 'correct' themselves, that is, balance the level of cooperation from too much to too little. These results would be supportive on the idea that agents, or characters, and the relationships existing between them change accordingly to their interactions, their existing social relationships and the environment they are placed on.

An alternative approach to generate collaboration between agents proposed by Puustinen & Pasanen is the employment of a Nash equilibrium [29], which is "a vector of action selection strategies, in which no agent can unilaterally change its strategy and get more utility"[28, pp. 1]. The premise behind this approach is that every single agent is always trying to maximize its own benefit, even if that means sometimes acting against the rest of the agents, while also trying to find a Nash equilibrium. In order to do so, each agent employs a utility function to evaluate which action given the current group's actions will yield the most utility. Each goal is described as a term or perception and has an assigned importance value; each round, every agent's utility function will verify the current state of the game and, by employing the weights of each term, calculate the resulting utility of possible strategies to take.

Each agent's strategy is recorded by a controlling module, which is in charge of verifying that the Nash equilibrium has been reached; if that is not the case, the agents are informed and they define another strategy. Once the Nash equilibrium has been found, each agent is informed and they proceed to execute their own strategies, which is surely to render the best utility. We could say that the controlling module acts in a similar way to what a chess player or dungeon master does when moving pieces across the board or controlling NPCs during battle: they analyze the possible actions to be performed and then decide which strategy will yield the most benefit; the difference in this case is that each agent will individually provide a possible strategy based on its own goals.

Another benefit of this approach is that the actions performed by the agents appear more realistic, as they are motivated by their own goals and act accordingly, and the group's actions and movements result more coordinated and intelligent, which adds a feeling of believability to the players [28]. One possible problem to take into account when using this approach is the total time it takes for a Nash equilibrium vector to be found; results found by Puustinen & Pasanen [28] indicate that, if the NPCs' number of possible actions is limited, as a result of providing fewer terms or by the existence of dominated strategies, the total time might be short..

3.4 Emotional NPC and Interactive Storytelling

We have reviewed some techniques and methods to create emotional NPCs and the relations between them, and explained how those can be affected by interacting with the player or other characters. As we have discussed, emotional NPCs can be used to add a higher level of realism to the game world as their actions and behaviours will vary depending on the actual state of the game world, their inner emotions and goals and their own social relationships. While emotional NPCs can be used in action or social simulation games (see [12],[28]), they also lend themselves nicely as helpers to create, enrich and unfold stories created using traditional narrative or, more interestingly, interactive storytelling methods and applications.

As Pizzi and Cavazza state, "the psychology and feelings of characters is an essential part of most dramas" [30, pp.1], so their usage of emotional NPCs and their relationships to construct, develop and unfold dynamic stories can be a very helpful technique. We review two approaches that address this idea in two different aspects for story generation.

Narrative can be divided into two main components: actions that can be executed by actors, and dialogues between characters to dramatize some of the performed actions [31]. Based on this premise, the model proposed by Cavazza and Charles focuses on the employment of the character's emotions and social relationships to generate realistic dialogues relevant to the current event being narrated to the player. They do this by implementing an affinity system between characters to indicate their social relationships and emotions towards one another, while a rule based system uses that information to generate the dialogue template to be used.

To test the model, the authors generated a group of authors which were individually being invited by another character to a party; each character would accept or refuse the invitation based on their emotions towards the inviting character, and their answer, either positive or negative would also be affected by the affinity between the characters. The results presented by Cavazza and Charles [31] show that constructing dialogues based on the character's emotions and relationships can result in the creation of more realistic situations and interactions, which could in turn, help develop the storyline in more interesting and non-linear ways.

The approach presented by Pizzi and Cavazza [30] employs character feelings and motivations as the defining variables that indicate how the story is unfolded. On this approach, every character has a defined set of goals and feelings defined as a set of rules in a STRIPS–like language; at a given moment, a planner module will analyze each character's emotions, goals and motivations, along with the current state of the game in order to determine the best action for them [30]. Once actions for each character have been selected, this information will be sent to the graphic engine which will update the game world accordingly.

The authors decided to test the model by employing a passage from the novel Madame Bovary, which focuses strongly on the psychology of the characters to tell the story of a bored high-society woman and her pursuit for happiness. Users would be able to have some input as characters interacting with the main NPCs, in order to affect their emotions and behaviours. The obtained results showed that interactions with the characters and the social relationships they establish can have an input on their behaviours, which in turn affects the actions they perform, thus changing the events presented in the story: one simulation ended with the main character leaving her husband for her lover, satisfying her need for happiness with him while other, on which another character empathized the joy of creating a family, resulted in the character leaving her lover to enjoy and protect her own family [30]. These experiments show the potential offered by emotional NPCs based techniques to support interactive storytelling.

4 Discussion and Future Direction

As we have seen with [9, 10, 15], when creating interactive storylines, the player's actions trigger a series of choices regarding which and how events may be presented and how non playing characters act and behave in response to those actions; however, this approach has the drawback of having to model all possible actions and behaviors that can be assigned to any NPC. A solution for this would be to have the NPCs react on their own to their environments, thus allowing them to relate more realistically with the world and their societies, which in turn will elevate the degree of interactivity for the story as, stated by Lankoski and Björk, "social relations in games are typically part of the storyline" [13]; one cannot deny that exploring the relationships between characters can provide better game experiences [4].

To generate more complex characters behaviours, as explained in [14], we could use flag or affinity systems to alter the behaviour of non playing characters as a result of the player's actions. A flag system is just a set of Boolean variables which change from 'yes' or 'no' values depending on the player's input; for example, being rude towards an NPC may prevent that character to help the player later in the game. A more complex approach is the affinity system on which the characters have a certain range of affinity towards each other, increasing and decreasing as a result of the interactions they have; so if a player is rude to an NPC, but later he saves his life, then the NPC may still be willing to help the player out as a result of the interactions they had. This type of relationships has been used in games such as The Elder Scrolls: Morrowind, or Star Ocean: The Second Story, which explore the relationships between characters and those relations, along with the player's decision's affect the way the story is unfolded.

A more detailed approach to achieve this is proposed by El Rhalibi et al. [12] [18][19] which use a rule based system (RBS) and iterated prisoner dilemma (IPD) to simulate the emotions and interactions of non playing characters. By using the emotional drives based model to manage the character's needs, their behaviours can be changed in order to fulfil those needs; then the RBS is used to decide which actions should be taken in order to satisfy the current needs; the agent's behaviour is then affected by the outcome of those actions [12][18][19]. To model the relationship between agents, the proposed approach uses the IPD to "give a straight forward interaction decision based upon the previous interaction with the agent" [12]. This way, we can obtain several interactions based on the previous actions and behaviour the player showed towards the NPCs, thus allowing for more realistic social relations between them which in turn can help to unfold the story.

One approach that has not been exploited much is to create storylines following the dynamic object oriented narrative, in which the overall storyline is divided into sets of episodes which in turn are divided into scenes, all of whom may be connected by another simpler technique such as linear or parallel narrative [14]. This approach to generate stories has the advantages of adding versatility to the storyline, as one player can begin the story in several defined points across a range of episodes and decide on its own how to advance through the scenes [14], and simplifying the way scenes are interconnected, while maintaining a global sense of the overall story. Another benefit is that it also can be used to maintain the three act structure, as suggested in [10], as each act can be comprised of several episodes.

Including emotional non playing characters would allow for more interactivity and immersion, as their relationships with the player would affect the way the story is created, as it occurs in the Storytron engine [15]. This feature can also be complemented by defining motivation instead of actions, as described in [9]; that way we can define the same motivation for several characters but the character or characters who will respond to that motivation may vary in response to other factors; finally, NPCs can be used to prevent the player from getting stuck and maintaining the flow of the story.

The implementation of emotional NPCs can be a very helpful resource in interactive storytelling to define how to present the story to players in a more realistic way; based on the methodologies reviewed in this paper, the authors believe that allowing characters to define their own emotional states and relationships based on their goals and needs, along with the implementation of a master control module in charge of examining the game state and deciding how the story events should be presented, can result in a very interesting framework to created dynamic stories.

Emotions and relationships could be modelled using an affinity system similar to the approaches presented in [20] and [23]: each character could employ a control module that, based on their motivations, goals and relationships, defines the current emotional state and behaviour for that character. A global control module would examine the current game state in order to define which event in the story should be presented next. That way, both players and NPCs emotions and motivations help shape the existing relationships between characters and the actions they make, thus affecting which events are presented to the player , generating more realistic dynamic stories. The implementation of such framework presents an interesting opportunity for future work.

A planning manager module can be implemented to analyze the state of each scene right at the beginning and, according to the player's actions, previous events and NPCs current behaviours and states, decide which actions should be included in a plan to keep the story flowing and which possible characters could perform them; this approach would employ techniques and ideas similar to the presented in [6, 7, 9, 10, 12].

As appealing as it may seem, one important thing to note regarding interactive storytelling is that, as pointed out in [14], it adds complexity to the whole development process of a game, as more pre-production and testing must be performed in order to create an enjoyable experience for the user. However, if handled appropriately, the inclusion of interactive storytelling can make a huge difference and add features that broaden the horizons in the field of not only games, but interactive entertainment as well.

5 Conclusions

As we have discussed in this paper, there are different techniques which can be used to achieve interactive storytelling in games, most notably the employment of planning algorithms to decide which and how events should be presented to the player at a given time, and the definition of non playing characters actions and behaviours as a response to the player's actions; the incorporation of narrative techniques into the storytelling used in games can help not only to increment the level of interaction between the player and the world and characters, but also to keep the story fluent, thus achieving more realistic narrative.

On this paper we have presented several approaches that can lead to interactive storytelling; however, while all approaches have strong advantages to address the generation of more dynamic stories, they also have some drawbacks to take into account, as some may be disrupted by complex stories [10], others may have it difficult to incorporate a formal set of rules for most modern genres [9] and some require several components to work properly [7].

While not perfect, all these approaches serve as bases to propose an alternative approach to create interactive storytelling, which utilizes the not so used dynamic object oriented narrative to handle the story arcs and employs some of the ideas and techniques presented in this paper in order to create a new framework which benefits from the strong points and tries to minimize the drawbacks of existing implementations.

We have also reviewed some techniques used to create emotional NPCs and to analyze and model the social relationships that can be created when they interact with the player or other characters. We have discussed some techniques to promote cooperation amongst NPCs, so that they can satisfy their own needs and motivations while also maximizing the gain value for the group they belong to.

As we have discussed, the inclusion of emotional NPCs and their social relationships to games can lead to a higher immersion level in the player, as players will get a more realistic feeling when dealing with them, since their actions and behaviours will be motivated directly from their own goals, emotions and past interactions with other characters, thus making them more believable.

While interactive storytelling can be applied most notably to games, there are also other fields where it could be used, such as medical simulations, training or educational software such as [16, 17], which currently may use defined and linear storylines. Introducing interactive storytelling into these types of applications, can increase their level of immersion, thus providing the user with a more enjoyable and attractive experience and a base for systems employing alternative types of interaction with users [21].

References

1. Rollings, A., Morris, D.: Game architecture and Design; The Coriolis Group (2000)
2. Rollings, A., Adams, E.: On game design. New Riders (2003)
3. Rouse III., R.: Game design, theory and practice. 2nd edn. Wordware Publishing, USA (2005)
4. Laurel, B.: Narrative construction as play. Interactions 11(5), 73–74 (2004)

5. Salovaara, A., Johnson, M., Toiskallio, K., Tiitta, S., Turpeinen, M.: Playmakers in multiplayer game communities: their importance and motivations for participation. In: Proceedings of the 2005 ACM SIGCHI international Conference on Advances in Computer Entertainment Technology (ACE 2005), Valencia, Spain, June 15 - 17, 2005, vol. 265. ACM, New York (2005)
6. Champagnat, R., Estraillier, P., Prigent, A.: Adaptive execution of game: unfolding a correct story. In: Proceedings of the 2006 ACM SIGCHI international Conference on Advances in Computer Entertainment Technology (ACE 2006), Hollywood, California, June 14 - 16, 2006, vol. 266. ACM, New York (2006)
7. Cai, Y., Miao, C., Tan, A., Shen, Z.: Fuzzy cognitive goal net for interactive storytelling plot design. In: Proceedings of the 2006 ACM SIGCHI international Conference on Advances in Computer Entertainment Technology (ACE 2006), Hollywood, California, June 14 - 16, 2006, vol. 266. ACM, New York (2006)
8. Shen, Z.: Goal-oriented Modeling for Intelligent. Agents and their Applications, PhD Thesis, Nanyang. Technological University (2005)
9. Ciarlini, A.E., Pozzer, C.T., Furtado, A.L., Feijó, B.: A logic-based tool for interactive generation and dramatization of stories. In: Proceedings of the 2005 ACM SIGCHI international Conference on Advances in Computer Entertainment Technology (ACE 2005), Valencia, Spain, June 15 - 17, 2005, vol. 265. ACM, New York (2005)
10. Barros, L.M., Musse, S.R.: Introducing narrative principles into planning-based interactive storytelling. In: Proceedings of the 2005 ACM SIGCHI international Conference on Advances in Computer Entertainment Technology (ACE 2005), Valencia, Spain, June 15 - 17, 2005. ACM, New York (2005)
11. Crawford, C.: Chris Crawford on Interactive Storytelling. New Riders, Berkeley (2004)
12. Chaplin, D.J., El Rhalibi, A.: IPD for emotional NPC societies in games. In: Proceedings of the 2004 ACM SIGCHI international Conference on Advances in Computer Entertainment Technology (ACE 2004), Singapore, June 03 -05, 2005, vol. 74. ACM, New York (2004)
13. Lankoski, P., Björk, S.: Gameplay design patterns for social networks and conflicts. In: Proceedings of the Fifth International Game Design and Technology Workshop, Liverpool, UK (November 2007)
14. Foundations of Interactive Storytelling [accessed February 2008], http://www.igda.org/writing/InteractiveStorytelling.htm
15. Crawford, C.: Storytron – Interactive Storytelling [accessed February 2008], http://www.storytron.com/index.html
16. Moreno-Ger, P., Blesieus, C., Currier, P., Sierra, J., Frenández-Manjón, B.: Rapid development for game-like interactive simulations for learning clinical procedures. In: Proceedings of the Fifth International Game Design and Technology Workshop, Liverpool, UK (November 2007)
17. Mansilla, W., Jung, B.: Emotion and Acousmêtre for Suspense in an Interactive Virtual Storytelling Environment. In: Proceedings of the Third International Game Design and Technology Workshop, Liverpool, UK (November 2005)
18. Rhalibi, A.E., Bendiab, A.T.: Harnessing Agent Based Games Research for Emerging Behaviour Analysis. In: Second GSFC/IEEE Workshop on Radical Agent Concepts (WRAC) Sponsored by IEEE CS Technical Committee on Complexity in Computing Corporate Sponsor – IBM, September 20-22, 2005. NASA Goddard Space Flight Center Visitor's Center, Greenbelt (2005)
19. El Rhalibi, A., Baker, N., Merabti, M.: Emotional agent model and architecture for NPCs group control and interaction to facilitate leadership roles in computer entertainment. In: Proceedings of the 2005 ACM SIGCHI international Conference on Advances in Computer Entertainment Technology (ACE 2005), Valencia, Spain, June 15 -17, 2005, vol. 265. ACM, New York (2005)

20. Sheldon, L.: Character Development and Storytelling. Thomson Course Technology, USA (2004)
21. Eladhari, M., Nieudorp, R., Fridenfalk, M.: The soundtrack of your mind: Mind music – adaptive audio for game characters. In: Proceedings of the 2006 ACM SIGCHI International Conference on Advances in Computer Entertainment Technology, Hollywood, California. ACM, New York (2006)
22. Bates, J.: The role of emotion in believable agents. Communication of the ACM 37(7), 122–125 (1994)
23. IGDA; Foundations of Interactive Storytelling [accessed March 2008], http://www.igda.org/writing/InteractiveStorytelling.htm
24. Bailie-De Byl, P.: Programming believable characters for computer games. Charles River Media, USA (2004)
25. Elliott, C.: Multimedia communication with emotion-driven Believable-Agents. In: AAAI Technical Report for the Spring Symposium on Believable Agents, pp. 16–20. AAAI, Stanford University (1994)
26. Hanneman, R.A., Riddle, M.: Introduction to social network methods. University of California, Riverside, CA (2005) [accessed March 2008], http://faculty.ucr.edu/~hanneman/
27. Hanseth, O., Monteiro, E.: Understanding Information Infrastructure [accessed March 2008], http://heim.ifi.uio.no/~oleha/Publications/bok.html
28. Puustinen, I., Pasanen, T.A.: Creating realistic collaboration for Action Games. In: Proceedings of the Fourth International Game Design and Technology Workshop, Liverpool, UK, November 15-16, 2006, School of Computing and Mathematical Sciences, Liverpool John Moores University, Liverpool, UK (2006)
29. Cohen, M., Riolo, R.L., Axelrod, R.: The Emergence of Social Organization in the Prisoner's Dilemma: How Context-Preservation and other Factors Promote Cooperation. Working papers. 99-01-002. Santa Fe Institute (1999)
30. Pizzi, D., Cavazza, M.: Affective storytelling based on character's feelings. In: AAAI Fall Symposium on Intelligent Narrative Technologies, Arlington, Virginia (November 2007)
31. Cavazza, M., Charles, F.: Dialogue generation in character based interactive storytelling. In: AAAI First Annual Artificial Intelligence and Interactive Digital Entertainment Conference, Marina del Rey, California, USA (2005)

Behavioural Reactive Agents to Define Personality Traits in the Videogame Überpong

Carlos Delgado-Mata[1,2], Jesus Ibáñez-Martínez[3], Felipe Gómez-Caballero[2],
and Oscar Miguel Guillén-Hernández[1]

[1] Nibbo Studios, Michoacán 200-B, CP 20270, Aguascalientes, México
[2] Universidad Panamericana, Aguascalientes, CP 20290, México
[3] Department of Technology, University Pompeu Fabra, Barcelona, Spain
carlos@nibbo.net, jesus.ibanez@upf.edu, fgomezc@up.edu.mx,
oscar@nibbo.net

Abstract. Nowadays, the video gaming experience is shifting from merely realistic to believable. The increasing graphic power of current graphic cards has made it possible to render near life-like images. Unfortunately, the behaviour of the computer driven player and non-playing characters is often poor when compared to their visual appearance. In this sense, there has been a recent interest in improving the video gaming experience with novel Artificial Intelligence (AI) techniques. This paper presents a robotics inspired behavioural AI technique to simulate characters' personalities in a multi-award winning commercial video game. Furthermore, the paper describes a study with users.

1 Introduction

The interest in Artificial Intelligence in Video Games has increased in recent years. The graphic power available in next generation console games (Nintendo's Wii, Sony's PS3 and Microsoft's XBox360) and graphics cards allows the artist to create visually near life-like virtual worlds, virtual objects and virtual characters. However, the behaviour of the virtual beings that populate these environments, often lacks believability. This is made more notorious, when the behaviour is compared against pristine graphical models (sadly, it is all-looks and no-brains). This mismatch aggravates the playability and believability of those virtual worlds. For that reason, there has been an interest in using traditional academic AI techniques (such as Neural Networks, Genetic Algorithms and Planning to name a few) within video games [1]. These techniques have been used instead (or in complement) of the good old Finite State Machines, that have been quintessential to video game's artificial intelligence. The novel approach presented herein is the use of behaviourally appealing opponents developed using an architecture inspire din behavioural robotics. Überpong, whose AI is the subject matter of this paper, is a video game that combines the genres of sports and action, and brings the classic game of Pong to the XXI century. To achieve this, several interesting algorithms of computational physics, collision detection and AI were developed.

The road map for this paper is as follows. Firstly, the state of AI in the video gaming industry is presented. Secondly, the use of behavioural inspired AI to provide different personality traits to different opponents is described. Thirdly, the implementation is presented. Fourthly, the user studies and results are explained. Finally, the conclusion and future work is discussed.

Z. Pan et al. (Eds.): Transactions on Edutainment I, LNCS 5080, pp. 135–149, 2008.

2 Related Work

Video games in particular, and virtual environments in general, have relied on artificial intelligence to create the 'illusion of life' in computer driven opponents and Non Playing Characters (NPC) for a few decades. Video games from previous generations had big resource restrictions. Therefore, the attention was focused in providing computer driven opponents with behaviours that only use a very small fraction of the scarse available resources. Furthermore, those developers used just a fraction of those available resources for AI. Nevertheless, some developers accomplished behaviours which were remarkable; one such example is Pac-man, developed primarily by Toru Iwatani of Namco, in which each of the computer driven opponents (ghosts) has a particular behaviour to simulate a personality trait. One ghost chases Pac-man (which can be construed as brave). A second ghost wanders randomly (which can be construed as silly). The last two ghosts seem to work as a team, and their behaviour can be construed as team work. This appalling restriction does not longer exist and the amount of resources available to developers now is vast and thence more resources can be used for developing interesting AI for the computer driven opponents and NPCs. Some examples are mentioned next.

2.1 Creatures

This game was designed by Steve Grand. In this very interesting game (Artificial Life Simulation), each of the creatures (Norns), is instantiated out of genetical information (digital genes). This information can be transmitted to future generations by mating, and that does provide their means to evolve into creatures with unique characteristics (systems). Examples of the latter is the digestive system and the action selection mechanism, which is made up of a simple neural network. Creatures presented an interesting in sight in artificial life creation[2] in video games.

2.2 Black and White

Peter Molyneux, of Lionhead Studios, produced the Black and White video game, in which Richard Evans developed complex AI for it. Techniques used therein furthered the AI seen in video games. The first novel AI technique used in Black and White is the use of Reinforcement Learning to teach the beasts (creatures) in the game. Teaching is performed by patting the back of the creature, if the player is happy with the creature's behaviour; or a by hitting it with a leach if the player is not pleased with the creature's behaviour. Also of interest is the influence of the player's decisions in the environment. If these are perceived to be good, the landscape is colourful; whereas, if these are perceived to be bad, the landscape turn into dark and evil. Other novel uses of AI that were introduced in this ground breaking game is the mouse gesture recognition used to cast spells, and finally, it is worth mentioning the use of psychologically plausible agents [3] with the implementation of a Belief-Desire- Intention agent architecture [4] for Non Player Characters.

2.3 F.E.A.R (First Encounter Assault Recon)

Jeff Orkin, of Monolith Productions, developed the game's AI for the F.E.A.R video game[5].This game has been critically acclaimed and commercially successful. The AI presented in this game is one of the most interesting seen in video games. The novel AI used for this video game is a planner which complements other techniques that are normally used in video games, like Finite State Machines and the A* algorithm for path planning. The novel use of this planner is that it simplifies the creation of interesting behaviours for NPCs or enemies.

Therein, a set of objectives are defined for the NPC, that are not coupled with the possible actions that the NPC can perform to achieve their goals. This makes the AI system configurable and manageable if the developer is to expand or change the NPC's repertoire of behaviours.

2.4 Unreal Tournament

Unreal Tournament (UT) provides a mean to configure a NPC behaviour via Unreal Script. Furthermore, an API (Game bots), which [6] is a modification to UT, allows characters in the game to be controlled via network sockets connected to other programs (for a detailed description of Gamebots see [7]). These features have been so successful that the UT has become a tool to do academic AI research. As pointed out in [8], although the development of realistic virtual environments is an expensive and time-consuming enterprise that requires expertise in many areas, computer games provide us with a source of cheap, reliable, and flexible technology for developing our own virtual environment for research. In this sense, the current trend is to use the UT engine as a development platform. UT is being used, for instance, to develop story telling systems [9][10][11][12], and AI-based bots in general [8].

2.5 Sims

Another interesting example of what could be considered A-Life exploration in video games is that of the Sim's. According to Forbus and Wright (The Sims author)[13], the Sims' world is created on top of Edith. A simulation in Edith consists of a set of objects. The simulation is evolved by running each of these objects in turn. Every object has a set of local data and a set of behaviours. The local data provide the parameters of an object, including handler to objects it is related to. The set of behaviours consist of a procedure that implements it, a procedure that checks to see whether or not it is possible to accomplish it, and a set of advertisements that describe its properties in terms of what needs it will satisfy. Sims (not under direct player control) choose what to do by selecting, from all of the possible behaviours in all of the objects, the behaviour that maximises their current so-called state of happiness. Once they choose a behaviour, the procedure for that behaviour is then run in the thread of the Sim itself, so that it has access to that Sim's parameters in addition to those of its defining environment. Sometimes there are a number of intermediate objects to implement behaviours. For instance, Social Interaction is an object that is created and used when two Sims interact.

The games mentioned above borrowed techniques from AI and Artificial Life techniques normally used in academy. Thereby, these games have improved the perceived believability of the Non Playing Characters' behaviours. Similarly, the work proposed here, benefits from AI techniques used in other fields.

3 AI to Produce Personality Traits

To put this work in perspective, it should be noted that the model described in this section is applied to control the user's opponent in the video-game Überpong, which is some how an evolution of the classic Pong. Pong, while not the first video game, was the first coin-op arcade game and the first mainstream video game that was available to almost everyone. Pong was invented by Ralph H. Baer in late 1960s, [14] and it was later licensed to Magnavox, which successfully marketed it, under the name Table Tennis. An arcade version of the game was developed (and marketed under the name Pong) by Atari, the company founded by Nolan Bushnel, in the 1970's. Pong was a pretty simple game with simple rules: hit the ball across the playing field and try your best to hit it past your opponents paddle on the other side. The origins of Pong lie with an abstract tennis game (called Tennisfor Two) created with an old oscilloscope and some vacuum tubes by Willy Higinbotham, way back in 1958 [15].

3.1 Background

As stated before, Überpong is a video game that combines the sports and action genres. The game provides different characters with distinctive perceived personality profiles. The aim of the game, as in most sport games, is to score more points (goals) than the opponent. The game is played via a paddle (composed of as pring and two small spheres). The paddle spring is affected by spring physics, and thus, the ball can be affected in several ways. One is by tightening and loosening the tension of the spring as the ball collides with it. Another is by moving the paddle direction as the ball collides with paddle, and thus, change the direction of the ball by applying an effect. The computer driven player uses different strategies to affect the ball's acceleration and direction, depending on their personality trait. The players are also provided with special items (power ups) that can be used to affect the properties of the ball, one's own paddle, and the opponent's paddle. The correct use of these so-called special items can be vital to win a game. Therefore, it is important for the computer driven player to select and use an effective and compelling strategies to attack, defend, apply effects to the ball and use items and thus became a worthy and believable opponent.

3.2 Behavioural Reactive Agents

Research in behavioural based robotics has demonstrated that with the use of simple rules, a robot can perform complex and compelling behaviours. This field of research was inspired by the influential work of Braitenberg [16]. Some of his proposed robots display behaviours that can be construed as more complex than the simple rules used to implement them. For example, he named some of the robots' behaviour: 'love', 'fear' and 'aggression'. In a similar vein, Brooks proposed a horizontal architecture [17] for robots, this in turn is the inspiration for an architecture (Behavioural Synthesis Architecture) first used for cooperating robots [18]. This architecture, has been expanded to communicate emotions through artificial scents in virtual conspecific mammals, first described here [19]. Later this architecture was expanded to affect a flocking behaviour via an emotion architecture, which is described here [20].

Herein, a horizontal behavioural architecture not dissimilar to the aforementioned was developed and is used to drive the response of the computer player (AI of the game) and is described next.

3.3 Behavioural Reactive Agents for Überpong

The AI of Überpong is defined using four parameters. These are shown in figure 1, where the stimuli is on the left; the four components are represented by the four black boxes; and the responses are represented by the arrows on the right.

1. How the computer driven opponent approaches the ball's destination.
2. First set of parameters to define the computer driven opponent personality profile.
3. Second set of parameters to define the computer driven opponent personality profile.
4. Third set of parameters to define the computer driven opponent personality profile.

It is not the aim of this work to develop a "deep" cognitive personality model, or to implement a Social– Psychological Model, like the one found in [21]. For an excellent overview on Synthetic Personalities the reader is refered to [22]. The aim of this work is, instead, to develop a simple architecture to give perceived personality traits for video game opponents. This personality traits are defined by the manipulation of "simple" parameters. Simplicity in the manipulation of parameters is important for the level designer of the Überpong game, a detailed explanation of the architecture can be found here [23].

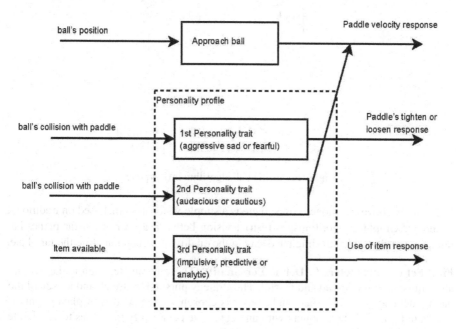

Fig. 1. AI architecture of Überpong

How the opponent approaches the ball's destination. These parameters are used to define the strategy on how the AI driven player paddle's will approach the ball. There are three methods used. The first is simply follow the ball. This method computes the difference (Δy) of the opponent's paddle position with the ball's position. The paddle position used to compute the oppoent's response depends on the status of the paddle's string, i.e. if the opponent's paddle spring is broken or not. This is shown in figure 2. If the spring is not broken the Δy used will be $\Delta y1$, if the spring is broken then Δy would be the smaller of $\Delta y2$ and $\Delta y3$. Depending on the sign of Δy and on the opponent's profile, defined in the XML described below, a velocity vector for the opponent's paddle is created. This vector is represented in to top right arrow in figure 1.

The second one, is an erratic version of the first one. That is, noise is added to the velocity vector response. The third one, is a predictive algorithm that computes where the ball is estimated to arrive when it crosses the plane described by the x position of the AI driven player, this algorithm uses our version of the death-reckoning algorithm shown in figure 3. V is the velocity vector of the ball and P is the opponent's paddle current position and P' is where the ball is going to cross the plane mentioned above. Δy is the distance of the paddle position with the ball's calculated future position. With those values time is computed. With time the velocity of the paddle is affected, so that the opponent can reach the ball at the same time as the ball at P'. The third strategy is used by the 'smarter' opponents.

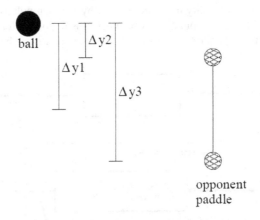

Fig. 2. Following ball algorithm inÜberpong

In all the above-mentioned cases, there is a simple vision system, based on traditional Computer Graphics algorithms, to restrict vision between a near and a far plane. Parameters we also added to simulate decay in the quality of perception close the far plane.

First Set of Parameters to Define Personality. These parameters define the personality traits: aggressive, sad and fearful. The strategy pursued to stretch and loosen of the paddle depends on which personality trait is chosen for the AI driven player. This is shown in figure 4. The opponent with an aggressive personality trait, tries to accelerate the ball by loosening the paddle before the ball approaches it and then the opponent

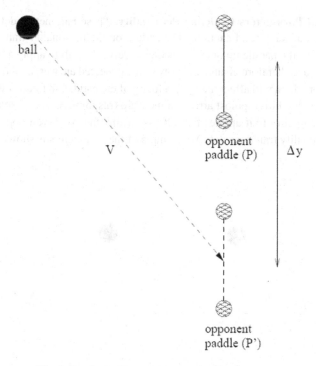

Fig. 3. Predict ball's position algorithm in Überpong

tightens the paddle as the ball is colliding with the paddle's spring. The fearful opponent tries to de-accelerate the ball by tightening the paddle before the ball approaches and then loosening the paddle as the ball collides, and the sad player just plays a safe game and keeps the paddle stretched all the time. An example of the parameters used is shown next. Depending on the strategy pursued by the computer driven opponent the ball's acceleration is affected using spring physics.

$$a = -k\frac{\Delta x}{m} \tag{1}$$

Where k is the spring constant, which depends on the opponent's profile, Δx depends if the spring was tightened or loosened and m is the ball's mass. The mass is useful as there is a special effect that in creases the ball's size and thence it's mass.

```
<personality1D
  consecutive_omissions="2"
  consecutive_changes="3"
  type="agressive"
  random_omissions="0"
  random_changes="0" />
```

The parameters listed above are for a computer driven player with an aggressive personality trait that will try to accelerate the ball three consecutive times followed by two consecutive times where it does not try to accelerate the ball.

Second Set of Parameters to Define Personality. These parameters define the personality traits audacious and cautious. Depending on the personality trait selected the opponent moves the paddle up or down as they receive the ball to apply a ball effect to their response and therefore change the flow of the expected answer, as shown in figure 5. *V* is a vector which will affect the final velocity of the paddle, in figure 1 this vector is represented by the third topmost arrow on the right (responses). The opponent with an audacious personality trait applies ball effects, whilst the AI driven opponent with a cautious personality trait does not. An example of the parameters is shown next.

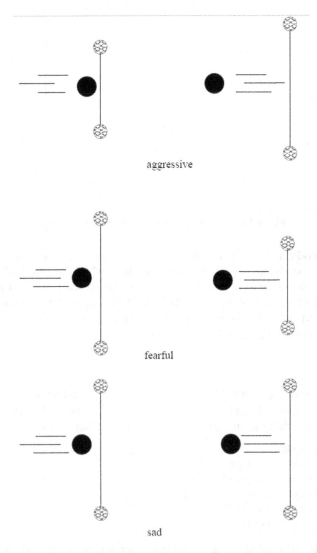

aggressive

fearful

sad

Fig. 4. First personality trait for the AI opponent

```
<personality2D
 delta_change="0.0"
 consecutive_omissions="0"
 consecutive_changes="0"
 type="cautious"
 probability_left="0.0"
 random_omissions="0"
 max_change="0.0"
 random_changes="0"
 probability_right="0.0" />
```

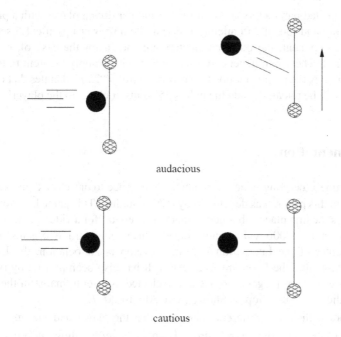

audacious

cautious

Fig. 5. Second personality trait the AI opponent

The above-listed parameters are used for a computer driven player with a cautious personality trait and thus it will not attempt to change the ball's direction by applying an effect to the ball.

Third Set of Parameters to Define Personality. These parameters define the personality traits impulsive, predictable and analytic. These parameters define the strategy of how the opponent will use the power-ups available to them. The opponent with an impulsive personality trait uses the power-up as they receive it (a knee jerk reaction), the opponent with a predictable personality trait will wait x seconds to apply the power up. The opponent with an analytic personality trait 'analyses' the moment to cause the most damage to the opponent. An example of the parameters is shown next.

```
<personality3D
 position_mirror="250"
 position_magnet="350"
 acceleration_to_big="50.0"
 wait_seconds="1.5"
 position_invert_control="250"
 position_stretch="250"
 acceleration_to_accelerate="50.0"
 variance="1.0"
 type="predictive"
 position_shrink="250" />
```

The above-listed parameters are used for a computer driven player with a predictive personality trait and thus it will attempt to use an item (power-up) after1.5 seconds of receiving the opponent, the other parameters are shown for the case of an analytic personality trait. These parameters are used as a trigger to apply the item to the opponent. For example, the parameter position invert control = "250", dictates that the invert control item will be released when the ball is 250 units or closer to the player's paddle x position.

4 Implementation

The video game Überpong, whose Artificial Intelligence to drive the computer player is described in this paper, was developed by Nibbo Studios. This game has won several awards; one is the first place (obtained with an alfa version)for a video game developed by company in the 2006 video game development competition organised by the Mexican chapter of the International Game Developers Association, the Electronic Gamming Show, and the Economy Secretariat. It has also been praised by two Independent Game Festival judges, and has been selected as a semi finalist in the international 2nd Indie Game Developers Showcase in August 2007.

In Überpong, there are different characters that the player and the opponent can select, some of them are shown in figure 6. Each character has different properties that affect their behaviour and performance. These depend on their personality traits. Relevant to the argument of this paper are the properties to create a personality profile with the AI personality traits described before. In figure 7 the opponent prepares its move. In figure 8 the opponent has returned the ball.

5 User Studies

Preliminary results discussed in [23] had shown that the users perceived the opponents as more "intelligent" and "beleivable" than previous versions.

An experiment was carried out to investigate whether the users perceive differences amongst the unique personality traits of the video game opponents.

For the experiment, the award winning video game Überpong was parametrised in order to show three personality traits: 1) Aggressive, 2) Fearful and 3) Sad.

Fig. 6. Some Characters in Überpong

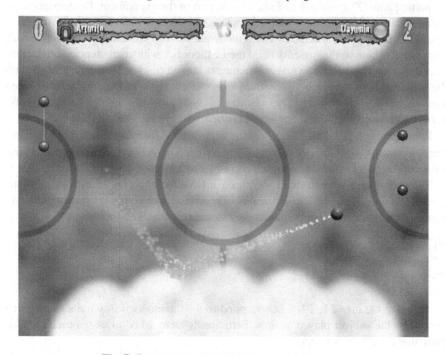

Fig. 7. Opponent (on the right) is preparing its move

Fig. 8. Opponent (on the right) has returned the ball to the player

5.1 Method

40 participants (27 male and 13 female) took part in the experiment. Participants were asked to rate their experience with computers, virtual environments and video games. The vast majority of participants had a moderate to very satisfactory experience with computers; whereas, the majority rated their experience with computers as satisfactory or better. Experience with virtual environments ranged from none to experienced, with the vast majority ranged between little to some experience. Experience with video games ranged from none to very experienced, with the vast majority rating their experience between reasonable and very experienced.

Participants played three matches of the video game Überpong (see figure 8) against three opponents with a unique personality trait; that is, aggressive, fearful or sad/boring. Order of the matches was randomised according to a latin design.

The participants were made to play three full matches. Later on, they were asked to complete a questionnaire. Participants were presented with three tags corresponding to various personality trais. In particular they were presented with these tags:

T1 Aggressive
T2 Fearful
T3 Sad/boring.

Note that the tags T1, T2, T3 correspond to the three personality traits of the three opponents the subject played against. Participants were asked to assign each tag to a particular condition (an opponent).

5.2 Results

The results are shown in figure 9. It displays the frequencies of tags for each condition that was studied. More concretely, it shows the number of participants that assigned eachtag (T1, T2 and T3) to each condition (Aggressive, Fearful and Sad). Most participants (23 out of 40) assigned the tag T1 (Aggressive) to the corresponding opponent with an aggressive personality trait. A relative majority of participants (17 out of 40) as signed the tag T2 (Fearful) to the corresponding opponent with a fearful personality trait. A relative majority of participants (16 out of 40) assigned the tag T3 (Sad) to the corresponding opponent with a sad personality trait. Thus, most participants perceived the intended personality traits of the opponents.

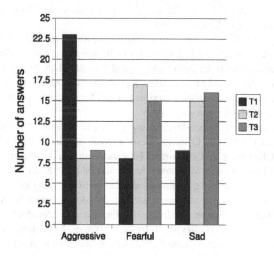

Fig. 9. Number of participants that assigned each tag (T1, T2 and T3) to each condition Agressive, Fearful and Sad

6 Conclusion and Future Work

The recent shift from graphical realism to believability in video games is the reason of the recent interest in the use of academic artificial intelligence to man-age computer driven opponents and non-playing characters. In this paper, an approach (inspired in behavioural robotics and behavioural reactive agents) for computer driven players with personalities is presented. This architecture was developed and is used successfully in a commercial video game. This video game has caught the attention of players and reviewers. The test, described in the previous section, have shown that the users of the video game detect different personality traits of a computer driven character. On the other hand, it would be desirable to improve the subject's perception on some personality traits, as there seems to be confusion between the fearful and boring/sad personality trait. An interesting approach would be to develop an emotional architecture using arousal-valence values (similar to that presented in [24]) to define each of the opponents' personalities.

Acknowledgements

The authors would like to thank Pier Paolo Guillén-Hernández (Programming lead) and the rest of the developers and artists involved in Nibbo Studios' Überpong.

References

1. Bourg, D.M., Seemann, G.: AI for Game Developers. O'Reilly Media, Sebastopol (2004)
2. Grand, S.: Creatures: an exercise in creation. IEEE Intelligent Systems Magazine (July 1997)
3. Bratman, M.E.: Intention, Plans, and Practical Reason. CSLI Publishing, USA (1987)
4. Wooldridge, M.: Reasoning About Rational Agents. MIT Press, USA (2000)
5. Orkin, J.: Three states and a plan: The a.i. of f.e.a.r. In: Game Developers Conference, CMP Game Group, SanJose, California (2006)
6. Adobbati, R., Marshall, A.N., Scholer, A., Tejada, S., Kaminka, G.A., Schaffer, S., Sollitto, C.: Gamebots: A 3d virtual world test-bed for multi-agent research. In: Second International Workshop on Infrastructure for Agents, MAS, and Scalable MAS, Montreal, Canada (2001)
7. Kaminka, G.A., Veloso, M.M., Schaffer, S., Sollitto, C., Adobbati, R., Marshall, A.N., Scholer, A., Tejada, S.: Gamebots: a flexible test bed for multiagent team research. Communications of the ACM 45(1) (January 2002)
8. Laird, J.E.: Research in human-level ai using computer games. Communications of the ACM 45 (1SPECIALISSUE: Game enginesin scientific research) (January 2002)
9. Robertson, J., Oberlander, J.: Ghostwriter: Educational drama and presence in a virtual environment. Journal of Computer Mediated Communication 8(1) (2002)
10. Young, R.M.: An overview of the mimesis architecture: Integrating intelligent narrative control into an existing gaming environment. In: The Working Notes of the AAAI Spring Symposium on Artificial Intelligence and Interactive Entertainment, Stanford, CA (March 2001)
11. Cavazza, M., Lugrin, J.L., Hartley, S., Libardi, P., Barnes, M.J., Bras, M.L., Renard, M.L., Bec, L., Nandi, A.: Intelligent virtual environments for virtual reality art. Computers & Graphics 29(6), 852–861 (2005)
12. Ibáñez, J., Aylett, R., Ruiz-Rodarte, R.: Storytelling in virtual environments from a virtual guide perspective. Journal of Virtual Reality, Springer 7(1), 30–42 (2003); Special Edition on Storytelling in Virtual Environments
13. Forbus, K.D., Wrigth, W.: Some notes on programming objects in the sims. Technical report, Northwestern University (2001)
14. Baer, R.H.: Television gaming apparatus and method. U.S. Pattent 3,659,285 (April 1972)
15. De Maria, R., Wilson, J.L.: High Score! The Illustrated History of Electronic Games. Osborne/McGraw-Hill, New York (2002)
16. Braitenberg, V.: Vehicles: Experiments in Synthetic Psychology. Papermac, Oxford, United Kingdom (1984)
17. Brooks, R.A.: A robust layered control system for a mobile robot. IEEE Journal of Robotics and Automation 2(1), 14–23 (1986)
18. Barnes, D.P.: A behaviour synthesis architecture for cooperant mobile robot. In: Gray, J.O., Caldwell, D.G. (eds.) Advanced Robotics and Intelligent Machines, UnitedKingdom. IEE Control Engineering Series 51, pp. 295–314 (1996)
19. Delgado-Mata, C., Aylett, R.: Communicating emotion in virtual environments through artificial scents. In: de Antonio, E., Aylett, R. (eds.) IVA 2001. LNCS (LNAI), vol. 2190, pp. 36–46. Springer, Heidelberg (2001)

20. Delgado-Mata, C., Ibanez, J., Aylett, R.: Let's run for it: Conspecific emotional flocking triggered via virtual pheromones. In: Butz, A., krüger, A., Olivier, P. (eds.) SG 2003. LNCS, vol. 2733, pp. 131–140. Springer, Heidelberg (2003)
21. Rousseau, D., Hayes-Roth, B.: A social-psychological model for synthetic actors. In: Creating Personalities for Synthetic Actors, pp. 165–172 (1998)
22. Trappl, R., Petta, P. (eds.): Creating Personalities for Synthetic Actors. LNCS, vol. 1195. Springer, Heidelberg (1997)
23. Delgado-Mata, C., Ibanez-Martinez, J.: Ai opponents with personalities in Überpong. In: Feiner, S. (ed.) INTETAIN 2008, Cancun, Mexico, ICST (2008)
24. Ibanez-Martinez, J., Delgado-Mata, C., Gomez-Caballero, F.: A novel approach to express emotions through a flock of virtual beings. In: Cyberworlds, IEEE Computer Society, pp. 241–248 (2007)

'Killer Phrases': Design Steps for a Game with Digital Role-Playing Agents

Ulrike Spierling

FH Erfurt, University of Applied Sciences,
Altonaerstr. 25, 99085 Erfurt, Germany
spierling@fh-erfurt.de

Abstract. The Killer Phrase game is a digital role-playing game where the player is the moderator of a discussion between two debating robots. In this article, the design steps for the creation are explained, such as building the simulation model, designing sub-games, implementing dialogues starting from a script, and testing and tuning the game. Concluding, advantages and disadvantages of the virtual game compared to a 'real' role-playing game are discussed.

Keywords: simulation game, digital agents, computer game design, interactive digital storytelling, authoring.

1 Introduction: Conversations with Digital Characters

The project *Interparolo* was an interdisciplinary project concerned with the endeavor to create e-learning content that offers interactive text chat dialogues for learning. 'Interparolo' is an Esperanto term for 'conversation'. Accordingly, conversations constitute the focus of exploration, not just the means of transferring the knowledge. The learning topic of 'moderation and mediation' is a course at the FH Erfurt, University of Applied Sciences, within the faculty of transport and communications. Students learn how to moderate a discussion between several parties with stakeholder interests in the context of urban planning. Naturally, these types of discussions bring together people with contrasting, even antagonizing positions and with varying skills in expression and discussion. As a moderator of a meeting, one can run into situations that are difficult to master. These include deadlocked positions that make discussion impossible, and dealing with difficult people, or with time pressure, to name a few.

The existing (non-electronic) course material included a collection of instructions and work sheets presenting factual background knowledge. However, the core skills necessary for moderation are foremost dependent on tacit knowledge, including the competence to identify situations and the ability to react accordingly. Hence, the traditional learning methods utilized within the seminar largely focus on learning by doing, for example, by employing live role-playing games, which allow simulations of cases and situations. Naturally, we were also thinking about electronic game material to address these requirements.

Within the project *Interparolo*, we explored the use of chatbots for learning. The term 'chatbot' (also: 'chatterbot' - recently becoming more popular on commercial

Z. Pan et al. (Eds.): Transactions on Edutainment I, LNCS 5080, pp. 150–161, 2008.

web sites) refers to a software robot program, which attempts to maintain a textual conversation with a person. Technically, current chatbots, such as the open source 'A.L.I.C.E.' chatbot [2] use the simplest pattern matching of written user input to find suitable answer patterns in a database, also called 'knowledge base'. Hence, the knowledge base created needs to contain these user text patterns that were either anticipated by the creators, or added consecutively during a test phase.

In order to achieve a digital role-playing game in the context of moderation, this concept has been implemented in a way that lets several digital agents converse with each other and the user, acting as conversational sparring partners. The user is able to interrupt the conversation of the virtual characters, either by typing text or by using control elements of the graphical user interface (compare Figure 1).

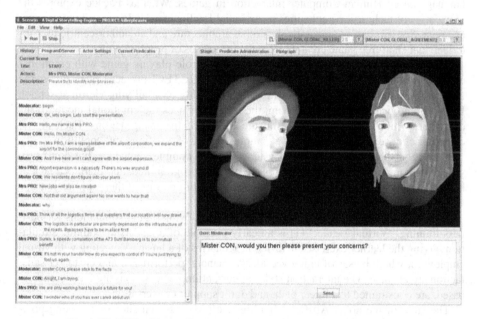

Fig. 1. The Killer Phrase Game prototype running in the *Scenejo* Platform

Technically, the virtual game is running with the platform *Scenejo* [9]. *Scenejo* connects several A.L.I.C.E. chatbots in a conversational loop of turn taking, which is controlled by a software component called 'drama manager'. Additionally, authoring of the conversations is supported by a graphical interface. The *Scenejo* architecture influences the possible interaction concepts of content to be created.

The resulting first learning game tackles the topic of how to identify and react to so-called 'killer phrases' within a discussion. Killer phrases are 'creativity killers', often used in a knee-jerk manner, which can destroy new ideas before they are discussed with solid arguments. The designed game assumes a scenario with two parties, planners and residents, arguing about upcoming plans for an airport expansion. The partly predefined conversation between the two parties, carried out across a table, contains such killer phrases. The learner plays the role of the moderator and has to manage the meeting (see game screen in Figure 1).

This paper presents the results of this experiment. The emphasis is on critical design questions and design steps, such as designing a suitable dynamic model, designing the story and the dialogue pieces, and tuning/testing. Further, a short discussion on the effectiveness of the learning game is provided.

2 Related Work

The Killer Phrase game resembles the player interaction offered in the avant-garde game 'Façade' [6], which is not designed for educational use, but is well-known within the research community of 'Interactive Storytelling' as a pilot study for a new form of language-based Human-Computer interaction in games. Whereas Façade explores the boundaries of technical complexities in Artificial Intelligence, dialogue and drama management, *Scenejo* has a comparatively simple architecture and an author-centric user interface that shall free game creators from the intricacies of programming.

A more educational implementation of a digital role-playing game with emotional characters is the demonstrator 'FearNot!' of the 'VICTEC' project [3]. In this game targeted at children, the user plays the role of a buddy of a bullying victim at school. By giving advice to the digital victim, the user influences the emotional model of the character, which leads to a change in the course of following actions. Each digital character chooses actions based on a complex model of emotions and cognition.

Currently, the above-mentioned systems support complex behavior, but don't provide authoring tools. The virtual actors are directly programmed, and there is a lack of best practice and design knowledge. This results in limitations of their application in a flexible learning context.

There is a current trend for 'Serious Games' employing digital simulations for business training. 'Virtual Leader' [1] is an early example of a leadership training simulation, giving the learner exercises in different scenarios of a business meeting with virtual employees, where biases of employee ideas, financial performance and customer satisfaction are at stake. The interaction styles in current implementations are mostly choice-based, are constrained to a linear path, and don't support conversations.

The state of the art in Artificial Intelligence (AI) research shows promising prospects for future learning games that employ role-playing with digital companions. However, there is a huge gap between these possibilities and their accessibility for the designers of learning games. The chatbot-based platform *Scenejo* shows reduced complexity in terms of AI, and it is equipped with an accessible authoring tool [8]. Nevertheless, with the design of the Killer Phrase game described here, we entered uncharted territories.

3 Design Steps

3.1 Initial Considerations

The envisioned digital role-playing game simulates a live role-playing game for learning (albeit up to a certain point), while showing several significant differences. These include disadvantages, since nothing seems to be as suited to training for a real–life situation as training with a live-action role-playing game. However, there are also advantages to using simulated environments over real ones. Therefore, there is no intention to substitute a virtual game for existing methods, but rather to enhance the learning material with additional possibilities. A list of identified advantages – as well as disadvantages - of the virtual role-playing game over real/physical role play shall be pointed out in the last section.

A critical design step is the design of a dynamic model of an emergent, open-ended conversation that can be operated and managed by the computer system. Figure 2 shows the general concept of transition functions building the core of a dynamic model [5]. According to Holland, a 'perfect model' would result in a complete detailed mapping of real world configurations to model states, and of laws of change in the real world to transition functions in the model. However, as he points out, the art of model building lies in selecting the right level of detail that is useful for the purpose, distinguishing salient features from detail, and capturing the laws of change at the chosen level. It is very unlikely that we could manage to observe the world successfully in every detail, and doing so would result in a way too complex model. The transfer of observed world states and 'laws of change' to a model is a creative, inductive process. Observation results depend on the applied monitoring and measuring techniques, as well as on the goals of the simulation. In the case of the moderation game, the identification of the phenomenon of 'killer phrases' already existed in the learning material, which was indeed an important 'critical incident' to start out with.

3.2   The Process of Finding a Model for Emergent Dialogues

Within this experiment, several developments had to be achieved in parallel: Imagining the content for the dialogues, accomplishing the learning goals of the game, making first experiences with the authoring process and, at the same time, addressing the feasibility conditions of the available technical platform by the design. Naturally, this

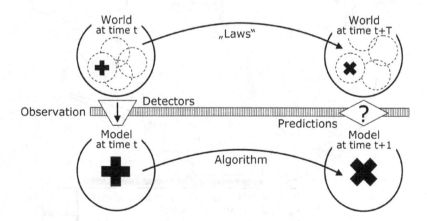

Fig. 2. The observed world configurations and their identified 'laws of change' have to be transferred to a dynamic model of states and calculable transition functions ('algorithm'). (Illustration adapted from [5]).

had to be done by an interdisciplinary team, consisting of the domain experts (the instructors of the seminar 'moderation and mediation') and the developers and designers of the platform, who were familiar with the logical frame for the calculation model. It turned out that the easiest way to develop the content was, at first, to let the domain experts come up with linear scripts of imagined conversations, such as a 'best case' and a 'worst case' scenario of an optimal and a dysfunctional moderation of a debate containing killer phrases. Starting out from these scripts, we categorized the individual utterances into groups. During brainstorming sessions, world states and possible transitions based on the groups of utterances had to be found. The emphasis was on identifying reasons for the occurrence of killer phrases, and their effects on participants in a meeting.

The resulting first draft of the virtual debate model was 'actor-centered' in the same sense as there is a character-centered approach to storytelling. Each individual agent was assigned individual internal states of a modeled 'mind' – and should then behave in accordance with those states. Figure 3 shows an abstract sketch of the conceived structural elements of this first game model. Agent utterances, which are part of the 'script', can influence the internal states of other agents while they are depending on their own current state values.

User utterances are compared with a prepared database of pieces of dialogue covering possible verbal interactions. The matched patterns influence the same set of character parameters by applying rules, which, in turn, are taken into account while the drama manager selects agent utterances from the prepared dialogue base. For example, offending one character with a certain killer phrase would count down the value

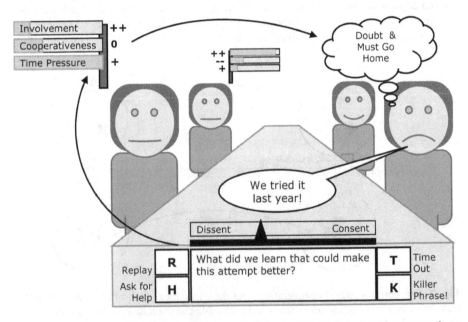

Fig. 3. Design sketch of the conceived structural elements of the 'killer phrase' game, such as the parameter states of each virtual actor

of that character's cooperativeness – the moderator may have to do something to raise this value again, since only with a high degree of cooperativeness would this character ever agree to a compromise.

3.3 Reducing the Complexity of the Model

Although this first attempt modeled a simple 'mind' for each actor, it was not based on approved psychological models. In order to achieve dramatic interactive storytelling, one could additionally model special personality traits for each actor. The traits would affect the transition rules for state changes in a way that lets different personalities react differently to the same actions and events. The vision of this endeavor is to finally achieve this complexity, in order to allow for emergent conversations providing novelty and surprises in the conversational turns, each and every time the game is played. As this is considered a crucial prerequisite for drama, it has been identified for a follow-up in future work, in order to achieve a level of Interactive Digital Storytelling going beyond simple game structures.

However, due to the difficulties of implementation, for the first prototype, the complexity had to be channeled down to even less complex interactions. As a next step after the modeling process, the states of the model had to be mapped with concrete utterances made by the virtual actors and potential utterances of users. With the current platform, these correlations had to be done explicitly during the authoring process while the utterances were being formulated. As a result, the initial model had been changed to an even more abstract and simple game-like model. Figure 4 shows the simplified model, which was then implemented.

Instead of modeling each character's mind, a generalized view is taken by only modeling overall levels of stress or mood – here: the 'Killer Phrase Level'. The idea is that the utterance repertoire of each character contains killer phrases, as well as valid arguments for its own position. As soon as an argument is played, it will lead towards a compromise. However, valid arguments of each party can only be triggered

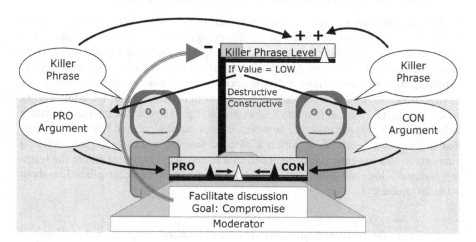

Fig. 4. Simplified model of states and transitions

by the system if the killer phrase level is low. Any occurrences of killer phrases raise this level, and it can only be kept low by the moderator's interaction.

3.4 Learning Game Design

With either model, there can be further designed games and sub-games with several stages of complexity:

1. Modeling, without a game element: The agents model an ideal or a dysfunctional interaction of the moderator, providing context information, with no interaction.
2. Situation-awareness: The player/learner has to simply identify occurring killer phrases, by hitting a 'buzzer'-like button and reading more information about the situation, earning points on hits.
3. Coaching: The player/learner plays moderator and has to interrupt and phrase verbal reactions to the virtual characters in order to influence the meeting in a positive way. In a first 'learning system' version, several game features, like wild cards, can help the learner. These are a time-out function to gain more time to phrase an utterance, as well as a Help-function, calling another agent working as a kind of coach or prompter. Game-like features include gathering points for managing a situation.
4. Simulation: The player/learner does the same, except that there is a simulation of a real meeting including the decision whether or not to interrupt, the time constraints for actions, and the experience of the outcome not measured by gained points, but by the reactions of the simulated meeting participants. Optionally, the influenced parameters are explicitly made visible, or hidden in order to let the player focus on the reactions only (such as in a real situation).
5. Reflection: Players/learners are able to replay their finished simulation, again with the option to either visualize internal parameter states or not. This can be embedded in a debriefing phase linked to the classroom course.

The aforementioned stages of possible virtual game designs with the created material relate to an often-used instructional design approach of 'Cognitive Apprenticeship' (CA). The simulation step, however, as a task of exploring the territory, occurs at a rather early stage compared to CA methods[1]. Instead it fosters the constructivist exploring of unknown territory with the opportunity to make mistakes in a risk-free environment. Stages 2 to 4 particularly benefit from digital material including agents, where the digital material is tolerant, uncomplaining, and repeated interaction with it is harmless. The digital material, however, cannot stand alone and has to be embedded in the course curriculum within a blended learning strategy. A game working similarly to this example can be included as a temporary component within the learning material. One run of the implemented prototype could be accomplished in about 10 to 20 minutes.

---

[1] According to Collins, Brown and Holum [4], the instructional design method of 'Cognitive Apprenticeship' sequences the learning content by increasing complexity through the steps 1) Modeling, 2) Coaching, 3) Scaffolding/Fading, 4) Articulation, 5) Reflection, 6) Exploration.

3.5 Implementation / Authoring and Design of the Dialogues

For the implementation of the first prototype in *Scenejo*, concrete dialogues for each actor had to be defined and implemented in AIML[2]. The initial best case / worst case scripts were taken as a starting point, followed by the definition of state changes invoked by each utterance, as well as the conditions under which an utterance is likely.

Figure 5 shows the advancement of the simple model of Figure 4 towards its implementation. The (over-)simplification of this model in comparison to reality was made not least due to the constraining conditions of implementation. The utterances in the resulting AIML database were classified as being Killer Phrases or Arguments. Simple counters are implemented to count the occurrences of killer phrases and, on the other hand, to count the occurrences of valid arguments. In the implemented simplified model, utterances of valid arguments only take place if the Killer Phrase level is low; however, the mere utterance of an argument is sufficient to raise the agreement level. Once a given value has been achieved either by killer phrases or by the agreement level, the game ends with either an escalation or a compromise of the parties.

Another advantage of this simplification is that the game play is independent of the domain knowledge needed by players to participate in the discussion, because all arguments are brought up by the virtual characters. The role of the player is only to moderate the discussion style. The disadvantage is, naturally, that this model is oversimplified and different from the real world. It is only suited to create awareness of Killer Phrases.

3.6 Tuning and Testing

Combining the first scripts (best case / worst case) with the simulation model led to the first implementation that could then be test-played. As is common practice in

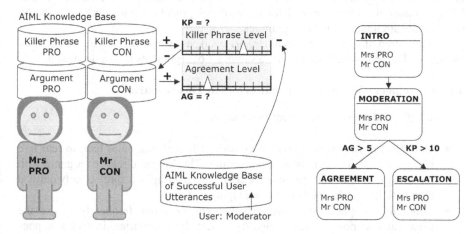

Fig. 5. Left: Implementation of utterances with state changes in AIML. Right: Implemented decision point for winning or losing the game.

---

[2] AIML: Artificial Intelligence Markup Language. The knowledge base for the chatbot A.L.I.C.E. [2] is implemented in AIML.

computer game design, at this stage, flaws in the game play become obvious and have to be fixed iteratively by testing and tuning the game play. For example, phases of lengthy dialogues between the virtual actors, without a possibility for the moderator to take a turn, have to be eliminated and cut into smaller segments. Resulting from the first linear scripts, single utterances suddenly appeared too long. Although, in reality, one conversational turn of a participant is likely to cover several sentences, it turned out to be not suitable within the implemented game, in which all utterances were spoken by a speech synthesiser. Together with the difficulty involved in interrupting the conversation at any possible point within a sentence, it shows that technical circumstances also have to lead to a redesign of the dialogues – mostly by shortening the single utterances of the virtual actors. The result is a game that has a specific (technical) pacing of conversational turns that is not the same as experienced in reality.

4   A First Evaluation of the Game

The game has been evaluated in a formative manner by the design team during the early design phases and the technical development process. Thus, major insights for a long list of possible advancements to be done in future work were found through self-criticism, especially addressing technical improvements.

Further, the implemented version was test-played with students of the seminar 'moderation and mediation', followed by a focus group discussion. At this point in the development, many technical aspects need improvement, and the tested game was not technically perfect. Nevertheless, the game was playable. Out of all who managed to play the game to the end, there was a reasonable 50/50 distribution of outcomes, winning or losing the game (winning: achieve a compromise, losing: escalation of the meeting). The questions discussed focused on the suitability of such a game for learning, as well as on acceptance issues. The majority of students understood the game as learning material with a potential for future developments, while some students did consider the attempt to only be a 'gimmick'.

Several strengths and opportunities, as well as weaknesses and risks, were identified. The following lists provide a summary of arguments in this discussion.

4.1   Advantages of Using the Virtual Actors in This Scenario

The strengths and opportunities identified include:

- Doll playing in general allows users to test boundaries more than in real live role play, which occurs in a social setting. The 'magic circle' of a game with digital agents - and thus the safe space of 'just playing' - is more clearly defined than with live participants in a role-playing game.
- Generally, people dealing with chatbot conversations frequently ignore the usual rules of polite behavior and try to test the boundaries. In fact, this phenomenon was debated within the project. On the one hand, this can be a chance to experiment with situations like this and experience the outcome directly. The counter-argument is the concern that students don't take it seriously and prefer to make fun of the resulting annoying situations. Given the background that

these games would be embedded in a classroom course, this objection was given minor importance.

- The digital environment allows for the adjustment of timing and pacing, for example, to stop and to play single scenes for more emphasis, to increase the time pressure intentionally, or to replay achievements and played games for reflection and debriefing.
- Through the text-only interface, phrasing can be judged explicitly, since parameters from the real world are missing that could have a disguising effect on recognition. Dealing with verbal language is the subject of interest being taught, so the choice of words plays an important role.
- For a live action gaming simulation, a classroom setting with participants and proper preparation is needed. Classroom realities dictate that this is not always convenient, especially when repetition is desired. Computer simulations can be beneficial as additional learning opportunities or for preparation of the live game in the preliminary stages. They are also useful for experiencing extreme situations, which are hard to create in real-life, and repetition of a given situation is possible.

4.2 Disadvantages of Using Virtual Actors

The weaknesses and risks identified include:

- General argument: A simulation never represents the real situation properly with all its complexity. A mapping of the experiences in the simulated world to (those of) the real situation has to be achieved. The computer simulation is even more abstract than the live role-playing game, so it may also confuse the issue more rather than contributing to a successful transfer.
- Nonverbal cues, such as body language and presence, are difficult to implement (or non-existent, as in our prototype). Verbal factors are presented in isolation, while life is more complex. Several emotional levels are left out, and the stress a learner experiences in the live situation is not part of the system. Voices of the characters are currently only represented electronically (by text-to-speech, which facilitates rapid prototyping during the design phase).
- The work involved in the creation of the necessary dialogues for the chatbot knowledge base - before a game can successfully be played - is significant. The technology base used to run the chatbot dialogues still needs technical development.
- There is an underlying risk that the typical flaws known from chatbot interactions also apply to the learning game, and that they may hamper the outcome of the game. The only way to work against this is an increased effort toward scripting, in order to be prepared for many possible situations. In the current prototype, this flaw led to user frustration.
- Risks can also be identified in the lack of experience of teachers as simulation designers. The quality of the simulation model is crucial to the success of the learning experience. This model can only be built in a cooperative effort between experts of the respective domain and experts in gaming simulation. In this sense, the greatest risk is that the designed model can be plain wrong, which results in learning mistakes.

5 Conclusion

The experiment of the Killer Phrase game has shown that there is a potential for learning games involving virtual actors based on digitally implemented agents. However, in order to achieve success exceeding a prototype implementation as shown here, there is a need for further developments, not only in available technologies. There is also a need for interdisciplinary design competence of domain experts and teachers/facilitators embracing these new possibilities. Within the design process of the presented game project, it became clear that the abstract modeling task is actually a question of designing 'the content' and, as such, not something that can be delegated to a programmer. However, the initial perception of the domain experts was that this task is 'technical stuff' – understandable, due to the necessity of understanding the platform mechanisms to come up with a calculable model. For success, the big challenge of designing learning games with digital role-playing agents will be the building of an abstract model of any learning subject that bridges 'reality' and computational conditions.

During the design phase, one obvious learning effect has been the increased reflection on the dependencies within the system dynamics while building the model, particularly experienced by the game designers and creators of the dialogues. As another conclusion it can be suggested that 'designing learning games' is an effective method for learning.

Acknowledgements

The project *Interparolo* has received funds from the German Federal State of Thuringia. Thanks to Dennis Linke and Sebastian Weiß for the technical support and implementation of the game in the platform *Scenejo*. Thanks to Rebekka Eizenhöfer and Heidi Sinning for the collaboration in model design and knowledge base creation in the seminar 'moderation and mediation'. A similar version of this article has been presented at ISAGA 2007 [7].

References

1. Aldrich, C.: Simulations and the Future of Learning. Pfeiffer & Company (2003) ISBN: 0-7879-6962-1
2. ALICE. Homepage of the A.L.I.C.E. Artificial Intelligence Foundation (Last accessed: 03.31.2008), http://www.alicebot.org
3. Aylett, R., Louchart, S., Dias, J., Paiva, A., Vala, M.: Fearnot! - an experiment in emergent narrative. In: Panayiotopoulos, T., Gratch, J., Aylett, R.S., Ballin, D., Olivier, P., Rist, T. (eds.) IVA 2005. LNCS (LNAI), vol. 3661, pp. 305–316. Springer, Heidelberg (2005)
4. Collins, A., Brown, J.S., Holum, A.: Cognitive Apprenticeship: Making Thinking Visible. In: American Educator, Winter Issue, 6-11, 38–46 (1991)
5. Holland, J.H.: Emergence: From Chaos to Order. Oxford University Press, Oxford (1998)
6. Mateas, M., Stern, A.: Procedural Authorship: A Case-Study of the Interactive Drama Façade. In: Proceedings of Digital Arts and Culture (DAC), Copenhagen (2005)

7. Spierling, U.: Killer Phrases: Design steps for a game with digital role-playing agents. In: Mayer, Mastik (eds.) Organizing and Learning through Gaming and Simulation, Proceedings of ISAGA 2007, Eburon, Delft, pp. 333–342 (2008) ISBN 978 90 5972 2316
8. Spierling, U., Weiß, S., Müller, W.: Towards Accessible Authoring Tools for Interactive Storytelling. In: Göbel, S., Malkewitz, R., Iurgel, I. (eds.) TIDSE 2006. LNCS, vol. 4326, pp. 169–180. Springer, Heidelberg (2006)
9. Weiß, S., Müller, W., Spierling, U., Steimle, F.: Scenejo – An Interactive Storytelling Platform. In: Subsol, G. (ed.) ICVS-VirtStory 2005. LNCS, vol. 3805, pp. 77–80. Springer, Heidelberg (2005)

From Pencil to Magic Wand: Tangibles as Gateways to Virtual Stories

Ana Paiva

GAIPS Grupo de Agentes Inteligentes e Personagens Sintéticas,
INESC-ID and IST, Tagus Park,
Av. Prof. Cavaco Silva, 2780-990 Porto Salvo, Portugal
ana.paiva@inesc-id.pt

Abstract. Interactive storytelling provides experiences to the users that go beyond the simple passive role of experiencing story events and situations in a third person perspective. Users are driven into taking an active role in a narrative by acting and interacting with characters, by feeling what characters feel, and thus influencing the outcome of that narrative. As such, when interactivity is brought into storytelling, a quite delicate balance needs to be found between the user's participation and the wishes and intended directions of the authors. Many different aspects of this "interactivity dilemma" have been raised over the past few years, either by taking an authors' centric perspective, or a perspective that is centered on the participant's experience. In this paper, I would like to raise a different view where interactivity is seen as the dynamics created on the boundaries between the virtual and the real. In that sense, the role of tangibles, as the gateways for interactive storytelling systems, is explored, and some issues related to their design are addressed.

1 Introduction

In the area of interactive storytelling, where computers, interaction and storytelling are brought together to generate dynamic stories, interactivity becomes an essential piece in this new form of digital content. Stories emerge from the combination of the users' actions and the author's creations, which means that authors must change the way to express narrative content, and, at the same time viewers must become active participants in computer supported narrative.

An author of non-linear narrative may construct a story representation that constrains the viewers to important and interesting situations or experiences, while at the same time, provides them with enough freedom to deviate from a pre-defined story line, perhaps established by a traditional linear narrative (Galyean 95). As argued by many researchers, in interactive narrative, the author's role is not only modified, but taken further, into one that allows for parallel interleaved stories and content to be part of the audience's experience of narrative. On the other hand, the audience is transformed from passive viewers to participants that are able to act, making a difference in the way the story progresses. Thus, getting engaged in an interactive storytelling experience implies

Z. Pan et al. (Eds.): Transactions on Edutainment I, LNCS 5080, pp. 162–171, 2008.

moving beyond the simple passive role of experiencing events and situations in a third person perspective into taking a more active role by feeling what characters feel and influencing the outcome of the story. As such, when interactivity is brought into storytelling, a quite delicate balance needs to be found between the user's participation and the wishes and intended directions of the authors.

Many different aspects of this "interactivity dilemma" have been raised over the past few years, either by taking an authors' centric perspective, or a viewer's centered perspective.

In this paper, I would like to raise a different point of view where interactivity is seen as the dynamics created on the boundaries between the virtual and the real, interleaving the influence one has over the other. For example, if the "real" world (the user) does not influence the virtual storytelling world, the link and thus influence is unidirectional, and we have the typical linear story with complete author's control. Thus, looking at interactivity in terms of the dynamics created on these boundaries may allow us to consider that in interactive storytelling one may take advantage of all elements of the physical world as ways to cross such boundaries. And, one way of doing that is by allowing for physical actions and physical elements in the real world (tangibles) to become gateways to the interactive storytelling virtual world. The idea of tangibles is not new and was defined by Ishi (Ishii 1997) as "giving form to digital information, employing physical artifacts both as representations and controls for computational media". This paper tries to address this idea, by looking at aspects of interactivity in interactive storytelling and by discussing design issues concerning the inclusion of tangibles used for such interactivity.

2   Modes and Modalities for Interactivity

Interactivity in storytelling systems assumes that users must be able to interact with the system influencing its outcome. Many modalities have been explored to this end. In some of the most influential and earlier works on interactive narrative, the user simply types commands in a command line, and those "actions" (commands) of the user lead to changes in the world he or she belongs. One of the most well known cases of this type of systems is Photopia, the winner of the 1998 Interactive Fiction Competition. Due to its rich content these systems may be extremely engaging and participants feel as part of the story. However, these systems may be limiting what the user wants to express, and, on the other hand, the richness of graphical worlds so popular in computer games, is not present. At the same time, the text approach may also be too limitative when the interaction is based on simple moving commands that can be captured so easily without text. Indeed, the most used mode for interactivity allows for participants to move and act in a virtual world, using actions like move, shoot, talk, or do some other semantically relevant action in the world, with just the touch of a key or the pressure of a joystick.

We can distinguish two different mechanisms by which the user influences the stories in interactive storytelling environments. In the first one the user controls a character (which may be its avatar in the graphical world) and the advancement of the story emerges by the actions of that avatar. This type of control needs to be rooted in the story for the user to feel engaged with the world, to the extent that he/she feels that his/her senses were extended by what character perceives of the virtual world. The second type of interaction is established between the user and elements of the virtual word, in particular other characters. When interacting with other characters users may want to ask questions, give orders and so on. These interactions lead to different story paths, and thus, different experiences. Figure 1 illustrates these differences in the different modes of interactivity.

Yet, with the amazing advancements in computer graphics, 3D worlds became also ideal settings for interactive narrative, taking advantage of the richness of the medium. These two modes of interaction can also be found in graphic based storytelling systems.

	Control oriended	Interaction oriented
Text and Command line	Simple commands in a command line controlling the actions of the characters	Natural language interface in a command line to interact with other characters
Graphic virtual worlds	Commands in a 3D/2D world directing/ controling characters	Interaction in natural language with graphical characters
Real Wold	Use of tangibles for directing characters	Speech and natural language interaction with characters

Fig. 1. Interactivity and Modality for Interactive Storytelling

On top of the different modalities of interaction, users can also take different roles, and thus influence the story in many different ways. Several different approaches have been explored in terms of roles. For example, in Cavazza et. al. (Cavazza et. al. 2003) the user is an invisible avatar in the 3D environment that acts like a "God" influencing the environment by removing or displacing props of narrative significance to change the direction of the story. Machado et. al. (Machado et. al.) proposed that users should also be considered actors, and their influence in the story is through their basic actions and their interactions. In Façade the user is a visitor (friend) of a couple with marital problems. Finally, in the case of FearNot! (Dias et al. 2007) children become friends with a victim of bullying (the main character in the story) and interact with it by suggesting ways of dealing with his/her problems. In FearNot! the user influences the way the story develops by providing goals and suggesting coping mechanisms to the main character.

More recently some systems have been designed where the interaction with the interactive storytelling, yet still through keyboard, is done using natural language with the system. For example, the approach taken in Façade (Mateas et. al. 04) allows for users to influence the story through natural language conversations established with the main characters, thus influencing its outcome. Similar to Façade, FearNot! also allows for children to participate in the story via natural language interaction (Dias et. a. 2007). However, this type of interaction has the drawback that it may lead the user to make assumptions about the capabilities of the characters, which are often not met, leading the user to disappointment.

But, all these systems, in spite of being quite advanced in the way users can influence the interactive narrative, rely mainly on keyboard input. And, although the area of tangible interfaces (Ishii et. al. 97) has been developing fast, and gesture based interfaces are now gaining the commercial world (se for example the case o EyeToy and Wii), the use of tangibles as a modality for interactivity in virtual storytelling is still new.

Tangibles can be used for both control and for interaction with other characters. As interaction mechanisms, tangibles can be used to express some actions towards other characters by using objects such as a sword or a hammer. As control mechanisms tangibles can be used for capturing control actions, such as walk, move, point, etc. Figure 1 shows the different modes for interaction in interactive storytelling environments.

3   Virtual Make Believe: Breaking the Fourth Wall with Tangibles

The goal of this research is for users to be able to explore their senses and use their body in their participatory story building. As such, multi-modality could become an emerging technology for enabling participants to engage differently in computer based interactive storytelling. Gestures, as in the case of Romeo and Juliet ((Nakatsu et. al. 1998) is a good example of the kind of bodily interaction that participants may have with the system. Another example is "Sam the Castlemate" (Ryokai et. al. 2002), a virtual playmate for children that is able to attend to childrens stories told around a physical castle they play with, and tell back relevant stories in return.

The use of tangible interfaces for storytelling makes the physical environment of the participants to be seen as part of the interface with the virtual world, where stories become a combination of shared worlds' experiences. Like in makebelieve activities, where transitional objects are gateways to the imaginary world, in computer based interactive storytelling, tangible interfaces can be gateways to the virtual world. As pencils turn out to be magic wands and transport their holder to a magic imaginary world, so can objects in the real worlds become gateways to the virtual narrative experiences. A participant can use a pen, which, in the virtual world, may turn out to be a fantastic powerful key. The reality of the physical world can be challenged, and somehow augmented with this new form of interaction.

In order to explore the role of tangibles and tangible interfaces for user participation in interactive storytelling, one must challenge the borderline between the real and the virtual.

But how can we build gateways to the virtual world that do actually work as interface metaphors in interactive storytelling? In most systems the interaction design presupposes that there is a clear boundary between the virtual story (and the characters that live in the virtual world) and the user (that is living in the real world) but at the same time influencing the virtual world. This is the case of FearNot!, Façade and others. But, as those boundaries become more diffuse, and an apparent dual presence of users in both worlds begins to be addressed, we need to find seamless couplings between these two parallel existences (see (Ishii 1997)). To address this topic we have structured the questions related with the design of tangibles for virtual storytelling into four different areas: Physicality versus naturality; Physicality, Attachment and Emotions; Physicality in direct control or influence; and Physicality in interaction.

3.1   Physicality and Naturality

Stories can be enacted through the gesturing with objects, tangibles, thus involving the body. However, what is the coupling between the gestures and their semantic meaning in the virtual world? And should the gestures be natural (and inspired in the way we use the objects themselves) or learned? If they are only based on the real gestures, how could a pencil become a magic wand or a key? On the other hand, if they are learned, doesn't that learning process impair the interaction and immersion we want to achieve? Or will it add to the challenge of the system?

From some of the research we have done at GAIPS, we believe that one should ground the interaction in the way people feel comfortable with. This leads to the involvement of the users right from the start of the system development, capturing the way people may be able to interact with the objects that are going to influence the story. Yet, grounding the interaction in natural gestures should not prevent the emergence and creation of learned gestures, as the virtual world may itself demand it.

One of the interfaces developed by GAIPS was SenToy (Paiva et. al. 2002), a tangible interface that has the shape of a doll and the ability to detect gestures that represent emotions expressed by the user. SenToy was used within a system with two elements, the doll itself which is responsible for acquiring all the information regarding its handling by the user, and the computer that receives the data from the doll and proceeds by doing its processing and interpretation giving as an output an emotion with a certain certainty value. SenToy initially worked as an interface to the role playing game (FantasyA) where players would exhibit a particular set of emotions and perform a set of actions as a way to evolve in the game (see (Paiva et. al. 2002)). The aim of SenToy was to "pull the user into the game" through the use of a physical, touchable affective interface. With sensors in its limbs, sensitive to movement and acceleration, SenToy captures certain patterns of movements from the users, which are associated with particular emotional expressions. During SenToy's design we raised several questions concerning the most appropriate gestures. We aimed at natural gestures, influenced by the body gestures that humans perform in certain emotional states. As such a set of initial patters of gestures were designed and tested with users in Wizard of OZ studies in order to determine if the movements idealised would be natural enough for the users. The patterns interpreted as emotions are described in table 1.

Table 1. Patterns associated with emotions

Gesture	Emotion
Move the doll up and down	Happy
Slightly bend the doll's head onward	Sad
Agitate the doll vigorously	Anger
Cover the doll's eyes with it's hands	Fear
Incline the doll's body backwards and making the doll move backwards	Surprise

The results showed that some of the initially identified patterns worked very well, and others (such as the gesture for disgust) did not work at all and this had to be changed or eliminated. The interleaving between natural gestures and learned gestures was essential but it required testing right from the start of the system development. Users may not learn the gestures we expect and if feedback from the application is not adequate, frustration may appear. In terms of modes, natural gestures are more used for interaction mode (for example using a sword to fight against an enemy) whereas learned gestures are more associated with control mode.

3.2 Physicality, Attachment and Emotions

People can create attachments with characters and objects in stories, and tangibles can be part of that emotional relation. The physicality of objects that one can touch, smell, cuddle, etc, may be also used as a way to break the boundaries of the interaction. By analyzing users interacting with two of our applications with tangibles (SenToy and I-Shadows (Lopes 2005)) we found that, in a natural way, they are lead into holding as if they were "alive" (for example, with SenToy users often hugged it).

So, one may ask if this attachment element can be explored as a form of allowing for stronger and more empathic relations between users and the characters in storytelling worlds.

In one of the investigations done to explore this relation, we allowed users to manipulate SenToy in an interactive storytelling situation and let them express

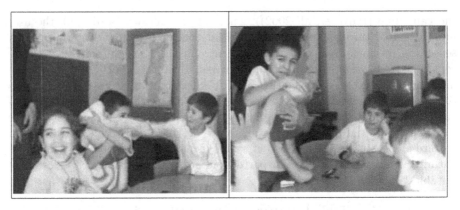

Fig. 2. Using SenToy for emotion expression in virtual storytelling

the emotional states associated with the stories emerging from the storytelling scenarios. To do that, SenToy's components were embedded into the FearNot! (Paiva 2005) storytelling application. Users were allowed to use SenToy and express what they "felt" along the story being shown. The results obtained (see (Figueiredo 2005)) were quite positive, not only because it confirmed once more that children really liked the tangible interface, but also because it allowed us to gather emotional data about the users while interacting with the interactive storytelling environment. From the logs obtained, the results show that the emotion that was expressed more often was sadness, which is in accordance with the contents of the displayed story. In fact, the results show that children did express the emotional states that the authors tried to evoke with the system.

3.3   Physicality for Direct Control or Influence

Is there any link between the use tangibles in virtual storytelling and the type of control the participant will have? Doesn't the use of objects makes the interaction metaphor less direct which in turn may impair the agency aspect of the interactive narrative?

As shown in Figure 1, tangibles can be used for control and for interaction. Yet, in terms of story progression, what is their role?

Plus, as mentioned before, participants of interactive narrative may take several roles in the story. Some involve more direct control (the participant controls his/her avatar in the world), and others, like for example M. Cavazza's work, or even FearNot!, the user influences the environment or the characters that make up the story. In general, the tangible should link the real world objects through the control of virtual events, and "influence", can be the kind of metaphor that allows it. On the other hand, direct control may also work, if the participant is seen as a kind of "God" that changes and updates the virtual world. Direct control is the most obvious form of use of tangibles, as participants can change the course of the story controlling some elements in the story interface. Yet, we can also consider that by acting through their characters and manipulating (phisically) the objects of the characters participants will influence the story flow. However, if our characters are smart enough, the direct control becomes influence, which may give extra challenge to the interaction.

3.4 Physicality and Interaction: Getting the Right Balance

When using objects, their design needs to be done so that the tangibles stay in the interactivity loop, adding to it, and making the story be influenced by their "virtual" state. So, some of the relevant questions are:

- Are any specific design issues in creating tangibles for interactive storytelling environments?
- What is the most adequate design methodology to develop them?
- How do we involve participants and authors in this design process?
- What are we designing? The tangible? The interaction? The system?

Although we do not have answers for the above questions, from the experience of GAIPS, we found that the involvement of the users from the start, using Wizard of OZ studies was crucial to understand the role that the tangible may have in the interaction loop. Also, the interaction loop needs to be carefully designed, as tangibles can impair the interaction itself. At GAIPS, one system was developed where cards are used as a way to influence how the story progresses and is told. Papous (see Figure 3) is a grandfather that tells stories. Users can change not only the emotional content of the story, by making it more happy or sad, but also the characters and scenes in the story. To make Papous change, children had to insert different cards (that picture not only scenes, but also characters) into a special type of mailbox (Sengers 2002).

Children that interacted with Papous felt not only that they influenced the story being told by the character, but particularly, that the physical interaction

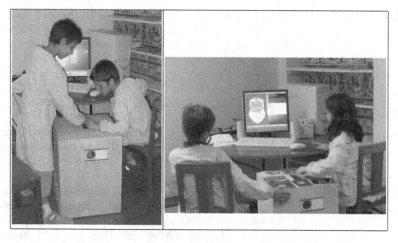

Fig. 3. Influencing the stories Papous tells through cards

was immensely enjoyable, and the enthusiasm and curiosity about the way it worked was obvious. However, we also found that the presence of the box distracted the users from getting engaged in the story, as the tangible was much more interesting than the story itself. The balance was not right.

4   Conclusions

I believe that the area of tangibles for storytelling will grow as new physical interfaces become more explored. The typical scenarios that we can witness nowadays, where physical commands like the Wii commands are mostly explored as extensions to the control interfaces in computer games, will change, and more scenarios, applications and games will be developed where the coupling between the physical objects and the virtual elements is so natural that the user feels the physical world as extended and his capabilities in the storytelling worlds is augmented by the tangibles.

Acknowledgements

This paper is supported by the eCIRCUS (Contract no. IST-4-027656-STP) project carried out with the provision of the European Community in the Framework VI Programme. The author is solely responsible for the content of this publication. It does not represent the opinion of the European Community, which is not responsible for any use that might be made of data appearing therein.

References

[Galyean 95]   Galyean T.: Narrative Guidance of Interactivity. MIT Ph.D. Thesis (1995)

[Machado et. al. 2001] Machado, I., Paiva, A., Prada, R.: Is the wolf angry or just hungry? Inspecting, modifying and sharing Characters' Minds. In: Proceedings of the International Conference on Autonomous Agents, ACM Press, New York (2001)

[Sobral and Paiva 2003] Sobral, D., Paiva, A.: Machiavellian Characters and the Edutainment Paradox. In: Rist, T., Aylett, R.S., Ballin, D., Rickel, J. (eds.) IVA 2003. LNCS (LNAI), vol. 2792, pp. 333–340. Springer, Heidelberg (2003)

[Marsella et. al. 2000] Marsella, S., Johnson, W., LaBore, C.: Interactive Pedagogical Drama. In: Proceedings of the Fourth International Conference on Autonomous Agents, pp. 301–308. ACM Press, New York (2000)

[Mateas et. al. 2004]   Mateas, M., Stern, A.: Natural Language Processing In Façade: Surface-text Processing. In: Göbel, S., Spierling, U., Hoffmann, A., Iurgel, I., Schneider, O., Dechau, J., Feix, A. (eds.) TIDSE 2004. LNCS, vol. 3105, pp. 3–13. Springer, Heidelberg (2004)

[Cavazza et. al. 2003]   Cavazza, M., Martin, O., Charles, F., Mead, S., Marichal, X.:
                           Interacting with Virtual Agents in Mixed Reality Interactive
                           Storytelling. In: Rist, T., Aylett, R.S., Ballin, D., Rickel,
                           J. (eds.) IVA 2003. LNCS (LNAI), vol. 2792, pp. 231–235.
                           Springer, Heidelberg (2003)
[Dias et. a. 2007]   Dias, J., Vala, M., Louchard, S., Aylett, R., Figueiredo,
                           R., Andr, E., Paiva, A., et al.: E-Circus Deliverable on
                           FearNot!v2.0. E-circus project (2007)
[Nakatsu et. al. 1998]   Nakatsu, R., Tosa, N., Ochi, T.: Interactive Movie: A Virtual
                           World with Narratives. In: Heudin, J.-C. (ed.) VW 1998.
                           LNCS (LNAI), vol. 1434, pp. 107–116. Springer, Heidelberg
                           (1998)
[Paiva et. al. 2002]   Paiva, A., Andersson, G., Höök, K., Mourao, D., Costa, M.,
                           Martinho, C.: SenToy in Fantasy A: Designing an Affective
                           Sympathetic Interface to a Computer Game. Personal and
                           Ubiquitous Computing 6, 378–389 (2002)
[Ishii et. al. 1997]   Ishii, H., Ullmer, B.: Tangible Bits: Towards Seamless In-
                           terfaces between People, Bits and Atoms. In: Proceedings of
                           Conference on Human Factors in Computing Systems (CHI
                           1997), ACM Press, New York (1997)
[Silva, A. 2004]   Papous: The Virtual Storyteller, MSc Thesis, Instituto Su-
                           perior Técnico (2004)
[Sengers et al. 2002]   The Enigmatics of Affect. In: Designing Interactive Systems-
                           Conference Proceedings, ACM Press, New York (2002)
[Figueiredo et. al 2005]   Figueiredo, R., Paiva, A.: Watch and Feel: an affective inter-
                           face in a virtual storytelling environment. In: Tao, J., Tan,
                           T., Picard, R.W. (eds.) ACII 2005. LNCS, vol. 3784, pp.
                           915–922. Springer, Heidelberg (2005)
[Ryokai et. al. 2002]   Ryokai, K., Vaucelle, C., Cassell, J.: Literacy Learning by
                           Storytelling with a Virtual Peer. In: Proceedings of Com-
                           puter Support for Collaborative Learning (2002)

Game-Based Learning with Computers – Learning, Simulations, and Games

Alke Martens[1], Holger Diener[2], and Steffen Malo[2]

[1] University of Rostock
Department of Computer Science and Electrical Engineering
Albert-Einstein-Str. 21
18059 Rostock, Germany
Fon: +49 − (0)381 − 4987650
martens@informatik.uni-rostock.de
[2] Fraunhofer IGD
Joachim-Jungius-Strasse 11
18059 Rostock, Germany
Fon: +49 − (0)381 − 4024110
{holger.diener,steffen.malo}@igd-r.fraunhofer.de

Abstract. For developing a sophisticated game-based training system it is important to consider both, the technical aspects of game development (i.e. games engineering) as well as the pedagogical aspects of games and technology enhanced learning (i.e. game didactics). How game-based training systems are engineered and how the underlying didactics is realized depends on the target group and on the learning objectives. A game-based training system, which requires a player to learn a wide variety of skills and strategies, has to be elaborate concerning content, interaction, and behavior. In order to describe the game aspects of a game-based training system more clearly, we separate them from engineering and didactic and discuss all three aspects separately. We analyze the components of game-based training systems and sketch useful game concepts for teaching and training. Finally, we describe pedagogical concepts like motivation and transfer, which support game-based learning.

1 Introduction

One question is why computer based games and game-based learning are interesting for research fields like computer science in general and in technology enhanced learning in particular. There are two answers for this question. First, games have a highly motivational character, which is often missing in traditional computer-based training systems. Secondly, computer games are interesting from the software development point of view, integrating diverse aspects like artificial intelligence and simulations, and other approaches e.g. the application of mobile devices (e.g. cell phones or PDA) [41]. Nowadays full price commercial computer games are highly complex software systems, which are developed by multidisciplinary teams. They require long development times, due to increasing demands of players regarding realistic computer graphics, intuitive user interfaces, and

Z. Pan et al. (Eds.): Transactions on Edutainment I, LNCS 5080, pp. 172–190, 2008.

realistic behavior of computer generated characters (see e.g. [10]). Since game-based training systems are mainly suited for a comparably small target group, the system developers usually cannot afford high budgets like full price games, which are potentially sold millions of times (e.g. The Sims [47]). Although a variety of tools for developing computer games exists for free, it is very demanding to create an appealing game with a small budget. Therefore, sad but not surprising, most of the teaching and training systems come in a comparably boring traditional learning guise.

Also another aspect has to be taken into account: the way the computer has become part of everyday life, and also of education, has dramatically changed over the years. Today's researchers and teachers stem from an era, which might be called pre-digital or at least "early-digital". Most of the people at the age of thirty plus have had no computers at school. In contrast to this, today almost every school-age kid has access to computers – be it at home or at school – and is working (and playing) with it in a quite natural way. It can be said that today's learners already have integrated digital media in their learning process. Prensky has observed this and stated it in [31] and [35]. Moreover, he stated that the old computer games have in most cases nothing to do with teaching and training (games like Poker, Chess or Go are excluded from this observation) [35]. Prensky noted that this has changed over the years due to the growing complexity of computer games. Even if they are developed without a pedagogical focus, today's computer games often support training at different levels, i.e. training of facts, of skills, of behavior, etc.

In the following we will focus on game-based learning with computers, and game-based training systems. We will start in the first section with a terminological delineation and with a closer look at games in general. To allow for a structured analysis we distinguish three essential aspects of game-based learning and game-based training systems:

- Pedagogical aspects, i.e. how to teach and train.
- Technical aspects, i.e. in the context of computer games: computer science aspects, e.g. mobile games, simulation and AI. In the following the focus here is on simulations.
- Game aspects, i.e. what kind of game is used.

Figure 1 shows the interplay of the three parts. In [42], Smith offers a similar comparison, but he has not included pedagogics. Our comparison of systems revealed that only if aspects of all three parts are realized in a training system, it can be called a real "game-based" training system. Leaving out learning aspects creates simulation games, which are either games purely for entertainment or serious games for controlling business processes (e.g. logistic). Leaving out simulation aspects creates mainly simple edutainment games for primary school. Finally, leaving out game aspects, creates simulation for training purposes only. Such training systems are used e.g. for military training (e.g. [33]), pilot training (e.g. [11]), and even in the medical domain (e.g. [23]).

With Prensky's work in mind and based on the distinction between different types of teaching and training systems described above (and in figure 1), the

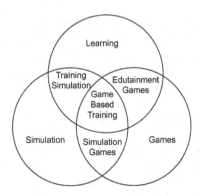

Fig. 1. Interplay of pedagogy, computer science and games

following questions arise: what is a pure computer game and what is a game-based teaching and training system? This question will be pursued in section two.

In [35] Prensky distinguishes between different types of games. He separates so-called "minigames" from complex games. Minigames are based on a trivial structure. As a game-based training they can only be used to teach and train facts. In contrast to this, "a complex game requires the player to learn a wide variety of often new and difficult skills and strategies." [35] The distinction between minigame and complex game thus takes place regarding the pedagogical complexity on one hand and the complexity of used computer science techniques on the other hand. Complex computer games are often based on simulations. In section three, the role of simulations in game-based teaching and training systems will be explored in more detail.

Not only the complexity of a teaching and training game plays an important role – also the size of the group, which will participate on the game, influences the selection of strategies. There are some pedagogical strategies, which lend themselves for specialized education in small groups. Other strategies must be used if a big and heterogeneous group takes part in a lecture. Especially game-based learning has to be carefully adapted to the intended group size and group structure. In most cases, game-based trainings with the wrong pedagogical concept can only reach small parts of a big heterogeneous group. What kind of didactics must be used for game-based learning and how can game-based learning support the transfer from game to reality or keeping the learner's motivation at a high level? Possible answers to this question will be given in section four, followed by a concluding discussion in the last section of the paper.

2   Game-Based X and Games

When looking at the comparably young field of computer based games for teaching and training, a large number of terms can be found: game-based learning and educational games, game-based training and digital games, training games, serious games etc. Given this amount of terms, this section shall start with a terminological delineation. Afterward we will look at different aspects of game-based training system development.

2.1 Game-Based X

The term game-based learning (GBL) is most commonly used for learning with games in the broad sense. This term is not necessarily related to computers, as game-based learning has a very long tradition in theory and practice of pedagogy and psychology (e.g. [17], [49]). Game-based learning can be found in early education, e.g. in kindergarten and at primary school (e.g. [9]). Children learn and train almost everything in a game-based manner. Game-based learning can take place with educational games – these are games specifically designed for educational purposes. Some of them are realized as computer games. For example, writing and first aspects of mathematics (e.g.[18]) are taught with educational games, and foreign language education can start in a playful manner, sometimes via song singing, sometimes by role play, classics education can take place by support of a website (see [8]). Small children train their social skills in games. Even in fields like biology or history, facts are presented in games and stories. Naturally, educational games can be computer based. This aspect will be focused in this article.

The term game-based training is often used as a substitute for game-based learning, especially if "training" is focused instead of the "learning". Surprisingly, this often takes place when adult education is addressed – the connotation exists that adults "train" to do something, whereas kids "learn". The term game based training system (GBT) is in most cases related to computer based training environments. The term training game often means the same, but also includes non-computer games. These systems are usually used in later stages of education, especially in adult education. Often, these GBTs are not even perceived as games. For example, case-based training (e.g.[29]), role-play (e.g. [32]), and storytelling (e.g. [7]) are part of game-based learning approaches in adult education. Case-based training is often used at Universities in medical, business, and in law education (e.g. [25]). Teaching and training based on role-playing is used in business, but also in management training, in psychology, and in seminars (e.g. leadership or communication seminars) (see e.g. [42]). Whereas the main purpose of computer based game-based training systems is teaching, from the engineering perspective quite a lot of them are based on modeling, simulation, and artificial intelligence (AI) techniques. Simulation of complex models and AI enable training systems to show reactive and proactive behavior. They allow the learner to act and interact with flexible and adaptive content and virtual characters, which can show quite realistic behavior.

Digital games are usually video, computer, or mobile games (see e.g. [4]). These games are not primarily designed or developed for educational purposes.

Even these games lead to some sort of learning, but this is not focus of our article. We focus on what is also called serious games [3] – these are the games developed for non-entertainment purposes. The term occurs in the late 1990s in the Anglo-American region. Located at the interface between entertainment industries and serious business training, it is used to contrast the traditional games for playing with the more serious educational approach.

2.2   Is It a Game?

The term game is traditionally often associated with winning or loosing, especially in the field of not-digital games. In Artificial Intelligence, but also in Bussiness Sciences, Social Sciences, and in Mathematics, game-theory has an important part in research. Salen and Zimmerman [38] give a good overview over different kinds of games, the related cultural and psychological aspects and approaches, and relations to fields like game-theory, information theory, and system theory, to name but a few. This field is much to broad to be covered in a single article. Thus, we keep our comparably narrow focused on the relation between what we call here "game-based" and the related special training systems, with our background in computer science and pedagogy.

As mentioned in the introduction, the development of a teaching and training system takes place based on pedagogy and computer science. If the system shall be "game-based", then game's aspects have to be integrated as well. Depending on how much of each of these three overlapping fields will be used (see figure 1), the system can be perceived to be a "game" or a "game-based training" system.

Nowadays, it is sometimes discussed that learning also takes place in playing computer games (see e.g. different articles at http://www.markprensky.com). The intention of a pure computer game is primarily having fun – but internally, these games often require the development of knowledge and of a certain strategy to reach the next level (see section 4.4). Even if it cannot be denied that this requires learning, the question remains what is learned, why is it learned, and which parts of this knowledge are transferred from the game to the real world (see section 4.4). Next to keywords like motivation and transfer, which will be discussed later, one of the keywords in the development of a game is intention: the intention of a teaching and training game is to facilitate acquisition of knowledge in a playful way, based on a clear pedagogical strategy [1]. The game-like part of the teaching and training system shall help to keep motivation of the learner at a high level. Todays learners often play complex computer games. Prensky [32] assumes, that these learners might be better motivated to learn with a teaching and training system based on game technology, as these game-based trainings are (at least) more interesting than traditional ones.

The decision whether to construct a pure game, a game-based training system, or a teaching and training system (ignoring the game aspects) must take at least the following aspects into account:

Teaching and training content: Not every content lends itself for realizing a game-based setting. A rule of thumb can be: teaching and training in a game-like, playful way can be used if a mere demonstration of something does not support the learning of facts, relations, and rules. This can for example be training of behavior. Training of knowledge and behavior in a game-based close to real life situation can encourage learning, as many aspects of reality are combined with the safety of the computer environment. An example is case based training in medicine [24]: students can train treatment processes without endangering patients or destroying expensive laboratory equipment. A game-based training system which supports this kind of learning can be used to complement classical teaching and training, and helps to deepen the acquired theoretical knowledge. Thus, if it is possible to develop models of close to real life situations, the realization of a computer game-based training system might be a good idea.

Learning theory: Role play and case-based teaching and training are examples of approaches, which quite naturally lend themselves to be realize in a game-based training system – meanwhile, as computer technology also allows for virtual interactive role plays, this is also possible in a computer based approach (e.g. Second Life http://secondlife.com/) . Another classical example is training with a microworld [40], which can be seen as a small world in a sense that it provides a closed environment which functions based on its own (and sometimes artificial) rules.

Realization as a computer system: From the computer system perspective, a wide variety of games exist. Even a simple HTML based quiz can be interpreted as a "quiz game", which is only a minigame by the categories of Prensky [35]. The more complex a game-based training shall be, the more demanding and sophisticated the used computer science technology must be. Complexity at this level of system development describes the underlying algorithms, the knowledge bases, the user interface, and some other technical aspects. For example, the technique to develop role-play games or role-play teaching and training environments is related to the research field of CSCW (Computer Supported Collaborative Work) [28]. In these settings, non-player characters can be based on certain models, which can be controlled by simulation engines. Another important aspect and future trend will be software engineering of computer games.

Kind of game: From the perspective of the world of games and related research, another level has to be added. This new emerging field is called ludology – a term which comes from the Latin word "ludus", which means "game". Ludology is said to be "the yet non-existent 'discipline that studies game and play-activities' [14] (see: http://www.ludology.org). Taking into account this level, it can be decided in advance, which type of game shall be developed. Examples for structurally simple games are puzzles and quizzes, which nonetheless can also be used in educational setting. Complex games, which are at the border between pure games and game-based trainings are strategic games, role play games, and adventure games. In areas like creativity research and the related learning theories, strategy games (e.g. where it is possible to construct cities, or develop companies or kingdoms) can be used.

3 Computer Science Aspects of Games: Properties and Simulations

When analyzing the field of game-based learning, as done in the previous section, some special properties of computer games occur, which are not easy to categorize. Thus, we have decided to integrate them in the following subsection. Additionally, as the field of computer simulations for game-based learning is a broad field, we offer a short overview and a special categorization of this field in an extra subsection.

3.1 Properties of (Computer-) Games

There are some special properties of games, which add to the list in the previous subsection, but which can not be part of the aspects' list above. These special properties are related to the collaboration and community aspect of games, the learning by watching (comparable to the learning theory's cognitive apprenticeship, see e.g. [2]), and the assumed relation between structure and motivation, which is special for games.

Collaboration and Games' Communities: Dyck et.al. [12] describe that players easily form communities. Many multi-player games quite automatically support to build "common interest" between players. This leads to forming of short time groups for a single task or of organized clans where every player has certain responsibilities (see e.g. [46]). The players meet online in massive multiplayer online games (MMOGs) or in real live (e.g. at a LAN party) to play their game as a group, to solve problems together or to fight against similar groups. Steinkuehler has observed and experienced this in playing the MMOG Lineage, and described it in her dissertation [46].

Learning by Watching: Beginners learn rules, first steps, and even complex game procedures simply by watching experienced players playing the game. Many games are offering learning by watching as part of the software: in-game tutorials offer playful step-by-step instructions to show the different possibilities without the necessity to read a reading written manual.

Structure and Motivation: Adventures and online role playing games contain complex structures, which are separated and capsuled in smaller quests. Quests are challenges and tasks a player has to solve in order to receive a reward. These quests are necessary to motivate players to do specific things, e.g. collect important items or learn essential skills and to stay in the game as long as possible. For this purpose quests are often overlapping. Players get new information and start new quests shortly before ending the last one. Therefore, it is quite seductive to play just a little bit longer after finishing the previous quest. Divide and conquer seems to be the strategy to keep the motivation of players high. The duration of quests depends on the complexity of its tasks, but the period of time between challenge and reward is decreasing over the last years. Game-based trainings also use this concept of segmentation in small tasks and rewards, and the crosswise joining of tasks (e.g. in case-based training). Within one task the learner already gathers skills for the next task – such that even after finishing the first one, the learner's motivation is still high to solve the next task.

3.2   Simulation in Computer Games

Next to the competitional aspects, which is also described as winning or loosing in 2.2 and [38], Caillois refers to different types of games as competitional, chance, vertigo, and also as simulation [5]. It is sometimes difficult to decide, whether a game is a simulation or not. This is due to the fact that the term "simulation" has a slightly different meaning in computer science than in the everyday language [27]. Many games are a simulation in the sense of 'simulating a real-life situation' (i.e. to act 'as if'), offering a artificial game reality, or even imitating real-life. In contrast to this, simulation in the sense of computer science explicitly implies the development of models and their simulation over time. Aim of the computer science approach is often to run experiments on the model, thus the term simulation is for example defined as: "A simulation is an experiment performed on a model" ([6], p. 6). In the following, the sketched simulations are interpreted based on this viewpoint as execution of models.

In computer based game-based trainings, simulation can be found at different places. A first categorization suggests to distinguish which role the simulation has in the game. Three different types of simulations have been found:

Character Simulation: The simulation steers and controls the virtual character. A virtual character is sometimes also called non-player character or simply character. Often the virtual character is related with a two or three dimensional visual representation. The underlying models can be realized with quite different complexity, ranging from simple behavior models, over interaction models, up to complex communication models (see e.g. [36]). Simulation of a virtual character means model execution in a sense that the simulation part of the system takes over the control and steers the virtual character. The development of the character might be triggered by external inputs, e.g. another non-player, a real player, or changes in the game environment (e.g. in the virtual world). If the player steers or influences the development of a virtual character, the player can be seen as the 'human in the loop' which pushes the simulation forward. In a narrow sense, simulation of a character is no experiment on a model.

Simulation of the Environment: If the environment in a game-based training is based on a simulation, the game's progress is mainly steered by the simulation. Similar to the perspective mentioned above, the human player (in this case often a learner) takes over the role of 'human in the loop'. The player steers and guides the experiment. His decisions and his actions decide about the simulation's development and thus about the continuation of the game. Classical examples can be found in the military training domain. Another example are flight simulations, which are sometimes located at the border between actual emulations of airplains for serious training and more simple simulations for gaming purposes.

Simulation of other models: Instead of steering a character or steering the basic system functionality, simulation can also be integrated in teaching and training system for other purposes, i.e. for experimenting with models. Most simulations of this type can be found in teaching and training systems which have hardly any connection to gaming.

Regarding the three ways to use simulations in (game-based) teaching and training systems, another distinction, which shifts the focus a bit toward the role of the learner, can be made in the following way. Character simulations, simulations of the environment, and also simulations of other models are in most cases somehow influenced by the learner's interaction. Thus, all of these three are part of another category, which is:

Interactive Training Simulation: The learner interacts with existing, predefined models. Via interacting with the models the learner steers the simulation, either implicitly or explicitly. Interaction can take place at different levels. For example, the learner might have access to predefined model parameters. By changing the parameter values, the learner can experiment with the model and investigate changes in the model's behavior and thus in the simulation (e.g. [22]). If the construction of a model is the task of the learner (e.g. [26]), only parts of the model are predefined or roughly sketched (e.g. [45]).

This category is contrasted with another type of teaching and training system, the **demonstrative simulation**. This approach is not at all linked to game-based learning. Simulation in this context is only used to demonstrate how models behave over time. They can be used as tutorials, to show and explain experiments, and to explain the functioning of machines.

The different approaches of using simulations in teaching and training can be mixed, e.g. in a simulated setting, a virtual character might be embedded (e.g. [44]). Well known examples which are based on simulations are Sim City (http://www.simcity.ea.com), The Sims (http://www.simzone.de or http://thesims.ea.com), as well as several different Tycoon games (e.g. ZooTycoon, http://www.microsoft.com/games/zootycoon, or RailroadTycoon, http://www.railroadtycoon.de).

4   Learning, Motivation, and Transfer

Coming from pedagogy, social sciences, or psychology, a difficulty when dealing with concepts like "game-based learning" is the following: while doing a closer examination of the game-based aspects, the aspects of learning get out of focus and vice versa. What is the reason for this difficulty? There exist many different definitions of learning and of games. Often it seems like games and learning are contradicting each other. Some of these definitions are analyzed in the following. Afterward, some examples are given.

4.1   Learning or Playing?

Several researchers (e.g. [21], [16], [39]) try to describe games and playing. Summarizing, games and playing can be seen as consisting of the following aspects:

- Playing a game is associated with freedom. Games often take place outside of the ordinary life's restrictions and rules.
- Games are fictitious and symbolic. Playing thus means to accept or become part of the fiction and learn how to act and interact on the symbolic level.
- Playing sometimes allows a look behind the barriers of the innermost feelings of humans.
- Playing ends in itself – to play usually follows no other goal than simply to play.
- Games have rules.

In contrast to these aspects, learning seems to be something completey different (e.g. [43]):

- There is usually no stop in learning – the brain always learns. Some researchers even state that also the body always learns.
- Interpreted as knowledge acquisition, learning is focused and goal oriented.
- Learning can be formal, non-formal, and informal.
- From the pedagogical perspective, learning can be formalized: "learning" is perceived to consist of the learning objective, the learning process, and the learning result.
- In contrast to the last point, it is also agreed that learning itself cannot be determinated. There seems to be no causal connection of formalized aspects which could give the reason why learning took place.

Despite these opposite interpretations of playing and learning, many examples of game-based learning can be found, e.g. playful aspects of learning processes, or support of learning processes by integrating the motivating aspects of games. The following subsections will first show some examples, which combine both aspects. Subsequently the motivating factor of games and the transfer of knowledge will be described. Within this paragraph motivation is understood as the fundamental aspect of activation and maintenance of the learning process. Accordingly, transfer of knowledge is the basis to use acquired knowledge in other contexts.

4.2 Examples

There are several different areas, where game-based training systems and game-based learning can be found. These games are based on a pedagogical background and on didactic design with the aim to support knowledge acquisition in a context, which is likewise game oriented and rule based. One area for game-based learning is sports. Here, mainly psychomotorical competencies are trained (e.g. coordination of the own body in interaction with others), but also competencies regarding social interaction (e.g. team play) and emotional compensation (e.g. anger and frustration). Another area of successful application of game-based learning is language learning. Mainly knowledge regarding the language itself (vocabulary and grammar), but also psychomotoric knowledge (e.g. articulation) is trained (e.g. Nintendo Flash Focus or Ubisoft my French Coach for Nintendo DS). In game-based language learning approaches also social and emotional aspects can be trained, both regarding the language itself (e.g. expressiveness) and the psychomotoric knowledge (e.g. cultural dependent habits of articulation). Last but not least, role-play offers a quite natural combination of games with teaching and training. To act "as if" occurs in every stage of education, and even small children train social interaction and psychomotoric abilities in role-play. Taking over other than the well-known traditional roles allows testing and trying different behavior, to explore new situations, to train how to act and react. Vice versa, observing role-play can lead to conclusions about own behavior. For example watching kids acting as 'mom' and 'dad' can sometimes give the parents a hint about how they behave. In the save context of the game the exploration of strange, possibly new, and often unknown situations can take place, without danger. Sometimes, role-play opens the door to establishing new behavior or understanding.

Whereas the mentioned sports game is somewhat far away from computer game-based training, sometimes it has been claimed that hand-eye-coordination is an aspect which is trained in human-computer interaction. However, hand-eye-coordination is no substitute for real life sport – and is in most cases not intended to be. As mentioned above, language learning can easily be supported by a computer program – as has e.g. been done by [13]. Both, human-human interaction in the classroom and human-computer interaction in a program, are somewhat artificial compared to real experiences made when visiting the foreign country and actually speaking the language. Regarding role-play, the main difference between computer based and real life training maps the differences between human-human interaction and computer-human interaction in teaching and training. The competencies, which can be acquired in computer game-based trainings are similar. Interaction with virtual characters are no substitute for face-to-face communication. Research in the pedagogical field of how media affects humans, especially in investigation of commercials and children, has not revealed a generalizable causal dependency between using modern media and social misbehavior or misuse of power. However, one result of the investigation has been the insight that time-intensive interacting with virtual worlds leads to a shift in realizing the difference between fiction and reality, which then lead to actions which should better stay in the virtual world (e.g. [30]).

The question of how playing and also teaching and training with the computer can affect knowledge acquisition leads to two 'magic' words: motivation and transfer. The following subsections will explore these fields a bit further.

4.3 Magic of Motivation

To keep learners motivated is very important for successful teaching and training. The notion of success in this context means, that learners are able to reach a teaching and training goal, that they remember the content, and moreover, that they are able to transfer the learned content to other situations. To keep the motivation on a high level is a goal, which is extrinsically very difficult to reach. One important aspect of games, which should be transferred to teaching and training, is the high intrinsic motivation. In this context, the psychological, cultural, and pedagogical aspects of "play" are important to consider. This has been done for example by Caillois in [5] and will not be focused here. Unfortunately, a high motivation in the context of playing does not necessarily lead to a high motivation when it comes to teaching and training.

Where does the motivation in the context of game playing come from? The combination of several different aspects makes games interesting and helps to keep the motivation of the players at a high level. Games usually provide a large amount of interactivity. At least, there is the interactivity between computer (the game software) and the player. In more complex games, interaction between different player and probably also non-player characters is realized (e.g. World of Warcraft http://www.worldofwarcraft.com or http://www.wow-europe.com/en/). Each games has its rules, but to a certain amount the player has control and power. In games like Black & White (http://www.lionhead.com-/bw/index.html (developer) or http://blackandwhite2.ea.com/ (publisher)) the player even has some "god-like" powers of creation and destruction. Equally important is the symbolic form: a game allows the player to take over other identities, to become part of the game, and to play another than the everyday role. As symbolic forms, these identities fit to secret wishes and ideas – the symbolic characters offered in games are often similar to characters in movies or in tales. This "role playing" allows player to examine and to solve problems on a symbolic level. Likewise important is the adaptability of games. Usually, games provide levels of expertise, such that the player is seldom confronted with a boring (i.e. too easy) or annoying (i.e. too difficult) situation. Boring and annoying situations lower the level of motivation, thus game developers strive to avoid them. Similar relations between adaptation and motivation can also be found in teaching and training systems (e.g. see [20]). The technical realization of a computer game can also be fascinating and thus motivating. Modern technology offers a large amount of possibilities to construct virtual worlds, which are even able to reach different human senses.

During playing the game, a relation between computer and player is established. Via connecting the players senses structurally to the game, an autopoietic construction of sense leads to a focused awareness [48]. The player, who is not aware of this connection, feels a strong intention to understand the game, and is highly motivated. Intrinsic motivation and stimuli offered by the computer system alternate [48]. Moreover, certain aspects of games can raise the player's level of interest even before the actual interaction, for example the type of game (e.g. strategy), the game's context (e.g. fantasy), and, not to forget, the marketing (e.g. a game related to a famous movie, like "Lord of the Rings", e.g. http://lotr.ea.com or http://rotk.ea.com).

Similar to Wesener [48], Fritz [15] stated that the interests of the player and the offer of the computer game overlap, which results in a stimulation of the player. This stimulation optimally leads to positive emotions, but sometimes to negative emotions. Having success in a game is from the player's perspective often not related to certain actions. Success is even not related to knowledge acquisition regarding the game's content. Often the effective usage of rules and relations which are the basis of the game, is most important. This can for example lead to a situation where the player uses the game's rules in another way than intended by the game developer. Success is for example to outwit the game. Thus, for having the feeling of success in a game, it is for some players more important to understand rules and relations than to grasp the game's content. The motivation to play shifts toward a motivation to learn how to play.

4.4 Magic of Transfer

Whether knowledge can be transferred to another context or not, whether it can be applied in another than the teaching and training context, is a sign for the applicability of the knowledge and of what is really "learned". At a top level, passive knowledge can be distinguished from active knowledge. Passive knowledge is available, but has no potential applicability and often a lack of transferability. Active knowledge can actually be used, i.e. transferred and applied to other than the original context.

Not much research has taken place in the context of transfer and transferability of knowledge between virtual worlds and the real world, neither in computer game-based training nor in computer games. In contrast to this, the examination of the transfer of knowledge is essentially important to understand how modern media, computer games, and new teaching and training scenarios affect the learning process.

In the context of learning, transfer can be distinguished in intramondial and intermondial. Intramondial means for example to re-use knowledge acquired in one computer game in another game. Transfer takes place in a certain world, e.g. a virtual one. In contrast to this, intermondial, i.e. transfer between worlds, means to re-use knowledge in everyday life. This distinction is more obvious in an quite negative example. If the knowledge of usage of weapons is intramondial, than the player is able to successfully act in similar games in a similar way. If the knowledge becomes intermondial, the player learns how to use weapons in everyday life. Combined with a shift between reality and game, this might be a disastrous and murderous mixture [37]. However, this transfer is difficult to reach and, moreover, difficult to prove.

Wesener tries to categorize different transfer processes according to a category of computer games [48]. The three categories he suggests are based on the content, the graphic complexity, the player's perspective and the potential interaction, and also aspects like the player's perception and activity.

Micro-virtual game worlds provide a linear structure of content. Player and non-player characters are represented as figurative substitutes – interaction in the game world takes place via these substitutes. The perspective on the game situation is subjective, only the direct environment is visible. Examples are HalfLife (http://half-life.com/) and Tomb Raider (http://www.tombraider.com).

Meso-virtual game worlds provide a primarily linear structure with some not-linear parts (e.g. capsuled as missions). Most of the time, the game combines a figurative substitution with partly direct interactions, e.g. via menu structures. As the game world is more complex than the micro-virtual world, it is necessary to have more parts of the environment visible. Often, an isometric perspective is taken. Examples are Empire Earth (http://www.empireearth.com/) and Spellforce (http://spellforce.com/).

Macro-virtual game worlds are not bound to a linear structure, as the game world is complex enough to let the player explore the world on his own. Usually, direct identification takes place, i.e. no representative is given. In some games, game characters or figurative substitutes are offered. The perspective allows supervision of the complete world and switching between different views. Examples are Civilization 3 (http://www.civ3.com/), The Settlers 4 (http://www.thesettlers.com), and Anno 1503 (http://www.anno1503.com/)

These game worlds have different transfer processes, which can be distinguished according to Fritz [15] as:

- Fact level – transfer is mainly related to content and knowledge of facts. Examples are historical data and development, basic economic knowledge, knowledge from the field of natural sciences.
- Script level – allows mainly the transfer of plot, i.e. how to act and react in a certain situation. An example is start and landing of airplanes.
- Print level – at this transfer level, only single isolated actions or reactions without related meaning are transferred. Examples stem mainly from sports, like tricks in soccer play.
- Metaphoric level – transfer of symbolic presentations and hints. The player gets knowledge about how to handle for example standard icons, like the disc symbol for data storage, and small game sequences with hidden hints.
- Dynamic level – transfer of knowledge from a computer game to everyday life. Here, the overall topic of the game plays a certain role in the player's life, e.g. acceptance orders and rules, having power (or not), fighting, wining and loosing.

Combining the game categories mentioned above with the levels of transfer processes, this leads to the following. Micro-virtual worlds usually only support transfer at print and script level. Meso-virtual worlds add the fact level. Due to the partly open game structure, knowledge application and development of strategies are required and support the acquisition of cognitive competencies, which then support transfer of knowledge to real worlds. In macro-virtual worlds, the success in the game depends on the player's ability to understand and to apply rules and relations. These rules and relations are often not that far away from rules and relations in the real world. Thus, as a first step, knowledge from the real world is taken to perform in the virtual world – which is another form of transferring knowledge. As a next step, strategies from the real world are adapted to game situations and game context. In a third step, the adapted strategies and behavior developed due to new experiences in the game setting are transferred again, but now into the real world (dynamic level of transfer). Here again a transformation of the knowledge might be necessary.

5   Conclusion: Drawing Connections – Game-Based Learning

Computer games and computer game-based teaching and training systems have strongly influenced each other in the last years [44] (see: http://gamestudies. org/). Especially in the context of graphical interfaces or the human computer interface design, the influence becomes obvious. Similar to computer games, modern teaching and training systems offer elaborate and technically ambitious graphical interfaces, optically fascinating gadgets, life-like virtual characters, and complex and well designed navigation structures. In contrast, after several years of focusing the graphical user interface, computer game developers nowadays re-orientate toward establishing complex and demanding computer science techniques as the basis of their games. There, the insight has rooted that a game is only interesting for the long term when it provides interesting and continuously motivating interaction scenarios in addition to the nice user interface. As Prensky stated: "While eye candy is important for some things, most game designers tell you that it is the 'game play' that really make the difference in holding the players' attention and getting them to compete until they win." [34]. Whereas teaching and training system developers aim at aspects like motivation and interest, game designers strive to provide fine grained interaction and adaptation to make their games even more interesting and reactive. Nonetheless, even teaching and training system developers should not turn completely toward eye candy, but combine the best of both: complex and demanding interaction scenarios and the well designed interface.

How to keep a learner's motivation on a high level has been subject of investigation in the research field of teaching and training systems for quite a long time, and even longer in psychology (e.g. [2], [49]). As mentioned above, one important aspect is to have a teaching and training system which is flexible enough to adapt to the learner's current state of knowledge, to support the learner if necessary, and to raise the level of difficulty if required. Thus, the notion of adaptability is important in teaching and training systems. Additionally, it should be taken into account that there are different types of teaching and training strategies – not all of which lend themselves for establishing game-based approaches. Case-based training is traditionally close to game-based approaches and can easily use motivational aspects like adaptation and emotional involvement of the learner. One possibility might be to combine case-based and fact learning in a interlace process: start with case-based learning to make the subject interesting for the learner, continue with less game-oriented approaches, and shift again to game-based scenarios if the learner get's bored.

Regarding the distinction of micro-, meso-, and macro-worlds, a connection to simulation and artificial intelligence suggests itself (see section 3.2). In a micro-virtual world usually no simulation (see section 3.2) and usually no AI is required. Even the figurative substitutes of player and non-player characters need no simulation, as the based on the linear structure interaction is prescribed. The game scenario is linear, thus the model is fixed in advanced. If simulation is used at all it would be a demonstrative simulation. However, in most cases the focus of these games is not on an elaborate basic computer science technology but on a complex graphical interface. The meso-virtual and the macro-virtual worlds are the playgrounds for simulations. Whereas in the meso-virtual world in most cases the character simulation can occur, the macro-virtual world usually contains both, complex character simulations and simulations of the environment. Depending on the complexity of the game world, the simulated character's ability to act, to react, and to interact differ, as well as its adaptability to the learner. Accordingly, the transfer of knowledge might be influenced. If virtual characters are very simple, no complex interaction patterns have to be learned by the players. On the opposite, if the virtual characters are quite complex, providing a so called close to real life interaction, players might be in a situation where they have to use and apply knowledge of human interaction to the virtual character. Then, transfer on a dynamical level (in both directions as described above) takes place. Simulation of the environment and of other model can realize parts of a meso-virtual world (e.g. special engines or missions). They are mainly found in macro-virtual worlds, where in some cases the complete game can be seen as a simulation. Again, the intensity of transfer of knowledge between virtual and real world depends on how elaborate, interactive, and adaptive the environment or the other model has been developed. From the player's perspective, this means: how much prior knowledge is needed to act and interact in the virtual world, and vice versa, how much knowledge is acquired by acting and interacting in the virtual world.

Micro-worlds with their linear structure can also be located in game-based or game-like learning environments, e.g. in case-based training in clinical medicine. Going away from the linear structure, as for example done in Docs 'n Drugs [24], the teaching and training system is similar to a meso-world. Here, the micro- or meso-world is a close to real life world, in the examples a virtual hospital, where the learner as physician has to interact with a patient. In a micro-world situation, the learner has no choice to influence the linearity of the training case. In a meso-world situation, the learner can decide how to proceed. Whereas in the micro-world situation only one cognitive process is trained – the process of diagnostic reasoning – the meso-world situation allows additionally to train the cognitive process of general knowledge application (see [25]). The cognitive process of diagnostic reasoning is close to the above mentioned fact-level. The cognitive process of general knowledge application is related to the script level and to the dyamic level – i.e. how to act and react in close to real life situations and to successfully transfer this knowledge to everyday life. It would be a nice to construct a macro-world for interactive game-oriented learning in case-based situations, especially in training domains like clinical medicine. However, these macro-worlds are difficult to develop, as in serious teaching and training systems the requirements regarding realistic depiction of the real world are on a very high level. Moreover, it is difficult to realize didactically elaborate content in a macro-world. For example, Docs 'n Drugs started as something similar to a micro-world, has then be extended towards a meso-world, as the linear guidance of the learner has been loosened, and finally reached a level which is a step in the direction of a macro-world. However, whereas the technical software level had reached the level of a macro-world, the teaching and training content (i.e. the training cases) remained on the level of meso-worlds. An interesting observation in supervising the students learning with Docs 'n Drugs has been that to loosen the structure of the training case has raised the learner's motivation to successfully solve the training case.

In teaching and training systems, the focus is on learning rather than on having fun. But learning, especially based on a technology like computers, can be fun. This has impressively been shown by the gaming industry, and by teaching and training system developers like [36], which combined Hollywood like storytelling and storyboards with simulations to get a very complex teaching and training setting. Motivation in learning is often compared with motivation to reach the next level in a game ("leveling up" [35]). In contrast to this, goals of teaching and training and goals in a game are hardly comparable. Even if a separation of teaching and training goals into different levels is possible and might be useful, the goals in a game are in most certainly not pedagogical oriented and cannot be mapped to the teaching and training goals. Sure the player of a computer game learns as well, as sketched in section 4.4. In pedagogical as well as in game settings, the transfer of knowledge between a virtual and a real world requires transformation and, initially, evaluation and validation of the knowledge. Based on different intensities of sensual input, human beings are usually able to distinguish between real world and virtual world (see [48]). They are in most cases able to separate different levels of reality. However, the question remains, which of these transfer processes can be used to successfully support learning processes. Research in this direction should follow.

References

1. Aldrich, C.: Six Criteria of an Educational Simulation (download 2004) (last visited March 2008),
   http://www.e-learningcentre.co.uk/eclipse/Resources/simulation.htm
2. Anderson, J.R.: Cognitive psychology and its implications. Worth Publishers, New York (2000)
3. Blackman, S.: Serious games... and less! SIGGRAPH Comput. Graph. 39(1), 12–16 (2005)
4. Bopp, M.: Didactical Analysis of Digital Games and Game-Based Learning. In: Pivec, M. (ed.) Affective and Emotional Aspects of Human-Computer Interaction (2006)
5. Caillois, R.: Man, Play, and Games. University of Illinois Press, Paperback Edition (2001)
6. Cellier, F.: Continuous Systems Modeling. Springer, New York (1991)
7. Chaitin, J.: Stories, Narratives, and Storytelling. In: Beyond Intractability (last visited March 2008),
   http://www.beyondintractability.org/essay/narratives/
8. Cincinnati Classical Public Radio Inc.: Classics for kids (last visited March 2008), at http://www.classicsforkids.com/

9. Compigs. Grundschuldatenbank - Spiele zur Lehre und zum Lernen. (download August 2005) (last visited March 2008), http://www.compigs.de/grundschuldatenbank/
10. Diener, H., Schumacher, H.: Game Based Interfaces. In: Short Presentation for Eurographics, Manchester, pp. 59–64 (2001)
11. Dörr, K., Schiefele, J., Kubbat, W.: Virtual Simulation for Pilot Training. In: Human Factors & Medicine Panel, NATO's Research & Technology Organization (RTO), Den Haag, The Netherlands (2000)
12. Dyck, J., Pinelle, D., Brown, B., Gutwin, C.: Learning from Games: HCI Design Innovations in Entertainment Software. In: Proceedings of the Conference on Human-Computer Interaction and Computer Graphics, Halifax (2003)
13. Felix, U.: Beyond Babel: Language Learning Online. Language Australia Ltd. (2001)
14. Frasca, G.: Ludology meets Narratology, http://www.ludology.org/articles/ludology.hmtl (1999) (download August 2005) (last visited March 2008), http://www.ludology.org/my_articles.html
15. Fritz, J.: Zur Landschaft der Computerspiele. In: Fritz, J., Fehr, W. (eds.) (Hrsg.): Handbuch Medien: Computerspiele (1997)
16. Fritz, J.: Das Spiel verstehen. Eine Einführung in Theorie und Bedeutung. Juventa (2004)
17. Gage, N.L., Berliner, D.C.: Educational Psychology. 4th edn., pp. 12–31. Houghton Mifflin, Boston (1988)
18. Gamecraft. Mathespiele (last visited March 2008), http://www.gamecraft.de/
19. Gebel, C., Gurt, M., Wagner, U.: Kompetenzförderliche Potenziale populärer Computerspiele. Studie des Instituts für Medienpädagogik in Forschung und Praxis (December 2005)
20. Harrer, A., Martens, A.: Adaptivität in e-Learning-Standards - ein vernachlässigtes Thema? In: Proc. der DeLFI 2004, 2.Deutsche e-Learning Fachtagung der Gesellschaft für Informatik, Paderborn, September 5-8, 2004, pp. 163–174 (2004)
21. Huizinga, J.: Homo ludens. Vom Ursprung der Kultur im Spiel. 19. Aufl. Rowohlt (2004)
22. Kinshuk, Oppermann, R., Rashev, R., Simm, H.: Interactive Simulation Based Tutoring System with Intelligent Assistance for Medical Education. Ed-Media, 715–720 (1998)
23. Kühnapfel, U.G., Cakmak, H.K., Maass, H.: 3D Modeling for Endoscopic Surgery. In: Proc. of the IEEE-SB Symposium on Simulation (1999)
24. Martens, A., Bernauer, J., Illmann, T., Seitz, A.: Docs 'n Drugs - The Virtual Polyclinic. In: Proc. of the American Medical Informatics Conference 2001, AMIA 2001, pp. 433–437 (2001)
25. Martens, A.: Ein Tutoring Prozess Modell für fallbasierte Intelligente Tutoring Systeme. DISKI 281. AKA Verlag infix, Germany (2004)
26. Martens, A., Himmelspach, J.: Combining Intelligent Tutoring and Simulation Systems. In: Proc. of the Internat. Conference on Simulation in Human Computer Interfaces, SIMCHI, Part of the Western Multi Conference WMC 2005, New Orleans, USA (January 2005)
27. Martens, A.: Simulation in Teaching and Training. In: Tomei, L. (ed.) Encyclopedia of Information Technology Curriculum Integration. IGI Global (2008)
28. McLaren, B.M., Koedinger, K.R., Schneider, M., Harrer, A., Bollen, L.: Toward Cognitive Tutoring in a Collaborative Web-based Environment. In: Proc. of the Workshop on Adaptive Hypermedia and Collaborative Web-based Systems (AHCW) (2004)

29. Merseth, K.: The Early History of Case-Based Instruction. Journal of Teacher Education 42(4), 243–249 (1991)
30. Pfeiffer, C., Windzio, M., Kleimann, M.: Kriminalität, Medien und Öffentlichkeit. Medientenor Forschungsbericht Nr.148 (2004)
31. Prensky, M.: Digital Natives, Digital Immigrants. On the Horizon - NCB University Press 9(5) (October 2001)
32. Prensky, M.: Game-Based Learning. McGraw-Hill, New York (2001)
33. Prensky, M.: True Believers: Digital Game-Based Learning in the Military (2001) visited (2006),
    http://www.learningcircuits.org/2001/feb2001/prensky.html
34. Prensky, M.: A Military Field and Training Game Developer Corps (2002) (download August 2005), http://www.marcprensky.com
35. Prensky, M.: Complexity Matters. Educational Technology 45(4) (July-August 2005)
36. Rickel, J., Gratch, J., Hill, R., Marsella, S., Swartout, W.: Steve goes to Bosnia: Towards a New Generation of Virtual Humans for Interactive Experiences. In: Proceedings of the AAAI-SS 2005, Spring Symposium on Artificial Intelligence and Interactive Entertainment (March 2001)
37. Rötzer, F.: Die Wahrheit über das Massaker in Erfurt. Telepolis vom 29.04.2002 (download January 2006),
    http://www.heise.de/tp/r4/artikel/12/12432/1.html
38. Salen, K., Zimmermann, E.: Rules of Play. Game Design Fundamentals. MIT Press, Cambridge (2003)
39. Scheuerl, H.: Das Spiel. Untersuchungen über sein Wesen, seine pädagogischen Möglichkeiten und Grenzen. Beltz (1994)
40. Schulmeister, R.: Grundlagen hypermedialer Lernsysteme. Oldenbourg Verlag, München, Wien, 2te. Auflage (1997)
41. Shin, N., Norris, C., Soloway, E.: Effects of handehld games on students learning mathematics. In: International Conference on Learning Sciences, Proc. of the 7th International Conference, pp. 702–708 (2006)
42. Smith, R.: Game Impact Theory: The Five Forces that are Driving the Adoption of Game Technologies within Multiple Established Industries. In: Games and Society (2007) (last visited March 2008),
    http://www.modelbenders.com/papers/Smith_Game_Impact_Theory.pdf
43. Spitzer, M.: Lernen. Gehirnforschung und die Schule des Lebens. Spektrum (2002)
44. Squire, K.: Game-based Learning - An X-Learn Perspective Paper. e-Learning Consortium (download August 2005), http://www.masie.com/xlearn/
45. Steed, M.B.: STELLA - A Simulation Construction Kit. Journal of Computers in Mathematics and Science Teaching 11(1), 39–52 (1992)
46. Steinkuehler, C.A.: Cognition and learning in Massively Multiplayer Online Games: A critical Approach. University of Wisconsin, Madison (2005)
47. The Sims: Computer Games (last visited April 2008), http://www.simszone.de/ and http://thesims.ea.com/
48. Wesener, S.: Spielen in virtuellen Welten. Verlag für Sozialwissenschaften (2004)
49. Zimbardo, P.G., Weber, A.L.: Psychology. 2nd edn. Longman, New York (1997)

Core Attributes of Interactive Computer Games and Adaptive Use for Edutainment

Myint Swe Khine[1] and Mohamad Shalleh Bin Suja'ee[2]

[1] Emirates College for Advanced Education, United Arab Emirates
mskhine@ecae.ac.ae
[2] Ministry of Education, Singapore
Mohamad_Shalleh_SUJA'EE@moe.gov.sg

Abstract. Playing computer games is a routine activity of children today. They play different genres of games in different settings and on varying platforms. In recent years educators beginning to take interest in this phenomena and explore the characteristics of the computer games that allure children of all ages. Many have agreed that interactive computer games enhance concentration, promote critical thinking, increase motivation and encourage socialisation. This paper examines the core attributes of some of the interactive computer games and suggests how these attributes can be adapted in the lessons as edutainment that can captivate and delight the students in day-to-day teaching in the classrooms.

Keywords: computer games, edutainment, learning, design, gameplay.

1 Introduction

The term "Edutainment" has been used since in 1970s to indicate the use of computer games partly educational and to some extent entertaining [1]. Recent research on computer games suggests that children and youths enjoy playing different genre of games and this activity become significant part of their daily life. There are gamers who play massive multilevel online role play games (MMORG) and also there are gamers who play with traditional stand-alone devices. Whichever platforms they choose to play these gamers spend considerable amount of their time in accomplishing the tasks set out by the game designers. Green and McNeese [2] suggest the characteristics of high quality games and promote its use to supplement the school curriculum.

Gee [3] also proposed that the design of the good quality games involve high degree of interaction, encourage exploration through rewards, and demand creativity. Besides the educational component is always a hidden agenda. Hutchison [4] explores the design of computer games and recommends some strategies for incorporating them into educational programs. However some educators warned that improper use of games can be harmful to the learners [5].

2 Interactive Games in Education

Kirriemuir & McFarlane [6] described that the use of games in education are still a relatively new phenomenon. However, teachers and parents recognize the fact that

Z. Pan et al. (Eds.): Transactions on Edutainment I, LNCS 5080, pp. 191–205, 2008.

gameplay can support skills such as strategic thinking, planning, communicating, negotiation skills, group decision-making and data-handling. They also observe that games promote higher levels of attention and concentration among students. There is a widespread view among educators that computer games can be a powerful tool if we can exploit the affordances and harness the application in classroom settings.

Shaffer [7] argues the need to foster rigorous learning for innovative work and he believes that technology can make this possible for students of all ages in preparing such skills. These technologies include computer games and simulations. He found that contemporary computer games are engaging and motivating to young people. In introducing digital games in learning, Pivec [8] raised questions on how the teachers can use in their teaching, under what circumstances is the game is good and efficient instructional strategy for supporting knowledge acquisition and how the teacher can support cognitive processes within this learning environment. Gee [9] has a strong view that good computer games can promote good learning. He pointed out that computer games are good if we play with thought, reflection and engagement with the world around us. He also think that computer games hold great potential for transformation of learning, changing how people think, value and live [10].

Brown [11] in his article discussed the use of games in the new learning environments for the 21st century. He noted that teaching new generation of students or digital native requires different sets of skills. He suggests that one way to find out how these students learn and how do they like to learn is to look at the computer and computer games. In this situation students immerse themselves in a complex, information-rich, dynamic environment where they must make sense, infer, decide and act quickly in order to win the race. Just-on-time decision making skills are important part of the game play. Paras & Bizzocchi [12] highlighted that game environments support immersive learning experience. They use flow theory to explain the potential of integrating games in the learning process. They argued that games produce a state of flow, which increases motivation and in turn support the learning process.

3   Computer Game Design and Adaptive Use for Edutainment

Over the last few decades educators have been interested in exploring the affordance of the computer games and how these can be used as part of the edutainment. Therefore it is worthwhile to explore the affordances of the games, examine the attributes and transform them into the teaching strategies. The following paragraphs enumerate the core attributes of interactive computer games and adaptive use for edutainment.

3.1   Capturing Learner's Interest

In every lesson, an introduction is important. Teacher needs to excite the children with some novelty to capture their attention. These can be in the form of interesting story, suspense and excitement. Quest Atlantis (http://atlantis.crlt.indiana.edu/) is a learning and teaching game that was created in 3D multi-user platform for the children ages 9-12 to engage in educational tasks. The developers of this game combine the educational theories and commercial game design knowledge and thus the program is educational and entertaining. The program allows the user to travel to virtual places with the aim of performing educational activities, communicate with other users, and build virtual identity. *Quest Atlantis* game was introduced as:

> *You may have heard of the legendary Atlantis, the island paradise that sank beneath the sea. For me your legend is more than just a story. In the distant solar system much like our own is the planet of Atlantis. Thousands of years ago a portal appeared between our planets and yours. Through this portal, my ancestors visited your's and shared our knowledge and culture. ...*
>
> *..... With the hope that we can make a difference, we formed a Council. We are small group that secretly work our Quest to rebuild the Atlantis. We use a special computer called the Otak to reconnect with the people of Earth. Each Council member using their own passions and knowledge has developed a virtual world in the Otak. The Council hopes that you will explore these places and share what you have learnt. To share your wisdom you can help us to help ourselves. Hurry Questers, we can not do this alone. Please work with the Council and with each other to save Atlantis and to avoid what may be our common fate.*

The above narration mixed with 3D graphics and music excites the students and arouses the curiosity. In computer games, instructions are given to the player in an interesting manner and inspire them to proceed. In *Quest Atlantis* learners are immersed in meaningful inquiry quest, often engaged in social interaction in forging collaboration to gather information on social and environmental issues to enlighten the citizens of planet Atlantis on how to build their lost world [13].

In many computer games players pursue the ultimate objectives through struggle, cooperation, or simply from engaging in social interaction with others, and all these build-up to a climatic finish. The goals are further layered into very short-term goals, medium-term goals and long-term goals. This is engineered to keep the students in alignment and focus on the higher purpose, and provide them with a sense of achieving "little victories" upon successfully completing these goals so they will be spurred on to overcome more difficult task.

While learning about geometry or circuits in computer games, students find themselves engage in a more fulfilling and meaningful pursuit that often requires them to "be the hero" by carry out complex task [14]. In *City of Heroes*, students are called upon to a place where everybody can be hero. In *Harry Potter and the Prisoner of Askaban*, students are urged to help Harry fights against the evil forces. And in the *Rise of Nations*, students are reminded how they are instrumental in helping save the entire human history. By linking the purpose of learning to a compelling cause at the same time making students "be the hero", students will be intrinsically motivated to learn even the most factual and dry subject.

Fig. 1. A player takes up a protagonist role (right) to keep the town free from criminals in *City of Heroes*

3.2 Anchoring Content to Reality

One of the features a player senses from playing computer games is that these are designed with the bias that requires the player to learn multiple skills, demonstrate the ability to research and collaborate with others players in order to be successful at playing. Often the players will find having to draw from relevant life experiences and perhaps some learning in school, and turn these into tools to help them overcome every obstacle they face. Those who fall short in these are compel to do their own research or learn from their peers. Failing to do this well entails them the prospect of being pushed out, an eventuality that no player can conceive after going through exciting experience from playing the game.

In other words, as they successfully progress from level to level, they would have acquired so much knowledge and skills across many disciplines, and gained an enhanced understanding from the authentic application of the knowledge and skills gained.

A classic example of such features can be found in the game *RuneScape* (www.runescape.com), a fantasy-themed world filled with several kingdoms, regions and cities. Players travel across various regions that offer different types of monsters and materials and engage in quest for meaningful play. To be successful in their quests, players need equipments and resources that can be obtained from trading. Players put on sale materials they obtained from questing for in-game currency and use them to purchase equipments in the market area called *The Grand Exchange*.

Prices of items traded fluctuate according the law of supply and demand. A successful player is also one who is competent in trading for profit. Some players with higher level specific skills like crafting advertise crafting services to players with inferior level crafting skills for payments in the game forum. Others form a group and may offer similar or other services to new players and also actively recruit new "workers", very much like how a company with considerable number of employees operates in the real world.

In this game kids as young as 10 year old are playing a typical in-game mini-economy. Upon successful completion of the game, a 10-year-old would have learnt economics lessons on the supply chain, division of labor, value added, supply and demand, business structure, control, human resource and management, wealth creation, capital building, corruption, business ethic, communication, and management training.

Fig. 2. How player put up a diamond for sale in *The Grand Exchange* in *Runscape*

When teaching teacher must relate the subject matter and how knowledge and skill that they learnt from the lesson can be applied real life situation. Just like in computer games, we need to draw lessons from all our life experiences and learning, and turn them into tools to help us prevail over life challenges. Skills and concepts learnt in school are often memorized with the hope of finding opportunity to apply them later in life, rather than to be learnt to apply them as tools to solve challenges for knowledge also resides in the context where they are used [15]. This realization has encouraged many educators to gear their lessons more toward problem-based centered, or work with fellow colleagues to present a more interdisciplinary approach in learning.

Teachers will find that every student is unique not only in their learning styles, but also in their neurological make up and diverse background, mould by race, culture and economic standing. Our brain is continuously engage in meaning making of the things that we learn and how we are applying them, and this process is mediated by our unique neurophysiology and experience [16]. How can we teach the curriculum in a class of 40 with unique neurological and life experience? It is possible to provide personalised instruction for every student or group the students with similar learning styles and life experience. However a more practical and less problematic approach is to adopt a interdisciplinary curriculum in order to respond to student diversity in all its forms.

Barab & Young [17] researched on the impact of anchors in instructional practice using a computerized lesson *Rescuing Rocky* that was developed applying the principle of anchored instruction. Their findings concurred with the study done by the Cognition and Technology Group at Vanderbilt University that indicated that "carefully design anchor help students to learn techniques, fact, and ideas in long-term and transferable ways" [15]. Furthermore, students scored higher on achievement test when compared to those who experience instruction without anchor, and more importantly they were able to make "connections among various disciplinary concepts, even seeing relations between the computerized lesson and other lessons, and between lesson and personal experiences" [17]. Carefully designed anchor should be able to capture the imagination, be perceived as important by learners, legitimize the disciplinary content they integrate, and accommodate a variety of learning approaches.

The advantage of anchoring content to reality is that teachers can present the curriculum in a multidisciplinary and problem-based approach. This approach provides a more authentic and better way of learning that would promote transfer of knowledge. Students will be able to see more relevance and connection in what they learn to their daily experience. They will be more motivated to learn and to participate actively regardless of their entry level competency and learning style.

3.3 Creating Learner Puzzlement

In a pursuing a compelling and worthwhile goals that build-up to a climatic finish, players are often confronted with challenges, puzzles and quests in computer games. For example, in a journey to the land of Aio, in the *Rise of Nations: Rise of Legends*, players embroil in an epic struggle between the forces of Magic and Technology. However, the gameplay involves more that just action in battlefields as players, guiding a young inventor's struggle to unravel his world's ancient past and unite its people against an inconceivable danger, have to brazen out challenges concern with loyalty and betrayal in a new world of heroes and monsters. In *Puzzle Quest: Challenge of the Warlord*, players have to create, develop and customize the ultimate hero to save the land of Etheria from the evil Lord Bane. In a multiplayer mode, players forge cooperation and take turn to overcome puzzle style games consisting of many challenging quests.

Challenges, puzzles and quests are not only instrumental in learning, but they are also important features in computer games [18]. Bates [19] indicated that they form the foundation of gameplay design. While learner puzzlement seems to be a common feature in many learning institutions and computer games, a closer examination reveals some disparity on how it is carried out. For problem-based learning approach to promote effective learning, authentic problem solving activities and access to wide

Fig. 3. A screenshot of a battle in *Rise of Nations: Rise of Legends*

range of data are essential components. In computer games the problem solving activities are wide range and plenty as player progress from level to level, working through achieving the short-term goals, medium-term goals and eventually, the long-term goals. Furthermore, the problem solving activities are graded in difficulty in line with the level progression (i.e. higher level will have more difficult activities as compared to lower level), and this is done on purpose to develop prayers with better skills or acquire more concepts, while maintaining their interest by keeping the activities challenging. Whereas in classroom that adopts problem-based learning approach, the lesson objective often sits on one problem solving activity, often very challenging and even if it seems to suggest that there other smaller and less difficult activities that built up to the main activity, they are usually not structured in the lesson or made explicit to the students (i.e. students are left to figure them out).

Amory [18] explained two theoretical arguments why challenges, puzzles and quests serve well as learning tools. Firstly he used Vygotsky's [20] Zone of Proximal Development that described "the distance between the actual development level as determined by independent problem solving and the level of potential development as determined through problem solving under adult guidance or in collaboration with more capable peers". So a well-designed computer game serves appropriately as the mentor or capable peers ("teacher") to help players move from their actual development level to their level of potential development [9].

Secondly, he explained that challenges, puzzles and quests in computer games are authentic examples for the realisation of flow taken from Csikszentmihalyi's [21] flow theory. Csikszentmihalyi detailed that a flow state is where you will find a person to be in the optimal state of intrinsic motivation. He will be giving focused attention, fully immersing himself in the thing that he does, without giving any attention to temporal concerns (like food, time, ego-self, etc) and how time flies. To achieve the flow state, a balance needs to be strike between the challenge of task and the skill of the person. If the task is too difficult or too easy, the flow cannot happen. While we may acknowledge experiencing a flow state during our schooling days, the feeling did not happen by default the moment we sat in class for lesson. But the moment our students start playing computer games, we start losing them for they are exhilarated by the flow.

According to Amory [18] "challenges-puzzles-quests appear to be the core of leaning activities associated with immersive learning environment where accommodation, assimilation, and puzzlement are supported through excess of explicit knowledge, conversations, and reflection and result in the construction of tacit knowledge after a flow state". By structuring plenty, wide range and graded problem solving activities, and tying progression to the next level to student being successful in completing the activities, educators are able to guide their students to acquire complex concepts and more than that, will result in the construction of tacit knowledge.

3.4 Providing Generous Choices

In solving challenges, puzzles and quests in computer games, players are often confronted with a number of choices to take. For instance, they have to choose a character (e.g. profession, race, etc) from dozens of choices that their avatar will be clothed in, and to what or who do they pledge alliance with (e.g. religion, guild, good or dark sides, etc), as skills and ability are distributed over different characters and interacting with people with a variety of different skills is crucial to be successful in playing the game. Then, they will have to make up their mind which path to take from a number of choices. By taking any of these choices, the players will find different scenario unfold before them.

To progress to the next level, it is instrumental that they make the right decision. While making the right choice will increase their chance of doing well, less than perfect decision will certainly hasten their demise in the game. These choices are equally difficult to decide upon and often they present as ethical dilemmas. What will be the consequences of my action? Should I take this path if there is a chance of success but at the risk of losing half of my team?

A successful player is a thinking player who will not leave his fate to chance by just choosing at random any choice. He will use the few seconds he has in his hand to weigh the pros and cons of each choices with regards to his strengths or weaknesses, his short-term objectives and long-term goals. Upon being successful in the activity, he will again be confronted with a number of choices in the next activity and subsequently in all the activities in every level of the game. Again, he will have to be careful and will weigh all the choices he has, thinking through what decision to make.

In an hour of playing, a player can find himself going through dozens of activities where he is called upon to decide what course of action to take. In each occasion, he has to draw from his intelligent and experience playing the game, be intuitive and envisage what will happen if he were to take any of the choices present before him, narrow his choices through self-rationalization on his stand mentally, and decide on the one and only life-saving choice to take. All these stimulate his thinking.

For example, In *Toontown* (www.toontown.com) players have to decide with who they feel most suitable to work with to form a lethal team, complementing on each other strength to defeat higher-level cogs. Choosing the wrong members can lead to total annihilation of the whole team. In *America's Army Operation*, potential recruits are taught more than just military doctrine, but also strategy and tactics of military confrontation. According to Prensky [22], many computer games designers see computer games as "a series of interesting and important decisions leading to a satisfying conclusion".

Fig. 4. Basic training to prepare player for real battle situations in *America's Army Operation*

In many schools, however, most of the decisions of what to do and how to go about with learning are already taken care of by the teachers. Students are told what they have to do for their intellectual well-being and to deviate from the instructions will only be detrimental to their learning. Their chance to stimulate thinking through decision making, if present, often will be few and far between and will likely be confined to limited choices like which mathematical formula to choose from in solving a mathematical problem or which text-type to use to best explain their ideas. Debates laden with ethical dilemma are most likely to surface in discussions over human-linked issues in language class. How is it possible for the mind to remain agile in classroom if the time between decisions can often be measure in hours?

Student needs to be encouraged to explore learning issues in multiple role-plays, and solve problems using unorthodox way and out-of-the-box thinking. Providing more autonomy for students to choose their learning path and consider multiple solving paths in working out authentic, multi-disciplinary, problem-based activities, will stimulate their thinking [14].

3.5 Focusing on the Flow

In extending the discussion on Csikszentmihalyi's *flow theory*, it is worth repeating that the flow state comes about from balancing the challenge of task and skill of learner. Prensky [22] brought up the concept of *adaptivity* and *levelling-up* to show how this is done in computer games.

The concept of *adaptivity* in computer games serves to keep a player in a flow state. Computer game has a built-in intelligence system that can senses player ability and allows playing experience that is neither too hard nor too easy for him. How this is done? A simplistic way of explaining this is as follow (although there is a more complex algorithm at play for more complex system). When a player is progressing faster than an average time taken to complete a particular level, the intelligence system senses that the quest is likely to be easy. The intelligence system will then present a slightly more challenging quest, monitor again the time taken by the player to complete the challenge, and work out again the difficulty level for the next quest.

When the intelligence system senses that the task is too difficult for the player, it will then give him more "power-ups" (e.g. more powers or ammunition), provide computer-generated allies to help overcome the more dangerous or difficult characters or situation, or present him with easier quest. This process of monitoring and accommodating challenge of the quest with the skill of the player as he moves from level to level in the game takes place throughout the game.

Levelling-up in essence means to progress to a higher level in the game. Players often get a sense of immense pleasure in getting better and better at playing and the number of levels chalk up serves to remind them how far they have progressed. Many players who have move to higher level will start the game with a new character just to see how good they are now at competing the lower level activities faster than before. This feeling of pleasure from *levelling-up* keeps player in the flow state.

Other discernible features of computer games design that are relevant to keep the player focus on the game are the way instruction is convey and learner accessing task. In school, when visual presentations are played to illustrate key concepts, they often run into 5-10 minutes movies. In computer games however, they come under 30 seconds. Also, instructions are conveyed verbally and in text during lesson in class, whereas in computer games, a multi-modalities approach is adopted. *Quest Atlantis*, an educational game, starts off with a movie introduction just like in the computer games *Rise of Nation: Rise of Legends* to present the context of learning. Subsequent instructions come in text, audio and graphics. In school, students are also accustomed to do all tasks in order. In computer games, learners have random access to all tasks.

Educators can consider providing students with random access to all tasks and to design wide ranging learning activities that not only accommodate different entry competency but also varying students progression rate. Instructions have to be presented using multi-modalities and "just enough" approach – not to lengthy that will bore student and at the same time not too little that provide vague description, but just right. Teachers should also develop strategies to celebrate successful completion of every level by students. A habit that is celebrated is a habit that gets repeated. While making public announcement for successful endeavour may be the most convenient and rational thing to do, this approach has it shortcoming too. Successful student will definitely be spurred to work hard, however those who only manage incremental progress are likely to feel that they are being highlighted unintentionally, and thus feel uneasy. Teachers need to be careful and be more creative.

3.6 Encouraging Collaboration

Collaboration is an instrumental component in learning, and this argument can be found in many contemporary theories of learning [23]. The advent of Internet helps to firmly establish collaboration as an integral part of computer games design by moving computer games from an individual-centric activity to a more social activity where many people meet online and solve quests together. Barab (2005) even argued that challenges, puzzles and quests in computer games not only support learning but afford learners a platform to collaborate in promoting social agenda.

Today, there are two types of multiplayer computer games; "multiplayer" and "massively multiplayer" computer games [22]. "Multiplayer" computer games confine interactions among members in the same team and these interactions exist only during play time. An example is the America's Army. In "massively multiplayer" computer games, players can interact with anyone they meet in the ongoing game world. Computer games like *Lineage, EverQuest, Asheron's Call* and *Dark Age of Camelot* serve good examples. *Lineages* for instance, boasts of having over 4 million registered users and often up to a million players are engaged in playing at any one time.

It is not an easy task for educators to get students to collaborate online even if they were to structure task that requires students to collaborate. Often, online discussions lack in rigor and depth to promote dialogic dimension of learning , and certain considerations and practices that work with one group of students are found lacking when employ with other groups. While there are broad issues that need to be worked out first in collaborative online learning environments, specific issues peculiar to a particular context can be discerned from observing group social dynamics in order to have a better likelihood for rigorous and meaningful interactions among learners online.

Using social network analysis tool to undercover the dynamics of interaction, it was found that low-interactivity resulted in a lack of reciprocity [18]. Jones & Issroff [24] put forth the issues of time, distribution of control, the nature of task, social affinity and development of a community to support "safe-for-learning" or "safe-for-disclosure" interactions as important considerations to encourage high-interactivity. Apart from providing the tools to enrich social networks (e.g. computer mediated tools), there is a need to provide network actors with tools to visualise their status within the network and to serendipitously bump into each other (e.g. broadcasts their intended activities and locations using SMS, IM, online journal and email) so as to extend their social network [25].

Veermans and Caserani [26] suggested that in order to support collaboration, activities must be structured and learners have to be informed and be made to understand the pedagogical considerations why learners must work together. Learners have the tendency to revert to the least demanding and easy approach to learning because of their understanding that learning is all about comprehension and memorization [27] or they will break up the task and just concentrate on their share of the task, if the pedagogical considerations why collaboration is necessary are not impressed upon them.

In computer games, there is a phenomenon that players not only interact on strategies online but offline. Dickey [28] discovered that in "massively multiplayer" online computer games players became so absorb in "complex, ill-structured, dynamic and evolving systems" suggesting that the focus of the computer games is primarily on the activity and not on the informational content. This finding suggests that there is a fine line that links all the lessons together in term on how content, learning activities and interactions are designed and packaged. The package that comes close to offer similar learning experience as computer games has the power to draw learners together to collaborate in carrying out the learning task, even extending the collaboration offline.

Learning is a social practice and dialogue is the foundation of social constructivism [18]. Educators who leverage on computer games design in teaching and learning do not see games as designed object but as a social practice. To be successful in promoting students to collaborate online, educators need to appreciate the intricacies of social dynamics and be well-versed with issues concerning contemporary collaborative online learning environment. They should work out the broad and specific issues in collaborative online learning environments, and in doing so they will find that their students will be engaged in dialogic dimension of learning online which is the starting tool for collaboration.

3.7 Promoting Creativity

With the advancement in communication and computer technologies the world economic structure is shifting from individual states to globalization and knowledge-based society. Innovations and creative spirit are highly desirable in order to attain the competitive edge [29]. Jobs in the future will demand more creativity and problem solving skills and those who can handle multi-tasks will have an advantage.

Helping students find their creative centre cannot happen in a vacuum as this is only possible in the context where students are allowed to create something. When students have the opportunity to create, they will experience a more active and experiential learning. Students are more likely to be motivated to take part for it allows learning to take place in a participatory framework, and affords them ownership of their design and creation. Learning activities that permits multiple problem solving approaches will challenge student creativity and ingenuity. In computer games design, students have the opportunity to create artifacts and share or sell their creations. In the *Monkey Wrench Conspiracy*, to be successful in rescuing Copernicus station from alien hijackers, players must design everything they need for the job, starting with a simple trigger for their gun to more sophisticated combat tools using a CAD programme. In *Quest Atlantis*, learners have many opportunities to build objects and fill their personal space in the immersive world with their creative creations.

Educators need to structure their learning activities with multiple problem solving approaches in a context of active, experiential and participatory learning, that allow students to create and have ownership of their own their design and creations. In doing so they will help their students discovered their creative centres.

4 Conclusion

The above examples illustrated the core attributes of the educational games that can be used as for edutainment in any classroom situations. We have examined some of the edutainment games and analyze the structures to find out how the game design captures the learner's interest and situate the content in real settings. When the students see the relevance of the materials that connects to their daily life they tend to participate actively in the learning process. Students also take more interests in the topic if it is presented in inquiry mode. Students come from the varying background and experience and they should be allowed to progress their learning at their own pace. Therefore having ample opportunity to choose the type of content, level of difficulty and mode of participation are important elements in lesson preparation. It is clear that such characteristics are prevalent in game designs.

Another factor that holds the attention and maintains the interest of the user is the ability to balance the challenge of task and skill of the user. In game situation varying level of difficulty is made available to hold the user and stay in the game. The games involve higher order skills that requires the player think strategically, analyze the opponent's characteristics and draw a strategy to win over. It also entails management of complex tasks and responds to rapidly changing situation and making swift and timely decisions. The main purpose of edutainment is to promote student learning through exploration, collaborative interaction and repetition with trial and error which make the learner fun [30].

The challenges lie ahead for educational institutions are to draw strategies and transform the traditional approaches to the adoption of new technology and redesigning the new learning model. Current research about how students learn is shifting to social constructivist approach and insight gains from the game design could help the learning situation more conducive, persuasive and productive. A number of higher learning institutions are setting up game design laboratories where experts in game design, digital artists, computer programmers and educational researchers work collaboratively with the aim of infusing edutainment into the curriculum [31][32][33].

We need to consider the fact that there is a significant change in the characteristics of children today as compared to those a decade ago. Children today are technology savvy and more exposed to all forms of communication media. They are discovering new things in their own environment as much as they learn in schools. While teachers are trying their best to gain attention from the students, traditional approach may not work with this generation of children. It is hoped that edutainment can help the teachers in engaging their students in day-to-day lessons.

References

1. Engenfeldt-Nielsen, S.: Third generation educational use of computer games. Journal of Educational Multimedia and Hypermedia 16(3), 264–281 (2007)
2. Green, M., McNeese, N.: Using edutainment software to enhance online learning. International Journal of E-Learning 6(1), 5–16 (2007)
3. Gee, J.P.: What video games have to teach us about learning and literacy. Palgrave MacMillan, New York (2003)
4. Hutchison, D.: Video games and the pedagogy of place. The Social Studies, 35–40 (January/February 2007)

5. Okan, Z.: Edutainment: Is learning at risk? British Journal of Educational Technology 34(3), 255–264 (2003)
6. Kirriemuir, J., McFarlane, A.: Literature review in games and learning. Futurelab, Bristol, United Kingdom (2004)
7. Shaffer, D.: How computer games help children learn. Palgrave Macmillan, New York (2006)
8. Pivac, M.: Play and learn: Potentials of game-based learning. British Journal of Educational Technology 38(3), 387–393 (2007)
9. Gee, J.P.: Pleasure, learning, video games, and life: the projective stance. E-Learning 2(3), 211–223 (2005)
10. Gee, J.P.: Good video games and good learning: Collected essays on video games, learning and literacy. Peter Lang, New York (2007)
11. Brown, J.S.: New learning environments for the 21st century: Exploring the edge. Change 38(5), 18–24 (2005)
12. Pras, B., Bizzocchi, J.: Game, motivation and effective learning: An integrated model for educational game design. In: DiGRA Conference, Vancouver, Canada (June 2005)
13. Barab, S., Thomas, M., Dodge, T., Carteaux, R., Tuzun, H.: Making learning fun: Quest Atlantis, a game without guns. Educational Technology Research and Development 53(1), 86–107 (2005)
14. Prensky, M.: Don't bother me Mum – I'm learning. Paragon House, St. Paul, Minnesota (2006)
15. Barab, S., Landa, A.: Designing effective interdisciplinary anchors. Educational Leadership 54(6), 52–55 (1997)
16. Ward, J.: The student's guide to cognitive neuroscience. Psychology Press, New York (2006)
17. Barab, S., Young, M.F.: Perception of the raison d' etre of content information: The purpose and mechanisms of anchored instruction. In: Paper presented at the annual meeting of the AECT, St. Louis, Missouri (1998)
18. Amory, A.: Game object model version II: A theoretical framework for educational game development. Educational Technology Research and Development 55(1), 55–77 (2007)
19. Bates, B.: Game design. Boston, Thomson (2004)
20. Vygotsky, L.S.: Mind in society: The development of higher psychological processes. Harvard University Press, Cambridge (1987)
21. Csikszentmihalyi, M.: Flow: The psychology of optimal experience. Harper and Row, New York (1990)
22. Prensky, M.: Digital Game-based learning. Paragon House, St Paul, Minnesota (2007)
23. Bigge, M., Shermis, S.: Learning theories for teachers. Allyn & Bacon, Boston, Massachusetts (2004)
24. Jones, A., Issroff, K.: Learning technologies: Affective & social issues in computer-supported collaborative learning. Computers & Education 44, 395–408 (2005)
25. Gros, B.: Digital games in education: The design of game-based learning environments. Journal of Research on Technology Education 40(1), 23–38 (2007)
26. Veermans, M., Cesareni, D.: The nature of the discourse in web-based collaborative learning environments: Case studies from four different countries. Computer and Education 45, 316–336 (2005)
27. Jonassen, D.H., Land, S.M.: Theoretical foundations of learning environments. Lawrence Erlbaum Associates, London (2000)
28. Dickey, M.: Game design and learning: A conjectural analysis of how massively multiple online role-playing games (MMORPGs) foster intrinsic motivation. Educational Technology Research and Development 55, 253–273 (2007)

29. Canton, J.: The extreme future. Dutton, New York (2006)
30. Green, M.: McNeeese.: Using edutainment software to enhance online learning. International Journal of E-Learning 6(1), 5–16 (2007)
31. London Knowledge Lab, http://www.lkl.ac.uk
32. Michigan State University, Games for Entertainment and Learning Lab, http://gel.msu.edu
33. University of Wisconsin, Madison, Games, Learning and Society Group, http://gameslearningsociety.org

Interactive Media Authoring Systems

Kok Wee Goh, Gangwen Mei, and Shuzhi Sam Ge

Social Robotics Lab, Interactive Digital Media Institute,
and Edutainment Robotics Lab
Department of Electrical and Computer Engineering
National University of Singapore
Singapore 117576
Tel.: (+65) 6516 6821; Fax: (+65) 6779 1103
samge@nus.edu.sg

Abstract. Advance in technologies has revolutionized the traditional mode of teaching and learning. Various media authoring systems have been developed in order to enhance the effectiveness of learning and teaching processes by supplementing traditional teaching materials such as text books and lecture notes with interactive digital media. In this paper, we are going to discuss two media authoring systems, KooBits and Web 2.0 Media Publisher, which incorporate creativity, innovation and cutting-edge technologies such as Artificial Intelligence and Asynchronous JavaScript and XML (AJAX). The major part of KooBits system is a client based e-book editor that is specifically designed to enhance interactivity, while Web 2.0 Media Publisher is a server based publishing platform. This paper describes various features, design consideration, implementation of KooBits and Web 2.0 Media Publisher, and compares them with other existing systems in terms of these aspects. Possible future developments for KooBits and some applications for Web 2.0 Media Publisher are also being discussed in the end.

1 Introduction

The advent of the information technology has allowed traditional documents to become livelier with the integration of images, animations and other multimedia components into one coherent interactive format [2]. The industry has witnessed one of the earliest manifestations of such documents in the form of powerpoint slides which integrates sound, images and other multimedia tools to assist people in creating better presentation [4,11]. In recent years, industrial trends have moved towards emulating these concepts into electronic books and other document types [13,30].

These new generation document types aim to enhance interactivity between the user and the media. Interactivity is enhanced through three aspects. Firstly, these documents must allow interactive authoring of documents. User must be given the freedom to create and manipulate the document. Secondly, it must also be able to support the authoring of interactive documents. This allows user

Z. Pan et al. (Eds.): Transactions on Edutainment I, LNCS 5080, pp. 206–230, 2008.

to manipulate different interactive media files in one interface. Lastly, it must also allow different authors of the same document to interact [3].

Interactive media authoring systems provide a viable solution to the problems discussed. A multimedia document aims to convey a message to its audience in an interactive and creative way [14]. Unlike traditional static documents, the multimedia support dynamic loading of data based on user input and generate required content in user demand. This allows user to interact with the system. In the past, to create a multimedia document requires the user to possess a certain amount of basic software knowledge. The user needs to learn some software skills to put different media files together. Therefore, it usually takes a user a significant amount of time to develop a multimedia document. Developers soon realized the potential in such documents and devoted efforts into cutting down development time. As a result, various software applications which allow the users to embed other types of media files such as images and videos into the documents were developed. A notable example of such software is the Microsoft PowerPoint. In Microsoft PowerPoint, users are able to import images into the software and allow limited animations. In view of the long development time needed, Hardman, Rossum and Bulterman have also developed a "Structured Multimedia Authoring" to address this problem [9].

This paper presents and discusses two separate media authoring systems – KooBits and Web 2.0 Media Publisher, which rely on two sets of technologies. KooBits contains a client-side application (ebook editor) that requires local installation on the clients' machine and a distributing network for the authors to create and exchange their interactive documents. There is no web 2.0 technology involved in the KooBits system. However, for Web 2.0 Media Publisher, this system makes use of web 2.0 technology to allow the users to author, store and publish their interactive documents completely on the server. In recent years, consumers need more customization that allows a higher level of manipulation on these multimedia documents. KooBits System had been developed as a platform with client side interactive e-book editor and server-side e-book publisher. It has since been introduced to the market to meet this demand [12]. Various novel concepts and features have been introduced with the release of KooBits:

1. As an interactive authoring tool, it significantly cut down the time taken to create dynamic multimedia content. This is in sharp contrast to traditional multimedia software which needs a much longer time to create the content. This is achieved by having a deep understanding on the cognitive process of user interaction and smooth integration of various multimedia types.
2. Various types of media files such as images and animations are combined in one single coherent interface and can be embedded in the electronic book. Conventionally, different software applications are used to support different types of media files. This makes integration of various media files very difficult. By putting everything in one coherent interface, this will greatly improve the user experience.
3. With inbuilt artificial intelligence module, the software is capable of interpreting the meaning of the user's text input and automatically generates

and modifies the graphics content. This is the revolutionary technology introduced by KooBits. With this feature, writing electronic books have transformed from a static, trivial task into one that is vibrant and interactive.

This process greatly enhances user experience for both the author and readers, thereby helping the author to convey ideas more clearly through visualization of the text content. It improves communication between the author and his readers. KooBits help users to clarify abstract concept and visualize the conceptual objects based on his input. Recently, rapid development of infrastructure has resulted in bigger bandwidth. Hence, server side technologies become more mature to support applications. As such, client side applications slowly shifted to server side for better communication. With the emergence of AJAX technology and Web 2.0 concepts, dynamic internet applications can be developed independent of console-based technology. This minimized data transfer and resulted in a more efficient system. Systems developed using this technology do not require the users to install additional software on the client side machine. Based on these concepts, Web 2.0 Media Publisher has been developed as a online media authoring system that allows the users to publish documents created using KooBits or other systems. This paper will first discussed the client based software Koobit which enhance interactivity by providing interactive authoring of documents and authoring of interactive documents. Discussion will then focus on the Web 2.0 Media Publisher which promote interactivity by allowing multiple authors to edit the same document concurrently.

2 Design Consideration

Building these media authoring systems requires various rigorous considerations. In order to make the application performing consistently across platforms, subtle details are scrutinized based on research done [21].

2.1 Browser Compatibility

In the design of web applications, browser compatibility is always a major issue. The three major internet browsers used at the present moment are Internet Explorer, Fire Fox and Safari. Different browsers interpret the HTML/CSS/JavaScript code in a slightly different way causing the webpage rendered on the computer screen to appear differently. Currently a popular solution to this problem is to use a conditional statement to check the type of browser the user is using and deliver the appropriate content to the browser accordingly. However, the drawback of this solution is that it significantly increases the size of the javascript program resulting in a longer loading time. For a complicated web application, this method tends to slow down the connection speed and thus reduce the responsiveness of the application.

The situation for mobile browser is even more chaotic. To develop successful content, one needs to consider the diversity of hardware in the market. As different mobile phones use operating system and different browsers, one needs to understand the technical limitations of these mobile browsers. Besides differences between hardware and operating systems between brands of mobile phone, one also needs to note that differences exist even within phones of the same brand. This difference is especially significant when one compares an old model phone with the latest model. As such, to develop the system for the mobile platform, catering to this diversity of hardware is a must. Typically, one needs to identify the model of phone that is requesting for the data before the server can send the appropriate content to phone. When a browser requests for content, it will send a HTTP request to the server. Hence, based on the HTTP request, one can interpret it and determine the model of the mobile phone. Based on the model of the phone, its capability can then be determined by comparing the particular model with a database (a collection of the capabilities of all the phone models in the world). By doing that, appropriate content can be send. The downside, however, is that determining the capabilities of the mobile phone takes time and will slow down the download speed. However, until a better solution is available in the market, this is currently the best possible solution in the market.

2.2   Server-Side Technology

Server-side technology is used to allow a Web server to serve dynamic Web content. Dynamic Web content requires the Web server to perform additional processing of the corresponding request to generate customized response. Server-side technology focuses primarily on delivering dynamically generated HTML documents to a user Web browser while the user interacts with a website. Various server side technologies are discussed in deciding the right technology for the system.

1. Active Server Pages (ASP) is a server-side technology developed by Microsoft. ASP uses embedded scripts in HTML documents to inform the Web server to generate the necessary HTML data dynamically. ASP supports multiple scripting languages like VBScript, JavaScript and PerlScript, with VBScript as the default scripting language. ASP includes support for Microsoft-specific Web technology like ActiveX, which provides useful functionality like file manipulation. ASP applications can only be developed and deployed on the Windows platform and Web servers like Internet Information Server (IIS) and Personal Web Server (PWS). Third party applications are required to port ASP to other platforms.

2. Macromedia ColdFusion, formerly from Allaire, uses a different approach to enable Web servers to generate dynamic content. Instead of embedding some programming language into the HTML document, ColdFusion uses its own proprietary ColdFusion Markup Language(CFML), which is a tag-based language. ColdFusion has about 100 built-in tags to access variables, databases and build conditions. In addition, ColdFusion allows the creation of custom tags, which can be created with CFML, or using C++ and ColdFusion API. ColdFusion documents end with a .cfm extension. The Web server hands over any .cfm document to the ColdFusion server. The ColdFusion server processes the document and sends the output back to the Web server,

which then sends it to the Web browser.While this approach makes it very easy to build Web applications, if a complex Web application is required, C++ is required to link to the ColdFusion server. This creates problems like memory-leak in complex codes that are not well-written. And since the code is running all the time inside the ColdFusion server, this can easily lead to disastrous consequences like crashing of server due to exhaustion of memory.

3. Personal Home Pages (PHP) is a server-side technology developed in the Open Source community. It is similar to technology like ASP and JSP in that PHP consists of a set of additional code tags placed inside the HTML documents. However, PHP is unique in that it is a language developed purely to serve Web pages rather than being based off an existing language such as Visual Basic or Java. PHP provides support for many kinds of Web applications, including database access, graph plotting and networking. PHP is available freely and supports a wide range of platforms.

2.3   Client-Side Technology

Client-side technology is used to add dynamic behavior to HTML content by executing certain routines on the Web browser. Client-side technology helps to ease the load on the Web server and shortens the response time for each request for dynamic content. This section looks at some of the common client side technologies available.

1. AJAX (Asynchronous JavaScript + XML) is a relatively recent web programming technology developed. With certain parts being known as Dynamic HTML and remote scripting, AJAX magically stretches a bunch of trivial old technologies such as JavaScript and CSS well beyond their original scope, and turns them into the powerful tool for building complicated web service. The public attention is attracted to AJAX when some major web application developer, such as Google, shows the general public what AJAX can do. The classic type of websites and web application is that visitor browse through the web page on the server one by one. In contrast, one of the main concepts in the AJAX technology is to put in some JavaScript control logics inside the web pages to monitor user actions and alter the HTML code and CSS styles. By doing so when user access the internet, what the server returns are not separate web pages, but a client application for the first access, then simply data in the following communication.

2. Macromedia's Flash is a system which is able to create interactive movies in a compressed vector graphics format, which is one of the strength of flash because other web application techniques lack this graphic support. For implementing the web application in flash, the server side need to be developed in Macromedia's Flex and open source Laszlo framework, and both framework need to be run under Java/Java 2 Enterprise Edition (J2EE) on the server. Moreover, the user's web browser needs to install flash player in order to run the application. The restricted running environment of flash serves as a drawback to this technology, despite its attractive graphic support which will enrich user experience.

3. ActiveX is the name Microsoft has given to a set of "strategic" object-oriented programming technologies and tools. The main technology is the Component Object Model (COM). Used in a network with a directory and additional support, COM becomes the Distributed Component Object Model (DCOM). A component is a self-sufficient program that can be run anywhere in the ActiveX network. This component is known as an ActiveX control. ActiveX is Microsoft's answer to the Java technology from Sun MicroSystems. An ActiveX control is roughly equivalent to a Java applet, and can be reused by many applications. An ActiveX control can be created using one of several languages or development tools, including C++ and Visual Basic, or with scripting tools such as VBScript.

3 KooBits System

A system called KooBits has been developed to address those problems mentioned in the previous section. To make the system functional on different platforms, a number of new problems occurred, which need to be appropriately dealt with. In the following sections, issues such as system overview, login system design, KooBits workspace design and KooBits applications implementation will be addressed.

3.1 KooBits System Overview

Fig. 1 presents a holistic view of the KooBits system. At the current stage, it consists of the following three major parts:

1. KooBits login system: this part manages the user authentication and registration processes. This login system has been designed with very high standard security levels. All the user inputs from the html forms are being filtered and extracted by functions to remove sensitive special symbols. This measure prevents the infiltration of unauthorized person who uses a combination of special sensitive symbols to undermine the database and server side code.
2. KooBits user workspace: this web page provides a user interface allowing the users to access the two main functions. First, the user can access to the virtual learning applications under the media authoring system, namely "KooBits electronic book publisher" and "web 2.0 slide show". The user can also access the system database by uploading or downloading various types of media files, such as images, videos and sound.
3. KooBits e-book publisher is one of the two main applications being developed under the interactive media authoring system. The application is an effective virtual learning tool for young users to create e-books in a wide variety of categories, such as electronic diary, story book, spelling book, dictionary and even multimedia text book. This software allows the user to merge image, sound, video, 3D animation and text into one user-friendly, coherent format, allowing easy creation of highly interactive electronic content.

3.2 Login System Design

To prevent unauthorized access, the system server checks the login credentials against user records stored on a database server. These user records contain information on authorized users to the system. In order to prevent outsider from accessing the content of the site directly, a session has been added into the page. As shown in Fig. 2, the session will verify whether a particular visitor is logged in, and will only display content of the page if he is logged in. The session works on the principle of providing verification with the cookie at the client side computer. When user login, a cookie will be planted in his computer and the browser will be sending the cookie whenever the user is requesting for a new page. The cookie value will then be verified with the system value and data will only be sent if both values agreed.

Visitors will be able to visit the website without logging in. However, there are certain privileges which are only enjoyed by registered users. For visitors, they can see the restricted profiles of current users. In addition, they will be introduced and provided an overview of the whole system. In order to use the application, the users have to log in.

3.3 KooBits Workspace Design

The user workplace is an essential part of the system. After successful login, the user will be directed to his workplace, from where the user can manage his files

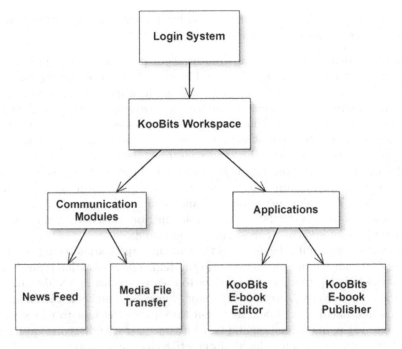

Fig. 1. System architecture design

or share those files with other users. User can organize their files into folders and put his shared files into shared folders. These files can be sorted or an advance search is incorporated into the application.

The layout of KooBits workspace is shown in Fig. 3. The workspace allows the user to upload media files to the system. Various types of media files such as flash, image, video and animation files are allowed [7]. It also supports a wide variety of file formats such as jpg, gif, wav, wmv etc. After uploading, it allows the files to be integrated into the electronic books created.

User can also create and publish the electronic books in the workspace to be shared within the system. The more books the users published, the more credits will the user earn. These credits can be used to earn further membership into the system or exchange for other services. Users can also add other users as friends in the workspace. This encourages cyber social networking in the workspace helping to build a closely knitted community within the system.

3.4 Client-Side Application: KooBits Editor

KooBits Editor allows authors to create next generation multimedia books. Traditionally, authors need to understand various multimedia software applications in order to create a multimedia electronic book. With the introduction of this software, authors now fully concentrate on content creation and focus less on technical aspects. Appropriate images and animations can be added in automatically as author types out stories in text. KooBits client-side application was

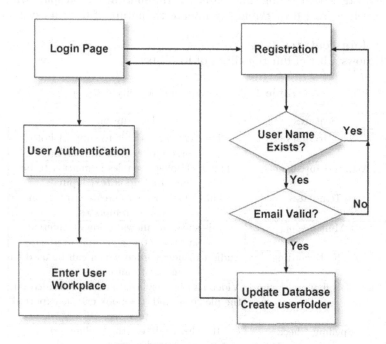

Fig. 2. Login system flowchart

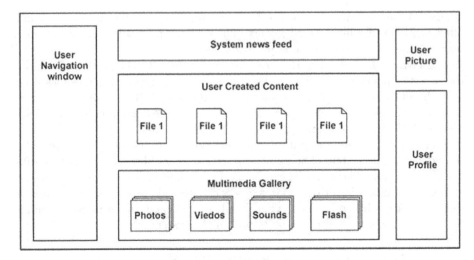

Fig. 3. User workspace layout

designed with special considerations to make the user interface straightforward and easy-to-use. The development team had done extensive research targeted at user end by organizing KooBits learning sessions in several primary schools in Singapore, the result shows users as young as 6 years old are able to learn how to use this software within a month. Research has shown that one of the major learning obstacle that young children face is the short attention span, which can be effectively extended by the highly interactive nature of KooBits system [5].

3.4.1   Main Features
Table 1 shows a list of functionalities of KooBits:

Table 1. Application functionality list

Features	Description
Text to Speech	This software is able to support both chinese and english translation
Artificial Intelligence	This technology enables animation to be generated upon text input
Templates	This allows users to create story from existing templates
Multimedia	This software allows fusion of different media files in one coherent interface
Audio Recording	Audio can be recorded which can be used to integrate into the file
Video Display and Export	Video can be displayed and transformed on the platform and, the book can be exported to video.
Spelling Check	It helps to detect the spelling errors committed when creating file

The client-side application integrates 3D, video, animation, graphics and text into one user-friendly, coherent format, allowing easy creation of interactive e-books. With the enhanced multimedia technology, KooBits Author further fosters a creative learning experience and allow individuals to express their emotions in different fashions. The system constantly seeks active inputs and activates pictures and animations on the fly. The final output products engage readers with multimedia, animations and Interactive Intelligent Motion whereby pictures and animations move in accordance to reader's interaction. KooBits shortens the creation cycle by letting users begin with formatted templates that they can use to compose various book types such as photo albums, diary entries, comic books and story books etc. Authors need only to focus on creating content. The client side application takes care of the tedious processes such as formatting and page adding before presenting the final product of a complete multimedia e-book ready for showcasing or publishing. Advanced users have the option of having total control over layout and graphics to achieve a more unique presentation. E-books created may be archived on KooBits's online bookshelves, stores and libraries; accumulated works may form part of author's own digital portfolio. They can also be burned into CDs for showcasing and distribution.

KooBits also allows users to easily link words or phrases of the written story to image, video and animation. During auto book playback, the text will appear gradually and triggers digital files to appear as story progresses. This feature engages the child in the writing and creation. "KooBits can be used to create comics, video books, storybooks, album, diaries, instructional text, teaching books, excursion recounts, science experiment reports, and many other book types" [12]. The content can be a mixture of flash, 3D, animations, videos, text and graphics. It is able to support English, Mandarin, Tamil, Malay and any other Unicode inputs. KooBits transforms writing from a passive subject into

Fig. 4. KooBits reading mode interface

a fascinating learning adventure for users. The created KooBits interactive e-books allow active input from readers and reward them with unique animated e-books to call their own. It encourages self-expression and heightens authors' propensity for independent work.

3.4.2   User Interface

KooBits is a user-oriented software application which places heavy emphasis on user experience. The graphical user interface of the software is designed based on the conventional design heuristics [10]. Firstly, it is taken into account that the electronic books editor is a novel concept and users may not get use to it initially. Hence, play, fast forward and stop buttons are imported from conventional music player to give user a sense of familiarity. Studies have also been made into commercial software applications to ensure that the presentation of user options follow industrial standards. This makes the software more user-friendly. Fig. 4 shows the KooBits user interface design.

The electronic book presentation is designed to simulate that of physical book and physical concepts such as flipping is emulated in the virtual space. With these features, users are able to relate their physical world experience into the virtual space thereby enhancing user experience. To open previous works, Fig. 5 indicates that the software provides a visualization using a bookshelf as a metaphor. Unlike conventional software, organizing books on the bookshelf allows better categorization. It also significantly improves software interface presentation by allowing the user to relate their daily experiences onto the virtual space by making use to metaphorical representations.

3.4.3   Client-Side Application Implementation

KooBits integrates 3D, video, audio, animation, flash, images and text all into one user-friendly, coherent format, through its advanced "Media Fusion" technology

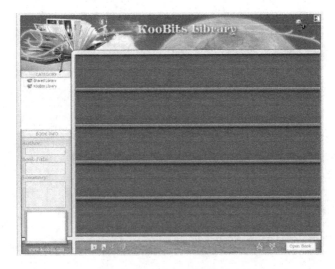

Fig. 5. KooBits book shelf interface

[24]. It shortens the content creation cycle by letting users import a wide range of digital formats under one editing environment, and facilitates the manipulation and editing of highly interactive content in real-time.

This software allows authors to publish next generation multimedia books. In the past, authors need to understand various multimedia software applications in order to create a multimedia electronic book. With the introduction of this software, authors now fully concentrate on content creation and focus less on technical aspects. Appropriate images and animations can be added in automatically as author types out stories in text.

Content-driven animation is another technical advance of this software application. Instead of using key frames to create animation, users of KooBits can use storyline to generate animations and trigger dynamic actions make up of various digital formats. This significantly shortens the process of creating an interactive media from hours to minutes. With embedded AI components, KooBits also allows users to create animation content based on user's text input. For instance, a fox avatar will be generated when the word "fox" is keyed in. It is primarily designed for users to aid them in expressing their creativity. This technology is redesigned to aid users in learning abstract concepts which are better explained pictorially. Developing an animations generator based on text input application, therefore, allows user to interact with the system. In this application, the system will generate the conceptual animation to aid users to visualize the conceptual objects. It also permits interaction by responding to users' text input to adjust the animation accordingly.

KooBits helps to create digital books in a fun and interesting way via its powerful built-in artificial intelligence system. This Artificial Intelligence system constantly seeks active user inputs and responds with picture and animation generation. It resulted in a final output - electronic books that engage readers with multimedia and animations coupled with real-time interactive intelligent motion. This electronic book can be used for playback with the story slowly unfold.

1) KooBits Text to Speech Converter

Another key technology of KooBits is its sophisticated text to voice converter which transforms user's text input into speech effortlessly. The current version supports all languages. This text-to-speech system is developed based on a text normalization component. The input text is converted into a series of words. Text normalization will isolate the words in the input text. The system then looks for significant symbolic representations to analysis. It will then be converted to words. If abbreviation is encountered, the normalizer will compare the abbreviation with the database to look up for the appropriate word. After the word is normalised, it is then passed on to the homograph disambiguation stage. This stage analysis the most appropriate pronunciation based on the context of the input text. After the disambiguation process, the information will be passed onto the pronunciation module. The pronunciation module will first look out for the appropriate word in the system pronunciation lexicon. If the word is not found in the lexicon, the engine will pronounce it using the letter to sound rule. With that, the appropriate sound will be determined and output to the user.

Using this feature greatly enhances interactivity which significantly improves user experience.

2) KooBits Text Parser

In order to understand the user's input and react to it by generating various animations. A text parser has been designed to filter the user's input and feed the filtered result into the application core modules. The text parser takes typed input from the user and simplifies it to something that KooBits can understand. Normally, words with similar meaning are converted into the same word, for example, the words "acquire" and "obtain" are filtered by the parser and classified into the same verb that means get. A database has been built up that relates different words and phrases with similar meanings. The KooBits Text Parser makes it much easier for the client side application to react on user's input. After text filtering, the system core modules does not have to check whether the command is "obtain the gem", "take the gem", "take gem", "get gem", "discover the precious gem", and so on, because the KooBits Text Parser has already stripped these various phrases down to something like "take gem".

For the users, the client-side KooBits application is more flexible. The users do not have to input exactly the right words, because the application can understand the same word or phrase that appears in a few different forms.

3.4.4 Applications of KooBits Editor

KooBits offers a high degree of freedom to customize, it can be used to create comics, video books, storybooks, photo albums, diaries, instructional text, excursion recounts, even science experiment reports. The content can be a mixture of flash, 3D, animations, videos, text and graphics. The software is able to support English, Mandarin, Tamil, Malay and any other Unicode inputs.

Fig. 6. Diary book

Fig. 7. Spelling book

As shown in Fig. 6, this software can be used as an interactive diary or blog for users. The current form of diary is either in the form of diary book or website blog. This will help to meet the market demand for the next generation electronic diary.

An extension of this technology can also be used to create an educational tool to helping user to learn spelling. This can be used as an educational for users to learn spelling. Assignment will be given to the user via the electronic books. Hints will be given to the users for them to key in the correct words. Upon keying

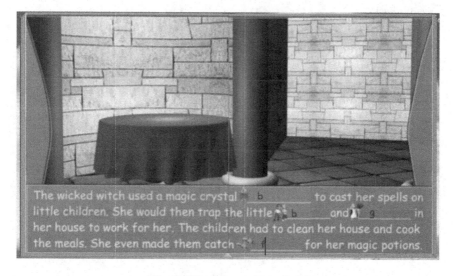

Fig. 8. Grammer exercise book

in, the software will feedback to the users on the results. If the result is correct, a relevant descriptive animation of the spelling word will appear on the interface. This helps the user to enforce what was learned. Fig.7 shown the spelling book.

KooBits can also be used as a language training book. The software is very powerful and efficient in detecting the correct grammar of the language. Thus, it can help the user to master a language on his own via the interactive feedback.Appropriate animation will be shown to enforce the learning when the user keys in the right grammar. When the grammar is wrong, the software application will feedback to the user the area he needs to improve on. This grammar exercise book is shown in Fig. 8.

It can also be used as an interactive dictionary. Traditional dictionary allows one to look up for the meaning of the words and detail description. In recent times, dictionary has moved online and people can easily search words via website. However, explanation of the words remains quite static. Using KooBits, a dynamic dictionary can be created. After the user keying in the words, the software application can provide the meaning of the words. In addition, relevant images and animations can be used to explain the meaning of the word much more effectively, thus speeding up the learning process substantially.

3.5   Server-Side Application: KooBits Publisher

KooBits Publishing Network is an online platform for all the users to publish their electronic books and also view the works done by other users. Within this website, all the registered users can upload the completed piece of works to the database and make it available for all the other users. "The book authors can also have the option to source, develop, share or market their e-books" [12]. Besides

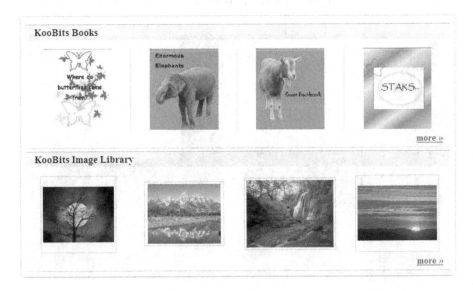

Fig. 9. KooBits publishing platform

uploading and downloading e-books, the users can also upload media files like photos, pictures, drawings, storylines, animations, music and video to co-develop and co-publish content with other users. Fig. 9 shows the layout of the KooBits publishing interface.

Registered users in this networks are able to earn Koobits credits through active participation of publishing activities. These Koobits credits in turn can be exchanged for free membership and other members benefits. In this way, users are being encouraged to publish more which results in large amount of user generated content. This enhances the value of the network.

4 WEB 2.0 Media Publisher

KooBits was primarily developed as a client based solution to address the interactivity issue. The industry has witnessed the migration of media authoring development to the World Wide Web in the recent years [1]. Web 2.0 Media Publisher extended the KooBits media authoring system and is developed as a server based alternative. This web based application allows the user to create multimedia documents. The documents created are being wrote into xml format [20]. This publisher is built upon the foundation of Tan and Wu [27, 29].These user created documents are stored in the system database and can be shared concurrently accessed by multiple users [24].

The client program in the last generation of web applications will send a request and load a new page from the server only when the user clicks on a button to trigger an event. The asynchronous HTTP call is different from the traditional http call in various aspects. Firstly, the http request is being processed in the background such that no refresh of the webpage will be created. The client-side program will only take the returned data to update the existing web page. Secondly, the asynchronous request allows the user to perform other actions before the reply is received from the server. As a result, it minimizes the user's waiting time for process completion and allows multiple requests to be made from the client.

4.1 Web 2.0 Slides Show

Web 2.0 slides show application is functionally similar to the desktop application - Microsoft PowerPoint. At the client side, HTML and CSS are used to create the graphical user interface, and JavaScript code controls the logic. The PHP scripts at the server side is responsible for handling request from function calls, and MySQL is used to store the content.

To make the system easier to develop and maintain, we have taken a modular approach to break down the control logic into different functional modules, with each of them perform certain specific tasks and provide functions that can be called by other modules. All these modules are implemented as different JavaScript (.js) files. Fig. 11 shows the structure of the application.

Every slide consists of a number of editable rectangular boxes. These boxes could be a text box, or an empty box containing picture or video. The edit box

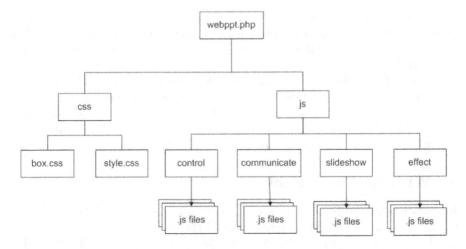

Fig. 10. Web 2.0 slides show structural diagram

is created and handled by the EditBox module, and each of them is editable, resizable and draggable.The edit box module is defined in the file editBox.js, in which there are two classes: editBox and editBoxBuilder. The class editBox is used to construct the static edit box, while the class editBoxBuilder is used to add events to the edit box. To create an edit box, the main module will call the editBoxBuilder class, which will in turn call the editBox class to create a static box, then adding events to it and return the final edit box to the main routine. The editBox class is used to create a static edit box. An edit box is created as a HTML div element with visible border. In this edit box, certain properties of the edit box will be kept track, including its x-position, y-position, width, length, state (idle, focus, editing). The contents of a edit box is empty by default, but it can also be used to contains contents like text, picture, video or geometric shapes.

The Slide module defined in JavaScript file slide.js is use to create a new slide. It is able to create a default empty slide with no content, or open the previously saved slide and use the stored content to create the new slide. Similar to the structure of edit box, the slide module has two classes defined. The slide class is used to build a static slide. The static slide is build by creating a HTML div element as the slide, and calls the editBoxBuilder class to build the various edit box inside the slide. The slideBuilder class is called by the main program to build the actual slide. The slideBuilder class calls the slide class to create a static slide, and adds the event functions to the slide so that it could respond to different user action.The addEditBox() function in the module is used to insert extra edit box into the slide. Hence multiple edit boxes could be used in the same slide to contains various content such as text, picture and video. To insert a new text box into the slide, click on the Insert button on the menu, then choose New Text Box. A new text box will be added to the current slide.

The slide show module is used for creating the slide show effects in the slide presentation. This module makes use of the JavaScript library provided by

Script.aculo.us, in which effects are implemented as functions. When an effect function is called with an object as a parameter, then the effect will be applied to the input object. For example, if the slide show module calls Fade(slide1), then the effect fade is applied on object slide1, and the slide will become more and more transparent and disappear eventually.

The slide show can be started by clicking on the slide show icon in the tool bar. A new window will appear to display the slide show. There are many slide show effects available, such as fade, slide down/up, blind down/up, grow, fly in/out. However, the various effects are a combination of a few numbers of simple core effects, including:

- Change of opacity – reduce the opacity of an object to make it more transparent;
- Translation – move an object in the left/right or up/down direction;
- Resizing – increase or decrease the size of an object, including all of its elements

These three fundamental effects are the building block of the many slide show effects implemented at the later stage. With the combination of the above core effects, plus time control, many Microsoft PowerPoint slide effects can be produced. For example, we can reduce the opacity of an object by certain percentage after a few millisecond to produce the fade effect; or we can make a small size slide to move in a spiral path with expanding size until it reaches the final full screen position, by increasing the slide size and changing its translation direction every few millisecond. This module runs on top of the Communication module and it is used to save the contents of the slide on the server. The Save function can be accessed by clicking on the Save To Server menu.

The dictionary module is a JavaScript widget added to the system. It allows the user to enter a word to search for its meaning. The searching of the definition of the key word is actually done on the server, by making use of some other online dictionary database. When a user enter a key word and click search, the client program will initialize an asynchronous HTTP call to the server, with the search key word as input. After receiving the word, the server side will call the dictionary handling function to connect to some online dictionary websites and do the searching. As these websites will return a web page containing the definition of the word together with other content like advertisement, the server side handling function will parse the result and filter out the irrelevant content. Afterwards, the function will reply the definition of the word to the client program, which will display the definition in the JavaScript widget. Fig. 12 shows the dictionary interface.

The dialog box consists of three parts: one is the text input field in which user can enter the word to be searched; another is the search button; the third one is a text area in which the meaning of the word will be displayed. In this module, two methods of searching are implemented. The first one is the normal search. User opens the dialog box and type the word in the input text field. After clicking "Search", the definition of the word will be displayed in the main text box, after the program receives the reply from the server.

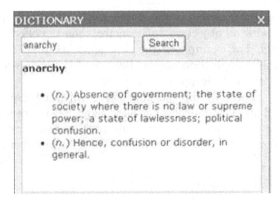

Fig. 11. Dictionary javascript widget

Another method of searching is the highlight search. In this way the user only need to highlight the work he want to look up, then open the dictionary dialog box following the same steps described above. The dictionary module will automatically check for highlighted words in the slide. If there is any highlighted word, it will initialize the search and display the result once it is obtained from the server.

It is also possible to implement the dictionary function by installing a dictionary database on the server side, and have the advantage of fast searching and less overhead since there is no content filtering. In , we use available online dictionary websites for the advantage of larger database and more information, without the need of database maintenance and update. It is a suggested practice in web application development, to make use of available online resource as much as possible. This technique could be further enhanced to connect the server to other powerful internet search engine, so it can perform various kind of searching.

User can add in geometric shapes, such as square, triangle, circle, star and arrow in the slide. These shapes are generated using the shape module, and then inserted into an editable box so that it can be moved and resized.

Although the system only provides predefined shapes for user, shape module is function that can be used to draw any arbitrary geometric shape. This module takes a point array as the function parameter. This point array is an array that contains the coordinates of all the vertexes, with the first array item as the coordinate of the first vertex (starting point). The function will start from the first vertex, then draw connecting line to the second vertex, and so on. When it reaches the last vertex, the function will automatically connect it to the first vertex to draw a closed shape. Vector Markup Language (VML) is used to draw the various shapes in the Shape module. VML is an application of Extensible Markup Language (XML) 1.0 which defines a format for the encoding of vector information together with additional markup to describe how that information may be displayed and edited. It supports the markup of vector graphic information in the same way that HTML supports the markup of textual information. Within

VML the content is composed of paths described using connected lines and curves. The markup gives semantic and presentation information for the paths.

Besides being resizable and draggable, the geometric shape created by the Shape module is able to rotate. When user double click the edit box that contains the geometric shape, the edit box will be in "edit" state, in which user could drag the shape to rotate it. The shape class defined in the module is the one that creates the geometric shape. The rotate() function in the class is used to produce the rotation of the geometric shape. The rotate() function is called when the mousemove and mousebuttondown event occurs in the edit box "edit" state. The function will detect the co-ordinate of the mouse and the one of the center of the shape. By comparing these two sets of co-ordinate, the function will decide the direction (clockwise or anti-clockwise) and turns the shape by a small degree. Rotation will continue as long as there is mouse movement and the mouse button is being pressed.

To access the upload picture function, click on the Upload Image menu. A dialog box will appears and allow user to browse the file in his local computer. After selection the user can click on the Upload button to transfer the file to the server. The Gallery module is developed to be used together with the Upload Picture module. This module is used to allow user to brows the image contents saved in the server, and the user could select and insert the picture into the slide.

To open the gallery function, click on the Gallery menu. A dialog box will appears in the workspace. In the Gallery dialog box, there is a panel which displays all the file names of the image files saved on the server. User is able to select the file in the panel, and the associated picture will be displayed in the Preview panel. After finding the desired image, user could click on the Insert to add the picture into the slide. At the current stage, the gallery is connected to the server and to view the contents in the user's folder.

4.2 Communication Modules

In order to allow users to communicate and collaborate on the media authoring system, both text and voice based communication modes are made available for the users to carry out discussion. Text-based communication is carried out in traditional chat-room style while voice-based communication allows the users to speak using desktop microphones. This combination creates a communication method that is highly interactive and at the same time less demanding in terms of bandwidth compare to other methods like video conferencing and video broadcasting.

4.2.1   Text-Based Communication

Users within can communicate with each other through text-based communication. This communication is conducted for users to interact with each other in real time. As an educational system, allowing users to interact with each other is an important feature as it allows ideas to be shared. Users can also clarify their doubts through this form of peer support.

4.2.2   Voice-Based Communication

In comparison, audio-based communication is more complicated due to its higher requirement in terms of bandwidth. As the transmission of audio data can generate significant amount of network traffic, measures should be taken to reduce the strain on the network. The interactive learning system conserves bandwidth through the use of audio compression techniques and exercises control over the audio transmission.

In our audio transmission module, Audio data stored in Pulse Code Modulation (PCM) format is compressed by GSM 6.10 audio codec, which is capable of achieving a transmission rate of 8-16 kbps. After compression, the compressed audio data is then sent across the internet to the all the listeners. Upon arriving at a listener's end of the connection, the client application converts the compressed audio data back to the PCM format and plays it through the PC speakers. Using this method, the audio communication process does not involve the transfer of large audio files, but instead it relies on the streaming of audio data packets. Thus, the network traffic can be lowered significantly.

4.2.3   Concurrent File Editing

In this system, users can collaborate with each other to work on group projects by working on the same documents concurrently [18, 22]. All the users are given the permission to create projects in the workspace. After creating the project, the creator can add his group mates into the project group and declares certain documents as shared files, enabling it to be accessed and edited by all the other group members. At the same time, the user database will be updated and these shared documents will appear inside the workplace of all other users in the project group.

In order to allow more than one user to edit a document concurrently, all the users should be mutually excluded from accessing the particular part of the content that the users are currently working on. This is to prevent problems from arising when one user overwrites the content of the same section which another user is still working on. Thus, mutual exclusion is necessary to protect the integrity of the data. The mutual exclusion rule in this system is such that when the first user accesses a certain section of a document, this section is blocked from all the other users until this user finishes editing and releases this section. For example, Fig. 13 shows a user's view when he is doing concurrent editing of an online power point document. The title text box appears in gray color indicating that this text box is currently being edited by another user.

The concurrent file editing feature is implemented through a few critical steps.

1. A module is written to send a signal to the server. The signal serves as an indication to the server should a user decides to edit a certain section of a document.
2. When the server receives this signal it will then update other clients who are working on the same document to reserve the textbox that the editor is currently working on.
3. The user is granted unique access to the selected section and starts updating data to the server using ajax communication model.

4. On the server side, all the updates from users are entered into a queue. The server periodically reads from the queue and sends requests to update all the documents stored on the user's computers. Fig. 13 shows how this mechanism works.

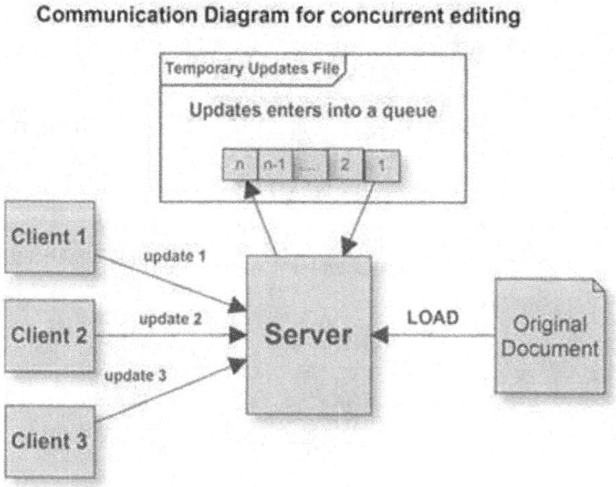

Fig. 12. Concurrent file editing

4.3   Future Development

The system can be further developed and evolve into a virtual online learning platform by integrating several different modules introduced in the above sections: text/voice communication, concurrent file editing and Web 2.0 Slides Show [23]. This will become a more interactive solution over existing technology which primarily promote one way communication [16, 17, 19]. In fact, developing this technology will enhance the effectiveness of distance learning [6, 15]. Fig. 14 illustrates how such a virtual online lecture network can be built and how the lecture can be carried out.

Only lecturers are assigned the permission to initiate new virtual lectures. An online power point document will be prepared in advance and attached to that lecture session. Under this system, it brings users from different regions to logon to the system and attend the lesson together. During each virtual lecture session, all the users will see the same online power point document on their client machine and receives voice communication from the lecturer in a way similar to broadcasting. However, a significant difference from conventional broadcasting is that all the users are allowed to signal to the lecturer by "virtual hand rising" [25]. If a user wants to interrupt the session to ask a question, an option button is provided to signal this intention to the lecturer. Upon receiving the request, the user can talk to the whole lecture room if the lecturer granted the permission to speak up via an accept request button provided. The users can then choose to

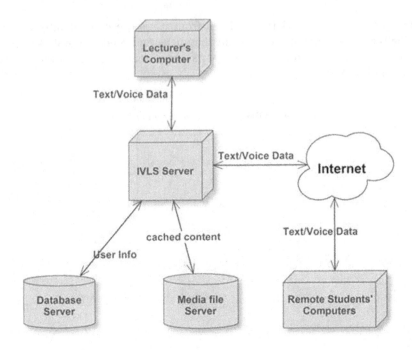

Fig. 13. Online virtual lecture

use either text or voice-based communication mode according to the bandwidth limitation of his/her internet connection.

Besides text/voice discussion, the lecturer can ask users to solve problems using the concurrent file editing feature. On the web 2.0 slides show system, each user can be assigned to work on a mathematics problem and write their answers in separate text boxes. They can look at each other's solution, compare and give comments, thus enhancing interactivity in learning.

At the end of each virtual lecture, all text-based communication and problem solving sessions will be automatically recorded in terms of history log on the system server. This can be accessed by users again for review purposes.

5   Conclusion

This paper discussed two different systems, KooBits Media Authoring System and Web 2.0 Media Publisher, which enhance the effectiveness of learning process. These two systems incorporate creativity, innovation and cutting edge technologies to facilitate this process. These systems promote interactivity which is a critical factor in effective learning. KooBits Media Authoring System is developed based on client based technology which requires installation. Web 2.0 Media Publisher build on the idea of KooBits and is developed into a Web 2.0 system. This enables the system to be more widely accessible and free the user from installation. Traditional client based applications have slowly developed into server based web applications. It is anticipated that this shift from client application to the server side is likely to continue in the future.

Acknowledgements. The authors thank the inputs from Xiaoyan Stanley Han and Xiangdong Chen, Personal e-Motion Pte Ltd.

References

[1] Mark, A.K.: Integrating open hypermedia systems with the World Wide Web. In: Proceedings of the Eighth ACM International Hypertext Conference, Southampton, UK, pp. 157–166 (1997)

[2] Bailey, B., Konstan, J., Cooley, R., Dejong, M.: Nsync - A Toolkit for Building Interactive Multimedia Presentations. In: Proceedings ACM Multimedia1998, Bristol, UK, pp. 257–266 (1998)

[3] Knightly, E., Templin, F., Banerjea, A., Mah, B., Zhang, H., Ferrari, D.: The Tenet Real-time Protocol Suite: A Demonstration. In: Proceedings of the second ACM international conference on Multimedia, San Francisco, California, United States, pp. 489–490 (1994)

[4] Seongbae, E., No, E.S., Kim, H.C., Yoon, H., Maeng, S.R.: Eventor: An Authoring System for Interactive Multimedia Applications. Multimedia Systems 2(3), 129–140 (1994)

[5] Essa, E.: A Practical Guide to Solving Preschool Behavior Problems, pp. 382–393 (2001)

[6] Sébastien, G.: Contextualizing Discussions in Distance Learning Systems. In: Proceedings of the 4th IEEE International Conference on Advanced Learning Technologies (ICALT 2004), Joensuu, Finland, August 30-September 1, 2004, pp. 226–230 (2004)

[7] Cruz, G., Hill, R.: Capturing and playing multimedia events with STREAMS. In: Proceedings of the second ACM international conference on Multimedia, San Francisco, California, USA, p. 466 (1994)

[8] Hamakawa, R., Rekimoto, J.: Object composition and playback models for handling multimedia data. Multimedia Systems. In: Proceedings of the first ACM international conference on Multimedia, Anaheim, California, USA, pp. 273–281 (1993)

[9] Hardman, L., Rossum, G., Bulterman, D.: Structured Multimedia Authoring. ACM Transactions on Multimedia Computing, Communications and Applications 1(1), 89–109 (2005)

[10] Nielsen, J.: http://www.useit.com/papers/heuristic/heuristic_list.html

[11] Wei, J.: Web page based dynamic book for document presentation and operation. US 0030719 A1 (2004)

[12] KooBits web site, http://www.KooBits.com

[13] Soares, L.F., Rodrigues, R., Saade, D.M.: Modeling, authoring and formatting hypermedia documents in the HyperProp system. Multimedia Systems 8(2), 118–134 (2000)

[14] Hardman, L., Bulterman, D., Rossum, G.: The Amsterdam hypermedia model: adding time and context to the Dexter model. Communications of the ACM archive 37(2), 50–62 (1994)

[15] Castro, M., Pérez-Molina, C.M., Colmenar, A., Mora, C., Yeves, F., Carpio, J., Peire, J., Daniel, J.: Examples of Distance Learning Projects in the European Community. IEEE Transactions on Education 44(4), 406–411 (2001)

[16] Microsoft's NetShow, http://www.microsoft.com/netshow

[17] Microsoft's Vxtreme, http://www.microsoft.com/netshow/vxtreme

[18] Streitz, N., Haake, J., Hannemann, J., Lemke, A., Schuler, W., Schtitt, H., Thuring, M.: SEPIA: A Cooperative Hypermedia Authoring Environment. In: Proceedings of the 4th ACM Hypertext Conference, Milan, Italy, p. 1122 (1992)

[19] Real networks, http://www.real.com

[20] Andrews, R.L., DeFilippis, J.M., Murphy, D.S.: Creating an HTML document from a source document. US 019489 (2003)

[21] Giachetti, R.E.: Integrating hypermedia design concepts with a systems analysis and design methodology to develop manufacturing web applications. Int. J. Computer Integrated Manufacturing 18(4), 329–340 (2005)

[22] Costa, R.M., Moreno, M.F., Rodrigues, R.F., Soares, L.F.: Live Editing of Hypermedia Documents. In: Proceedings of the 2006 ACM symposium on Document engineering, pp. 165–172 (2006)

[23] Benjamin, R., Davenport, G.: Structured content modeling for cinematic information. ACM SIGCHI Bulletin 21(2), 78–79 (1989)

[24] Deshpande, S., Hwang, J.: A Real-Time Interactive Virtual Classroom Multimedia Distance Learning System. IEEE Transactions on Multimedia, 432–444 (2001)

[25] Ge, S.S., Tok, M.Y.: Enhancing Online Education Using Collaboration Solutions. Journal of Educational Technology Systems 31(4), 361–380 (2003)

[26] Antonio, S., Fox, E.A., Hix, D.: The Integrator: A Prototype for Flexible Development of Interactive Digital Multimedia Applications. Interactive Multimedia 2(3), 5–26 (1991)

[27] Tan, C.K.: Web-based Desktop Application. B.Eng Final Year Project Thesis, ECE department, Faculty of Engineering, National University of Singapore (2002)

[28] Thuong, T.T., Roisint, C.: A Multimedia Model Based on Structured Media and Sub- Elements for Complex Multimedia Authoring and Presentation. International Journal of Software Engineering and Knowledge Engineering 12(5), 473–500 (2002)

[29] Wu, Z.: WEB 2.0 Slide Show Presentation System. B.Eng Final Year Project Thesis, ECE department, Faculty of Engineering, National University of Singapore (2007)

[30] Nicole, Y., Meyrowitz, N., Dam, A.: Reading and writing the electronic book. IEEE Computer 18(10), 15–30 (1985)

A Review of Using Virtual Reality for Learning

Elinda Ai-Lim Lee and Kok Wai Wong

School of Information Technology, Murdoch University, South Street Campus,
Murdoch, Western Australia 6150
{elinda.lee,k.wong}@murdoch.edu.au

Abstract. The major concern of educators is how to enhance the outcome of education. Better education media used to assist teaching has constantly been sought by researchers in the educational technology domain. Virtual Reality (VR) has been identified as one of them. Many have agreed that VR could help to improve performance and conceptual understanding on a specific range of task. However, there is limited understanding of how VR could enhance the learning outcomes. This paper reviews types of VR that have been used for learning, the theoretical framework for a VR learning environment, and instructional design for VR-based learning environment. Further research is suggested for VR-based learning environment.

1 Introduction

Virtual Reality (VR) has been used as education tools for some time in applied fields such as aviation and medical imaging, and it has also been used in schools and colleges in the recent years [1]. One of the main reasons why VR has been used for educational and training purposes is the support of high interactivity and the abilities to present a virtual environment that resembles the real world. With this technology, learners can explore and manipulate three-dimensional (3-D) interactive environment. However, VR is just an educational tool which can be used to support learning, which might not work for all kind of learning [2]. This paper reviews the types of VR that have been used for learning but does not attempt to cover all VR technologies mainly because this technology is developing rapidly and new methods are continually emerging everyday [3]. In addition, this paper also reviews theoretical and instructional design models that have been developed specifically for VR-based learning environment.

2 Definition and Types of VR

Basically, VR can be classified into two major types based on the level of interaction and immersive environment. In non-immersive virtual environment, computer simulation is represented on a conventional personal computer and is usually explored by keyboard, mouse, wand, joystick or touch screen [1, 2]. On the other hand, immersive VR environments are presented on multiple, room-size screen or through a stereoscopic, head-mounted display unit [1, 2, 4]. Special hardware such as gloves, suits and high-end

Z. Pan et al. (Eds.): Transactions on Edutainment I, LNCS 5080, pp. 231–241, 2008.

computer systems might be needed in immersive VR environment. Lately, VR computer simulation has been defined as a highly interactive, 3-D computer generated program in a multimedia environment which provides the effect of immersion to the users [5]. Users are able to become a participant in abstract spaces which is a computer generated version of real world objects (for example, chemical molecules or geometric models) or processes (for example, population growth or biological). These simulations could take many forms, ranging from computer renderings of 3-D geometric shapes to highly interactive, computerized laboratory experiments [1].

Allen et al. [3] have classified three levels of immersive VR:

i)   Partially or semi immersive VR
     A system that gives the users a feeling of being at least slightly immersive by a virtual environment [6] where users remain aware of their real world [3]. For example, a workbench that uses a table-top metaphor where special goggles are used to view the 3-D object on a table-top; a fish tank VR which uses monitor-based systems to display stereo image of a 3-D scene that is viewed by using shutter glasses; or a sensor-glove is used to interact with the world by using natural movement with the glove through a desk-top screen for visualization.

ii) Fully immersive VR
     A system that uses special hardware where users are completely isolated from the physical world outside, to fully immerse in the virtual environment [6]. Head-mounted device, sensor gloves and sensors are attached to the user's body to detect, translate real movement into virtual activity. For example, CAVE, a projection-based VR system is a room with multi walls where the stereoscopic view of the virtual world is generated according to the user's head position and orientation, and users can move around the 'cave'[7].

iii) Augmented Reality
     A system where users can have access to a combination of VR and real-word attributes by incorporating computer graphics objects into real world scene [3, 5]. It is also known as Mixed Reality. For example, a user dissects a virtual dummy frog using head-mounted device, or table-top display and a real scalpel.

Depending on the level of interaction and the complexity of the ambience, Silva, Cardoso, Mendes, Takahashi & Martins [8] classify two types of VR: VR on-line and VR off-line. With VR off-line, more complex simulation and perfect modeling objects in terms of textures, materials and animation is possible. As for VR on-line, there is more limitation in their multimedia aspect because care need to be taken for the size of files transmitted through the internet. VR on-line and VR off-line by Silva, Cardoso, Mendes, Takahashi & Martins [8] is somehow parallel to immersive and non-immersive VR respectively.

There are a number of methods to generate a non-immersive virtual environment on a personal computer. Web3D open standards, such as X3D (eXtensible 3D Graphics) and VRML (Virtual Reality Modeling Language) are used to generate 3-D interactive graphical representations that can be delivered over the World Wide Web [9, 10]. VRML provides a language that integrates 3D graphics, 2D graphics, text, and multimedia into a coherent model, and combines them with scripting languages and network capabilities (Carey & Bell 1997, cited in, [11]). Whilst X3D is the successor of VRML which was approved by the ISO in 2004 [11]. X3D inherits most of the design choices and technical features of VRML and improves upon VRML mainly in three areas: adds new nodes and capabilities; includes additional data encoding formats; and divides the language into functional areas called components [11]. On the other hand, Quick Time VR which is a type of image file that allows the creation and viewing of photographically captured panoramas can also be used [12]. Users can explore the objects through images taken at multiple viewing angles [12].

The virtual world used in learning could be of two types: virtual world that mimics the real world scenario (for example, a virtual museum is created to study the history, art and heritage of a place or a virtual scene shows how bacteria enter human body) or just computer simulation with 3-D geometry objects in an interactive multimedia environment (for example, ripping and unfolding a cube or generating a bottle design from a 2-D diagram). What makes VR an impressive tool for learning is in addition to multimedia, VR allows learners to immerse in a 3-D environment and feel 'in the middle of another environment' that extremely close to reality [13, 14] .

3   Application of VR in Educational Settings

VR is becoming increasingly popular for a variety of applications in today's society. It has become well suited and a powerful media for use in school [15], especially for science and mathematics which involve the study of natural phenomena and abstract concepts. The reason being the ability of this technology to make what is abstract and intangible to become concrete and manipulable [1]. Nevertheless, the application of VR in arts and humanities studies should not be ignored. For example, the ability to model on places that cannot be visited, such as historical cities and zoos could be beneficial in social studies, culture and foreign languages. Students could immerse themselves in historical or fictional events filled with foreign cultures and explore them first hand [1, 4].

There are quite a number of research reports mentioning VR computer simulations to be an effective approach for improving students' learning in both non-immersive and immersive virtual environments as discussed below.

3.1 Non-immersive VR Applications

The VRML-based 3-D objects used by Song and Lee [16] to teach geometry in middle school shows a positive effect on students' learning of geometric topics. And the VR Physic Simulation (VRPS) which is created by Kim, Park, Lee, Yuk, & Lee [17] helps students to learn physics concepts such as wave propagation, ray optics relative velocity and electric machines at the level of high school and college has also shown that students understand the subject matter better. An interactive VR distance learning program on stream erosion in geosciences is developed by Li et al. [18] with the aim to help motivate learners with concrete information which is perceptually easy to process and understand. In their project, VR is used to visualize the effects of related earth science concepts or phenomena, and the result shows that the VR of stream erosion may enhance students' learning in geosciences [18].

3.2 Immersive VR Applications

Complex spatial problems and relationships can be comprehended better and faster than with traditional method when Construct3D, a 3-D geometric construction tool is used [19]. The Construct3D uses a stereoscopic head-mounted display and a Personal Interaction Panel developed by Kaufmann et al. [19] for used in mathematics and geometry education at high school and university level. The Virtual Reality Gorilla Exhibit is an immersive VR developed at Georgia Institute of Technology for Zoo Atlanta to help educate people about gorillas, their lifestyle and their plight as an endangered species [20]. The positive reactions from the users suggest that it is possible to use VR as a general educational tool to teach middle school students the concepts about gorilla behaviors and social interactions [20]. These learning objectives normally cannot be achieved just by visiting the zoo [20].

Liu, Cheok, Lim and Theng [21] have created a mixed reality classroom. Two systems are developed: the solar system and the plant system. In the solar system, users sit around an operation table and used a head-mounted device to view the virtual solar system. Cups are used for the interactions between the users and the virtual objects. For instance, users can use the cup to pick up part of the earth to observe its inner structure. As for the plant system, four topics regarding plant are created: Reproductive, Seeds Dispersal, Seeds Germination and Photosynthesis. For example, in seeds germination, users have to set the right conditions to see a bug growing. The preliminary study conducted by Liu et al. [21] indicates participants' intention to use mixed reality for learning which is influenced directly by perceived usefulness, and indirectly through perceived ease of use and social influence.

In spite of the positive findings of some research, it would be premature to make broad recommendations regarding the use of VR as a curriculum enhancement [1]. It should not be used indiscriminately in any educational program [22]. The pedagogical benefits of VR as a learning tool need to be examined in a more comprehensive way. A broad framework that identifies the theoretical constructs or participant factors and their relationships in this domain should be developed further. Relevant constructs and their relationships need to be examined for the effective use of VR in education because all these constructs plays an important role in shaping the learning process and learning outcomes [23]. Strangman and Hall [1] also mention that factors that influence the effectiveness of computer simulations have not been extensively or systematically examined. Sanchez et al. [22] mention that it is a challenging and an outstanding task to study the right and applicable use of VR in education. Questions posed by them remained unanswered [22]: What are the appropriate theories and/or models to guide the design and development of a VR learning environment? What disciplines or subjects and what sorts of students require this technology? How are VR systems capable of improving the quality of student learning? When and why VR is irreplaceable?

Study on the use of VR for learning has been endeavoured with most of the efforts focus on implementing special-purpose systems or limited-scope prototypes [22]. Nevertheless, a matured framework still needs to be formalized to answer those questions mentioned above.

4   Reviews of Theoretical Model

The literature search shows only one model that has been developed to understand how VR influences the learning process and learning outcomes in a VR learning environment. Although designers and evaluators of VR systems know that this technology has significant potential to facilitate and improve learning, but little is known about the aspects of this technology that are best leveraged for enhancing understanding [23, 24]. In other words, we need to know when and how to use VR's features to support different learning tasks and various learners' needs to maximize the benefits of employing this technology in learning [23].

Knowing that VR's affordances and other factors of a learning environment all play a role in shaping learning process and the learning outcomes, through Project ScienceSpace, Salzman, Dede, Loftin and Chen [23] develop a model for understanding how VR aids complex conceptual learning in an immersive virtual learning environment. ScienceSpace project consists of three immersive virtual environments for science instruction: Newton World, Maxwell World and Pauling World. In Newton World, learners can become a ball that moving along an alley to learn Newton's laws of motion. Multisensory cues are used to direct users' attention to important variables such as mass, velocity and energy [23]. In Maxwell world, learners can build and explore electric fields. They can directly experience the field by becoming a test charge and be propelled through the field by the electric forces [25]. In Pauling World, learners explore the atoms and bonds of a simple and complex molecule for a lesson in chemistry [23].

This immersive virtual learning model describes how VR's features work together with other factors such as the concept that is to be learnt, learner characteristics, the interaction and learning experience that influence the learning process which, in turn, affect the learning outcomes (see Fig. 1). The learning process of this model is defined as the understanding development process that occurs while a person is completing lessons within the VR learning environment. In other words, it means the ability to do predictions, observations, and comparisons during the process of learning [23]. The assessment of the value of the VR's features is done through students' comments during the learning process, administrator observations during the lesson, usability questionnaires, interview feedback, and pre- and post-lesson knowledge assessments. The model stresses on the type of relationships that are important to examine rather than the direction (positive or negative) or strength (strong or weak) of the relationships which will differ depending on the specific nature of the virtual learning environment [23].

According to the model of Salzman et al. [23], before designing and developing an immersive VR learning environment, it is important to analyze the concepts to be mastered for the appropriate usage of VR's features because VR's features can support the learning of one concept, and at the same time hinder the learning of another. The three features afforded by the VR technology in this model are immersive 3-D representations, multiple frames of references and multisensory cues. The model shows that the relationships between the VR's features and learning may be moderated by the learner characteristics such as gender, domain experience, spatial ability, computer experience, motion sickness history and immersive tendencies. And these learner characteristics may also influence the learning and interaction experience as each individual has a unique experience in a learning environment. Finally, the VR's features also influence the quality of the interaction and learning experiences which,

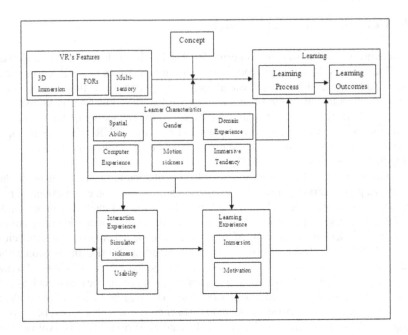

Fig. 1. Model describing how VR's features, the concept one is being asked, learner characteristics, and the interaction and learning experiences work together to influence the learning outcomes in VR learning environments [23]

in turn, affect the learning. The learning experience such as motivation and presence, and interaction experience such as usability and simulator sickness are the identified variables that can be affected by VR's features. Additionally, the interaction experience may also influence the learning experience which, in turn, affects the learning.

The model by Salzman et al. [23] can be a useful guide in designing, developing and evaluating VR learning environment. For instance, which concepts to address, which features are appropriate, and how interfaces should be designed to support usability. This model might have shed some light on what sort of students might gain benefits through VR learning and how VR enhances learning by looking into the interaction and learning experience. Nevertheless, more research is definitely needed to look into the appropriate theories and/or models to guide the design and development of a VR learning environment; how are VR systems capable of improving the quality of student learning by investigating the psychological learning process of the learners; and to investigate how other relevant constructs or factors work together to influence VR learning environment. Further investigation on the role of individual characteristics in VR learning environment is also needed.

5   Instructional Design Theoretical Framework

In order to use VR as a learning tool, an appropriate instructional design that guides the development of a VR-based learning environment is imperative because it is the

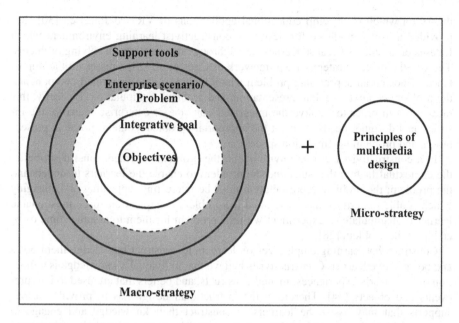

Fig. 2. Theoretical framework for designing a desktop VR-based learning environment [28]

instructional implementation of the technology that determines learning outcomes [26]. Clark [27] claims that *"if learning occurs as a result of exposure to any media, the learning is caused by the instructional method embedded in the media presentation."* Chen, Toh and Wan [28] have proposed an instructional design theoretical framework that offers design guidelines for desktop VR-based learning environment. Based on this instructional design theoretical framework, Chen et al. [28] have designed and developed a VR-based learning environment to assist novice car drivers to better comprehend the traffic rules. The framework comprises macro-strategy and micro-strategy (see Fig. 2). The macro-strategy combines the concept of integrative goals proposed by Gagné and Merill [29] and the model of designing constructivist learning environment proposed by Jonassen [30]. Whilst the micro-strategy is based on the cognitive theory of multimedia derived by Mayer [31] which is used to guide the design of the instructional message.

Goals that are to be achieved from learning are presumed to be the starting point of the instructional design process [29]. Thus, this framework starts with identifying the instructional goal which is a combination of several individual objectives that are to be integrated into a comprehensive purposeful activity known as enterprise. This is the concept of integrative goal proposed by Gagné & Merill [29]. These individual objectives may fall in the category of verbal information, labels, intellectual skills, or cognitive strategies (Gagné 1985, cited in [28]). The instructional designer then needs to design instruction that enables the learners to acquire the capability of achieving this integrated outcome, which is called the enterprise scenario [28].

VR is capable of affording constructivist learning because it provides a highly interactive environment in which learners are active participant in a computer-generated world [17, 32]. Winn [33] mentions that constructivism provides the best learning theory on which to develop educational applications of VR and Jonassen [30] has provided a useful guidance for designing constructivist learning environment which focuses on problems because learners learn through their attempt in solving problems. Thus, in the macro-strategy, the framework of Chen et al. [28] stresses on the importance of posing an appropriate problem which includes three integrated components: the problem context, problem presentation, and problem manipulation. Basically, this means that in order to achieve the integrated outcome or enterprise scenario, the instructional designer needs to select the appropriate problem context, problem presentation, and problem manipulation space.

In a constructivist learning environment, the problem statement must describe all the contextual factors that surround the problem to enable the learners to understand the problem; the problem representation must be interesting, appealing and engaging which is able to perturb the learner; and the problem manipulation space must enable learner to manipulate or experiment with the problem for them to assume some ownership of the problem [28].

Constructivist learning emphasizes on learners to construct knowledge themselves and be an active learner. Constructivists believe that individual's knowledge is a function of one prior's experiences, mental constructs, and beliefs that are used to interpret events and objects [34]. Therefore, the instructional design has to provide various supports that may assist the learners to construct their knowledge and engage in meaningful learning in the learning environment. These support tools include related cases, information resources, cognitive tools, conversation and collaboration tools, and social or contextual support [28]. Related cases refer to a set of related experiences or knowledge that the learner can refer to. Information resources refer to the rich sources of information that help learners to construct their mental models and comprehend the problems. Cognitive tools are tools that can scaffold the learners' ability to perform the task. Conversation and collaboration tools allow learners to communicate, collaborate and share ideas. Whilst social or contextual support stresses on the importance of considering contextual factors, such as physical, organizational, and cultural aspects of the environment [2].

To complement the macro-strategy, Mayer's [31] principles of multimedia design is served as the micro-strategy to guide the design of instructional message in the

Table 1. Principles of Multimedia Design (Mayer, 2002)

Principle	Description
Multimedia Principle	Learners learn better from words and pictures than from words alone.
Spatial Contiguity Principle	Learners learn better when corresponding words and pictures are presented near rather than far from each other on the page or screen.
Coherence Principle	Learners learn better when extraneous words, pictures, and sounds are excluded rather than included.
Modality Principle	Learners learn better from animation and narration than from animation and on-screen text.
Redundancy Principle	Learners learn better from animation and narration than from animation, narration, and on-screen text.

learning environment for a more effective learning. The five principles of multimedia adopted by Chen et al. [28] are multimedia principle, spatial contiguity principle, coherence principle, modality principle and redundancy principle. A description of these five principles is shown in Table 1.

The instructional design theoretical framework by Chen at al. [28] can be used to guide the design of a desktop VR-based learning environment that fits the constructivist learning environment. Empirical findings by Chen [2] show that this framework may function as an initial structure to guide the instructional design of a VR-based learning environment which can be further refined and/or revised to generate a more robust model.

6 Conclusions

This paper has given a review of the VR used for learning. We first started by examining the definition and types of VR available to be used for learning. From literature search, it can be observed that there are already some applications of VR for learning that have been implemented. However, implementing VR for learning without examining the pedagogical theories and the effect of using VR for learning would not be convincing. We have reviewed frameworks that have been applied in this domain. However, we realized that the framework is still immature. There is a need of a detailed theoretical framework for VR-based learning environment that could guide future development efforts. Key factors related to learning effectiveness in a VR-based learning environment and the influence of VR technology on psychological learning process should not be ignored. A critical step towards achieving an informed design of a VR-based learning environment is the investigation of the relationship among the relevant constructs or participant factors, the learning process and the learning outcomes. And only through this investigation that we would be able to answer to those implementation questions.

References

1. Strangman, N., Hall, T.: Virtual reality/simulations. National Center on Accessing the General Curriculum, Wakefield (2003), http://www.cast.org/publications/ncac/ncac_vr.html
2. Chen, C.J.: The design, development and evaluation of a virtual reality-based learning environment: Its efficacy in novice car driver instruction. Centre for Instructional Technology and Multimedia. University Science Malaysia (2005)
3. Allen, K., Austin, T., Beach, R., Bergstrom, A., Exon, S., Fabri, M., Fencott, C., Fernie, K., Gerhard, M., Grout, C., Jeffrey, S.: Creating and using virtual reality: A guide for the arts and humanities (2002), http://vads.ahds.ac.uk/guides/vr_guide/sect11.html
4. Dalgarno, B., Hedberg, J., Harper, B.: The contribution of 3D environments to conceptual understanding. In: ASCILITE 2002, Auckland, New Zealand, pp. 149–158 (2002)
5. Pan, Z., Cheok, A.D., Yang, H., Zhu, J., Shi, J.: Virtual reality and mixed reality for virtual learning environments. Computers & Graphics 30, 20–28 (2006)

6. Fällman, D.: Virtual reality in education: On-line survey (2000), http://www.informatik.umu.se/~dfallman/projects/vrie
7. Cruz-Neira, C., Sandin, D.J., DeFanti, T.A.: Surround-screen projection-based virtual reality: the design and implementation of the cave. In: 20th Annual Conference on Computer Graphics and Interactive Technique, pp. 135–142. ACM Press, New York (1993)
8. Silva, L.F., Cardoso, A., Mendes, E.B., Takahashi, E.K., Martins, S.: Associating non-immersive virtual reality and cognitive tools for Physics Teaching. In: 9th International Conference on Engineering Education, San Juan, Puerto Rico (2006)
9. Ashdown, N., Forestiero, S.: A guide to VRML 2.0 and an Evaluation of VRML Modelling Tools (1998), http://www.agocg.ac.uk/train/vrml2rep/cover.htm
10. Ieronutti, L., Chittaro, L.: Employing virtual humans for education and training in X3D/VRML worlds. Computers & Education 49, 93–109 (2007)
11. Chittaro, L., Ranon, R.: Web3D technologies in learning, education and training: Motivations, issues, opportunities. Computers & Education 49, 3–18 (2007)
12. Wikipedia: Quick time VR (2008), http://en.wikipedia.org/wiki/QuickTime_VR
13. Inoue, Y.: Effects of virtual reality support compared to video support in a high-school world geography class. Campus - Wide Information Systems 16, 95 (1999)
14. Kommers, P.A.M., Zhao, Z.M.: Virtual reality for education, http://projects.edte.utwente.nl/proo/trend4.htm
15. Roussou, M.: Learning by doing and learning through play: An exploration of interactivity in virtual environments for children. Computers in Entertainment 2, 10–23 (2004)
16. Song, K.S., Lee, W.Y.: A virtual reality application for geometry classes. Journal of Computer Assisted Learning 18, 149–156 (2002)
17. Kim, J.H., Park, S.T., Lee, H., Yuk, K.C., Lee, H.: Virtual reality simulations in physics education (2001), http://imej.wfu.edu/articles/2001/2/02/index.asp
18. Li, F.C., Angelier, J., Deffontaines, B., Hu, J.C., Hsu, S.H., Lee, C.H., Huang, C.H., Chen, C.H.: A virtual reality application for distance learning of Taiwan stream erosion in Geosciences. In: International Conference on Computers in Education (2002)
19. Kaufmann, H., Schmalstieg, D., Wagner, M.: Construct3D: A virtual reality application for mathematics and geometry education. Education and Information Technologies 5, 263–276 (2000)
20. Allison, D., Hodges, L.F.: Virtual reality for education. In: ACM Symposium on Virtual Reality Software and Technology, pp. 160–165. ACM Press, NY, USA, Seoul, Korea (2000)
21. Liu, W., Cheok, A.D., Lim, C.M.L., Theng, Y.L.: Mixed reality classroom - learning from entertainment. In: Second International Conference on Digital Interactive Media in Entertainment and Arts, Perth, Australia (2007)
22. Sanchez, A., Barreiro, J.M., Maojo, V.: Design of virtual reality systems for education: a cognitive approach. Education and Information Technologies 5, 345–362 (2000)
23. Salzman, M.C., Dede, C., Loftin, R.B., Chen, J.: A model for understanding how virtual reality aids complex conceptual learning. Presence: Teleoperators and Virtual Environments 8, 293–316 (1999)
24. Barnett, M., Yamagatah-Lynch, L., Keating, T., Barab, S.A., Hay, K.E.: Using virtual reality computer models to support student understanding of astronomical concepts. Journal of computers in Mathematics and Science Teaching 24, 333–356 (2005)
25. Salzman, M.C., Loftin, R.B.: ScienceSpace: Lessons for designing immersive virtual realities. In: CHI 1996, Vancouver, Canada (1996)
26. Collins, A.: Anticipating the impact of multimedia in education: Lessons from the literature. computers in Adult Education and Training 2, 136–149 (1995)

27. Clark, R.E.: Media will never influence learning. Educational Technology, Research and Development 42, 21–29 (1994)
28. Chen, C.J., Toh, S.C., Wan, M.F.: The theoretical framework for designing desktop virtual reality-based learning environment. Journal of Interactive Learning Research 15, 147–167 (2004)
29. Gagné, R.M., Merrill, M.D.: Integrative goals for instructional design. Education Technology Research and Development 38, 23–30 (1990)
30. Jonassen, D.H.: Designing constructivist learning environment. In: Reigeluth, C.M. (ed.) Instructional-design theories and models: A new paradigm of instructional theory, vol. 2, pp. 215–239. Merrill Prentice Hall, NJ (1999)
31. Mayer, R.E.: Multimedia learning. Cambridge University Press, Cambridge (2002)
32. Salis, C., Pantelidis, V.S.: Designing virtual environments for instruction: concepts and considerations. VR in the Schools 2, 6–10 (1997)
33. Winn, W.: A conceptual basis for educational applications of virtual reality (1993), http://www.hitl.washington.edu/projects/learning_center/winn/winn-R-93-9.txt
34. Mergel, B.: Instructional design & learning theory (1998), http://www.usask.ca/education/coursework/802papers/mergel/brenda.htm

The Mental Vision Framework - A Platform for Teaching, Practicing and Researching with Computer Graphics and Virtual Reality

Achille Peternier, Frederic Vexo, and Daniel Thalmann

Virtual Reality Laboratory (VRLab)
Ecole Polytechnique Federale de Lausanne (EPFL)
{achille.peternier,frederic.vexo,daniel.thalmann}@epfl.ch

Abstract. Despite the wide amount of computer graphics frameworks and solutions available, it is still difficult to find a perfect one fitting at the same time many constraints, like pedagogical intents and user-friendliness or speed with high rendering quality and portability. In this article we describe our contribution to the topic: the Mental Vision platform. Mental Vision is a framework composed of a teaching/research oriented graphics engine simplifying the users needs in computer visualization and a set of corollary tools specifically designed for practicing and learning of computer graphics and virtual reality. In this dissertation we explain our approach design and the contribution brought into a series of study cases to show how concretely Mental Vision satisfies existing needs not addressed by other solutions.

Keywords: Computer Graphics, Virtual Reality, Teaching and learning, CAVE, Mobile devices, Immersion.

1 Introduction

Virtual Reality (VR) is a science that has gained an increasing amount of popularity and applications during the last years. This increasing interest has also produced a very wide amount of both software and hardware technologies to support and improve creation of VR environments. Unfortunately, most of these innovations are often accessible only by skilled users with a good background knowledge in VR and Computer Graphics (CG) and through cumbersome and expensive devices. VR applications require also a significant amount of time to be developed, because of the complexity introduced by the generation and adaptation of 3D objects to fit into a specific realtime software. Finally, VR is a complex matter by itself and difficult to learn because of the points previously cited and also because of the heterogeneity of notions (mathematics, networking, physics, etc.) a user needs to practice with before attempting to implement a full Virtual Environment (VE).

With the Mental Vision project we aim to tackle theses issues, by creating a framework for virtual reality intended to be very intuitive, powerful and low-cost.

Z. Pan et al. (Eds.): Transactions on Edutainment I, LNCS 5080, pp. 242–260, 2008.

Mental Vision has been created by mainly targeting to the needs and constraints of the educational and scientific community, notably reducing the learning curve and time required to create VEs, limiting the cost of immersive or wearable frameworks without compromising their quality, and improving understanding of VR concepts and techniques by directly practicing with them. Moreover, such a framework has been designed to fit into a wide range of heterogeneous devices, spacing from low-end student PCs through mobile devices up to Cave Automatic Virtual Environments (CAVEs) [1], across different operative systems and hardware setups.

Our framework is composed by two main entities: a multiplatform, multidevice 3D graphics engine called MVisio (see 3.1) and a set of tools ranging from pedagogical interactive demonstrators to 3D model exporters and file format converters (see 3.2).

We introduced our first results about the Mental Vision platform in [2]. In [3] we separately described the mobile aspects of the platform, while in [4] we published the first adaptation of our system to work in a CAVE. In this dissertation we insisted in making complex things easier and more affordable for the users, in order to widen the fruition and application scenarios of VR-oriented technologies. Our experience with students and researchers has shown that this approach effectively responds to a need that is not only welcome but also required. In this work we expose in detail each step of the creation and design of the Mental Vision framework, comparing our approach against other similar scenarios, and we conclude with a series of case-of-study of concrete utilizations and applications developed through the use of our framework *in toto*, pointing out the contributions brought.

2   Related Work

A wide effort has been invested during the last years into the production of tools to standardize and simplify access to 3D visual contents. Industry, researchers and the open-source community released a large amount of platforms to fit the different needs, covering almost each possible device and operating system.

2.1   Open and Closed Source 3D Graphics Engines

Ogre[1], Crystal Space[2] and Irrlicht[3] are among the most used and complete open-source graphics engines available so far that could be used as foundation for virtual reality applications. Similar to MVisio, they feature high quality rendering but suffer from being available only on PC, without support for mobile devices or CAVEs. There are also many differences between the application programming interface (API): such open-source engines are mainly oriented to performance and game development, while MVisio aims at simplicity and compactness.

Industry graphics engine are state-of-the-art frameworks featuring the most recent effects available and extremely optimized for speed. Among these systems

---

[1] http://www.ogre3d.org
[2] http://www.crystalspace3d.org
[3] http://irrlicht.sourceforge.net

there are Cryengine2 from Crytek[4], Unreal Engine 3 from Unreal Technology[5], Half Life 2 from Valve Software[6] or Doom 3 from ID Software[7]. All these closed-source software are extremely powerful engines but limited by their licence costs, the lack of a full access to the source code for adaptations and modifications required to move the system to other platforms/devices not originally aimed by their developers (like CAVEs or Smartphones) and are very difficult to program for not specialists. Such engines are also very complicated and poorly documented, requiring a good amount of time to get used with as pointed out by Kot et al. in [5]. Kot et al. also complained about the limitations and bugs of some of the GUI available in these engines: with MVisio we implemented our own integrated GUI, offering the same basic user interface functionalities independently from the system/device the engine is running on.

Virtools[8] is a professional framework conceptually very similar to our one, offering support for a wide range of devices and platforms and includes a visual editor for quickly developing applications. With MVisio we preferred to directly simplify programming without recurring to an *ad hoc* visual editing tool and by targeting mobile devices, not supported by their platform. Virtools is also more hardware demanding than MVisio, which has been programmed to work on older student machines too.

Recently Microsoft released XNA 2[9] which is a free development framework oriented to game developers. XNA aims at reducing the complexity of this task by offering all the basic tools and source code to immediately start working on the application itself instead on corollary tasks. XNA is unfortunately very oriented to videogames and limited to Microsoft systems (Windows or XBox consoles) and lacks support for VR and mobile devices. XNA is also accessible only through C# and the .NET framework, a limitation for our students and researchers using also Linux or MacOS systems.

Java3D is acquiring more and more interest thanks to the support for hardware acceleration and availability of the J2ME platform on several recent devices. We used C++ and Windows Mobile instead because at the beginning of our project hardware acceleration on mobile devices was not as robust and as accessible as today. This evolution is summarized by Soh et al. in [6].

2.2   Educational Frameworks

Towle et al. first identified in 1978 with GAIN [7] the interest in offering interactive applications to use at home as an option to practical work sessions, done in cooperation with other students, and as a more intuitive way to learn than with just a manual or a workbook. We extended this idea with our pedagogical demonstrators, by integrating them directly with the class documentation and

---

[4] http://www.crytek.com
[5] http://www.unrealtechnology.com
[6] http://www.valvesoftware.com
[7] http://www.idsoftware.com
[8] http://www.virtools.com
[9] http://www.xna.com

by making them mobile for at-desk support during practical sessions. The benefits offered by multimedia contents for CG teaching purposes are also shown by Song and al. in [8]: interactive modules reduce learning time and improve use and diffusion of contents over the web, potentially targeting more people without additional costs. Meeker used a learning by practice approach in [9] through the use of the free software Anim8or[10] to let students practice about basic notions of 3D modeling during the course. Our system is more oriented to the use of models already created by artists, for example by exporting them through our plugin from 3D Studio Max directly into the graphics engine.

Many CG and VR topics can also be taught by recurring to games: for example Hill and al. used in [10] puzzles and games to reinforce the learning objectives. Similarly, Becker in [11] used video-games as motivator for programming applications on Computer Science classes. We already had a positive feedback by offering gaming projects during the course of advanced Virtual Reality in [12]: with MVisio, we want to provide to the learners a tool allowing them to benefit more from this option, by giving them all the instruments they need in an easy and comfortable way. Korte et al. also reported that creating videogames may also be an innovative method for teaching modeling skills in theoretical computer science [13].

About the creation of pedagogical oriented graphic engines, when 3D graphics accelerator cards for micro computer weren't available, Clevenger and al. developed a graphics engine to supply students with a learning platform (called TUGS) in [14]. Their goal was to offer a support to students to immediately render some images and to allow them to substitute parts of code of the TUGS engine with their own later in the semester, in order to have a full working platform since the beginning of the class. Their approach was particulary useful before the large introduction on personal computers of graphics APIs based on 3D hardware acceleration like OpenGL and DirectX, which substituted the expensive need to develop a custom rasterizer. Coleman et al. created Gedi [15], an open-source game engine for teaching videogame design and programming in C++. Based on the same principle to create a pedagogical engine, with MVisio, we want to provide a more generic software that can be used not only for games but also for Computer Graphics and Virtual Reality applications, by adding for example support for VR devices like head-mounted displays or CAVE systems. Tori et al. used Java 3D, small videogames, and customized software in [16] to introduce CG to students. They also relied on a more complex Java 3D graphics engine (called enJine) for the development of semester projects. The main advantage of their approach is the operative system independency offered by Java, very useful when addressing a wide user audience like a student class, using different PCs and operative systems. With our system we more aim at Virtual Reality and supporting devices other than standard personal computers.

In [17], Wilkens pointed out the advantages and disadvantages of using more than one API to access graphics functionalities during a computer graphics course, resulting in a excessive burdening of both students and teachers demanding more extra-time than the time normally expected for the class.

---

[10] http://www.anim8or.com

In the next sessions we describe first the goals and design of our framework and we analyze then different concrete uses of our platform on different projects and classes, to evaluate the contribution brought by our approach.

3   Mental Vision Platform

Mental Vision is a computer graphics and virtual reality framework oriented towards education and scientific research needs. We decided to create our own system after comparing the different already existing solutions without finding a perfect one fitting at the same time to all our constraints. We can enumerate our requests in ten points:

1. Multiplatform (across different operative systems) and multidevice (running on handheld devices, PCs and CAVE environments).
2. Very compact in sizes and resources, reducing external dependencies, improving compatibility between recent and older machines and project deployability.
3. Extremely simple to use, reducing the learning curve and the lines of code to write to achieve results and getting rid of all the corollary aspects CG usually requires.
4. Featuring an embedded GUI system with basic windowing, text management, buttons, etc. without requiring external additional dependencies.
5. Robust, for uses during public demonstrations, classes and conferences.
6. Not dependant from costly software or hardware, being aimed to education and science, often very budget-limited.
7. Fast and modern, featuring a good rendering speed, quality, and satisfying at the same time teaching and research needs in our field.
8. Virtual-Reality aware, easily supporting VR specific devices like Head-Mounted displays or haptic devices.
9. Including the necessary tools to import models, textures, videos and animations from other programs.
10. Including tutorials and demonstrators about the framework itself, CG and VR concepts as well.

With our framework we address and propose a solution to these points. Our work is divided into two main entities: the 3D graphics engine itself (called MVisio) and the pedagogical tools (like modules and tutorials) that rely on the top of MVisio. We describe them both in the next subsections.

3.1   MVisio 3D Graphics Engine

The MVisio 3D graphics engine is a generic, multi-platform and multi-device library giving access to modern computer graphics via a very simple API (see figure 1).

We insisted into simplifying things usually complex like advanced shading techniques or CAVE/mobile devices porting by making them almost invisible

Fig. 1. High-quality rendering with dynamic soft-shadowing, depth of field and bloom lightning

for the user. We extended this idea of simplicity to each aspect of the engine design, aiming at the same time to an apprentice user and a more experienced one. New users can have immediate results with just few lines of code: initializing the engine, loading a scene with lights, cameras, textures and many 3D models and displaying it on the screen takes as low as five lines of code. Advanced users can later accessing and modifying dynamically each element, by looking more deeply into the engine design or just use the highest-level instructions when they don't need unnecessary full control on specific details. One of the key points of MVisio making it very different from the game-oriented graphics products is the automatization of almost each feature through high-level methods taking care of everything but still offering experienced users to by-pass high-level calls to fine tune their needs. We can consider MVisio as a dual-head entity, exposing at the same time high and low level interfaces to the intrinsic features that can be accessed at the same time, according to the context and user needs. This is not only an advantage for new students who can have immediate results but also to experienced users to quickly build up a 3D scenario to use for their goals.

A MVisio-based application source-code for Windows is identical to its relative under Linux. Porting the same application from PC to mobile devices is just a matter of linking against different libraries and modifying a constant, switching from PC to CAVE just needs to specify the IP addresses of the CAVE-client computers. The following piece of C++ source code shows a very basic MVisio application supporting loading and rendering of a 3D scene on PDA, PC and CAVE:

```
//#define MV_PDA // <-- uncomment this for a PDA build
//#define MV_CAVE // <-- uncomment this for a CAVE build
#include <mvisio.h>

int main(int argc, int argv[])
{
    // CAVE build require to specify client PC IP addresses:
#ifdef MV_CAVE
    MVCLIENT *front = new MVCLIENT();
    front->setIP("192.168.0.1");
    front->setID(MV_FRONT);

    MVCLIENT *right = new MVCLIENT();
    right->setIP("192.168.0.2");
    right->setID(MV_RIGHT);

    // Etc...
#endif

    // Initialize the graphics engine:
    MVISIO::init();

    // Load full scene (textures, lights, models, etc.):
    MVNODE *scene = MVISIO::load("bar.mve");

    // If in the CAVE, update user head coordinates
    // for correct projection computation:
#ifdef MV_CAVE
    MVCLIENT::putUser(1.175f, 1.6f, 1.25f);
#endif

    // Display the scene:
    MVISIO::clear();
    MVISIO::begin3D();
        scene->pass();
    MVISIO::end3D();
    MVISIO::swap();

    // Free everything:
    MVISIO::free();
}
```

MVisio also natively satisfies most of the recent computer graphics standards, featuring direct support for complex model loading, advanced shading techniques and post-processing effects, skinning and animations, terrain rendering, integrated GUI systems, video2texture, etc. The user can just decide to activate

or load one of these items and let MVisio automatically manage everything, or
specifying each parameters through a very wide set of parametrization options
featured in each class.

Another advantage of MVisio is the coherence of the design. Each element,
either 2D (for the graphics user interface) or 3D, derives from the same base
structure and exposes the same functionalities, thus reducing learning time for
understanding how each MVisio object works and reducing code sizes. Advanced
users can create and add new objects to MVisio by simply deriving from this
base class, as shown in the following source code example. Users just need to implement the *render*() method that will be called by MVisio to display the object,
when other functionalities like scene-graph compatibility and instancing will be
natively managed by MVisio, reducing user tasks to perform when implementing
new entities:

```cpp
typedef class MY_SKYBOX : public MVNODE
{
public:
    MY_SKYBOX() { type = MV_NODE_CUSTOM; }

    bool render(void *data = 0)
    {
        MVELEMENT *element = (MVELEMENT *) data;

        // Scenegraph node base position:
        glLoadMatrixf((float *) element->getMatrix());

        // Setting OpenGL flags for this object:
        MVOPENGL::blendingOff();
        MVMATERIAL::reset();
        MVSHADER::disable();
        MVLIGHT::lightingOff();
        // Etc...

        // Perform native OpenGL calls:
        glColor4f(1.0, 1.0, 1.0,1.0f);
        glTranslatef(position.x,position.y,position.z);
        glScalef(0.5f, 0.5f, 0.5f);

        // Display the skybox with OGL triangles
        glBegin(GL_TRIANGLES);
        glVertex3f(20.0f, 20.0f, 20.0f);
        // Etc...

        return true;
    }
} MY_SKYBOX;
```

3.2 Pedagogical and Corollary Tools

The MVisio graphics engine is the core product of our framework, but not the only one. When MVisio is aimed mainly to concrete practice and developing of applications, we also created a set of corollary tools oriented to aid a more *ex cathedra* teaching approach. The Mental Vision platform is then completed by three additional tools: a set of pedagogical modules, a series of tutorials, and other utilities to reduce and simplify development times with MVisio.

Pedagogical modules are compact and interactive demonstrators created to practically illustrate a specific algorithm, method or technique introduced during the class. Modules are concretely executable files created on the top of the MVisio engine (thus inheriting the same robustness and smoothness) working as small stand-alone applications that both students and teachers can download and use as learning support. Moreover, modules can be used on handheld devices that assistants may use during practical sessions to directly illustrate additional explains on the desk. Modules are distributed along with their source code that can be used by learners as an example of uses of the MVisio graphics engine itself.

Tutorials refer to the use of the graphics engine. They are a suite of HTML pages with downloadable examples (conceptually similar to the very popular tutorial sites like Nehe[11] or Gametutorials[12]) illustrating step by step how to start working with MVisio. Tutorials are used for introductory notions and first practice with MVisio, while modules aim to cover more specific aspects by letting users reading their source code to find out how an algorithm or technique has been implemented.

Besides the graphics engine, modules and tutorials, the Mental Vision framework comes with a series of extra tools like Autodesk[13] 3D Studio Max plugins or FBX converters to easily import 3D contents from third-part products into MVisio. Extra tools include also optional classes for using a joypad to control 3D cameras or some basic artworks to improve the aspect of the embedded GUI.

4   Implementation

This section gives an architectural and technical overview about the main components of the Mental Vision platform, namely the MVisio 3D graphics engine and pedagogical demonstrators.

4.1   System Architecture

The Mental Vision framework is a multi-platform and multi-device system featuring a 3D graphics engine with an unique and same interface independently from the operating system or device we want to use, and cross-platform and

---

[11] http://nehe.gamedev.net

[12] http://www.gametutorials.com

[13] http://www.autodesk.com

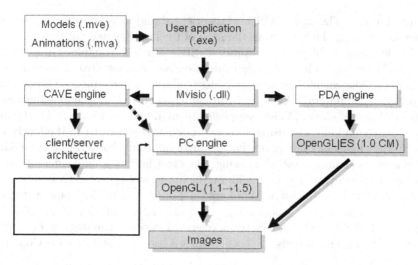

Fig. 2. MVisio multi-device rendering pipeline overview

cross-device pedagogical demonstrators and tools. Users adopting MVisio as graphics engine just need to link their code with the appropriate library created for each OS/device and let our software manage the rest. Students practicing or reviewing class notes through our modules just need to pick the appropriate version supporting their platform and run it.

MVisio automatically tunes its internal pipeline through different code-paths, according to the context. For example a typical PC application (x86 architecture on a Linux or Windows based system) directly uses the graphics hardware available to perform the best rendering approach. CAVE systems require a more complex approach: a local instance of MVisio (that runs on the same machine the user is developing on) becomes the server of the CAVE system. This server version of MVisio communicates with the several CAVE client machines, each one running a daemon service waiting requests from a server. Locally, each CAVE client (one per wall) starts a MVisio version for PC and reproduces all the high-level methods invoked server-side by the user. We can consider MVisio for CAVE as a remote playback of methods called on the server PC (see figure 2).

MVisio for mobile devices is very similar to the MVisio for PC version, but is optimized for fixed-maths ARM processors and uses only the basic graphics functionalities of the engine, that is the only ones that may run on the very limited resources available on handheld devices. It is important to mention that the only differences for the end user between running his/her application on a PC, CAVE or mobile device concern only the version of MVisio to link with: no other modifications are required.

4.2   Technical Details

The Mental Vision software is entirely written in C++. The graphics engine is distributed as a stand-alone dynamic-link library (DLL) to link against using its

.h and .lib files. The entire API is class-oriented and uses an internal resource manager releasing the users from the need of freeing allocated entities.

MVisio uses a slightly customized SDL version (Simple DirectMedia Library[14]) for basic platform independent output window creation, event and threading management. Low-level graphics rendering is performed via OpenGL[15] on personal computers/CAVEs and through OpenGL|ES[16] on mobile devices.

On PCs and CAVEs, MVisio supports OpenGL version 1.1 up to 1.5, by automatically compiling and using different code-paths according to the hardware quality the engine is running on. For example on a full OpenGL 1.5 compliant PC hardware skinning, soft-shadowing, per-pixel lightning and different post-processing effects (like depth of field and bloom-lightning) are activated.

On mobile devices (based on Windows CE 4 or better) MVisio comes with two different versions: a generic one, using a software implementation of OpenGL|ES (made by Hybrid) and a hardware accelerated version, running on PowerVR MBX-lite[17] graphics boards. In both cases we used OpenGL|ES 1.0 Common Lite profiles.

MVisio for CAVEs uses TCP/IP communications for data transmission between server and clients (refer to [4] for more details).

5   Cases of Study

This section presents several cases of study related to concrete uses of our platform, ranging from educational/practicing to scientific applications. Each case will be briefly summarized and followed by a discussion about the advantages brought by the adoption of the Mental Vision framework.

5.1   Mental Vision for Education During the Lessons

Teaching topics like splines, clipping planes or vertex skinning may be a difficult task because of the abstract notions required by the learning process. Teachers often recur to schematics or videos to support their explains with visual feedback. Despite the clearness contribution yielded by images to the learning process, practice and interactivity are not covered by these supports.

Pedagogic Modules. To improve these aspects of teaching, we developed a series of interactive modules to be used during lessons to concretely and dynamically show how an algorithm, technique or concept work. Teachers have a more robust and dynamic support to visualize on a large screen notions they're explaining, other than a blackboard or a video. Modules allow both teachers and students to directly interact with the topic discussed and have a direct relationship between the modifications they apply and the results they get (What

---

[14] http://www.libsdl.org
[15] http://www.opengl.org
[16] http://www.khronos.org/opengles
[17] http://www.imgtec.com

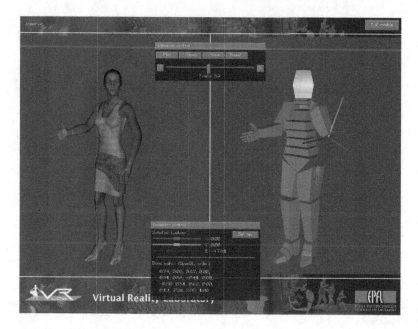

Fig. 3. Animation module: students can create, manipulate and export short animations for later usage within the MVisio 3D engine

You See Is What You Get approach). Moreover, modules can be downloaded and used at home for reviewing the class content and their source-code read for potential implementations during practical work sessions: being both modules and practical sessions based on the top of the MVisio engine, the course get a coherent guiding thread between the theoretical aspects and the practical ones, reducing the patchwork-like approach many courses suffer from using some tools during the lessons, other ones in the class-notes and different ones again during workshops and practice. Modules show also a great utility in e-learning contexts, offering students remotely following the class to still be able to practice and repeat the experiences taught.

For example the module about skinned animation allows students to create short animations by setting different key-postures on a time-table affecting a virtual character (see figure 3). This way, teachers don't need to rely on cumbersome and expensive software like 3D Studio Max or Maya to demonstrate and practice with this topic. Furthermore, animations created through this compact module can be saved and exported on a file for later usage in MVisio for practical work or class projects, connecting theoretical course lessons with practical sessions.

Other modules also feature this editing options, like the particle engine and terrain engine related ones: these modules can be used as teaching support during the lesson time and as particle or terrain editors during the practical sessions. Users can export to a file the particle system or terrain created through the

Fig. 4. Our CAVE used during young student visits to disseminate scientific technologies

module and load them directly into MVisio, thus reducing dependencies from external software and improving coherence with the theoretic aspects.

Modules are even more connected between *ex cathedra* lessons and practical sessions by their mobile versions, running on handheld devices. During practical sessions, assistants can freely sit at the student desks with their handheld devices and support their additional explains by reusing the mobile version of a module as a portative blackboard.

CAVE and Dissemination. We integrated a visit to our laboratory to the course plan in order to let students seeing and experiencing with our VR equipments. Particular attention has been used for the CAVE part of this visit, by using it to furthermore fix concepts like spatial level of detail and terrain rendering techniques. Students can enter the CAVE and experience these techniques by seeing them concretely used around them, with stereographic and immersive rendering. CAVE systems have the advantage of being very curious and rare devices that will attract students attention and give them a long term remember of the experience.

We also use our CAVE as attraction during public demonstrations for external visitors, like secondary or high school students, for disseminating technologies we use in our field through user-friendly and interesting demos (see figure 4).

Thanks to the automatic multi-device support of MVisio and the easiness of its calibration support for the CAVE rendering, it is straightforward and very time effective to run, maintain or improve such demos: in less than 5 minutes the entire system can be started, calibrated and ready for visitors.

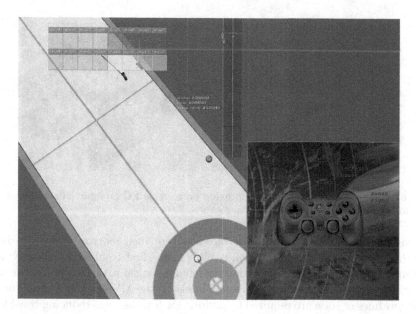

Fig. 5. A curling simulation game made by students with animations, dynamic lightning and GUI

5.2 Mental Vision for Practical Works

Theoretical classes are coupled with practical sessions where students may concretely apply the knowledge introduced during the different lessons. We already observed in [12] that proposing the creation of little game-like applications, including most of the VR and CG related aspects taught during the class, was an interesting motivating factor. We improved this aspect by introducing the MVisio 3D graphics engine as the standard tool for semester projects and workshops.

The Curling. Students of a virtual reality course were asked for developing a simulation of a curling match (see figure 5). With such a project, we aimed to make students practice with several aspects of virtual reality by integrating in the same work realtime graphics, basic physics, stereographic rendering, force feedback (through a vibrating joypad) and some game mechanics to implement curling rules. The practical sessions lasted one semester in reason of one hour per week and projects were done by groups of two students. We gave for the first time MVisio to students, a basic DirectInput library, 3D models and some guidelines for the physics and game related aspects.

At the end of the semester we evaluated about twenty projects. Compared to previously years projects, made by using other tools or letting students to freely choose which software adopt, a clear improvement in both the quality and completeness of the work were noticeable. Despite the low amount of time accorded weekly on this task, they managed to take care of all the aspects and improved their global vision about the creation of a VE. The immediate results available

Fig. 6. Virtualized CAVE to locally preview on a single PC an immersive application developed with MVisio

through the lightweight MVisio interface also kept their motivation high, reducing the gap from the documentation reading to the first results considerably: for example at the end of the first session students managed to display and move the different scene elements on the screen. Thanks to the MVisio API compactness, only few lines of code are required to perform such tasks, thus reducing considerably the amount of information users have to understand in order to be operative.

Semester Projects. We have been offering bachelor/master level projects about specific VR/CG topics for students who decide to pass their semester projects in our laboratory. Such project topics may be very heterogeneous, like implementing state-of-the-art techniques in our software or helping assistants in their researches. For example we offered many projects related to mobile devices or our CAVE, like a 3D GPS-like handheld remote controller to perform tele-operations on a real blimp or implementing a full immersive game in the CAVE. Unfortunately, we just have a single CAVE and very few mobile devices that may be shared among all the persons needing them. Thanks to the multi-device portability of MVisio, we can get rid of this problem by letting users work on the PC version and just run their projects later on the hardware they need. For CAVE users requiring a wider overview we also developed a Virtual CAVE (see figure 6) featuring a single PC preview about how their application will look like once ran on the real device.

5.3   Mental Vision for Research and Prove of Concept

We exposed so far minor uses of the MVisio engine on semester projects, course practical works or similar: in the following examples we describe deeper and more long-term applications of MVisio for thesis research projects.

MHaptic. MVisio has been integrated into a haptic engine (called MHaptic [18]) to manage the visual output of the system, featuring the Immersion[18] Haptic Workstation and a user-worn HMD (see figure 7).

---

[18] http://www.immersion.com

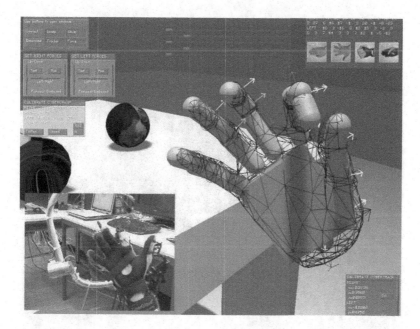

Fig. 7. MHaptic haptic engine using MVisio for visual rendering

MHaptic relies on an external editor, MHaptic Scene Creator, which is a 3D Studio Max-like software to add haptic proprieties to a 3D scene (like weight, collision detection, physics, etc.). This software has been developed by largely using the GUI system and advanced functionalities of MVisio (see figure 8).

The MHaptic project shows how far MVisio can be used not only to simplify teachers and students needs but also to develop very complex and advanced applications.

Human Animation. MVisio native support for large screens, CAVEs and head-mounted displays has been widely used in [19] to test and validate inverse kinematics reaching techniques authors introduced. Thanks to the MVisio portability, they could repeat the experience by giving visual feedback to users on PC, through an HMD or in front of large screens with no need of major modifications to the applications they developed (see figure 9).

6   Conclusions and Future Work

This publication describes motivations, approaches and results we obtained by creating our graphics framework called Mental Vision. We used it for teaching, practice and research in the field of computer graphics and virtual reality. We cite many different cases of study where the MVisio graphics engine and pedagogical tools have been successfully used, showing advantages and benefits. The MVisio 3D graphics engine simplifies the creation of virtual environments

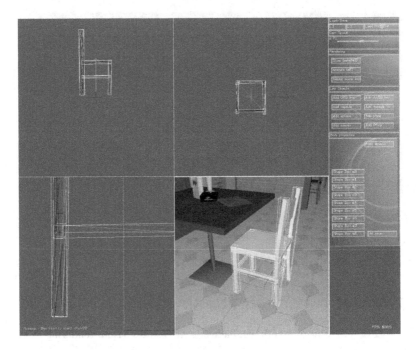

Fig. 8. MHaptic editor for adding haptic properties to virtual objects, entirely developed using MVisio and its GUI support

Fig. 9. User testing the different reaching techniques in the CAVE

and the adoption of less programmer-friendly platforms like handheld devices or CAVE systems. MVisio satisfies at the same time a very wide range of needs and perfectly fits into a series of different cases that usually would require more than a single software and approaches. Thanks to MVisio, our entire laboratory is working on the top of the same system, from researchers to students, improving inter-personal cooperations, reducing learning times and facilitating the maintaining of software written by other persons or members who left the crew.

We are now planning to make the CAVE and mobile device support more generic. CAVE support should become useable on CAVE installations other than ours, with an arbitrary shape and number of walls, while the hardware accelerated support for handheld devices should be extended to more recent mobile phones and personal digital assistants, supporting OpenGL|ES 1.1 or higher.

MVisio version 1.6.4 and pedagogical modules are freely downloadable for teaching and researching purposes on our website[19].

Acknowledgments. Mental Vision has been sponsored by the EPFL Funding Program for Teaching and Learning (FIFO). MVisio has been recently used and extended in the framework of the INTERMEDIA Network of Excellence.

References

1. Cruz-Neira, C., Sandin, D.J., DeFanti, T.A., Kenyon, R.V., Hart, J.C.: The cave: audio visual experience automatic virtual environment. Commun. ACM 35(6), 64–72 (1992)
2. Peternier, A., Thalmann, D., Vexo, F.: Mental vision: a computer graphics teaching platform. In: Pan, Z., Aylett, R.S., Diener, H., Jin, X., Göbel, S., Li, L. (eds.) Edutainment 2006. LNCS, vol. 3942, pp. 223–232. Springer, Heidelberg (2006)
3. Peternier, A., Vexo, F., Thalmann, D.: Wearable Mixed Reality System In Less Than 1 Pound. In: Proceedings of the 12th Eurographics Symposium on Virtual Environment (2006)
4. Peternier, A., Cardin, S., Vexo, F., Thalmann, D.: Practical Design and Implementation of a CAVE Environment. In: International Conference on Computer Graphics, Theory and Applications GRAPP, pp. 129–136 (2007)
5. Kot, B., Wuensche, B., Grundy, J., Hosking, J.: Information visualisation utilising 3d computer game engines case study: a source code comprehension tool. In: CHINZ 2005: Proceedings of the 6th ACM SIGCHI New Zealand chapter's international conference on Computer-human interaction, pp. 53–60. ACM, New York (2005)
6. Soh, J.O.B., Tan, B.C.Y.: Mobile gaming. Commun. ACM 51(3), 35–39 (2008)
7. Towle, T., DeFanti, T.: Gain: An interactive program for teaching interactive computer graphics programming. In: SIGGRAPH 1978: Proceedings of the 5th annual conference on Computer graphics and interactive techniques, pp. 54–59. ACM, New York (1978)
8. Song, W.C., Ou, S.C., Shiau, S.R.: Integrated computer graphics learning system in virtual environment: case study of bezier, b-spline and nurbs algorithms. In: Information Visualization, 2000. Proceedings. IEEE International Conference, pp. 33–38 (2000)

---

[19] http://vrlab.epfl.ch/~apeternier

9. Meeker, P.H.: Introducing 3d modeling and animation into the course curriculum. J. Comput. Small Coll. 19(3), 199–206 (2004)
10. Hill, J.M.D., Ray, C.K., Blair, J.R.S., Curtis, A., Carver, J.: Puzzles and games: addressing different learning styles in teaching operating systems concepts. SIGCSE Bull 35(1), 182–186 (2003)
11. Becker, K.: Teaching with games: the minesweeper and asteroids experience. J. Comput. Small Coll. 17(2), 23–33 (2001)
12. Gutierrez, M., Thalmann, D., Vexo, F.: Creating cyberworlds: experiences in computer science education. In: International Conference on Cyberworlds, 2004, pp. 401–408. Virtual Reality Lab., Swiss Fed. Inst. of Technol, Lausanne, Switzerland (2004)
13. Korte, L., Anderson, S., Pain, H., Good, J.: Learning by game-building: a novel approach to theoretical computer science education. In: ITiCSE 2007: Proceedings of the 12th annual SIGCSE conference on Innovation and technology in computer science education, pp. 53–57. ACM, New York (2007)
14. Clevenger, J., Chaddock, R., Bendig, R.: Tugs: a tool for teaching computer graphics. SIGGRAPH Comput. Graph. 25(3), 158–164 (1991)
15. Coleman, R., Roebke, S., Grayson, L.: Gedi: a game engine for teaching videogame design and programming. J. Comput. Small Coll. 21(2), 72–82 (2005)
16. Tori, R., Jo ao Luiz Bernardes, J., Nakamura, R.: Teaching introductory computer graphics using java 3d, games and customized software: a brazilian experience. In: SIGGRAPH 2006: ACM SIGGRAPH 2006 Educators program, p. 12. ACM, New York (2006)
17. Wilkens, L.: A multi-api course in computer graphics. In: CCSC 2001: Proceedings of the sixth annual CCSC northeastern conference on The journal of computing in small colleges, USA, Consortium for Computing Sciences in Colleges (2001)
18. Ott, R., De Perrot, V., Thalmann, D., Vexo, F.: MHAPTIC: a Haptic Manipulation Library for Generic Virtual Environments. In: Haptex 2007(2007)
19. Peinado, M., Meziat, D., Maupu, D., Raunhardt, D., Thalmann, D., Boulic, R.: Accurate on-line avatar control with collision anticipation. In: VRST 2007: Proceedings of the 2007 ACM symposium on Virtual reality software and technology, pp. 89–97. ACM, New York (2007)

Making the Real World as a Game World to Learners by Applying Game-Based Learning Scenes into Ubiquitous Learning Environment

Maiga Chang[1], Stis Wu[2], and Jia-Sheng Heh[2]

[1] School of Computing and Information Systems, Athabasca University, Canada
maiga@ms2.hinet.net
[2] Dept. of Information and Computer Engineering, Chung-Yuan Christian Univ., Taiwan
stis@mcsl.ice.cycu.edu.tw, jsheh@ice.cycu.edu.tw

Abstract. A ubiquitous learning environment provides learners opportunities of observing and touching the learning objects around the learners according to their preferences and/or interests. Learners can solve problems, answer questions, and propose their own questions, in the ubiquitous learning environment. However, it is still a serious topic to learners and most of them only do learning when they really have to, because it is a learning task. Games have many features which make learners have higher motivation in learning and have willing in learning actively. Moreover, the 'stage' concept in the games is also a big factor which might attract learners doing continuous learning, because the learners feel they really accomplished something and want to challenge further. In this paper, we first use small stories and activities to figure out what the learners interests with, which means, make learners call; and, build the personalized knowledge structure for the learner according to his/her choices and interests. With the helps of the context-awareness knowledge structure, we designs and builds learning scenes to offer learners the personalized learning services based on the 'stage' concept in the game. Each learning scene may cover one or many learning spots, and each learning spot has different learning objects. We can construct a series of learning scenes dynamically for individual learner based on the learner's choices, preferences and interests. Furthermore, a learning path involves learning scene switching is also generated automatically for the learner. A scenario with several exhibition rooms and artifacts in a museum is used to demonstrate the idea and mechanism proposed by this research.

Keywords: game-based learning, scene, ubiquitous learning, pervasive learning.

1 Scenario

Stis and A-bin are good friends in the high school. One day, A-bin calls Stis and invites Stis to go to the Zoo with him. The reason that A-bin wants to go to the Zoo is because his teacher, Miss Claire, asked each student in the class to do a .biological report. A-bin chose the butterfly topic, hence, he needs to go to the Zoo to gather enough data, take some pictures, and even shooting some fantasy video-clips.

Z. Pan et al. (Eds.): Transactions on Edutainment I, LNCS 5080, pp. 261–277, 2008.

When Stis and A-bin arrived at the Zoo, they take out their smartphones. The smartphones have been installed the individual ubiquitous learning service which provides the learners different game-based learning scenes automatically and dynamically according to the learners' requests and/or interests. Due to Miss Claire's project, A-bin makes his choice immediately in the butterfly topic. The individual ubiquitous learning service then comply his order and builds a series of learning scenes which cover different learning areas in the Zoo. The learning areas include the Amazon River, the Butterfly Exhibition Hall, and the Amazing Flower Hot-house.

In each learning area, there is at least one learning spot. For examples, the Amazon River has three major learning spots, The Woods, The People, and The Lifes; the Butterfly Exhibition Hall has a lot of exhibition rooms, each room has its own exhibition topic; and, the Amazing Flower Hot-house is also divided into different zones for showing different species. So, the learning scenes for A-bin's request will cover partial learning spots in the three learning area. Even that, the individual ubiquitous learning system will not ask A-bin to see all of the learning objects in the selected learning spots.

The individual ubiquitous learning system then guides A-bin moving in the Zoo with the learning path which is planned for the first learning scene. During A-bin moves in the Zoo according to the learning system's suggestion, he keeps observe learning objects and touch learning objects with his eyes, ears, and hands, at mean time, he keeps take pictures, shoot video-clips, and take notes, with his smartphone.

The ubiquitous learning system will keep tracing A-bin's completeness degree for the first learning scene and filter some redundant learning objects and learning spots out according to A-bin's progress. Once the learning system detects A-bin's completeness degree reaches the threshold, the system will see the learning missions in the first learning scene are accomplished, that is, 'stage clear' in game's term. At this moment, the system tells A-bin that he complete the first stage by pop-up messages followed by beeping and suggests A-bin to challenge the next stage.

Unlike A-bin, Stis does not have particular objective in the Zoo. The individual ubiquitous learning system installed in his smartphone first tells him several small stories and allows him to choose his favorite one(s). Also, the system will guide Stis to some learning spots which cover the Zoo's major topics. For examples, the system might tell Stis that, "you know? The chimpanzee's DNA is 99.99% similar to the human beings, but why they didn't evolve like us?"; and, the system might also ask Stis to see something first and do some small activities. If Stis expresses his interest in specific story, learning object(s), or activities, then the system builds the learning scenes and learning paths for him dynamically.

2   Introduction

In the traditional way of teaching, most of time is spent by lecturing and the learners are always just sitting there watching and listening. The learners work individually on assignments and do indoor learning. In 21st–century learners have different learning ways from earlier, for examples, doesn't like their teachers used to use papers and pens, learners now have used to use different information technologies; and, doesn't like their teachers used to do survey and self-learning in library, learners are familiar with using World Wide Web to do survey and self-learning [1].

In recent year, ubiquitous learning extends e-learning from indoor to outdoor, moreover, not like most of mobile learning applications which usually only provides the knowledge of single domain in particular environment, the ubiquitous learning emphasizes to offer learners interdisciplinary knowledge domains in the real world [8]. Ubiquitous learning also provides the learning activities which allow learners to observe and touch the learning objects in the real world based on learners' choices and preferences [19]. If learners want, they still can do suchlike solving problems, answering questions, expressing and organizing questions, and even brainstorming, during their learning processes [7].

Active learning makes learners learning better because they are doing what they feel interesting and they feel that they are controlling everything. Games can encourage learners to learn after classes. Learners are usually 'actively' to play their favorite games. So, it might be work if we apply game concepts, scenes and scenes switching, to help learners 'active' learn and have fun in the ubiquitous learning environment.

Frankly speaking, playing games is really more interesting to users rather than learning things, no matter the learning activities are occurred in classroom, websites (e-learning), mobile devices (mobile learning), or real world (ubiquitous learning). However, all of the successful factors we see the games achieved are building on the free-will of players. The meaning of the free-will of players is leaving the players to decide what games they want to play with, which also means, the games allow the players make calls.

This paper uses two game concepts, "control" and "challenge", to develop a game-based ubiquitous learning environment in which learners (players) can make their own decisions in the learning topics and can challenge different learning scenes step by step.

Section 3 introduces the related works of ubiquitous learning environment, game-based learning, different knowledge structures, and different learning strategies. The relations and definitions between the elements of the learning scene are described in Section 4. Section 5 uses a way to construct learning scenes and introduces how to switch between the scenes. In Section 6, a real example of ubiquitous learning in the museum with learning scenes is built to demonstrate the effects of this research. Finally, Section 7 makes a conclusion and discusses the possible future works about individual scenes layout and switching.

3 Research Backgrounds

3.1 Ubiquitous Learning and Game-Based Learning

In traditional teaching way, the classroom is the major place in which the teachers and learners get face to face at the same time. The learners can only get the learning materials prepared in advance by the teacher. Hence, the learning activities are limited by what the teacher has arranged and the materials and courses are difficult to be modified immediately according to students' learning status. E-learning uses computer and internet technologies to allow teachers teaching and learners' learning [1]. E-learning provides a new learning method to allow learners doing learning activities with e-mail, web-camera, and web-based testing, even if the teacher and learners are not getting together. Mobile learning extends the learning from indoor to outdoor, gives learners opportunities to understand the learning materials via touching, observing, and feeling the learning objects in real environment [4][5][10].

Mobile learning provides both teachers and learners a new learning way in the e-learning field, however, there is still an unsolved research issue, which is the flexible learning issue. The learners' learning activities will be limited in the specific learning environment and/or the specific domain knowledge arranged in advance. Ubiquitous learning not only extends e-learning from indoor to outdoor but also extends mobile learning from specific learning environment and specific knowledge domain to any-place and multidiscipline [9].

Some researchers have thoughts that there are four characteristics of games could enhance learning effects: (1) challenges; (2) fantasy; (3) curiosity; and, (4) control [11]. Regarding the first characteristic, the challenges, Malone has offered the instructional activities which have a various difficulty levels to different learners according to learners' abilities [12][13]. The different learners then will face different challenges.

Many researches indicate that by using games in teaching can encourage learners to learn after school and increase learners learning motivation. This paper not only focuses on the first game characteristic, the challenges, but also makes learners "control" what they want to learn according to their interests in the ubiquitous learning environment.

3.2 Knowledge Structure

In order to make learners control the learning activities in the ubiquitous learning environment, first of all, the ubiquitous learning system has to know what the learners interest with and what the learners have already known. Usually, the knowledge structure is a good way to represent and store the information that a ubiquitous learning system may require.

Ogata and Yano have proposed a knowledge awareness map [16], which is a kind of knowledge structures, visualizes the relations between the sharing knowledge and learners' interactions. Computer-assisted learning system tries to find the useful things out for learners and pick the most appropriate one up to help the learners. However, the learners might have different demands, for examples, different learning preferences and different learning places. Therefore, the technology, such as Perkam [6] (PERsonalized Knowledge Awareness Map), which is used to support learning according to individual learner's preference is very important.

Morton and Bekerian have proposed two features about knowledge structure, which are Semantic Network and Schema Theory. Semantic network emphasizes the knowledge organization in human brains, which is also called the knowledge structure. Schema theory emphasizes the operational process of knowledge in human minds [14]. Furthermore, Novak and Gowin have also applied the knowledge structure in education, which is called Concept Map [15]. Learners can concrete the concepts and the knowledge they have learned from the courses by drawing their own concept maps, and the teacher can examine the individual learner's concept map to know the learner's learning status and learning effect.

3.3 Learning Path

Ubiquitous learning involves the real learning environment, therefore, a ubiquitous learning system has to take not only suitable learning objects but also distance into consideration when plans a personalized learning path for the learner.

Chang and his colleagues have provided a way to create learning path for learners [2][3]. After the learner takes a test, Chang and his colleagues use the concept map closeness for each learning object between the teacher's and the learner's to know what learning objects which a learner should learn first.

Although the learning path is useful to learners, in a ubiquitous learning environment, learners may not always familiar with the environment. Kuo et al. have developed a way to generate the guidance message by using information theory [10].

3.4 Learner Profiles

In order to apply the game features into the learning system, the learner profile have to add several game-based characteristics. In game-based learning system, learner profile should have the abilities or skills to describe the learner's individual information, for examples, "ID", "ability", "training level", and "major preference".

Because the most important game feature is "control", the game-based learning system should allow learners chose what they want to learn and/or what they interest with. Therefore, the major preference stored in the learner profile can be very useful. A learner's major preferences might be divided into several different parts (or says knowledge domains), take learning in a museum for example, the major preferences could be "Sung dynasty", "Ming dynasty", "wood", and "Bamboo".

This research uses context-awareness knowledge structure to store the domain knowledge and personalized preference. In a ubiquitous learning environment, the knowledge structure not only focuses on learning materials' characteristics but also the different knowledge domains which are covered by the learning objects around the learners. The different knowledge domains might be covered the same learning object set, for example, both of the free-falling theory in physics and architectural engineering are covered by the learning object, the Piazza del Duomo, in Italy.

4   Scene Analysis

4.1 Scene Definitions

For storing knowledge and learning object information, this research defines "learning scene" to record all learning locations and objects in the ubiquitous learning environment. Besides, the scene is also used to gather the information about what learning objects exist in different learning locations.

A scene will cover many learning areas; each learning area is a physical place, for example, an exhibition room in a museum. In each learning area, there is at least one or more learning spot. A learning spot may cover one or many learning objects. Take a museum for example, there are many exhibition rooms (the learning areas). Each room has at least one learning spots. When the visitor stands at each learning spot, he/she can see one or many artifacts (the learning objects).

There are two major elements in a scene as Fig. 1 shows: (1) Learning spot (spot), indicates a learning location which covered the learning objects in a personalized knowledge structure; (2) Learning object (object), denotes possible learning objects for the learning spot.

The context-awareness knowledge structure can be used to extract the personalized context-awareness knowledge structure in order to provide individual services according to the learner's preferences, for example, to decide which learning objects in the learning spots should be learned by the learner.

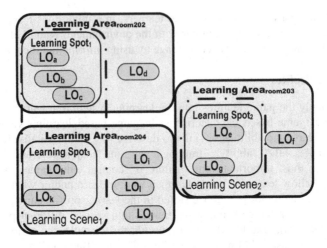

Fig. 1. Learning environment elements

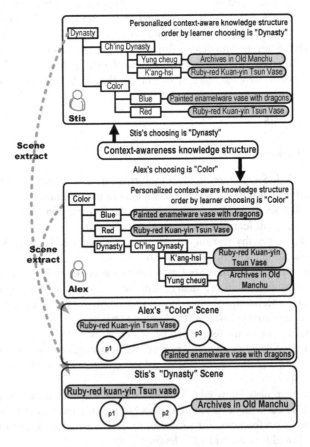

Fig. 2. Examples of two personalized context-awareness knowledge structures

4.2 Relations between Scenes and Personalized Context-Awareness Knowledge Structure

A personalized context-awareness knowledge structure can represent individual learner's preference in the ubiquitous learning environment. Furthermore, the ubiquitous learning system can provide different learners different learning objectives according to their personalized knowledge structure automatically.

The personalized context-awareness knowledge structure then can be used to build learning scenes for learners. Because different learners with different preference will feel differently even when they are looking the same learning objects in the real world, hence, the suitable learning scenes to the learner can be built once the ubiquitous learning system has the personalized knowledge structure. Moreover, different learning activities can be given to learners depends on their preferences and learning objects' characteristics.

In Fig. 2 there are two learners, Alex and Stis, have different viewpoints and/or preferences about the artifacts in the museum. The top part of Fig. 2 shows Stis' personalized context-awareness knowledge structure. Stis prefers the "Dynasty" characteristic rather than the "Color", hence, his personalized knowledge structure is constructed based on "Dynasty" characteristic. On the other hand, Alex has more interest in "Color", therefore his personalized knowledge structure root is constructed based on "Color" characteristic.

According to Wu's personalized knowledge structure [18], the major scene subject for Stis is "Dynasty". The bottom part of Fig. 2 shows how the ubiquitous learning system selects all learning objects related to the subject, "Dynasty", which Stis interests with to form a learning scene for Stis. Similarly, Alex's learning scene can be also constructed.

4.3 Game-Based Measurement with Learning Scenes

As the bottom part of Fig. 2 shows, there are many learning objects matched the preference of a learner. The next problem is what learning object should the ubiquitous learning system suggests the learner learning and observing first.

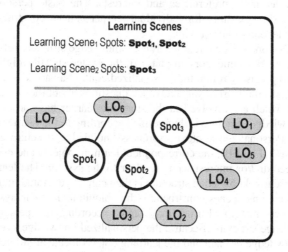

Fig. 3. Example of learning scene and objects

Fig. 3 shows an example of two learning scenes cover three learning spots and some learning objects. Assuming a learner stands at the learning spot$_2$. At learning spot$_2$, the learner can find two learning objects, $\{LO_2, LO_3\}$. Each learning object has its own characteristics about "Dynasty" subject. For example, the learning object LO_2 may have characteristic suchlike "Items of daily use were specially produced for the Ming imperial court". Moreover, the degree of realizing these story-like characteristics of learning objects can be seen as a quantitative measurement of learners' abilities and/or skill points based on the game-based learning theory.

This research defines the game-based measurement with the personalized learning scenes based on the probability theory. If a learner gets the idea from the questions, then the probability of specific characteristic will be raised and the probability represent the learner's degree of mastery in the specific characteristic. When the overall probability of a learning scene achieved a threshold, the ubiquitous learning system can say that the learner clears the stage or levels up, and ready to challenge another stage or level (another learning scene).

5   Scenes Construction and Switching

5.1   Scenes Construction

This research develops a way to extract scenes from the personalized knowledge structure. The whole scene construction flow involves 5 phases as Fig. 4 shows:

1. Phase I: Learning materials analysis, the learning objects in real environment have a lot of information (or also called characteristics), which might cover different domains or places. In this phase, we need to analyze the learning objects and its characteristics in the real world first. After this phase, the context-awareness knowledge structure can be built.

2. Phase II: Basic personalized context-awareness knowledge structure construction, because the personalized context-awareness knowledge structure should be created according to the learners' preferences and interests. The basic personalized context-awareness knowledge structure for individual learner can be constructed depends on which stories the learners interest with.

3. Phase III: Personalized context-awareness knowledge structure refinement, even if two learners choose the same story in phase II, their interests still might be a little different. In order to precisely refine the personalized context-awareness knowledge structure, the system asks the learner some advance questions about the characteristics of the learning objects which are involved in the story the learner has chosen. The personalized context knowledge structure is then refined according to the learner's feedback.

4. Phase IV: Personalized context-awareness knowledge structure generation, after repeating the phase II and III, the correspondent learning objects and characteristics the learner might need and/or interest with are clear to the system. The learner's personalized context-awareness knowledge structure is then can be generated in this phase.

5. Phase V: Learning scenes construction, the ubiquitous learning system can extract the learning objects that the learner may prefer according the personalized context-awareness knowledge structure. Because the personalized knowledge structure can represent different knowledge domain and the learning objects locate at different locations, the ubiquitous learning system then construct the game-based learning scenes based on the distinction features of the selected learning objects, such as "location" and "domain", as Fig. 4 shows.

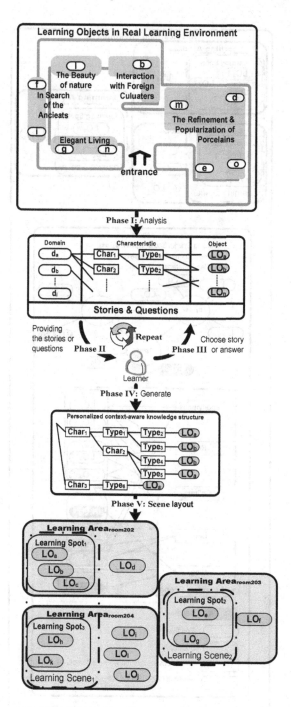

Fig. 4. The five phases to build individual scene

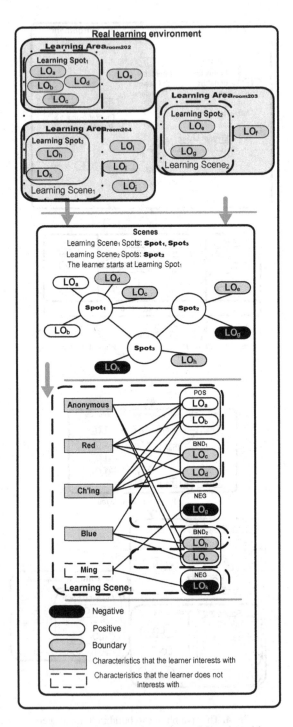

Fig. 5. The relation between characters and learning objects

5.2 Scenes Switching Principles

This research uses rough set theory [17] to develop scene switching methodology. In the rough set theory, data will be divided into three sets, including the Positive Set (POS), the Negative Set (NEG), and one or more Boundary Sets (BNDs). This research defines the positive set data as the learning objects which have more than one characteristic the learner is interesting with, the learner has to observe the learning objects in the positive set. On the contrary, the learning objects in the negative set don't have any characteristic that the learner interest with. Unlike the positive set and the negative set, there are many boundary sets in the learning scene. The learning objects in a boundary set also have the characteristics that the learner interests with. The difference between the positive set and the boundary set is that all of the learning objects in the same boundary set have the same characteristics, and the learner only needs to observe one of the learning objects for the same boundary set when he/she does learning activities in the ubiquitous learning environment.

Fig. 5 shows an example of using rough set to categorize learning objects involved in learning spots. At top part of Fig. 5, there are two learning scenes cover three learning areas. Each learning scene has one or more learning spots, and each learning spot contains one or more learning objects. In the middle part of Fig. 5, every learning object has many characteristics. The learning objects can be categorized into three sets. Table 1 lists a summary of the three sets and its learning objects.

Table 1. Three sets and its learning objects

POS	LO_a, LO_b
NEG	LO_g, LO_k
BND_1	LO_c, LO_d
BND_2	LO_e, LO_h

From Table 1 the ubiquitous learning system knows that the learner has to observe the learning object LOa. If the scene only includes four characteristics, including "Anonymous", "Red", "Ch'ing", and "Blue", then the ubiquitous learning system can do scene switching after the learner finished observing the LOa and LO_b.

6 Complete Example

6.1 Game-Based Learning in Museum

By using the game concept to help learner learning in the ubiquitous learning environment, the first thing is to define the learner profile suchlike "ID", "ability", and "major preference". The major preference includes the characteristics in the personalized context-awareness knowledge structure suchlike "dynasty", "color", "function", and "author", in Fig. 6. Ability is the learning object characteristics which learner has been observed. ID is the learner's name.

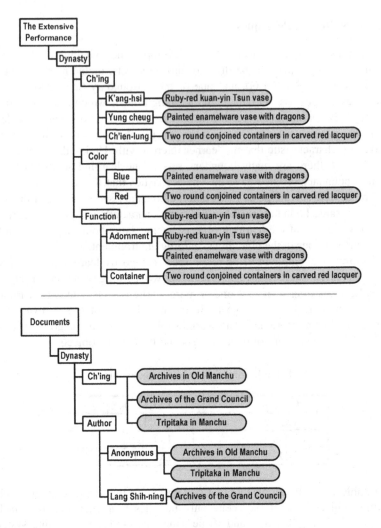

Fig. 6. The partial context-awareness knowledge structure in a museum

6.2 Scenario

This paper takes learning in a real museum for example. In a museum, there are many artifacts with different subjects and/or topics exhibiting in the different rooms. For example, the Room 203 in a museum as Fig. 7 shows, the "gray area" represents different subjects and/or topics (learning spots) suchlike "Elegant Living", "In Search of the Ancients", and "The Beauty of Nature"; "black circle" represents the artifacts (the learning objects) in the room; the number is the artifacts number. There are eleven learning objects in Room 203. This research considers a room as a learning area.

According the Phase I in Fig. 4, Fig. 6 shows the analysis results of learning objects. Fig. 6 represents how to use context-awareness knowledge structure to store a museum's learning objects and its characteristics.

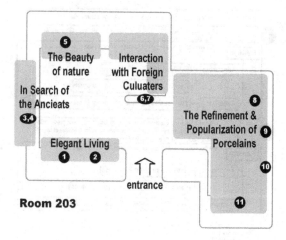

Fig. 7. Room 203 in a museum

The personalized context-awareness knowledge structures and game-based learning scenes are constructed based on with the learners' choices and their answers about the questions of artifacts' characteristics as Fig. 8 shows. The width or depth of personalize context-awareness knowledge structure depends on how much the learners' interest with and how exquisite they know.

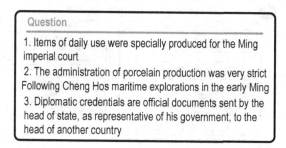

Fig. 8. Example of the questions about "The Fashionable vs. the Antiquarian"

Fig. 9 shows the process of constructing the learning scenes after the learner answered the questions. After the learner answered the questions, the ubiquitous learning system can revise the personalized context-awareness knowledge structure and find the preference learning objects and interesting characteristics from the personalized context-awareness knowledge structure. Furthermore, the bottom part of Fig. 9 shows how to use the personalized knowledge structure to realize the learning preferred objects' locations, to define the learning spots, and to construct the learning scenes for individual learner.

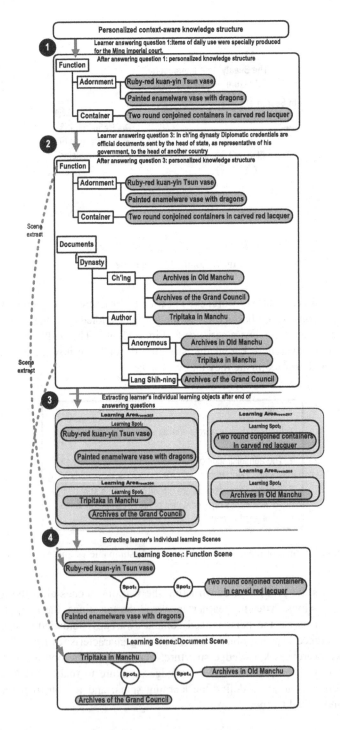

Fig. 9. Scenario constructing process

6.3 Individual Learning Path in Museum

With the learning scenes, this research uses the distances to plan the observation sequence for the learning objects in the positive set and boundary set that the learner may interest with.

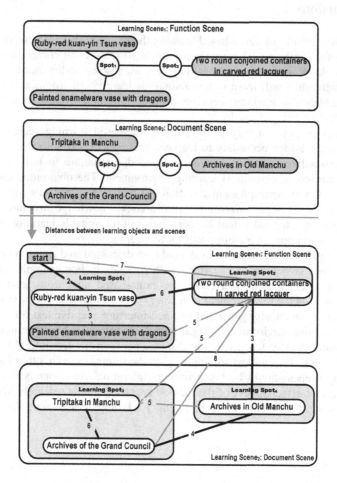

Fig. 10. Function scene and document scene relationship in scenario

The ubiquitous learning system then first picks the learning objects in the POS set, including "Ruby-red kuan-yin Tsun vase", "Two round conjoined containers in carved red lacquer", "Tripitaka in Manchu", "Archives of the Grand Council", and "Archives in Old Manchu". The learning path has to route every POS set learning objects.

Fig. 10 uses the "white ellipse" to represent the learning objects in the POS set, the must be observed learning objects. The scene can be switched from the Function Scene to the Document Scene after the learner has finished observing the white ellipse learning objects. According to the distance, the ubiquitous learning system generates the learning guidance path: start → "Ruby-red kuan-yin Tsun vase" → "Two round conjoined containers in carved red lacquer" → "Archives in Old Manchu" → "Archives of the Grand Council" → "Tripitaka in Manchu".

7 Conclusions

There are two features of game-based learning theory are taking into this research, the control and the challenge. This research uses small stories and correspondent simple questions to let learners chose what they feel interesting and/or need. The learner "controls" what they will learn in the ubiquitous learning environment. The learners have to complete one learning scene before they can move to next one. They "challenge" the different stages one by one.

This paper proposes a way to construct game-based learning scenes and scene switching methodology according to learners' preferences and abilities. The research uses the personalized context-awareness knowledge structure to build the learning scenes for learners in ubiquitous learning environment. The ubiquitous learning system uses story and correspondent questions to realize the learner's preference and interests, refines the personalized context-awareness knowledge structure, constructs the learning scenes for individual learner, finds out the suitable learning objects, and plans the most appropriate learning path for the learner.

There are still some research issues could be discussed and done in order to improve the scene switching and learning path generation. For example, as we mentioned, the challenge issue. Currently, the game-based ubiquitous learning system uses probability as the measurement of learner (player) abilities. The next step is how to provide an automatically generated and non-interrupt adaptive test for such kind of ubiquitous learning environment. Regarding the learning path generation issue, the current research and system uses only distance between the learning objects. As we all know, it is just the simplest solving way, in the future research, other factors suchlike learning scenes should be taken into consideration. Also, our next step should measure the cost effectiveness of the method proposed in this research. We are planning to do several different field experiments for biology course with the elementary schools.

References

1. Brodersen, C., Christensen, B.G., Dindler, C., Grønbæk, K., Sundararajah, B.: eBag—a Ubiquitous Web Infrastructure for Nomadic Learning. In: Proceedings of the 14th International Conference on World Wide Web Conference, Chiba, Japan, May 10-14, 2005, pp. 298–306 (2005)
2. Chang, A., Chang, M.: Adaptive Mobile Navigation Paths for Elementary School Students Remedial Studying. In: Proceedings of the IEEE International Conference on Interactive Computer Aided Learning (ICL 2006), Villach, Austria, September 27-29 (2006)
3. Chang, A., Chang, M.: A Treasure Hunting Learning Model for Students Studying History and Culture in the Field with Cellphone. In: Proceedings of the 6th IEEE International Conference on Advanced Learning Technologies (ICALT 2006), Kerkrade, The Netherlands, July 05-07, 2006, pp. 106–108 (2006)

4. Chang, A., Chang, M., Heh, J.S.: Implementing a Context-aware Learning Path Planner. In: the Proceedings of the 6th WSEAS International Conference on E-ACTIVITIES, Tenerife, Canary Islands, Spain, December 14-16, 2007, pp. 237–241 (2007)
5. Chen, Y.-S., Kao, T.-C., Yu, G.-J., Sheu, J.-P.: A Mobile Butterfly-Watching Learning System for Supporting Independent Learning. In: Proceedings of the IEEE International Workshop on Wireless and Mobile Technologies in Education, Chung-Li, Taiwan, March 23-25, 2004, pp. 11–18 (2004)
6. El-Bishouty, M.M., Ogata, H., Yano, Y.: Personalized Knowledge Awareness Map in Computer Supported Ubiquitous Learning. In: Proceedings of the 6th IEEE International Conference on Advanced Learning Technologies (ICALT 2006), Kerkrade, The Netherlands, July 05-07, 2006, pp. 817–821 (2006)
7. Felder, R.M., Brent, R.: Learning by Doing. Chemical Engineering Education 37(4), 282–283 (2003) Retrieved on January 15, 2008 from, http://www4.ncsu.edu/unity/lockers/users/f/felder/public/Columns/Active.pdf
8. Hwang, G.-J.: Criteria and Strategies of Ubiquitous Learning. In: Proceedings of the IEEE International Conference on Sensor Networks, Ubiquitous, and Trustworthy Computing (SUTC 2006), Taichung, Taiwan, June 5-7, 2006, pp. 72–77 (2006)
9. Hall, T., Bannon, L.: Designing ubiquitous computing to enhance children's learning in museums. Journal of Computer Assisted Learning 22(4), 231–243 (2006)
10. Kuo, R., Wu, M.-C., Chang, A., Chang, M., Heh, J.-S.: Delivering Context-aware Learning Guidance in the Mobile Learning Environment based on Information Theory. In: Proceedings of the 7th IEEE International Conference on Advanced Learning Technologies (ICALT 2007), Niigata, Japan, July 18-20, 2007, pp. 362–366 (2007)
11. Lepper, M.R., Malone, T.W.: Intrinsic motivation and instructional effectiveness in computer-based education. In: Aptitude, Learning, and Instruction, III: Conative and Affective Process Analysis, pp. 255–286. Lawrence Erlbaum Associates, Hillsdale (1987)
12. Malone, T.W.: Toward a theory of intrinsically motivating instruction. Cognitive Science 5(4), 333–369 (1981)
13. Malone, T.W., Lepper, M.R.: Making learning fun: A taxonomy of intrinsic motivations for learning. In: Aptitude, Learning, and Instruction, III: Conative and Affective Process Analysis, pp. 223–253. Lawrence Erlbaum Associates, Hillsdale (1987)
14. Novak, J.D.: Applying learning psychology and philosophy of science to biology teaching. The American Biology Teacher 43(1), 12–20 (1981)
15. Novak, J.D., Gowin, D.B.: Learning How to Learn. Cambridge University Press, New York (1984)
16. Ogata, H., Yano, Y.: Knowledge awareness for a computer-assisted language learning using handhelds. International Journal of Continuous Engineering Education and Lifelong Learning 14(4/5), 435–449 (2005)
17. Pawlak, Z.: Rough Sets: Theoretical Aspects of Reasoning about Data. Kluwer Academic Publishers, Norwell (1992)
18. Wu, S., Chang, A., Chang, M., Liu, T.-C., Heh, J.-S.: Identifying Personalized Context-aware Knowledge Structure for Individual User in Ubiquitous Learning Environment. In: Proceedings of the 5th IEEE International Conference on Wireless, Mobile, and Ubiquitous Technologies in Education (WMUTE 2008), Beijing, China, March 23-26, 2008, pp. 95–99 (2008)
19. Yatani, K., Sugimoto, M., Kusunoki, F.: Musex: A System for Supporting Children's Collaborative Learning in a Museum with PDAs. In: the Proceedings of the IEEE International Workshop on Wireless and Mobile Technologies in Education, Chung-Li, Taiwan, March 23-25, 2004, pp. 109–113 (2004)

VR Bio X Games

Y.Y. Cai[1,2], C. Indhumathi[1,2], W.Y. Chen[1,2], and J.M. Zheng[3]

[1] School of Mechanical & Aerospace Engineering
[2] Bio-Informatics Research Center
[3] School of Computer Engineering
Nanyang Technological University,
Republic of Singapore, Singapore 639798
myycai@ntu.edu.sg

Abstract. Many students voluntarily seek out challenges while playing computer games. Such high engagement is desirable in school education. We are interested in exploring VR-based game technology for educational use. This paper reports a VR game project for bio-molecular learning. Specifically, extreme game concepts are applied in biological context aiming to create a new biological learning experience on protein structure for secondary or primary students. With the aid of immersive visualization, VR interface and game-based interaction, this learning through gaming solution can help to introduce concepts of bio-molecular structures in classrooms or science museums. Through gaming, students can have better ideas about bio-molecular structure at different levels.

Keywords: Interactive Games, Learning Through Playing, VR.

1 Introduction

Computer games are already part of children's culture today [1]. Interactive computer games as a tool have a good potential for learning [2]-[4]. The Games-To-Teach project was jointly conducted by MIT and Microsoft to develop conceptual prototypes for the next generation of interactive educational entertainment [5]. Kafai *et al* discussed game design for fostering students' and teachers' mathematical inquiry [6]. While many people see the potential of using computer games for education, systematic research on computer games for learning is still relatively new [7]. Game interactivity is most crucial for computer game based learning. It is interactivity that fosters engagement and hence the playful nature of a good computer game is often based on its interactivity. Other critical issues with a computer game involves in story, graphics, characters, sound and interface.

This project aims to integrate VR enabled game technology and educational technology for creative biological study. While it is important to understand the models and driving factors of VR games, our emphasis is placed on the development of new methodologies in terms of VR game interactivity, interface, immersive and spatial perceptions for VR-based game learning. Special efforts are made to design/develop the game contents based on school curriculum. Prototyping work is performed in line

Z. Pan et al. (Eds.): Transactions on Edutainment I, LNCS 5080, pp. 278–287, 2008.

with the teaching needs, through partnering with pilot schools, in collaboration with school teachers and educational experts, as well as taking into account the student feedbacks.

2 VR Games-To-Teach Solution

To meet the high competition in education market, educational technology has been moving fast to provide various solutions supporting broad and interdisciplinary education, problems solving and enquiry-based learning, and so on. The basic challenges remain, however, in motivating students to gain knowledge and acquire skills. VR Games-To-Teach solution hopes to take the advantages of VR technology in terms of immersion, presence and interactivity to help developing student's curiosity and interest in study, especially for those difficult and complicated topics. Basically, it is to create a 3D, immersive and virtual learning environment by integrating VR-enabled game technology and educational technology. To do so, we need to develop new approaches, new techniques and new algorithms for this VR solution.

2.1 Three-Dimensionality

Different to conventional 3D games, VR games use a stereographic approach to enable the true 3D. Such 3D VR environments maintain a sense of realistic depth cues thus allowing users to have immersive experience in virtual world. To support this, 3D geometrical and physical modelling, 3D interaction and stereographic visualization are thus developed. Our 3D solution is powered by motion capturing, Graphics Processing Unit (GPU) based collision detection [8], and digital geometry including subdivision techniques [9][10].

2.2 Integration

In this research, we adopt an integrated view in developing VR Games-To-Teach solution. These include software and hardware integration, geometrical modeling and physical modeling integration, virtual space and physical space integration. The integrated VR environment provides a high-level interface for human-computer interaction enabling communication between virtual and real worlds.

2.3 Immersion and Presence

Immersive experience is important in learning which can increase the level of learning interest. VR Games-To-Teach solution is able to produce a reach-in environment allowing students to be present and immersed in the virtual space. In particular, bio-molecules and other learning objects appear with pop-up effects. Students can walk through the nano-world of bio-molecules. They can also interact with the bio-molecules. Here physical size is no more a constraint. Among many enabling technologies, 3D modelling, stereographic visualization and human-computer interaction play a crucial role [11][12].

3   Game Design for VR Games-To-Teach

Scientists in many generations contribute to advance the Science and Technology. Science learning today is more and more technology-dependent. With the rapid advancement of VR and gaming technologies, curriculum teaching is entering a new phase where content delivery is increasingly integrated with educational technology in the interactive fashion.

3.1   Interactivity

The integration of VR game technology and educational technology creates a synergy in designing game-based curriculum content. Our 3D technology makes it feasible to have high quality interaction with the educational games designed. Our GPU algorithm enhances the interactive efficiency in 3D virtual environment. Our immersive visualization improves the realism of interactive games. All these facilitate the classroom teaching and offer new channels for student-student and student-teacher interactions. As interactivity design is essential to bridge the virtual and real worlds, simple yet efficient

Amino Acid	Symbol	Structure*	Amino Acid	Symbol	Structure*
Glycine	Gly or G	H-CH-COOH NH₂	Asparagine	Asn or N	H₂N-C-CH₂-CH-COOH O NH₂
Alanine	Ala or A	CH₃-CH-COOH NH₂	Glutamic Acid	Glu or E	HOOC-CH₂-CH₂-CH-COOH NH₂
Valine	Val or V	H₃C CH-CH-COOH H₃C NH₂	Glutamine	Gln or Q	H₂N-C-CH₂-CH₂-CH-COOH O NH₂
Leucine	Leu or L	H₃C CH-CH₂-CH-COOH H₃C NH₂	Arginine	Arg or R	HN-CH₂-CH₂-CH₂-CH-COOH C=NH NH₂ NH₂
Isoleucine	Ile or I	H₃C CH₂ CH-CH-COOH H₃C NH₂	Lysine	Lys or K	H₂N-(CH₂)₄-CH-COOH NH₂
Serine	Ser or S	HO-CH₂-CH-COOH NH₂	Histidine	His or H	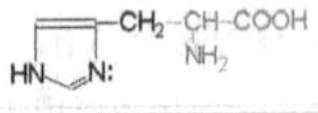 CH₂-CH-COOH NH₂ HN N:
Threonine	Thr or T	H₃C CH-CH-COOH HO NH₂	Phenylalanine	Phe or F	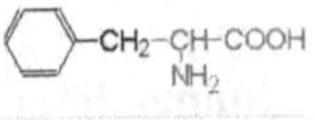 CH₂-CH-COOH NH₂
Cysteine	Cys or C	HS-CH₂-CH-COOH NH₂	Tyrosine	Tyr or Y	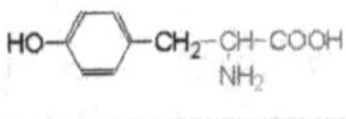 HO-⬡-CH₂-CH-COOH NH₂
Methionine	Met or M	H₃C-S-(CH₂)₂-CH-COOH NH₂	Tryptophan	Trp or W	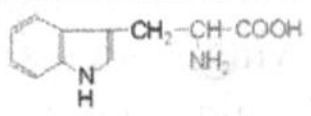 CH₂-CH-COOH NH₂
Aspartic Acid	Asp or D	HOOC-CH₂-CH-COOH NH₂	Proline	Pro or P	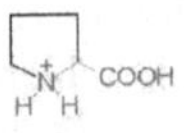 N COOH H H

Fig. 1. Amino acids

interaction is of practical importance for this communication goal. Several different types of interactive devices such as VR glove, magic wand, steering wheel, etc, are used in this project.

3.2 Content

In the post-genome era today, structural and functional biology therefore becomes the center of bio research and education. This, however, poses challenges to teachers and students. We are interested in using VR Game-To-Teach solution to assist the learning of structural biology in secondary or even primary schools. In particular, bio X-games are developed with an emphasis on interactive and immersive features for students to learn bio-molecular concepts. Through playing the 3D extreme games, students can have a better understanding of protein amino acid sequence structure (Figure 1), protein secondary structure (Figure 2) and protein surface structure (Figure 3).

There are great numbers of educational games developed in the market. We, however, focus on a niche area of bio education for curriculum linked teaching in classrooms or science museums.

3.3 Graphics Modeling and Visualization

Visualization technology can be helpful in learning difficult subjects, especially for those related to complicated structures. Compared to static images, animated, immersive and interactive visualization has the advantage in delivering more complete and

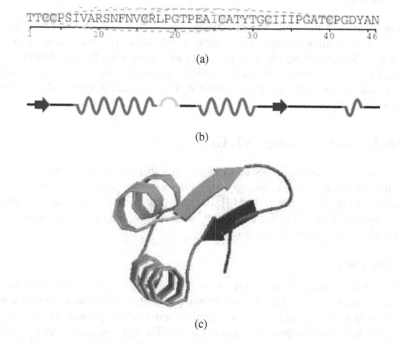

(a)

(b)

(c)

Fig. 2. (a) Protein amino acid sequence for protein 1crn; (b) secondary structure in 2D symbolic form; and (c) secondary structure in 3D representation

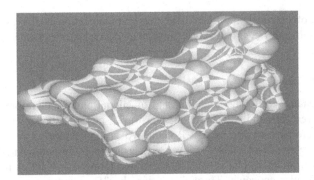

Fig. 3. 3D graphic modeling of protein surface

vivid information for concepts, especially for those difficult to present or can be easily misunderstood. Graphics design is not just for fancy display. Instead, it serves the purpose to assist better presentation of insight of the learning objects. Immersive visualization can forge students' interest in learning of tiny bio-molecules with complicated structures and other information. For instance, we use colors to illustrate the molecular properties such as electrostatic, hydrophilic and hydrophobic. We use latest GPU technology to achieve real-time interaction for students to reach-in the virtual molecular world and hands-on various proteins.

3.4 Interface

As pointed in [13], the game interface design is a critical task. A good interface design can improve attractiveness with a game and facilitate the interaction when playing a game. We prefer simple design as long as it serves the basic functions and is also easy to make control. In terms of usability, we choose plug-&-play game device for easy integration under the game interface. This way can actually help shortening students' learning curve.

4 Bio Learning Through VR Gaming

Many diseases including AIDS and cancers are still yet to have cures today. As such structure biology is increasingly becoming a central topic in Life Sciences. As highlighted in the book Bio 2010 [14], the changing paradigm of research calls for innovations and changes in the education of scientists along the spectrum of K-12, undergraduate and graduate education.

4.1 Motivation

This project is interested in using VR visualization and games to develop new teaching approaches allowing secondary or even primary students to learn basic concepts about structure biology. VR game technology is applied here to develop innovative and interactive educational games for protein structure learning. Through interactive gaming, students can easily gain basic knowledge about protein structure. We hope to have these VR games to stimulate students' interest in their further study of advanced topics of biology.

4.2 Learning Goals

The learning goal of this VR games is to introduce multi-level structures of bio-molecules. Students will learn 1) protein primary structure in terms of amino acids sequence, 2) protein secondary structure of α-helices, β-strands and loops, 3) tertiary structure of folded protein and 4) protein surface structure.

Students from secondary schools and high schools are target gamers. This VR Game-To-Teach solution can be used for primary schools as well. Students may choose proteins they are familiar as a target object in the VR games, e.g., hemoglobin for secondary students, and vitamin proteins for primary students.

4.3 Structure of the Game

It is a single-player game having two components: protein structures and avatar(s). The protein structures have primary, secondary, tertiary and surface levels. Users can choose to display some or all of them. These protein structures can be modeled in conventional fashion or realistic fashion. In conventional fashion, proteins are modeled following the biological convention in the form of ribbons, etc. In realistic fashion, protein structures are modeled as physical entities in real world such as Great Wall as protein secondary structure. The avatar(s) created can be controlled using interactive device.

4.4 Protein Roller Coaster Game

Proteins are bio-molecules made of a sequence of amino acids at a primary level. There are over 20 types of amino acids forming polypeptides (Figure 1). The back-bone structure of a protein can be modelled as a ribbon pattern. At the secondary level, proteins can be visualized in the forms of α-helices, β-strands and loops. Protein folding can generate tertiary and quaternary structures. At surface level, proteins can be viewed as van der Waals surface, solvent accessible surface or solvent excluded surface.

Fig. 4. (a) A physical roller coaster; (b) A protein roller-coaster

Motivated by the roller-coaster in entertainment theme park, we design roller-coasters for protein molecules. Protein α-helices and β-strands can be modelled as virtual roller-coastering for very exciting riding. These structures are unlikely available with any physical theme park (Figure 4(a)) worldwide today due to the safety concerns, if not impossible to construct. VR protein roller-coaster (Figure 4(b)) is modelled based on the protein backbone structure with α-helices displayed in pink, β-strands in blue and loops in yellow. The amino acids are modelled as a set of balls.

Protein roller-coaster is an immersive VR game. Apart from the use in classroom teaching, this protein roller-coaster was also exhibited in Singapore Arts Museum (Gallery #10) from Sept 2002 to Oct 2003.

4.5 Bio Motor-Biking Games

We have also developed a motor-biking game, another extreme sports game, in relation to bio-molecular structure. Through playing this motor-biking game, students can learn protein amino acids sequence, α-helices and β-strands of protein secondary structure. Figure 5(a) shows the graphic user interface with this Bio X-game. A scoring system is implemented in this game. Gamers can score if their motor-bike is able to hit the amino acid groups. Depending on the skills of extreme jumping with the motor-bike, gamers can have different score when cycling along the protein secondary structure. Different levels of games in terms of difficulty and time constraint are designed in this immersive VR game. Protein Great Wall is another game exhibited in China Science and Technology Museum (Oct 2006). In this Bio X-game, the protein secondary structure is modelled as Chinese Great Wall (Figure 5(b)). A slightly modified version of the game called Protein Rendition is currently being exhibited at the Genome Exhibition with the Singapore Science Centre (2006 to 2010).

The protein roller-coaster and motor-bike were trial used in Singapore Chinese High School. Students over there formed their own VR club and three workshops were organised by the VR club for other students.

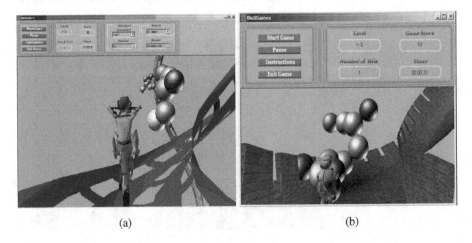

(a)   (b)

Fig. 5. (a) Protein motor biking; and (b) Protein Great Wall Game

4.6 System Architecture

The VR Game-To-Teach solution requires a high end and high performance graphics PC. For stereographic visualization, either high refresh rate CRT monitors or high lumen projectors/screen system can be used (Figure 6). Interactive game pad device is used as well.

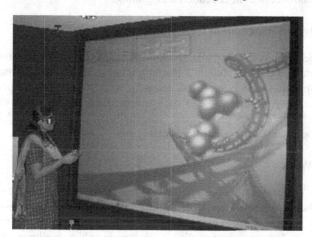

Fig. 6. Immersive Bio X game using rear projection

5 Conclusion

Computer games offer tantalizing potential for educational application. Many students enjoy playing computer games and voluntarily challenging themselves when gaming. Can we, as educators, develop our student with similar engagement to drive them for serious learning? While Games-To-Teach solution is encouraging, we are keen in exploring immersive game based learning. This paper presents our work on using VR-enabled X games for Life Science education. Using VR, students and teachers are able to enter the micro world of bio-molecules. Protein roller-coaster and motor-bike game are two VR games developed. The study is promising but meanwhile challenging.

5.1 Results and Evaluation

The VR project has received very positive responses from students and teachers. Using this innovative approach, secondary students or primary students are able to learn basic concepts of protein structures through VR gaming. The immersive visualization with the VR game contributes significantly attracting students to learn bio-molecular structure, which is often very complicated. Follow-up study shows this hands-on game can help motivating student gamers to choose advanced study in biology. The VR games are currently also being exhibited in science museums and we are interested to have more feedbacks for further evaluation.

5.2 Challenges

The primary advantage of computer games is the interactivity that fosters engagement. While game interactivity design is a challenge, content development suitable for serious learning is another. There are large numbers of games commercially developed but the successful use of them for learning is still beyond the expectation. Technology is offering help in design of compelling VR games. One of the issues one should consider that games must also accommodate the evolution and diversity of technologies and practices in education and gaming.

5.3 Curiosity and Imagination

Our VR games integrate VR game technology and educational technology for the purpose of better motivating student's learning interest. By visualizing and interacting with the complicated objects in virtual learning world, students may potentially develop their curiosity in other subjects such as mathematics, physics or chemistry. At this stage, we hope serious gaming can potentially stimulate students' imagination, which could be essential for scientific research.

5.4 Future Work

Currently the VR games of roller-coaster and the motor-bike game are single-player based. We plan to further develop them into multi-player or even massively multi-player games. Good interactivity is dynamic and compelling. So there are always rooms to improve in terms of interactivity. Biology is only a small part of the learning world, there are plenty new areas for us to explore further.

References

1. Fromme, J.: Computer games as part of children's culture. The International Journal of Computer game Research 3(1) (2003)
2. Betz, J.A.: Computer games: increase learning in an interactive multi-disciplinary environment. Journal of Educational Technology Systems 24, 195–205 (1996)
3. Broadie, R.: Measuring impacts and benefits of ICT-for-learning. Computer Education 105, 3–8 (2003)
4. Rieber, L.P.: Seriously considering play: designing interactive learning environments based on the blending of microworlds, simulations, and games. Educational Technology Research and Development 44(2), 43–58 (1996)
5. Squire, K., et al.: Design principles of next-generation digital gaming for education. Educational Technology 43(5), 17–33 (2003)
6. Kafai, Y.B., Franke, M.L., Ching, C.C., Shih, J.C.: Game design as an interactive learning environment for fostering students' and teachers' mathematical inquiry. International Journal of Computers for Mathematical Learning 3(2), 149–184 (1998)
7. Prensky, M.: Digital Game-based Learning. McGraw-Hill, New York (2001)
8. Cai, Y.Y., Fan, Z.W., Fan, H.G., Gao, S.M., Lu, B.F., Lim, K.T.: Graphics hardware to accelerate the collision detection for VR game. Simulation and Gaming 32(4), 476–490 (2006)
9. Zheng, J.M., Cai, Y.Y.: Interpolation over arbitrary topology meshes using a two-phase subdivision scheme. IEEE Transactions on Visualization and Computer Graphics 12(3), 301–310 (2006)
10. Sederberg, T., Zheng, J.M., Sewell, D., Sabin, M.: Non-uniform recursive subdivision surfaces. Proceedings of ACM Siggraph 1998, 387–394 (1998)

11. Cai, Y.Y., Lu, B.F., Fan, Z.W., Chan, C.W., Lim, K.T., Qi, L., Li, L.: Protein immersive games and computer music, Leonardo 39, pp. 135–138. MIT Press, Cambridge (2006)
12. Cai, Y.Y., Lu, B.F., Fan, Z.W., Chandrasekaran, I., Lim, K.T., Chan, C.W., Jiang, Y., Li, L.: Bio Edutainment: Learning Life Science through X gaming, Computers & Graphics 30, pp. 3–9. Elsevier, Amsterdam (2006)
13. Thomas, P., Macredie, R.: Games and the design of human-computer interface. Educational Technology 31, 134–142 (1994)
14. National Research Council, Bio 2010 – Transforming Undergraduate Education for Future Research Biologists, The National Academies Press, Washington

Online Learning and Clinical Procedures: Rapid Development and Effective Deployment of Game-Like Interactive Simulations

Pablo Moreno-Ger[1], Carl Blesius[2], Paul Currier[2], José Luis Sierra[1], and Baltasar Fernández-Manjón[1]

[1] Dpt. Ingeniería Artificial e Ingeniería del Software - Universidad Complutense de Madrid
Facultad de Informática, 28040 Madrid, Spain
{pablom,jlsierra,balta}@fdi.ucm.es
[2] Harvard Medical School / Massachusetts General Hospital
50 Staniford St, 7th Floor. Boston, MA, 02114, USA
{cblesius,pcurrier}@partners.org

Abstract. Traditionally, medical education has used live patients to teach medical procedures. This carries a significant risk to patients. As learning technology advances, the early integration of computer-aided medical simulations into medical training before patient contact is becoming an ethical imperative, yet development costs are constraining. In this paper, we describe the use of a gaming engine to create rapidly a game-like interactive simulation for medical training at a low cost. Our process model, driven by the simulation storyboard provided by the instructors, allows for easy simulation refinements and permits an early evaluation of the educational outcome. We also describe its initial integration into the existing matrix of low-tech simulation (procedures practiced on mannequins) and an educational platform (e-learning system) used to support and track novice physicians within a large academic training center.

Keywords: game-like simulations, game-based learning, development process model, development costs, virtual learning environments, learning management systems, clinical procedures, e-Adventure, IMS Learning Design, .LRN.

1 Introduction

Over thousands of years, medical education has relied on a master-apprentice system where patients are the primary learning tool for first-time medical procedures. This has created an ethical tension between the need to hone the skills of health professionals on live patients while insuring patient safety and well-being [1]. The emergence of high-powered computing, which allows real-time virtual interaction with haptics, is putting us in a position where we can mitigate this ethical tension by developing healthcare workers' skills early on by using realistic patient simulators without putting patients at risk. While this kind of advanced simulation technology may allay this tension, it also introduces a new problem: the development cost of highly advanced computer-driven simulators and their integration into existing educational infrastructure.

Z. Pan et al. (Eds.): Transactions on Edutainment I, LNCS 5080, pp. 288–304, 2008.
© Springer-Verlag Berlin Heidelberg 2008

Presently, visual and tactile realism in immersive simulations can only be achieved with significant investment. However, when dealing with specific procedures of limited application, lower-cost computer-based educational games and game-like simulations can still offer advantages over other forms of training (e.g., practice exercises using mannequins or live patients), allowing a broader range of experimentation, feedback and reflection on mistakes. Game-like simulations can be played by the trainees at home, as many times as desired, and at their own pace. They are free to explore, to try different approaches, without fear of breaking the equipment (or harming the patient) and, potentially, with the guidance and feedback provided by the simulation itself.

These products cannot match state-of-the-art simulations in terms of the development of motor skills, but those skills are often only a small part of what needs to be honed when learning to do a procedure. Most procedures require a combination of motor skills and the memorization of a large number of steps required before, during, and after the procedure. Learning with game-like simulations can provide important prior knowledge, so that motor-skill training and face-to-face exchange can be the focus when practicing the procedure in the presence of a clinical educator. This can reduce the total face-to-face time needed, increase the value of the teaching encounter, and ultimately reduce the risk involved in training on live patients.

Additionally, in order to coexist with the modern Technology-Enhanced Learning (TEL) settings, educational games and game-like simulations cannot be independent artifacts, but must be integrated with co-existing courses and training modules. Take, for example, The Hub, a community-driven learning and knowledge management system used by physicians and staff at Harvard Medical School's teaching hospitals. The Hub is built on top of the opensource .LRN e-learning platform [2], with several training courses already deployed there. The community value and the results achieved through The Hub encourage us to seek new applications of these technologies and the educational games and simulations used in training should not be disconnected from these environments. On the one hand, it should be possible to launch the games from within the online training environment, just as if they were a document or a streamed video. On the other hand, the game should monitor automatically the performance of the student, measuring the time required to complete each task, committed errors and level of completion. Finally, the data gathered from the monitoring of the student should be available as a report for the instructors as well as an automatically generated grade to be stored with the student's profile and achievements.

This work describes a design and implementation methodology for medical simulations that avoids the high development costs of VR-like simulations, and successfully addresses the integration requirements with the existing e-learning platforms (in particular, those identified in the context of The Hub, although the results apply for other training platforms). For this purpose we conceive simulations as game-based modules and we use <e-Adventure>, an educational game engine created at Complutense University of Madrid for their implementation.

The work is therefore organized as follows: in section 2 we present the design and implementation methodology. In section 3, we illustrate the methodology with a case study. In section 4 we discuss the conclusions derived from the development of the case study and in section 5 we summarize our conclusions and discuss future work.

2 The Design and Implementation Methodology

Clinical procedures do not only require motor skills or tactile tasks, but also the memorization of a large number of related steps required before, during, and after the procedure. For this purpose, we propose a blended-learning approach, where a simulation can be used to get an overview of complex procedures and the additional skills required can later be exercised in focused practical sessions. In our approach, simulations are conceived as point-and-click adventure videogames. Adventure videogames have been already identified as a suitable game genre for education [3-5], especially when it comes to learning complex procedures that involve sequences of steps. We have defined a process model to create these adventure-like simulations from already established clinical procedures, following a number of steps (see Fig. 1). The following subsections detail each of these steps.

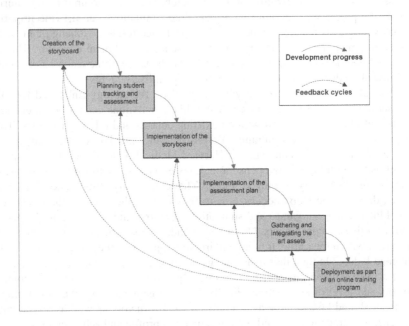

Fig. 1. Outline of the complete process. The red arrows indicate expected feedback cycles, although the process is flexible and can be iterated as a spiral development model.

2.1 Creation of the Storyboard

When creating a clinical procedure simulation, the initial storyboard is created with the physicians responsible for the face-to-face training. Typically, clinical procedures take place in a number of locations: a procedure could involve, for example, some activities in the patient's room, a visit to the lab to get some results, and checking with the nursing station for updates. The storyboard should include descriptions of all these locations or *scenes*.

Additionally, other participants in the procedure (patients, nurses, etc.) populate the diverse locations. In the adventure game jargon, those participants are described as *characters* that the trainee can interact with during the execution. In addition, the procedures involve interacting with objects, which can be described in the storyboard as *items*.

Finally, as described in [6], a network of scenarios that can simply be navigated and where every object and character always exhibits the same behavior does not create a meaningful game. Clinical procedures have steps and possible branches depending on certain conditions (e.g., "Is the patient conscious? "What are the test results?"). That is to say, the simulation must include a notion of state, and performing a specific activity within the simulation usually requires having performed some other activities first. Thus, the storyboard should contemplate sequenced steps, and include branches that may have an effect on what should be done next.

2.2 Planning Student Tracking and Assessment

One of the most important requirements identified in our experiences with Technology-Enhanced Learning is the need to monitor and assess the performance of the learners who interact with the different learning artifacts. Indeed, we identify it as a primary requirement for integrating simulations in the context of The Hub, as described in section 1, and we consider that it deserves a distinctive phase in our methodology. For this purpose, once the storyboard is ready, the instructor also prepares documentation describing the evaluation profiles. Since we want to monitor the performance of the student, it is necessary to identify what constitutes "good performance".

The assessment plan should cover the objectives that the formalized procedures try to accomplish. Questions that should be answered include "which steps are critical in the procedure?", "which branching decisions are correct?", and "what final states in the procedure are considered a success?" With this assessment plan, it should be possible to define rules that will transform the path followed by the trainee into a final grade and a written report with grading and self-evaluation purposes.

2.3 Implementation of the Storyboard

Once a detailed storyboard is available, the next step is to choose an appropriate technology for its implementation, with special attention to cost-effectiveness. Since these game-like simulations are only used to support part of the training (i.e., they do not substitute for the rest of the training program) the cost is definitely an issue.

The opensource <e-Adventure> platform was originally developed for the creation and execution of educational adventure games with modest technical requirements at a low cost. We found that the adventure game engine included in the platform covered most of the requisites outlined in the previous section, such as efficient involvement of the instructor physicians, while the cost-efficiency of the development process provided by the platform was ideal.

<e-Adventure> uses an XML (eXtensible Markup Language) notation [7] to describe the games that are interpreted by the engine and offers an authoring approach that facilitates the transition from the storyboard to a running game [8]. This helps us guarantee that no vital information is lost in the process of implementing the script. As described in [9], the center of the entire implementation process is the actual storyboard. The platform also includes a simplified graphical editor that facilitates the entire authoring process (Fig. 2).

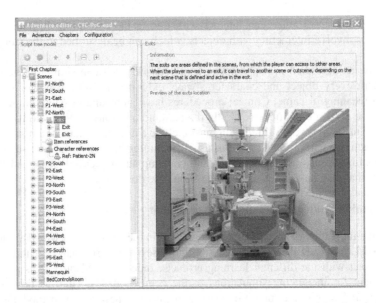

Fig. 2. The <e-Adventure> graphical editor being used to define a scene with exits on the sides that lead to other scenes

2.4 Implementation of the Assessment Plan

To track and assess the performance of the trainee during the simulation, <e-Adventure> uses a built-in assessment mechanism that supports the objectives related to monitoring and reporting the activity of the learner [10].

The configuration of this mechanism can be performed using the supplied graphical editor to define the so-called *assessment rules* (Fig. 3). These rules identify specific internal states of the simulation as relevant from a pedagogical perspective and describe the actions that should be performed if the rule is activated during the execution of the simulation. The payload of these rules can include generating a human readable entry in a report, measuring the time elapsed between two states and computing the grade that will be assigned to the student [11]. With this approach, implementing the assessment plan is a straightforward process that requires transforming the questions outlined during the "Planning Student Monitorization and Assessment" activity into <e-Adventure> assessment rules.

2.5 Gathering and Integrating the Art Assets

Often one of the most costly aspects of game and simulation development is obtaining the art assets that will be included with the game, as well as integrating these assets in the final videogame. Again, we focused on developing a sustainable methodology with a low cost.

Given that these procedures are being taught in the context of a healthcare institution, we used actual photographs of the environment in which the procedures take place and the items employed. In other words, we found that one of the cheapest and most effective ways of modeling a patient's room was to take a photo of that room.

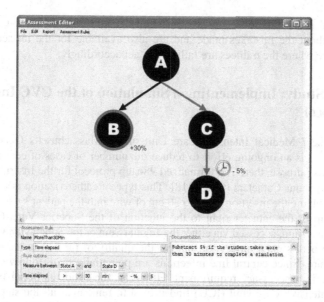

Fig. 3. Using the <e-Adventure> editor to create an assessment rule that measures the time elapsed between two states of the game and computes part of the student's grade

We hope the use of photorealistic environment will help familiarize trainees (often recently arrived residents) with their workplace. If the simulation requires going to the nursing station to check some information and this action is performed by navigating a series of pictures of the actual hallways, the trainee will find it easier to find the station when working on the medical wards depicted.

The <e-Adventure> platform clearly separates the treatment of the script from the treatment of the art assets, which facilitates both processes. It is possible to implement the script while the assets are gathered and then it is a straightforward process to include the assets in the simulation by using the supplied editor.

2.6 Deployment as Part of a Training Program

Finally, <e-Adventure> was designed with the objective of integrating the educational games with online learning environments compliant to the IMS Learning Design (IMSLD) specification [12, 13]. This specification allows the formalization of complex instructional designs including collaborative activities, branching and adaptive learning [14] and is currently considered the reference specification for educational modeling [15]. The .LRN platform supports this specification [16].

The <e-Adventure> platform includes plug-ins that enable the communication between the game engine and different IMSLD-compliant environments, .LRN included. This compatibility means that the simulations can be launched from a web environment and then, the assessment mechanism built into the engine, sends the grades and reports to the learning environment as the trainee executes the simulation [17].

The latest scores achieved by each trainee are stored in the environment along with their results from other tests of their training program. In addition to the final score, the engine also generates human-readable reports explaining all the criteria included in the final score. These documents are shown to the trainees so that they receive feedback about the mistakes made and are also available for the instructors so that they can see where the trainees are failing and act accordingly.

3   Case Study: Implementing a Simulation of the CVC Insertion Protocol

In the Blake-7 Medical Intensive Care Unit of the Massachusetts General Hospital (MGH), there is an ongoing effort to reduce the number of cases of central line infection. For this purpose, there is a formalized 98-step protocol for the Insertion Procedure of Central Venous Catheters (CVC) [18]. This type of catheterization is a delicate procedure, involving the insertion of 20 to 30 cm of wire into the patient's chest, in order to drive the tip of the catheter right to the junction of the Superior Vena Cava and the heart's right atrium, accessed via either the Jugular vein or the Subclavian vein.

The protocol's main aim is to improve the quality of the sterile technique during the procedure. Since central line infections are potentially fatal, following this protocol closely is a necessary requirement. However, the residents being trained at the Medical Intensive Care Unit (ICU) find it hard to remember all the steps, especially when working under the additional pressure they experience the first few times that they perform this aggressive procedure.

For this reason, there are ongoing training sessions using specially designed mannequins. These mannequins have the corresponding anatomical landmarks that allow the localization of the targeted landmarks and emulate the texture and anatomy of real tissue. During these sessions, one or two residents start the CVC protocol guided by an experienced physician (the clinical educator), who takes notes on trainee performance.

However, these sessions take longer than they should, making it hard to find enough time to perform them as frequently as desirable. Additionally, the feedback gathered from the residents after the training sessions suggests that the procedure itself is not as difficult for them as following all the preparatory steps required by the protocol. Thus, we decided to create a game-like simulation in which the trainees could go through all the steps of the protocol. The game-like elements were provided by adding a time pressure and by introducing competition by comparing and publishing individual results.

It must be noted that having a simulation of this procedure cannot substitute the training sessions with mannequins (let alone with live patients) due to the lack of tactile feedback and the fact that the trainee is not really practicing the landmark localization and the actual movements during the procedure. However, having a simulation of this 98-step protocol helps the trainee practice and memorize the required steps so that they are well prepared for sessions with an instructor.

This approach should save on-site instruction time and increase the confidence of the residents when performing the procedure with live patients. Next, we describe how our design and implementation approach has been applied in the development of this game-like simulation.

3.1   Creation of the Storyboard: Description of the CVC Game

The game storyboard reflects all the steps indicated in the 98-step protocol for CVC insertions applied at the Massachusetts General Hospital. The game starts with the

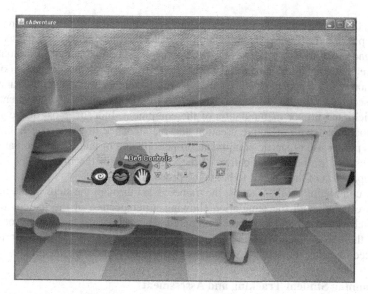

Fig. 4. During parts of the procedure, the bed should be in Trendelenberg (head down) position in order to facilitate vessel engorgement and optimize conditions for the procedure. The controls for the bed are the same controls the trainees will find on the beds at the Blake-7 Medical ICU.

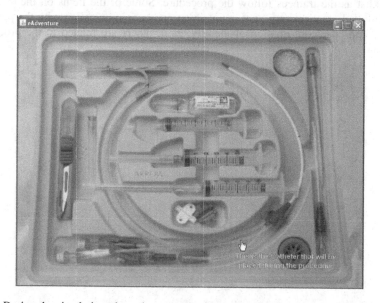

Fig. 5. During the simulation, the trainees get familiarized with the actual line kits used at the Hospital, including descriptions of all the components and their use

trainee standing in the corridor of the Blake-7 Medical ICU at the MGH. From here, the first step is to proceed to the actual location of the supply room to gather the supplies required for the procedure (except for those already available in the patient's room).

Then, the trainee enters the room and begins the initial stages of the procedure, including bed positioning (Fig. 4), identification of anatomical landmarks, and the use of the Ultrasound probe to locate the vessel. Other general aspects which are occasionally ignored are encouraged and monitored, such as proper use of disinfectant gel, good communication with the patient (if conscious), and redundant identification of the patient.

The second (and critical) stage of the simulation deals with the deployment of the sterile field and proper manipulation of the equipment. Indeed, most of the steps of the protocol deal with effective creation and maintenance of the sterile field, which includes proper use of sterile equipment, proper opening of the line kit, preparation of the Ultrasound probe, identification of the components in the line kit (Fig. 5), and final preparation of the line kit to begin the procedure.

After completing all these steps, the trainee is led through the steps of the insertion procedure itself, with the simulation showing a perspective of the patient with the sterile field deployed and the line kit prepared. This part of the simulation focuses on helping the trainee memorize the sequence of steps, but cannot substitute practicing the procedure using the actual components of the line kit and a mannequin.

3.2 Planning Student Tracking and Assessment

As mentioned previously, an instructor monitors and assesses trainee performance during training sessions for the CVC Insertion. During the session, the instructor completes a checklist as the trainees follow the procedure. Some of the items on the checklist deal with bad practices (e.g., not maintaining good communication with the patient - Fig. 6-, improper confirmation of identity, etc.), others are related to the procedure

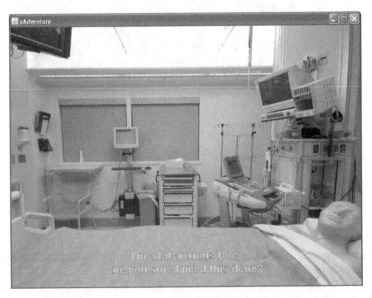

Fig. 6. Proper communication with the patient is not always mentioned in the materials explaining this procedure, an essential component that can get sidelined while the trainee is focusing on the task at hand. The simulation integrates patient communication reminders into the virtual encounter so it is less likely to be forgotten during the real encounter.

itself (e.g., correct sterile technique), and general safety practices (e.g., correct disposal of sharps or contaminated materials).

Every omission of an item from that checklist is a mistake made by the trainee. Therefore, each mistake results in a reduction of the score of the procedure. A simulation completed in a timely manner and without any mistakes represents a score of 100%. Each omission results in a deduction, with some omissions being considered more grave than others. Using excessive time to complete the simulation also results in a deduction (Table 1 summarizes some of the aspects included in the final calculated score). The final score is thus an estimation of how familiar the trainee is with the protocol, and can be used as an indicator of whether the trainee is ready to move on to training sessions with mannequins or even live patients. The score is accompanied by a full report with feedback explaining all the deductions. The trainees can consult the report in order to see on which steps they failed.

Table 1. A partial list of score deductions for different concepts. Grades below 80% mean a failed procedure.

Checklist Item	Grade	Checklist Item	Grade
Calstat used prior to entering room	-10%	Patient told to expect needle stick prior to injecting lidocaine	-5%
Bed adjusted to proper height, patient brought to head of bed	-2%	Lidocaine used at insertion site with ultrasound in real time	-5%
Patient in Trendelenberg position when examining vessels with ultrasound	-5%	Appropriate technique to reduce risk of air embolism (finger over needle hub)	-10%
Patient returned to supine position after ultrasound to avoid vessel collapse	-5%	Pressure tubing (if available) used to assess that needle is in vein	-5%
Landmarks appropriately identified	-5%	Guidewire always kept in hand and under control	-10%
Time out with nursing noted	-5%	Sharps returned to needle holder and scalpel retracted after use	-5%
Chlorhexidine properly applied w/ sterile gloves	-10%	After insertion, flushed air, flushed w/ saline, & clamped to keep closed system	-5%
Gown, gloves, and goggles/face-shield used; gowned w/ hands inside sleeves	-10%	CVC left 3 cm out and sutured in with soft clamp and box clamp	-5%
Sterile sheet from line kit used to cover field; opening matted down on patient	-5%	More than 30 minutes to complete the simulation	-5%
Tray and items set up completely prior to use including loading of suture	-5%	More than 45 minutes to complete the simulation	-10%
Line flushed and clamps placed prior to removing syringe when flushing	-5%	More than 60 minutes to complete the simulation	-20%

3.3 Implementation of the Storyboard

The implementation of the storyboard with <e-Adventure> started with an initial effort focused on the adaptation and evolution of the <e-Adventure> platform to this new domain. This evolution essentially supposed passing from a second-person perspective to a first-person one, more suitable for game-like clinical simulations.

However, even with this side-effort, the global implementation effort was reasonable (see Table 2 in the next section for a summary of the resources invested on each stage of the development). Once the tools had been adapted, the implementation simply required using the <e-Adventure> editor to turn the storyboard into a game.

3.4 Implementation of the Tracking and Assessment Plan

The implementation of the tracking and assessment plan was performed using the assessment features of <e-Adventure>. The process consisted on turning all the potential errors (most of them are described in Table 1) into <e-Adventure> assessment rules. Most of the rules followed the same pattern:

1. Identify the simulation state that indicates that the student failed to comply with the indications and express it in terms of game flags.
2. Add a *computation* payload to the rule, indicating the percentage that should be deducted automatically from the grade.
3. Add a *description* payload to the rule, with the texts from Table 1, in order to generate text reports indicating all the steps in which the student was penalized.

The exceptions to this pattern were the last three rules, related to measuring the time required to complete the entire procedure. These rules were created as *time measurement rules* (see Fig. 3), which require identifying two states and also carry a payload. In this case, the two states were the initial state of the game and the final step of the procedure, while the payload was similar to the rest of the rules (a score deduction and descriptive feedback).

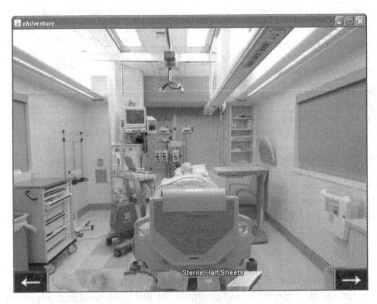

Fig. 7. All of the scenarios and objects displayed during the simulation are photographs of the actual rooms and equipment used in the Blake-7 Medical

3.5 Gathering and Integrating the Art Assets

The graphics for the simulation were obtained in three photo sessions. In the first session, we visited the Medical Intensive Care Unit at the Massachusetts General Hospital and photographed one of the rooms where this procedure is usually performed. The second session included taking close-up photographs of all the materials used in the procedure (Fig. 7). The third and final session simply provided additional assets for those materials that were identified as required during the testing and improvement stage.

3.6 Deployment as Part of the Training Program

The integration between <e-Adventure> and the .LRN platform described in section 2.6 gives busy residents access to the CVC training at any of the hundreds of clinical workstations available in the hospital and allows its integration into the existing e-learning infrastructure (The Hub) where individual trainee's progress is tracked and evaluated. This can be exemplified in the following hybrid-learning scenario (combining *e-learning* tools with other approaches), which can be fully supported using <e-Adventure> and .LRN:

> *Dr. X is scheduled to start his first rotation on the intensive care unit (ICU) on Monday. On Friday, relevant learning materials show up in his portal page in The Hub, because the administration has made the CVC game-like simulation part of the ICU curriculum. Dr. X knows it is also a requirement to take part in the face-to-face CVC skills training so he takes it until he exceeds 80% in the game. His progress is reported to The Hub, is added to his e-Portfolio, and results in him being scheduled for a CVC skills training session on a mannequin with a clinical educator (Dr. C) on Wednesday. He does well. On Friday a patient comes in that requires a CVC and 30 minutes before the procedure is planned Dr. C calls Dr. X to get ready to test what he has learned. Dr. X quickly reviews the steps required in the CVC game using the computer downstairs. After a successful unproblematic placement of the CVC, Dr. C fills out the evaluation form on The Hub for Dr. X. Later that night, Dr. X adds the successful procedure to his procedure log. Afterwards the administration can show that they have fulfilled their mission (and ethical obligation).*

4 Discussion

The development methodology supported by the <e-Adventure> platform suggests in this work could be potentially used to develop low-cost instructional content that improves training outcomes. The prototype developed from the case study shows some promising results as discussed in this section.

4.1 Development Costs

The work in [19] presents the results of a survey made during a session on serious games at the 2005 edition of the Game Developers Conference (http://www.gdconf. com/). The survey included questions about the costs of the initiatives that were being developed at the time, and most answers (26,23%) fit into the $100.000-$500.000 range (with also a significant 14,75% in the $1,000,000-$10,000,000 range). Similarly, the results introduced in [20] estimate costs for the development of a "next-generation simulation" on the 15-30 person-years range. These figures are far beyond the typical budgets available for learning specific procedures at individual institutions. Even if it were possible to generalize such simulations and apply them in different hospitals, it would be difficult to recoup such enormous development costs. One of the causes of this excessive cost is that developing even the simplest 3D simulation environment has a high cost.

In most application scenarios, the investment needs to be several orders of magnitude lower in order to be aligned with the educational budgets of most institutions, even if it means sacrificing part of the benefits. The simulation described in this work replaces pure interactive 3D environments with virtual spaces consisting of navigable series of photographs. This simplification is the key element in the reduction of development costs, although it sacrifices realism, interactivity and depth, taking a leap back from the current state of commercial videogames. The total effort for the development of this case study, as described in Table 2, took about 410 hours or roughly 2.5 person-months, which is a figure much more aligned with realistic budgets for a learning module focused on a single procedure at a specific institution. However, there is a concern in whether this approach really retains the educational value and the attractiveness that game-like simulations should provide, as discussed in the next section.

Table 2. Approximate number of man-hours required for each of the stages of the project and the profiles of the personnel involved (I = Instructors, SD = Software Developers, A = Artists, T = Trainees)

Concept	Cost	Profiles
Modification of the \<e-Adventure\> engine	50 hours	SD
Conception of the storyboard / Creation of the initial XML script	80 hours	I
Monitoring and Assessment Planning / Creation of assessment and grading profiles	50 hours	SD, I
Creation of the art assets	150 hours	A, I, SD
Deployment, testing and improvement	80 hours	I, SD, T
Total:	**410 hours**	

Additionally, it must be noted that there may be training scenarios where a higher level of interactivity (with its associated cost) is required. Even in those cases, this simplified methodology can have an impact. In those developments, it is usually difficult to appreciate the potential usefulness of a simulation project before it is completed. When dealing with complex and costly projects, an often-feared scenario is the possibility of the resulting product failing to deliver the expected educational results. In these cases, the approach presented here is still worthy as a prototyping methodology. This low cost-low risk approach can deliver a functioning product to demonstrate how the completed simulation would work. Indeed, these simplified games would act as interactive storyboards of the completed product.

4.2 Educational Value

As several academic authors defend, the use of videogames and simulations can improve the learning process [21-25]. This is partially a result of a closed game cycle, where the actions result in immediate feedback [26]. However, this feedback does not only provide the grounding for the acquisition of knowledge. In fact, this cycle also engages the player in wanting to interact more with the environment. Games are motivational and engaging, and motivated or engaged students learn better and retain more information [27-30].

When this approach is examined in terms of educational value and engagement, the concessions to interactivity and pacing made for the sake of reducing the development costs can raise concerns about their effectiveness. The resulting products are not nearly as interactive and fast-paced as modern commercial videogames or training simulations. In fact, moving back a few years, these games behave much more similarly to the originally best-selling series Myst™. However, these games have lost their impact in the commercial videogame scene, suggesting that current players prefer more intense action. Can this be an issue in terms of motivation? To prevent trainees from disengaging, we introduce game-like elements such as a time pressure and the publication of rankings and results. With this, we add objectives, performance measurement and an established rule-set, which are the basic ingredients for any form of game.

Additionally, there is a concern that the lower interactivity (when compared with a fully-featured 3D environment) may have an impact on the educational value. Training sessions performed with either mannequins or live patients with the close guidance of an experienced instructor can not be replaced by the approach proposed in this work or a fully interactive 3D emersion . However, as it has already been stated, the residents are not actually overwhelmed with the delicacy of the procedure itself, but with the requirements of the strict protocol devised to reduce the risk of infections. In these terms, the performance of this simplified game when it comes to memorizing the 98-step protocol is similar to the potential results of a more complex 3D simulation.

Additionally, the <e-Adventure> platform offers some other pedagogical advantages, such as the built-in assessment mechanism provided by <e-Adventure> can be employed to automatically compute the score of the player, a task that in other game-based approaches is usually performed by an instructor during the play sessions. The trainees can perform the procedure as many times as they want and get an instant report on how well they followed the protocol and whether they are ready for a practice session with an actual instructor that will not result in a waste of time.

4.3 Integration with the Existing E-Learning Infrastructure

Given that the <e-Adventure> platform can be integrated with .LRN, we can use it to deploy and serve the games as any other kind of instructional content delivered through the platform. When the games are launched they establish a communication with the server, allowing scenarios as the one described in section 3.6 to occur. The assessment mechanism is connected to .LRN through this link, and can interact with the rest of the modules on the course through the server's implementation of the IMS LD specification described in [16].

When the execution is completed, the calculated score can be sent back to the IMS LD engine, which, in turn, stores that information for further executions of the game and can publish the score along with the completion time to the student's profile. This publication of the score, apart from leveraging the competitive nature of students, serves a clear educational purpose. The instructors can check the grades of all the residents and decide which of them are ready to start participating in the instructor-guided practical sessions.

It should also be noted that the use of existing e-learning standards such as the IMS LD specification does not limit this kind of integration with the e-learning infrastructure used at this specific site, but allows it to be deployed wherever standards compliant e-learning tools are used.

5 Final Remarks

Although there is broad agreement in the need of improving medical training that precedes the interaction with live patients in order to maximize safety, the realities of daily life at a major hospital constrain the opportunities for training experiences. The current use of low-technology mannequins is a good approach for training before proceeding to live patients, but finding time for these guided training sessions is almost impossible.

The use of advanced forms of simulation would deliver an improved experience, but their costs are far beyond the training budgets of specific units such as the MGH Medical ICU. The use of educational adventure games, however, can reduce the time associated with guided sessions and offers the trainees a way to focus on learning complex procedures that consist of a number of steps and branching decisions beforehand, so that the steps do not subtract face-to-face time needed for practicing the necessary motor skills.

The genre of adventure games has proved efficient for acquiring this type of knowledge [3]. Even without featuring amazing graphics and sophisticated interaction, they can provide an engaging experience. The experiences with portable consoles like the Nintendo DS suggest the existence of a market for engaging titles without last generation graphics or interactions (like the specifically educational Brain Training™ or the simple but engaging gameplay of Phoenix Wright: Ace Attorney™, both on the Nintendo DS console). Therefore, there is room for lower budget educational adventure games, provided that the contents engage the players.

If we are willing to accept the reduction of interactivity and eye-candy and use specific educational game engines, there is a potential rapid development process that incurs higher costs than traditional teaching materials for clinical procedures, but is still within the boundaries of most training budgets.

Acknowledgments. The Spanish Committees of Education and Science / Industry (TIN2005-08788-C04-01, FIT-360000-2007-23 y TIN2007-68125-C02-01), the Regional Government of Madrid (4155/2005), the Complutense University of Madrid (research group 921340 and Santander/UCM PR34/07-15865 project), and the US National Library of Medicine Research (Training Grant 5T15LM007092-15) have partially supported this work. We would also like to thank Robin Ty and Katherine M. Lau for their help reviewing the final manuscript.

References

1. Ziv, A., Wolpe, P.R., Small, S.D., Glick, S.: Simulation-Based Medical Education: An Ethical Imperative. Academic Medicine 78(8), 783–788 (2003)
2. Blesius, C.R., et al.: LRN: Learning Inside and Outside the Classroom: Supporting Collaborative Learning Communities using a Web Application Toolkit. In: Fernández Manjon, B., et al. (eds.) Computers and Education: E-learning - from Theory to Practice. Springer, Heidelberg (2007)
3. Ju, E., Wagner, C.: Personal computer adventure games: Their structure, principles and applicability for training. The Database for Advances in Information Systems 28(2), 78–92 (1997)
4. Amory, A., Naicker, K., Vincent, J., Adams, C.: The Use of Computer Games as an Educational Tool: Identification of Appropriate Game Types and Game Elements. British Journal of Educational Technology 30(4), 311–321 (1999)
5. Van Eck, R.: Building Artificially Intelligent Learning Games. In: Gibson, D., Aldrich, C., Prensky, M. (eds.) Games and Simulations in Online Learning: Research and Development Frameworks. Information Science Publishing, Hershey (2007)
6. Moreno-Ger, P., Martinez-Ortiz, I., Fernández-Manjón, B.: The <e-Game> project: Facilitating the Development of Educational Adventure Games. In: Cognition and Exploratory Learning in the Digital age (CELDA 2005), IADIS, Porto, Portugal (2005)
7. Birbeck, M., et al.: Professional XML. 2nd edn. Wrox Press (2001)
8. Moreno-Ger, P., Sierra, J.L., Martínez-Ortiz, I., Fernández-Manjón, B.: A Documental Approach to Adventure Game Development. Science of Computer Programming 67(1), 3–31 (2007)
9. Moreno-Ger, P., Martínez-Ortiz, I., Sierra, J.L., Fernández-Manjón, B.: A Content-Centric Development Process Model. Computer 41(3), 24–30 (2008)
10. Moreno-Ger, P., Sancho Thomas, P., Martínez-Ortiz, I., Sierra, J.L., Fernández-Manjón, B.: Adaptive Units of Learning and Educational Videogames. Journal of Interactive Media in Education 2007(05) (2007)
11. Moreno-Ger, P., Burgos, D., Sierra, J.L., Fernández-Manjón, B.: Educational Game Design for Online Education. Computers in Human Behavior (in Press)
12. IMS Global Consortium. IMS Learning Design Specification, Version 1.0 Final Specification (2003) (cited March 2008), http://www.imsproject.org/learningdesign/index.html
13. Koper, R., Tattersall, C. (eds.): Learning Design - A Handbook on Modelling and Delivering Networked Education and Training. Springer, Heidelberg (2005)
14. Burgos, D., Tattersall, C., Koper, R.: Representing adaptive e-learning strategies in IMS Learning Design. In: TENCompetence Conference, Sofia, Bulgaria (2006)

15. Fernández-Manjón, B., Sierra, J.L., Moreno-Ger, P., Martínez-Ortiz, I.: Uso de estándares aplicados a TIC en Educación, CNICE (National Center for Educational Information and Communication), Report #16, NIPO 651-06-344-7 (2007)

16. Escobedo del Cid, J.P., de la Fuente Valentín, L., Gutiérrez, S., Pardo, A., Delgado Kloos, C.: Implementation of a Learning Design Run-Time Environment for the. LRN Learning Management System. Journal of Interactive Media in Education, 2007 (07) (2007)

17. Martinez-Ortiz, I., Moreno-Ger, P., Sierra, J.L., Fernández-Manjón, B.: Production and Deployment of Educational Videogames as Assessable Learning Objects. In: Nejdl, W., Tochtermann, K. (eds.) EC-TEL 2006. LNCS, vol. 4227, Springer, Heidelberg (2006)

18. Graham, A.S., Ozment, C., Tegtmeyer, K., Lai, S., Braner, D.A.V.: Central Venous Catheterization. New England Journal of Medicine 356(21), 21 (2007)

19. Michael, D., Chen, S.: Serious Games: Games that Educate, Train, and Inform. Thomson, Boston (2006)

20. Aldrich, C.: Learning by Doing: A Comprehensive Guide to Simulations, Computer Games, and Pedagogy in e-Learning and Other Educational Experiences. Pfeiffer, San Francisco (2005)

21. de Freitas, S., Oliver, M.: How can exploratory learning with games and simulations within the curriculum be most effectively evaluated? Computers & Education 46(3), 249–264 (2006)

22. Garris, R., Ahlers, R., Driskell, J.E.: Games, Motivation and Learning: A Research and Practice Model. Simulation & Gaming 33(4), 441–467 (2002)

23. Jenkins, H., Klopfer, E., Squire, K., Tan, P.: Entering the Education Arcade. ACM Computers in Entertainment 1(1) (2003)

24. Mitchell, A., Savill-Smith, C.: The Use of Computer and Videogames for Learning: A Review of the Literature. m-learning, Trowbridge, Wiltshire: Learning and Skills Development Agency (2004)

25. Squire, K.: Game-Based Learning: An X-Learn Perspective Paper, MASIE center: e-Learning Consortium (2005)

26. Pivec, M., Dziabenko, O.: Game-Based Learning in Univeristies and Lifelong Learning: Unigame: Social Skills and Knowledge Training Game Concept. Journal of Universal Computer Science 10(1), 4–12 (2004)

27. Cordova, D.I., Lepper, M.R.: Intrinsic Motivation and the Process of Learning: Beneficial Effects of Contextualization, Personalization, and Choice. Journal of Educational Psychology 88(4), 715–730 (1996)

28. Lepper, M.R., Cordova, D.I.: A desire to be taught: Instructional Consequences of Intrinsic Motivation. Motivation and Emotion 16, 187–208 (1992)

29. Malone, T.: What makes computer games fun? Byte 6(12), 258–276 (1981)

30. Malone, T.: Toward a Theory of Intrinsically Motivating Instruction. Cognitive Science 5, 333–369 (1981)

Author Index

Lecture Notes in Computer Science

Sublibrary 3: Information Systems and Application, incl. Internet/Web and HCI

For information about Vols. 1– 4656
please contact your bookseller or Springer

Vol. 4831: B. Benatallah, F. Casati, D. Georgakopoulos, C. Bartolini, W. Sadiq, C. Godart (Eds.), Web Information Systems Engineering – WISE 2007. XVI, 675 pages. 2007.

Vol. 4825: K. Aberer, K.-S. Choi, N. Noy, D. Allemang, K.-I. Lee, L. Nixon, J. Golbeck, P. Mika, D. Maynard, R. Mizoguchi, G. Schreiber, P. Cudré-Mauroux (Eds.), The Semantic Web. XXVII, 973 pages. 2007.

Vol. 4823: H. Leung, F. Li, R. Lau, Q. Li (Eds.), Advances in Web Based Learning – ICWL 2007. XIV, 654 pages. 2008.

Vol. 4822: D.H.-L. Goh, T.H. Cao, I.T. Sølvberg, E. Rasmussen (Eds.), Asian Digital Libraries. XVII, 519 pages. 2007.

Vol. 4820: T.G. Wyeld, S. Kenderdine, M. Docherty (Eds.), Virtual Systems and Multimedia. XII, 215 pages. 2008.

Vol. 4816: B. Falcidieno, M. Spagnuolo, Y. Avrithis, I. Kompatsiaris, P. Buitelaar (Eds.), Semantic Multimedia. XII, 306 pages. 2007.

Vol. 4813: I. Oakley, S.A. Brewster (Eds.), Haptic and Audio Interaction Design. XIV, 145 pages. 2007.

Vol. 4810: H.H.-S. Ip, O.C. Au, H. Leung, M.-T. Sun, W.-Y. Ma, S.-M. Hu (Eds.), Advances in Multimedia Information Processing – PCM 2007. XXI, 834 pages. 2007.

Vol. 4809: M.K. Denko, C.-s. Shih, K.-C. Li, S.-L. Tsao, Q.-A. Zeng, S.H. Park, Y.-B. Ko, S.-H. Hung, J.-H. Park (Eds.), Emerging Directions in Embedded and Ubiquitous Computing. XXXV, 823 pages. 2007.

Vol. 4808: T.-W. Kuo, E. Sha, M. Guo, L.T. Yang, Z. Shao (Eds.), Embedded and Ubiquitous Computing. XXI, 769 pages. 2007.

Vol. 4806: R. Meersman, Z. Tari, P. Herrero (Eds.), On the Move to Meaningful Internet Systems 2007: OTM 2007 Workshops, Part II. XXXIV, 611 pages. 2007.

Vol. 4805: R. Meersman, Z. Tari, P. Herrero (Eds.), On the Move to Meaningful Internet Systems 2007: OTM 2007 Workshops, Part I. XXXIV, 757 pages. 2007.

Vol. 4804: R. Meersman, Z. Tari (Eds.), On the Move to Meaningful Internet Systems 2007: CoopIS, DOA, ODBASE, GADA, and IS, Part II. XXIX, 683 pages. 2007.

Vol. 4803: R. Meersman, Z. Tari (Eds.), On the Move to Meaningful Internet Systems 2007: CoopIS, DOA, ODBASE, GADA, and IS, Part I. XXIX, 1173 pages. 2007.

Vol. 4802: J.-L. Hainaut, E.A. Rundensteiner, M. Kirchberg, M. Bertolotto, M. Brochhausen, Y.-P.P. Chen, S.S.-S. Cherfi, M. Doerr, H. Han, S. Hartmann, J. Parsons, G. Poels, C. Rolland, J. Trujillo, E. Yu, E. Zimányie (Eds.), Advances in Conceptual Modeling – Foundations and Applications. XIX, 420 pages. 2007.

Vol. 4801: C. Parent, K.-D. Schewe, V.C. Storey, B. Thalheim (Eds.), Conceptual Modeling - ER 2007. XVI, 616 pages. 2007.

Vol. 4797: M. Arenas, M.I. Schwartzbach (Eds.), Database Programming Languages. VIII, 261 pages. 2007.

Vol. 4796: M. Lew, N. Sebe, T.S. Huang, E.M. Bakker (Eds.), Human–Computer Interaction. X, 157 pages. 2007.

Vol. 4794: B. Schiele, A.K. Dey, H. Gellersen, B. de Ruyter, M. Tscheligi, R. Wichert, E. Aarts, A. Buchmann (Eds.), Ambient Intelligence. XV, 375 pages. 2007.

Vol. 4777: S. Bhalla (Ed.), Databases in Networked Information Systems. X, 329 pages. 2007.

Vol. 4761: R. Obermaisser, Y. Nah, P. Puschner, F.J. Rammig (Eds.), Software Technologies for Embedded and Ubiquitous Systems. XIV, 563 pages. 2007.

Vol. 4747: S. Džeroski, J. Struyf (Eds.), Knowledge Discovery in Inductive Databases. X, 301 pages. 2007.

Vol. 4744: Y. de Kort, W. IJsselsteijn, C. Midden, B. Eggen, B.J. Fogg (Eds.), Persuasive Technology. XIV, 316 pages. 2007.

Vol. 4740: L. Ma, M. Rauterberg, R. Nakatsu (Eds.), Entertainment Computing – ICEC 2007. XXX, 480 pages. 2007.

Vol. 4730: C. Peters, P. Clough, F.C. Gey, J. Karlgren, B. Magnini, D.W. Oard, M. de Rijke, M. Stempfhuber (Eds.), Evaluation of Multilingual and Multi-modal Information Retrieval. XXIV, 998 pages. 2007.

Vol. 4723: M. R. Berthold, J. Shawe-Taylor, N. Lavrač (Eds.), Advances in Intelligent Data Analysis VII. XIV, 380 pages. 2007.

Vol. 4721: W. Jonker, M. Petković (Eds.), Secure Data Management. X, 213 pages. 2007.

Vol. 4718: J. Hightower, B. Schiele, T. Strang (Eds.), Location- and Context-Awareness. X, 297 pages. 2007.

Vol. 4717: J. Krumm, G.D. Abowd, A. Seneviratne, T. Strang (Eds.), UbiComp 2007: Ubiquitous Computing. XIX, 520 pages. 2007.

Vol. 4715: J.M. Haake, S.F. Ochoa, A. Cechich (Eds.), Groupware: Design, Implementation, and Use. XIII, 355 pages. 2007.

Vol. 4714: G. Alonso, P. Dadam, M. Rosemann (Eds.), Business Process Management. XIII, 418 pages. 2007.

Vol. 4704: D. Barbosa, A. Bonifati, Z. Bellahsène, E. Hunt, R. Unland (Eds.), Database and XML Technologies. X, 141 pages. 2007.

Vol. 4690: Y. Ioannidis, B. Novikov, B. Rachev (Eds.), Advances in Databases and Information Systems. XIII, 377 pages. 2007.

Vol. 4675: L. Kovács, N. Fuhr, C. Meghini (Eds.), Research and Advanced Technology for Digital Libraries. XVII, 585 pages. 2007.

Vol. 4674: Y. Luo (Ed.), Cooperative Design, Visualization, and Engineering. XIII, 431 pages. 2007.

Vol. 4663: C. Baranauskas, P. Palanque, J. Abascal, S.D.J. Barbosa (Eds.), Human-Computer Interaction – INTERACT 2007, Part II. XXXIII, 735 pages. 2007.

Vol. 4662: C. Baranauskas, P. Palanque, J. Abascal, S.D.J. Barbosa (Eds.), Human-Computer Interaction – INTERACT 2007, Part I. XXXIII, 637 pages. 2007.

Vol. 4658: T. Enokido, L. Barolli, M. Takizawa (Eds.), Network-Based Information Systems. XIII, 544 pages. 2007.